Japan in Australia

Japan in Australia is a work of cultural history that focuses on context and connection between two nations. It examines how Japan has been imagined, represented and experienced in the Australian context through a variety of settings, historical periods and circumstances.

Beginning with the first recorded contacts between Australians and Japanese in the nineteenth century, the chapters focus on 'people-to-people' narratives and the myriad multidimensional ways in which the two countries are interconnected: from sporting diplomacy to woodblock printing, from artistic metaphors to iconic pop imagery, from the tragedy of war to engagement in peace movements, from technology transfer to community arts. Tracing the trajectory of this 150-year relationship provides an example of how history can turn from fear, enmity and misunderstanding through war, foreign encroachment and the legacy of conflict, to close and intimate connections that result in cultural enrichment and diversification.

This book explores notions of Australia and 'Australianness' and Japan and 'Japaneseness', to better reflect on the cultural fusion that is contemporary Australia and build the narrative of the Japan–Australia relationship. It will be of interest to academics in the field of Asian, Japanese and Japanese-Pacific studies.

Dr David Chapman is Associate Professor of Japanese Studies in the School of Languages and Cultures at the University of Queensland in Australia. His research interests include history, identity and citizenship. He is the author of *The Bonin Islanders 1830 to the Present: Narrating Japanese Nationality* (2016), coauthor of *Koseki, Identification and Documentation: Japan's Household Registration System and Citizenship* (Routledge 2014) and author of *Zainichi Korean Identity and Ethnicity* (Routledge 2007).

Dr Carol Hayes is Associate Professor of Japanese Language and Studies in the College of Asia and the Pacific at the Australian National University. Her research interests include literature, identity and language teaching methodologies and practice. She is the author of 'Sashiko Needlework Reborn: From Functional Technology to Decorative Art' (*Japanese Studies* 2019) and 'Women Writing Women: "A Woman's Place" in Modern Japanese Women's Poetry' (*JSOA* 2016), and coauthor of *Reading Embraced by Australia: Oosutoraria ni Idakarete* (2016).

Routledge/Asian Studies Association of Australia (ASAA) East Asia Series
Edited by Morris Low
Editorial Board: Professor Geremie Barmé *(Australian National University)*,
Emeritus Professor Colin Mackerras *(Griffith University)*,
Professor Vera Mackie *(University of Wollongong)*
and Professor Sonia Ryang *(University of Iowa)*.

This series represents a showcase for the latest cutting-edge research in the field of East Asian studies, from both established scholars and rising academics. It will include studies from every part of the East Asian region (including China, Japan, North and South Korea and Taiwan) as well as comparative studies dealing with more than one country. Topics covered may be contemporary or historical, and relate to any of the humanities or social sciences. The series is an invaluable source of information and challenging perspectives for advanced students and researchers alike.

Routledge is pleased to invite proposals for new books in the series. In the first instance, any interested authors should contact:

Associate Professor Morris Low
School of History, Philosophy, Religion and Classics
University of Queensland
Brisbane, QLD 4072, Australia

Japan's New Left Movements
Legacies for Civil Society
Takemasa Ando

Chinese Stories of Drug Addiction
Beyond the Opium Dens
Guy Ramsay

Anti-nuclear Protest in Post-Fukushima Tokyo
Power Struggles
Alexander James Brown

Japan in Australia
Culture, Context and Connection
Edited by David Chapman and Carol Hayes

For more information about this series, please visit: www.routledge.com

Japan in Australia
Culture, Context and Connections

**Edited by
David Chapman and Carol Hayes**

LONDON AND NEW YORK

First published 2020
by Routledge
2 Park Square, Milton Park, Abingdon, Oxon OX14 4RN

and by Routledge
52 Vanderbilt Avenue, New York, NY 10017

Routledge is an imprint of the Taylor & Francis Group, an informa business

© 2020 selection and editorial matter, David Chapman and Carol Hayes; individual chapters, the contributors

The right of David Chapman and Carol Hayes to be identified as the authors of the editorial material, and of the authors for their individual chapters, has been asserted in accordance with sections 77 and 78 of the Copyright, Designs and Patents Act 1988.

All rights reserved. No part of this book may be reprinted or reproduced or utilised in any form or by any electronic, mechanical, or other means, now known or hereafter invented, including photocopying and recording, or in any information storage or retrieval system, without permission in writing from the publishers.

Trademark notice: Product or corporate names may be trademarks or registered trademarks, and are used only for identification and explanation without intent to infringe.

British Library Cataloguing-in-Publication Data
A catalogue record for this book is available from the British Library

Library of Congress Cataloging-in-Publication Data
A catalog record for this book has been requested

ISBN: 978-0-367-18469-8 (hbk)
ISBN: 978-0-429-19648-5 (ebk)

Typeset in Times New Roman
by Apex CoVantage, LLC

The editors would like to dedicate this book to the Japan Foundation Sydney Office and to all those who have contributed (participated) in the experiences of Japan in Australia over many years.

Japanese cane cutters in front of loaded cane trucks, Hambledon Mill, near Cairns, ca. 1890

Two Japanese women on the driveway to the overseer's house, Hambledon Sugar Plantation, Cairns, ca. 1891

Contents

List of figures   ix
List of tables   x
Acknowledgements   xi
List of contributors   xii

Prologue: celebrating Japan in Australia   1
ALAN RIX

1 **Japan in Australia, an introduction**   4
DAVID CHAPMAN AND CAROL HAYES

2 **Youthful first impressions: Tsurumi Kazuko and Shunsuke in Australia, 1937**   25
TOMOKO AOYAMA

3 **Forging an Australian artistic modernity: how Japanese woodblock prints informed Margaret Preston's early paintings and prints**   44
PENNY BAILEY

4 **Japan-Australia friendship through bat and ball: the Yomiuri Giants' baseball tour of Australia in 1954**   63
AI KOBAYASHI

5 **Japan at the 1956 Melbourne Olympics**   81
MORRIS LOW

6 **Japanese sleeping beauties abroad: Australian retellings of Kawabata Yasunari's fairy-tale novella**   96
LUCY FRASER

7	**The irrepressible magic of Monkey: how a Japanese television drama depicting an ancient Chinese tale became compulsory after-school viewing in Australia** REBECCA HAUSLER	113
8	**Nikkei Australian identity and the work of Mayu Kanamori** TIMOTHY KAZUO STEAINS	130
9	**Trans-Asian engagement with Japan in/and Australia** KOICHI IWABUCHI	149
10	**The Australian literary scene and Murakami Haruki: Nobel laureate heir apparent or marketing overhype?** LAURA EMILY CLARK	161
11	**Why introductory Japanese? An Australian case study** CHIHIRO KINOSHITA THOMSON	179
12	**Mobility and Children Crossing Borders** IKUO KAWAKAMI	198
	Coda ROGER PULVERS	215
	On the streets of our town VERA MACKIE	229
	Index	240

Figures

1.1	Grave of Ewar Dicinoski (likely Sakuragawa Rikinosuke), first naturalised Japanese in Australia. Toowong Cemetery, Brisbane, Queensland	9
1.2	The Heathen Japee	11
2.1	Mr Yūsuke Tsurumi's visit to Adelaide (1937)	28
2.2	Father, daughter and son (1937)	32
3.1	Margaret Preston (*Still life with teapot and daisies*) (1915)	50
3.2	Margaret Preston. *Nasturtiums* (circa 1916)	52
3.3	Suzuki Harunobu. *Courtesan of the Motoya Looking at the Face of a Komusō Reflected in Water* (about 1769–70)	53
3.4	Margaret Preston. *Sydney Bridge* (circa 1932)	56
3.5	Margaret Preston. *Western Australian gum blossom* (1928)	58
8.1	Kathleen and Y on buggy	142
10.1	Google trends graph	162
11.1	Reasons to continue studying Japanese of university learners	185
11.2	Word cloud of student evaluation comments (2014–2016)	191
12.1	Concept of CCB	201
BM2.1	Akira's store in the Strand Arcade, Sydney	230
BM2.2	The Uniqlo Store in Sydney	232
BM2.3	The Uniqlo Store in New York	233
BM2.4	Sculpture by Akio Makigawa, Melbourne	235

Tables

11.1	Numbers of learners of Japanese in top five countries in 2015	181
11.2	Introductory Japanese A course students by faculty by stage (2017)	184
11.3	Japanese names that Introductory Japanese students knew in 2007	186
11.4	The top five names that introductory Japanese students knew by year between 2007 and 2016	187
11.5	Respondents of the survey (99 respondents; about 30% response rate)	189
11.6	'Why do you want to continue?' $N = 55$ (Multiple responses)	190

Acknowledgements

The editors would like to thank the Japan Foundation for its generous support of this project in providing funding for the Japan in Australia Conference in 2016. This funding enabled the contributors to come together at The University of Queensland, present their work and receive feedback. This book is the result of that conference.

Contributors

Tomoko Aoyama

Dr Tomoko Aoyama is an associate professor of Japanese studies in the School of Languages and Cultures at the University of Queensland in Australia. Her research interests include parody, humour and intertextuality in modern and contemporary Japanese literature, manga and film, especially women's texts. Her recent publications include 'Ame no Uzume Crosses Boundaries' (in Laura Miller and Rebecca Copeland [eds.], *Diva Nation: Female Icons from Japanese Cultural History*, 2018), and 'The Girl, the Flower, and the Constitution in 1945 (2015)' (in Yasuko Claremont [ed.], *Civil Society and Postwar Pacific Basin Reconciliation: Wounds, Scars and Healing*, (Routledge 2018). She has also translated Kanai Mieko's novels: *Indian Summer* (with Barbara Hartley, Cornell East Asia Series 2012) and *Oh, Tama!: A Mejiro Novel* (with Paul McCarthy, 2019).

Penny Bailey

Dr Penny Bailey is a researcher in Japanese studies and art history at the University of Queensland. Her research is primarily focused on art historical discourse of the modern period featuring Japanese/Korean art and design. Her doctoral thesis examines the ways in which the founder of Japan's Mingei (folk craft) movement, Yanagi Sōetsu, theorised Korean visual cultures during Korea's colonial period (1910–1945). She has published articles in *Monumenta Nipponica, International Review of Korean Studies, Asian Currents* and *The Asian Arts Society of Australia Review*, along with numerous book chapters and reviews and annotated translations.

David Chapman

Dr David Chapman is Associate Professor of Japanese studies in the School of Languages and Cultures at the University of Queensland in Australia. His research interests include history, identity and citizenship. He is the author of *The Bonin Islanders 1830 to the Present: Narrating Japanese Nationality* (2016), coauthor of *Koseki, Identification and Documentation: Japan's Household Registration System and Citizenship* (Routledge 2014) and author of Zainichi Korean Identity and Ethnicity (Routledge 2007).

Laura Emily Clark

Laura Emily Clark is an early career academic, having undertaken her postgraduate studies at the University of Queensland, writing a dissertation on Murakami Haruki and contemporary Japanese gender issues. She specialises in gender and Japanese fiction, exploring how mainstream discourses and values are present in popular cultural products, with an emergent interest in popular reception of Murakami. She has published on the theme of masculinity in Murakami Haruki's *A Wild Sheep Chase* in the electronic *Journal of Contemporary Japanese Studies* and *New Voices in Japanese Studies*. Laura was a Japan Foundation Fellow at Waseda University during her doctoral years and is currently teaching Japanese language and culture at the University of Queensland.

Lucy Fraser

Dr Lucy Fraser is Lecturer in Japanese studies in the School of Languages and Cultures at the University of Queensland, where she teaches Japanese popular culture, literature and language. She researches fairy-tale studies in Japanese and English, with particular interests in ideas of gender as well as animal-human interactions in retellings of folktales and traditional stories. Her publications include *The Pleasures of Metamorphosis: Japanese and English Fairy Tale Transformations of 'The Little Mermaid'* (2017) and 'Dogs, Gods, and Monsters: The Animal-Human Connection in Bakin's *Hakkenden, Folktales and Legends*, and Two Contemporary Retellings' (*Japanese Studies* 2018). She has translated short stories by well-known authors such as Kawakami Hiromi and Hoshino Tomoyuki, and literary and cultural studies criticism by scholars such as Kan Satoko, Fujimoto Yukari and Honda Masuko.

Rebecca Hausler

Rebecca Hausler is a doctoral candidate at the University of Queensland. Her thesis investigates fictional representations of Australian internment and prisoner of war camps which housed Japanese detainees during WWII. She graduated with a Bachelor of Arts (Hons I) in Asian studies and English literature. Her broader academic interests are Japan's transcultural connections with Anglophone nations through popular culture, literature and film. She has published in the interdisciplinary women's studies journal *Hecate* and written articles for the academic news analysis website *The Conversation*.

Carol Hayes

Dr Carol Hayes is Associate Professor of Japanese language studies in the College of Asia and the Pacific and Distinguished Educator at the Australian National University. Her research interests include Japanese cultural production, with a focus on modern Japanese poetry and Japanese language teaching methodologies and practice, particularly e-teaching and e-learning. Her recent publications include 'Baba Akiko: Intabyū' (2018, in Japanese), *Reading Embraced by Australia: Oosutoraria ni Idakarete* (with Yuki Itani-Adams, 2016) and 'Women Writing Women: "A Woman's Place" in Modern Japanese Women's Poetry' (*Journal of the Oriental Society of Australia* 2016). She has translated many works of poetry published in such journals as *Transference* and *International Tanka*. Carol has served as the President of the Japanese Studies Association of Australia (2015–2017) and continues to serve on the board and was awarded a Japanese Foreign Minister's Commendation (2016).

Koichi Iwabuchi

Dr Koichi Iwabuchi is Professor of media and cultural studies in the School of Media, Film and Journalism at Monash University. His main research concern is cultural globalisation and transnationalism, trans-Asian cultural flows and connections, cultural citizenship, diversity and multicultural inclusion in Japan and East Asia. His recent publications include 'Media and Communications' (with Nick Couldry et al., Rethinking Society for the 21st Century: Report of the International Panel on Social Progress Vol. 2); 'Globalization, Culture, and Communication: Renationalization in a Globalized World' (2018) and 'Introverted Jingoism in a Post-Imagined-Community Digital Era: The Upswing of Hate Speech Demonstration in Japan' (Chih-Ming Wang and Daniel PS Goh [eds.], *Precarious Belongings: Affect and Nationalism in Asia*, 2017). Iwabuchi is the editor of the book series *Asian Cultural Studies: Transnational and Dialogic Approaches* and coeditor of the *TransAsia: Screen Cultures* book series.

Ikuo Kawakami

Dr Ikuo Kawakami is Professor of applied Japanese linguistics at Waseda University and Honorary Professor in the School of Languages and Cultures at the University of Queensland. His research interests include Japanese language education and applied linguistics, with a focus on cultural and linguistic identity, citizenship and ethnicity. His recent publications include '*Kokusai idō suru nihongo shiyōsha no gengo jissen to aidentiti* [Linguistic Practice and Identity of Cross Borders Japanese Language Users]' (2017) and 'Children Cross Borders and Their Citizenship in Japan' in *Language and Citizenship in Japan* (Taylor & Francis 2012).

Ai Kobayashi

Dr Ai Kobayashi is an associate of the School of Historical and Philosophical Studies at the University of Melbourne. Her research focuses on the history of Japan-Australia relations, particularly the Japanese perspective on diplomatic relations and sporting contacts during the early post-WWII period. Her recent publications include 'Advantage Receiver: Australia and Japan's Return to the Davis Cup after World War II' (2014); 'Australia and Japan's Admission into the Colombo Plan' (2014) and a historical biography, *W. Macmahon Ball: Politics for the People* (2013).

Morris Low

Dr Morris Low is Associate Professor of Japanese history at the University of Queensland in Australia. His research interests include the history of Japanese science and technology, the history of Australia-Japan relations, Japanese visual culture and issues relating to identity. His recent publications include

'Contemporary Sino-Japanese relations on the screen: a history, 1989–2005' (2017) and coauthorship of *World's Fairs on the Eve of War* (2015), *East Asia Beyond the History Wars* (Routledge 2013, 2015), *Urban Modernity* (2010) and *Science, Technology and Society in Contemporary Japan* (1999). He wrote *Japan on Display* (Routledge 2006, 2012) and *Science and the Building of a New Japan* (2005). He edited *Building a Modern Japan: Science, Technology, and Medicine in the Meiji Era and Beyond* (2005) and coedited *Asian Masculinities* (2003, 2011).

Vera Mackie

Dr Vera Mackie is Senior Professor of Asian and international studies in the School of Humanities and Social Inquiry at the University of Wollongong and Director of the Centre for Critical Human Rights Research. She is Chief Investigator, with Sarah Ferber and Nicola J. Marks, on an Australian Research Council Discovery Project on 'IVF and New Reproductive Technologies: The Global Experience' (2015–2017) and Chief Investigator, with Diane Kirkby, Tanya Fitzgerald and Tangerine Holt, on an Australian Research Council Linkage Project on 'Fostering Women Leaders Through Educational Exchange, 1930–1980'. Her publications include *Remembering Women's Activism*, coauthored with Sharon Crozier-De Rosa (Routledge 2019); *The Reproductive Industry: Intimate Experiences and Global Processes*, coedited with Nicola J. Marks and Sarah Ferber; *The Routledge Handbook of Sexuality Studies in East Asia*, coedited with Mark McLelland (Routledge 2015); *The Social Sciences in the Asian Century*, coedited with Carol Johnson and Tessa Morris-Suzuki (2015) and *Relationships: Japan and Australia, 1870s–1950s*, coedited with Paul Jones (2001).

Roger Pulvers

Roger Pulvers, author, playwright, theatre and film director, translator and journalist, has published more than 50 books in Japanese and English, including novels such as *Star Sand*, *Liv* and *The Dream of Lafcadio Hearn*. In 2017 the feature film of *Star Sand*, written and directed by him, had wide release throughout Japan. In 2019 he published his autobiography, *The Unmaking of an American*. Roger was assistant to director Oshima Nagisa on the film *Merry Christmas, Mr. Lawrence*. He received the prestigious Miyazawa Kenji Prize in 2008 and the Noma Award for the Translation of Japanese Literature in 2013; in 2018, Japan's highest honour, the Order of the Rising Sun and in 2019, the Order of Australia. Over the past 50 years he has translated prose, drama and poetry from Japanese, Russian and Polish. His plays have been widely performed in Australia, Japan and the United States.

Alan Rix

Emeritus Professor Alan Rix was previously Professor of Japanese studies and Pro-Vice-Chancellor at the University of Queensland. He has researched and published widely on contemporary Japan and Australia-Japan relations, notably in political and economic fields, especially trade relations. He was one of the pioneers of research on Japan's foreign aid, and his book *Japan's Foreign Aid Challenge: Policy Reform and Aid Leadership* (Routledge 1993) was republished in 2011.

Timothy Kazuo Steains

Dr Timothy Kazuo Steains is an early career academic at the University of Sydney, teaching in gender and cultural studies, education and English. His primary research interests are in mixed race, Nikkei and Asian Australian identity. He is on the executive committee of the Asian Australian Studies Research Network and is a member of Nikkei Australia. His recent publications include 'The Mix Temporalities of Transnationalism in Dreams of Speaking' (2017) and 'Going With the Transnational Flow in Bondi Tsunami' (2016).

Chihiro Kinoshita Thomson

Dr Chihiro Kinoshita Thomson is Professor of Japanese studies at UNSW, Sydney. Her research interests focus on Japanese language education, particularly Japanese language learner agency, motivation, learning environment and its design based on sociocultural approaches. Her recent publications include *Foreign Language Learning Communities of Practice: Mechanisms for Participatory Learning* (2017, in Japanese), *Japanese Language Education: Connecting People, and Connected to the World* (2016, in Japanese) and 'Japanese Communities of Practice: Creating Opportunities for Out-of-Class Learning', *Language Learning Beyond the Classroom* (in Nunan and Richards [eds.] 2014 Routledge, with T. Mori). Chihiro has served as the President of the Japanese Studies Association of Australia (2009–2011) and represented Australia in the Global Network of Japanese Language Education (2004–2017). She has received a number of awards, for example, UNSW Vice Chancellor's Award for Teaching Excellence in the Category of Research Supervision (2017), Japanese Foreign Minister's Commendation (2016) and Australian Federal Government's Citation for Outstanding Contribution to Student Learning (2012).

Prologue
Celebrating Japan in Australia

Alan Rix

It is a pleasure to introduce this rich and fascinating collection of chapters on Japan in Australia and aspects of Japan's cultural influence in this country. In particular, this is because most of these chapters are by scholars based at Australian universities, who have become immersed in understanding the variety of Japanese influences in and on Australian history and society.

The Japanese presence and influence in Australia go back to the latter part of the nineteenth century, as is well documented in the recent compilation of historical research by David Sissons on the Australia-Japan relationship (*Bridging Australia and Japan, Volume 1*, ANU Press, 2016). Some of the earliest Japanese cultural influences were seen in northern Australia as a result of extensive Japanese involvement in the pearling and pearl shell industries. That presence still resonates faintly through the descendants of some of those workers and immigrants.

In 2017 the two countries celebrated the 60th anniversary of the signing of the Australia-Japan Agreement on Commerce, a landmark development in Australia's trade policy, which signified the beginnings of the shift in Australia's alignment towards Asia, and notably Japan. As a part of this transition, we are now also 40 years on from the establishment of the Australia-Japan Foundation (AJF) by the Australian government in 1976 – the Foundation took as its theme the advancement of 'people-to-people' contact, and much that is discussed in this book exemplifies how that contact has flourished, especially in education.

Japanese language education in Australia started in the first part of the 20th century, notably in some of the universities and at the Royal Military College at Duntroon, around the time of World War I. It grew strongly after the 1960s, as trade imperatives took hold and more teachers became available. I trained in Japanese at the Australian National University (ANU) under Professors E.S. Crawcour and Anthony Alfonso, as part of the ANU's extensive program of Asian languages and studies, but Japanese language education at some other universities had less conventional origins.

For example, although the University of Queensland (UQ) in postwar years recommenced its study of Japan and the Japanese language in 1966, when Professor Joyce Ackroyd was appointed from ANU, Japanese was in fact first taught at UQ before the war. In 1938 the university hired a Japanese lecturer, Professor Seita Ryunosuke, to teach the language. He had been selected by the Japanese

Foreign Office after interest was expressed by the Queensland government and the university in strengthening cultural relations.

Because of the international tensions of the time, from the outset Seita was under suspicion from the authorities for being a spy, but this was never proven. He was certainly active in teaching and lecturing and fulfilled his university duties. On the outbreak of hostilities, he and his daughter were interned first in Brisbane and later in Tatura in Victoria before being repatriated to Japan. Seita died during the war, but in the early 1950s his daughter sought to have their household effects returned to her in Japan, but they had been sold by the Australian government (as they were entitled to do under the Peace Treaty) as former enemy property.

One wonders how many other teachers of Japanese in Australian schools, universities and private colleges in 1941 were interned and/or repatriated.

Japan in Australia

It is clear from the contributions to this book that work on the Australia-Japan relationship remains vibrant and that there is strong postgraduate activity in these research areas. This model has been effective in advancing the study of Japan in this country for many decades, underpinned by the high standard of Japanese language teaching in Australian schools and universities and the effective combination of language and disciplinary expertise.

The 12 chapters in this collection cover a truly wide remit of the Japanese presence and influence in Australia – literature, art, history, sport, poetry, language education, media, fashion and migration. This is an impressive and fascinating analysis of the multidimensional presence of Japan in this country.

There are also many more important stories still to be told. For example,

- The Japanese trading community in Australian before the war – who were these men and their families who lived in Australia, who were so well-versed in dealing with Australians and who developed lifelong personal connections with their Australian colleagues? What were their economic, social and political connections in the Australian community, indeed, connections so close that the wool buyers were among the first Japanese back into Australia in 1951?
- The history of technology transfer and development from Japan to Australia. Take the car industry, for example – there were Japanese car imports pre-war (Datsun) and heavy engineering and machinery products. After the war came the Snowy Mountains Scheme, which brought the importation of Toyota vehicles for that project and subsequently for the mining industry.
- The links between the Australian and Japanese horse racing industries – jockeys and a Japanese vet were allowed in 1953 to assist with Australian horse sales to Japanese interests. These links are still strong.
- The vexing topic of when and how Japanese were allowed to enter Australia (including the issues of visas and immigration) both before and after the Second World War. This is a rich field for analysis.

Prologue 3

- The Japanese and Australian arts communities, notably ceramics – for example, the impact of the Japanese folk arts movement on Australian ceramic arts and crafts. The influence of the David Jones Art Gallery in Sydney in promoting and popularising Japanese art and craft to Australian collectors is a good case study.
- What about the links between Australian and Japanese churches and, at least in the early years after the war, the peace movements? The first Japanese visitor to Australia after the war in June 1950 (and a rather controversial episode in the granting of his visitor's visa) appears to have been Bishop Yashiro Hinsuke, Anglican Bishop of Kobe and a well-known opponent of the war.
- What does Japan know of Australian literature and what has been translated over the years? Certainly, Patrick White and Christina Stead's works were translated into Japanese – what else has been made available in translation?
- Finally, given the 40 years since the Australia-Japan Foundation began, it would be valuable to analyse the impact of AJF funding and projects over that period, through a detailed analysis of the activities of its grantees. There will certainly be much to draw from and a wealth of strong intercultural impact.

Thank you to the editors and the contributors of this volume for continuing to advance the important study of the cultural relationship between our two countries.

Emeritus Professor Alan Rix
University of Queensland
October 2017

1 Japan in Australia, an introduction

David Chapman and Carol Hayes

Introduction

Contemporary Australia's engagement with Japan continues a relationship of some 150 years that has deeply impacted Australia's social, cultural, economic and political landscape. Australia's proximity to Asia has meant it has developed close ties with neighbours in the region, and perhaps its relationship with Japan has become one of the most intimate. Such familiarity has been equally the result of nation-level interactions as it has been of everyday, personal and community contacts. However, this relationship has seen both extremes, and tracing its trajectory provides an example of how history can turn from fear, enmity and misunderstanding through war, foreign encroachment and the legacy of conflict to close and intimate connection that results in cultural enrichment and diversification.

This book incorporates a diverse range of disciplinary approaches to comprehend the countless ways in which Japan has been imagined, represented and experienced in the Australian context. At the same time, this approach furthers our understanding of the contribution from Japan in Australia's course as a nation. As a part of this, the contributors to this book have interrogated definitive notions of Australia and 'Australianness', and Japan and 'Japaneseness', where tensions emerge alongside attempts to place Japan and Australia into definable and distinguishable categories that are often labelled for consumption, representation and reassurance.

The critical approach of this book identifies and underscores a blurring of lines and smearing of borders that emphasise an interconnectedness that is transnational, translingual and transcultural. Moreover, as this interfolding continues, the necessity to rethink what we believe to be Australian and, equally, what we consider to be Japanese becomes more apparent. Even today, the juxtaposition of Japan and Australia often evokes notions of a binary of Oriental and Occidental, Asian and non-Asian and East and West. In this book we ask how we can better understand how dichotomies of Self and Other are challenged and disrupted when we explore the ways in which Japan and Australia intersect and interrelate. In doing so, we confront and unsettle commonly held notions of Japan, Japanese culture and Japanese society through scholarly engagement within diverse settings. This book is the result of the 2016 Japan in Australia conference held at the University of Queensland and generously supported by The Japan Foundation.

Book structure

The book is structured in loose chronological order starting with early contacts between Japan and Australia. The 12 chapters reflect the diverse and dynamic context in which we find Japan's presence in Australia through overarching themes such as early contact, war and rebuilding relationships, cultural fusion, identity and intercultural relations, contemporary culture and Japanese language education. The book is topped and tailed by two personal contributions, beginning with University of Queensland Emeritus Professor Alan Rix's reflections on the importance of exploring Japan and Australia's shared cultural relationship and concluding with an afterword from Professor Vera Mackie, a leader in the field of Japanese studies.

Drawing on his long and celebrated academic engagement with Japan in Australia, Rix reflects on a number of pivotal points in the bilateral relationship and argues the importance of recording both the 'people-to-people' contact and the myriad multidimensional ways our two countries are interconnected, from the wool trade to horse racing, from the tragedy of war to shared engagement in peace movements, from technology transfer to community arts. He celebrates this book for the new stories it adds to the narrative of Japan and Australia's shared relationship. Concluding the manuscript, Vera Mackie provides an afterword for the book reflecting on how Japan is imprinted on the very streets of our Australian cities, from high fashion to Muji and Uniqlo-style mass production, from haute cuisine to sushi trains and supermarket sushi, all speaking to the deep interconnectedness between these two cultures.

In this introductory chapter we provide a sketch of Japan in Australia from the earliest contact in the late Tokugawa Period through to the present, touching on the themes of the chapters within the volume. In it we posit that not only will we benefit by understanding more about Japan through this research, we suggest that a greater understanding of Australia is also gained through this work. Japan is well positioned as an important voice both within Asia and globally. Australia, too, stands in an important geopolitical sphere, part of and yet separate to Asia, with strong past links to the United Kingdom and United States but also a country with deep ties to Japan, China and other neighbours in the region. At a time when tensions between different religious, ethnic and other identities have escalated, we offer an example of how greater interaction and involvement can create lasting connectedness. We begin at the first recorded contacts between Australians and Japanese in the nineteenth century.

Early contacts

> Contacts between Australia and Japan are as old as the treaties that marked the end of Japan's seclusion.
>
> (Sissons 1972, 193)

It is impossible to discuss Japan and Australia without recognition and reference to the research of Australian historian David Sissons (1925–2006). Serving in the

6   *David Chapman and Carol Hayes*

Australian Army, Sissons learned Japanese through the military from 1944–47 and then studied in Tokyo 1957–60 (Sissons 1998, 40; Stockwin 2016, 1). Much of Sissons's meticulous research on the history between the two nations is stored away in '60 capacious boxes at the National Library of Australia Manuscripts Collection in Canberra' (Stockwin 2016, 3). Thankfully, the public now has greater access to this material with the recent publication of two volumes entitled *Bridging Australia and Japan*. In Volume 1, Sissons (2016, 87) divides nineteenth-century Australian contacts with Japan into three periods: the *sakoku*[1] period (1633–1866), the second period (1867–1891) and the third period (1892–1902). In the *sakoku* period, he focuses on the last years of Japan's seclusion from the West and the influx of foreign residents as well as Japanese travelling abroad. The second period, says Sissons, is characterised by 'unfettered but infrequent and small-scale contact' with important and increasing labour for the pearling industry sourced from Japan, and 'the appearance of the Japanese prostitute', or '*karayuki-san*' throughout much of Australia. The third period was one of increased Japanese emigration to Australia sponsored by large companies that ended with the 1901 introduction of the Immigration Restriction Act excluding non-European migrants and forming the basis of the White Australia Policy (*hakugōshugi*).

Although the first of Sissons's three periods includes the very beginning of the Tokugawa period through the opening up of Japan, not much happened between Japan and Australia before 1859. Therefore, the total length of time between the bookending of Japan's opening up after *sakoku* and Australia's clamping down on immigration of non-whites in 1901 constitutes just over 40 years. This was only a brief period of time, within which both countries interacted on many levels and in multiple ways.

Although the time prior to 1859 is like a black hole in Japan's interaction with the West, there are some recorded instances of Australians and Japanese encountering one another. Sissons (2016, 41, 88–89) speculates that the first encounter was with the 1831 landing of the Sydney whaler the *Lady Rowena* in Hamanaka Bay on Hokkaido. The Australian crew, according to a *Sydney Gazette* article, destroyed a village and fired upon its people (The Sydney Gazette 1831, 2). On this point, Sissons (2016, 42) playfully declares that, '[i]f this was in fact the first encounter between our two peoples, then the relationship got off to a bad start'. However, it seems that encounters soon after this one on Hachijōjima and with other Japanese junks were amicable and friendly, with the captain of the *Lady Rowena*, Bourne Russell, making purchases of food and supplies on the same trip without incident (Sissons 2016, 89). In fact, the *Lady Rowena* safely returned to Sydney Harbour in July 1832, with 600 barrels of whale oil from Japan (Japan Club of Australia 1998, 25).

Sissons's assertion of this being the first encounter between Australians and Japanese, however, may require revising. There is evidence that a landing on Japanese shores by an Australian vessel took place the year before the *Lady Rowena* in 1830. In 2017, an English teacher in Japan, Nick Russell, came across documents that provide strong evidence of the arrival of the *Cypress* on 16 January 1830 off the town of Mugi on Shikoku Island (Robertson 2017). The crew of the *Cypress* were escaped convicts who had mutinied in 1829 while on their way from Van Diemen's Land (Tasmania) to Macquarie Harbour (The Sydney Monitor 1829, 3). Although this event may take precedence, Sissons's claim about early Japanese-Australian relations getting off to a bad start still holds. Initially, the encounter was one of mutual curiosity with some limited interaction, but suspicion took over and the convicts were lucky to escape with their lives, being hastened away under cannon fire from the Japanese.

Interestingly, Japanese accounts record an illustration of a gift offered by the convict crew to the Japanese villagers that looks much like a boomerang. Other details recorded by the Japanese are of one of the crew who produced 'a big glass of what appeared to be an alcoholic beverage and indicated that we (the Japanese) should drink' (Robertson 2017). 'We declined by waving our hands, upon which they passed the glass around themselves, one by one tapping their heads as they drank to indicate the good feeling it brought them, and finished the lot'. Mima, a local commander, suspicious of the ship and its crew, stated, 'The men on the ship do not look hungry at all and in fact they seem to be mocking us by diving off the stern and climbing back onto the ship again, it is very strange that everyone who goes out for a closer look returns feeling very sorry for them. I think they are pirates. We should crush them!' (Robertson 2017). The *Cypress* eventually made its way to Macau and China, where she sunk due to the holes in her hull from Japanese cannon fire (The Sydney Gazette and New South Wales Advertiser 1831, 2). The convicts were then recaptured. Two were executed and one, William Swallow, was sent back to Van Diemen's Land, dying four years later.

There was another instance in 1850 in which an Australian vessel, the *Eamont*, intruded upon a closed Japan not far from where the *Lady Rowena* had landed 19 years earlier. The crew of the *Eamont* remained in custody for four months and were eventually transported to Nagasaki to be sent away aboard a Dutch ship to Batavia. One crewmember, James Higgins, died during a storm at sea and was buried amongst the Dutch graves in the grounds of Goshinji temple. According to Sissons (2016, 90), Higgins was the first Australian to be buried on Japanese soil. During the storm that killed Higgins, the crew saved the life of the Japanese officer who had accompanied them. This officer then gave orders that they be released from confinement, and they were then taken to Matsumai accompanied by 500 Japanese (Geelong Advertiser 1851, 2).

Although the brief landings of the *Cypress*, the *Lady Rowena* and the *Eamont* are recorded as the very first encounters between Australians and the Japanese, as Sissons's quote above clearly outlines, sustained interaction only began with the end of *sakoku*. Twenty-nine years after the *Cypress* left Japan's coastline, the country ended its more than two-century seclusion policy and opened selected ports and harbours to trade and foreign residents. The first from Australia[2] to encounter the newly opened Japan were Alexander Marks (1838–1919)[3] and his brother Henry (?–1871), who took up residency in Yokohama and set up a business in 1859. Henry Marks, alongside another brother, Lawrence, died in a typhoon aboard the Schooner *Julie* in 1871. Alexander Marks left Japan and returned to Australia the following year in 1872. After returning to Melbourne, he became the first Honorary Consul for Japan for the Australian colonies from 1879 to 1896. Marks was appointed by the Japanese government because of increasing court cases concerning the exploitation of Japanese crew by unscrupulous British captains who had recruited the men in Treaty ports in Japan (Sissons 2016, 93). From 1896, Marks went on to become Honorary Consul for Japan in Victoria, a position he held until 1902.

Following Marks, John Reddie Black (1826–1880) was the next from Australia to engage with Japan. Originally a Scotsman, Black arrived in Japan from Australia in 1862, and he remained there for more than 11 years. Black was a singer and newspaper publisher, and also the father of Henry James Black (1858–1923). Australian-born Henry Black lived in Japan from the age of 3 and became famous as a kabuki actor and the first foreign-born *rakugoka*. He performed as *Kairakutei Burakku* (Pleasure Black) and was eventually adopted as a Japanese, changing his name to Ishii Black. He died of a stroke at the age of 64. Not long after Black Senior's arrival in 1867, British-born politician John Henry Brooke (1826–1902) moved from Melbourne to Yokohama. Taking over from Black as proprietor and editor of the *Japan Daily Herald*, he wrote a series of articles for *The Australasian* newspaper in 1867 under the pseudonym 'An Australian Colonist' and remained in Japan until his death on 8 January 1902.[4]

The migration of Japanese to Australia was a little slower and did not begin until after the Sakoku Edict, which restricted travel outside of Japan, was lifted on 23 May 1866. Although some Japanese left Japan without permission or passports before 1866 (Yamamoto 2017, 8), sanctioned travel did not begin until late in 1866, or, in the case of the first Japanese to visit Australia, 1867. These first travellers were acrobats and jugglers, with the very first group of 12 members being part of 'Lenton and Smith's Great Novelty for the Colonies – The Great Dragon Troupe of Japanese – 12 Wonders from Yeddo' (Sissons 2016, 50), who performed at the Princess Theatre in Melbourne. The first naturalised Japanese in Australia was also an acrobat. He was Ewar Dicinoski (likely Sakuragawa Rikinosuke), who performed with the Royal Tycoon Troupe, a group of 13 members that came to Australia in 1871. Dicinoski decided to stay on and, 11 years later, in 1882, naturalised as an Australian (Armstrong 1973, 3; Sissons 2016, 51). His grave can be found in the Toowong Cemetery in Brisbane (see Figure 1.1).

In the 1860s, alongside the arrival of these first Japanese was an emerging interest in the cultural products of Japan. The earliest encounters with things Japanese were not only the result of interactions with Japanese performers and official delegations, but also came through the accounts of returning travellers and visitors from Europe, where the flood of Japanese exports entering European markets prompted a wave of interest in all things Japanese known as *Japonisme*. Japan's first participation in an international exhibition was not until 1867 in Paris (although fragments of Japanese wares were on display at earlier exhibitions).[5] This first involvement was prompted by Fukuzawa Yuichi's 1866 explanation (*seiyōjijō*) of his visit to the International Exhibition in London in 1862 (Kornicki 1994, 17).

Japan in Australia, an introduction 9

Figure 1.1 Grave of Ewar Dicinoski (likely Sakuragawa Rikinosuke), first naturalised Japanese in Australia. Toowong Cemetery, Brisbane, Queensland

Source: Grave of Ewar Dicinoski (likely Sakuragawa Rikinosuke), first naturalised Japanese in Australia. Toowong Cemetery, Brisbane, Queensland (photograph by David Chapman).

Not only was there interest in many things Japanese in Australia in these early days, there was a reciprocal interest in Australian products by the Japanese. This mutual curiosity prompted the earliest visit to Australia by Japanese official government dignitaries in 1875. It consisted of a small entourage of five representatives, including commissioners Hashimoto Masato and Sakata Haruo, and agriculturalists Funaki and Iida,[6] who were to make a detailed study of agriculture in the colonies of Australia and to accompany exhibits that were from private interests in Japan destined for display at the Intercolonial Exhibition in Melbourne. Englishman Robert Page was employed by the Japanese government as the secretary of the delegation (Kornicki 1994, 23).

The Japanese presence at the exhibition can be attributed to the President of the Victoria Commissions for the Philadelphia Exhibitions Sir Redmond Barry (1813–1880), a British immigrant and senior judge of the Victorian Supreme Court who had also presided over the trial of Ned Kelly (Kornicki 1994, 19). Barry had approached Sir Harry Parkes, the British Minister Plenipotentiary in Tokyo, making the suggestion that Japan's participation in the exhibition would make it attractive and 'extend competition beyond the limits of Australia' (Kornicki 1994, 20). At the time, speeches by Barry and Hashimoto demonstrated a very favourable response to the presence of Japan at the exhibitions, where they were met with enthusiastic applause. Barry emphasised the prospect of further cooperation between the two nations and also underscored the plans and wishes by Australia for furthering relations with Japan, which aimed for:

> Still more intimate relations of intercourse, and the reciprocal advantages of an expanded trade between the 35,000,000 who inhabit that great Empire [Japan], and the loyal and dutiful subjects of our Queen in Australasia.
>
> (Kornicki 1994, 24)

The press at the time was also enthusiastic about the Japanese wares on display and the favourable prices of the goods (Kornicki 1994, 26). For example, *The Age* (1875, 3) exclaimed that, 'No one department in the exhibition will be viewed with greater interest than that in which the industries of Japan are represented' and '[t]he Japanese, in the manufacture of the first-named goods, have reached a degree of perfection never attained by any other nation'. However, motivated by mounting hostility and racism toward the Chinese immigrant community in Victoria, the *Melbourne Punch* was less than enthusiastic and singled out the Japanese exhibit as the only display worthy of criticism. The picture (Figure 1.2) appearing in the *Morning Punch* of a man with a long top knot more resembled a caricature of a Chinese merchant than a Japanese.

> But after all said about the Japanese collection, why is it we see nothing of one really useful product of this polished or polishing people – where is the famed blacking of Japan, where are those mighty exhibitors whose bills have been posted on the pyramids and whose bottles have been shied at by the larrikins of Tartary . . .?
>
> (Melbourne Punch 1875, 7)

The exhibition and extended stay by Funaki and Iida resulted in a detailed two-volume report on Australia compiled by Hashimoto with the assurance that the activities over 1875–1876 would result in the establishment of a trading relationship of great benefit to Japan (Kornicki 1994, 29). Trade between Japan and Australia emerged in the late 1800s, with some industries flourishing, as evidenced by the number of bales of wool exported by F Kanematsu (Aust) Ltd rising from 200 a year in 1890–91 to 100,000 by 1930 (Sissons 2016, 93–94). The company founder, Fusajiro Kanematsu, had many business interests in Kobe and Osaka, including banking and merchant shipping, and he was the owner and editor-in-chief of the *Osaka Mainichi* newspaper (Sono 1998, 34; Sissons 1983, n.p.). The Japanese Consulate-General in Sydney had been established in 1882 to facilitate trade such as that established by Kanematsu as well as to help with bilateral relations.

Figure 1.2 The Heathen Japee
Source: *Melbourne Punch* 16 September 1875, 368

Prior to WWII, Japanese immigrant communities consisted primarily of the diving community in the Torres Strait and the Broome area, the cane farmers in North Queensland and diplomats and businessmen in Melbourne and Sydney. Fifty contracted Japanese cane workers arrived in 1892,[7] mostly on three-year contracts, and demands for Japanese workers led to an increase of a further 520 men the following year in 1893 (Bryce 1998, 42–43).[8] Working with cane was hard work, with grueling 10-hour days for the equivalent wage of 10 yen per month. However, with three meals a day and accommodation provided, it was an attractive option, as farm workers in Japan received as little as 20 zeni per day.[9] Interestingly, the contract for the Japanese workers, in addition to the import of Japanese products such as tea, soy sauce and pickles, also included a clause about the provision of a Japanese-style bath, and in one instance when the bath water had not been heated for the end of the day, the Japanese workers went on strike (Murakami 1998, 31). By 1896, Townsville and surrounding areas were home to 952 Japanese (including 20 women) as compared to 618 Japanese (35 women) in the diving communities around Thursday Island. The numbers of Japanese in Queensland peaked in 1898 with 1,865, including 117 women, the majority of whom were '*karayuki-san*' prostitutes.[10] Prior to 1900 and federation, as many as 3,247 Japanese had at some time resided in Queensland,[11] with the Japanese government supportive of contract labour rather than an immigration agreement.

The population of Japanese in Australia in the 1890s was small and remained so because of the introduction of restrictive legislation on immigration between 1893 and 1901. In 1888, the mainland colonies of the United Kingdom signed the 'Memorandum on Chinese Immigration' prohibiting immigration of Chinese citizens and naturalisation of Chinese residents. These restrictions on Chinese citizens led to a refocus on all North East Asian entry, including the Japanese, who were beginning to dominate the pearl-diving industry in Northern Australia and the indentured cane labour in Queensland (Meaney 1999, 17–18). Under pressure from the British government, which in 1894 entered a commercial treaty with Japan, some colonies in the late 1890s removed from their immigration restriction legislation the designation of any particular race. Instead, an education test, modelled on that used for some years by the colony of Natal, was to be administered by a customs officer in ways dependent on the discretion of that officer. This was represented by Britain as more tactful, but the same discriminative outcome was ensured. In 1901, a version of the Natal test was established under the Commonwealth Immigration Restriction Act (Willard 1923, 108–118; see also Clark and Ely 1888). Immigrants could be prohibited if 'when asked to do so by an officer fails to write out at dictation and sign in the presence of the officer a passage of fifty words in length in a European language directed by the officer' (Commonwealth of Australia 1901, 1). As with the pearlers, the promulgation of the Act and its European language dictation test, targeting both guest workers and immigrants of colour, resulted in very few Japanese workers remaining in the sugar industry (Murakami 1998, 30–31).

The Immigration Restriction Act eventually saw the Japanese population decrease dramatically. The 1921 census records a total of 2,639 Japanese nationals, including 150 women, living in Australia, of whom 92% were born in Japan. By the 1933 census, the total number of Japanese had decreased by more than half to 1,218 (76 women), the declining trend increasing as the war years approached (Australian Bureau of Statistics 1940, 554). For example, in the 1920s there were as many as 2,000 Japanese living on Thursday Island, although by 1936 only 350 or so, mostly divers, remained there (Jotani 1998, 18). According to the October 1940 census, there were 178 Japanese living in rural Queensland, generally engaged in the sugar industry (Murakami 1998, 30–31).

Someone who managed to negotiate his way around these restrictive conditions was businessman Takasuka Jo, who, having represented Ehime Prefecture in the Japanese House of Representatives from 1898 to 1902, arrived in Melbourne in 1905 and was given a 12-month exception from the dictation test. He established the Takasuka, Dight & Co export-import business to serve as a business gateway to Japan (Matsudaira 2018). Moving from business to land lease and farming, Takasuka battled the Australian elements, to a large extent unsuccessfully, to produce the first rice in Victoria, although by 1927 he abandoned his attempts to grow rice and tried other vegetable crops, which again met with little success, and in 1939 he returned to import-export. Takasuka died in 1940 in Matsuyama only a year after he had returned to Japan to set up a Kobe office as Australia Barter Trade & Co., leaving behind his wife Ichiko, his daughter Aiko and two sons, Shō and Mario, who had by this time become successful tomato farmers and orchardists in Fosterville, Victoria (Sissons 1990). Interestingly, his younger son Mario was Australian born and so served in both Crete and New Guinea in the 2/3 Australian LAA Regiment, while the older Shō was interned in 1941 in the Tatura camp, although happily he was soon released after enormous support from his neighbours (Whiley 2018; Sissons 1998, 38–40).

The other areas of commercial activity involving Japanese in Australia were, as mentioned above, mostly pearling, cane farming and prostitution. The first Japanese pearlers were seamen, starting with Nonami Kojiro in 1876. These Japanese men became well regarded for their abilities as divers, with many being recruited in the early 1880s through to the 1890s working in Torres Strait, Thursday Island and Western Australia. The first Japanese diplomatic mission in Australia,[12] no doubt due to the influx of Japanese cane workers, was established in Townsville, QLD, in 1896 (it closed in 1908), with Nakagawa Tsunejiro as the first consul. The Sydney Consulate was established the following year in 1897 and Nakagawa moved from Townsville to take up the role of Sydney Consul. In 1901 the Sydney Consulate was upgraded to a Consulate-General (Consulate-General of Japan 2012).

The closeness of the bilateral relationship shared by Australia and Japan in the late 1800s and early 1900s is further demonstrated by the fact that during World War I, as a result of the Anglo-Japanese Treaty of Commerce and Navigation signed by the United Kingdom and Japan on 16 July 1894, the Japanese navy shared some of the responsibility for patrolling the Australian coastline and participating in the transport of military personnel from both Australia and New Zealand to the European front (Miyaji-Lawrence 1998, 341–342).

Around this time in 1888, Scottish-born James Murdoch (1856–1921), the first Australian scholar of Japanese history, made his way to Japan to work as a teacher and journalist. While in Japan he became a professor at Tokyo First High School and taught the famous Japanese novelist Natsume Sōseki (1867–1916). It was during his time in Japan that Murdoch began researching and scribing the first comprehensive history of Japan to be written in English. In 1917, Murdoch returned from Japan and took up concurrent positions at the Royal Military College, Duntroon and the University of Sydney (Sissons 1982, n.p.).

Early recorded contacts between Japan and Australia can also be found in the field of horse racing. An Australian horse named 'Sydney' was reported as winning a race in Japan in 1867 (The Argus 1867, 7), the year before the Meiji Restoration began. Further, in Harold Williams's book (Williams 1958, 179) on the earliest foreign settlements in Japan, there is mention of 'fast racehorses and crooked jockeys' imported from Australia into Japan. At the turn of the twentieth century, the *Maitland Weekly Mercury* (1905, 13) published an article about a Mr Masuda (Matsuda), a Japanese horse buyer, who was in Australia to purchase horses for breeding purposes. The well-travelled Matsuda considered Australian horses superior to any others he had encountered. He believed the abundance of grass feed and the climate to be advantageous, but he remarked on how the wildness of Australian horses was a drawback. Matsuda's intentions were to purchase Australian horses for breeding with Japanese horses, which he believed to be the 'best in the world for the improvement of the Japanese horse'. From these early days of interest in Australian horses and horse racing, there has been a steady bilateral engagement in this industry, with Japanese horses racing in important Australian events and vice versa, and with Japanese buyers prominent in the Australian market, like Queensland's Magic Million yearlings sale (Bartley 2018).

As discussed above, interest in things Japanese began to expand in Australia in the late 1800s in parallel with increasing global interest. The influence on the art scene in Australia is worthy of note. Penny Bailey's chapter in this book explores the historical context of Australian artists such as Lionel Lindsay (1874–1961) and Violet Teague (1872–1951) who experimented with *Japonisme* as a platform for expressive experimentation. She also writes about how Margaret Preston (1875–1963) was drawn to the aesthetic conventions and techniques employed in Japanese woodblock prints for their radical departure from the Western methods of pictorial representation championed by the Academy. Bailey argues that Preston was unusual amongst these Australian artists because of her sustained reference to the Japanese pictorial modes (repetitive patterning, flat areas of colour and strong black outlines) that ultimately became synonymous with her hallmark style. Preston, she explains, secured her place as a champion of Australia's modern visual culture by incorporating Japanese pictorial conventions into her aesthetic practice throughout her career.

Further into the twentieth century, trade between Japan and Australia hit a rough patch. In 1936 a trade dispute erupted with Japan over Australia's decision to increase tariffs on imported goods with the hope of increasing the Australian manufacturing sector. Japan retaliated by looking for alternative sources for such primary goods as wool and wheat. Although resolved by the end of 1936, this dispute marked Australia's increasing concern with Japan's progressively aggressive 'southward advance policy' that was later seen as a prelude to war (Parliament of Australia 2000). It was the following year that Tsurumi Yūsuke, a member of the Japanese Diet, visited Australia with his two children. In this volume, Tomoko Aoyama provides a glimpse of the impact this visit had on Tsurumi's two children. After his visit to Australia, Yūsuke continued to get to know Australia better and eventually published a book on Australian nature and society. Further, Aoyama uses resources from a number of archives to illustrate how Tsurumi's daughter Kazuko, 19 at the time and gifted in traditional dance and poetry, appeared in the Australian media and continued to contribute to the relationship between Australia and Japan after the visit. Tsurumi's son Shunsuke, on the other hand, was more challenged by his experiences. While in Adelaide, he was shown an English translation of the *Kojiki*. The fact that this translated version of the famous anthology of Japanese origin myths presented a different interpretation of the work, challenging the imperialist interpretations widely accepted in Japan, influenced Shunsuke's thinking and led him to complete a collection of critical essays, *Ame no Uzume Den* (Tsurumi 1991). Sociologist Kazuko's poetry and dance and Shunsuke's writings, both as a scholar and a philosopher, were equally highly influenced by their visit to Australia.

War and rebuilding relationships

From 1940 relations between Australia and Japan cooled rapidly, with the 1941 economic sanctions against Japan leading to the freezing of Japanese assets that required all Japanese residents in Australia to return to Japan or face internment. With the outbreak of war, 4,300 Japanese residents in Australia, including Australians of Japanese heritage and some who were arrested outside of Australia, were declared 'enemy aliens' and interned in five of the eight main internment camps. Allocation to these camps was determined by where they had resided in Australia, their social status and their gender – in Hay NSW (1940–46), Cowra NSW (1941– 47) and Enoggera (Gaythorne) Queensland (1914–15 and 1940–46), Holsworthy (Liverpool) NSW (1939–46), Tatura (Rushworth) VIC (1940–47) and Loveday SA camp (1941–46) (National Archives of Australia; also see Nagata 1996). Most returned to Japan after the war, losing their assets in Australia with no compensation provided even after hostilities ceased.

However, some, like Tomitaro Fujii, were able to return to their previous lives. Known as the last Japanese diver on Thursday Island, Fujii had arrived from Kobe in 1923 when he was only 17 years old. Working as a diver, he married into a wealthy Chinese merchant family, until war broke out and he was interned in Hay NSW. After the war, he returned to Thursday Island, and while working for a Japanese pearling company, he toiled to re-establish the Japanese cemetery, placing as many as 200 grave markers on broken or unmarked graves (Mogi 1998, 22).

Another such example is Furusawa Hajime, who served as the secretary to Mr Alexander Marks, Honorary Consul for Japan in Victoria mentioned above.

Born in Uwajima in Ehime in 1868, Furusawa took up a position with the Japanese Department of Foreign Affairs in 1891 and was sent to serve as Marks's secretary in the Melbourne Consulate established in 1879, travelling on the *Sagami Maru* together with the 520 guest cane workers. Furusawa married the daughter to Japanese artist Kagami Godaiyu, and remained in Australia until his death in 1936. His whole family, including three daughters and his father-in-law, all rest in St. Kilda cemetery in Melbourne (Bryce 1998, 42).

These older Japanese graves scattered across the country make up an important part of the Japan in Australia story and are recognised in both Australia and Japan. In 2017, Japanese Ambassador Kusaka celebrated Cowra as a symbol of Japan and Australia's strong relationship. Kusaka noted that the Japanese War Cemetery, made up of 522 graves of Japanese nationals who passed away during WWII, is now jointly maintained by the Japanese government, through their embassy in Canberra, the City of Cowra and the Australian government, while the Japanese gardens and cherry-blossom-lined street in Cowra are kept in order by the commitment of the local community, serving as a good example of the closeness and depth of the bilateral relationship rising above the horrors of war.

The post-WWII period required the rebuilding of the relationship between Australia and Japan. Following the Japanese surrender on 2 September 1945, Australia played an important role in the 37,000-strong British Commonwealth Occupation Force (BCOF) stationed in occupied Japan from 21 February 1946 until the end of occupation in April 1952 (Wood 1998, 32). From the early 1950s, the racial-nationalism of the White Australia ideology was increasingly contested and stood at odds with Australia's desire to strengthen ties with Asia, particularly in terms of trade. Under the newly elected liberal government of Robert Menzies, which defeated the Chifley government in 1949, Immigration Minister Harold Holt developed a scheme to gradually approve entry and eventual assimilation of Japanese war brides, and on 27 March 1952, the Australian Cabinet approved the 'admission of Japanese wives of Australian servicemen and ex-servicemen' into Australia, provided they were approved by the Australian embassy in Japan, creating a new group of Japanese Australians, Japanese war brides and their children (ANZAC Day Commemoration Committee). The legalisation of Japanese war bride immigration was an important step towards reconciliation and forgiveness, serving to break down the restrictions on Japanese immigration and weaken the White Australia Policy (for a personal story on this topic, see De Matos and Huggett 2010).

As many as 650 new brides would emigrate to Australia throughout the 1950s (Tamura 2011, xi). Mrs Teruko Blair was one such war bride. Born in Hiroshima in 1925, Teruko experienced the horrors of the Hiroshima atomic bomb, and later, working as a waitress in the Officers Mess in Kure, where the British Commonwealth Occupation Force were stationed, she met her future husband William Dickson Blair. Living together in secret for two years, they were not able to formally marry until after the signing of the San Francisco Peace Treaty in 1952, and in December 1953, Teruko arrived in Australia with their eldest son Billy a babe in arms (Blair 1991, 10). Through her research into the lives of these war brides and their families, historian Keiko Tamura argues the importance of their individual narratives to the Japan in Australia story (Tamura 2011, xii).

With reports of the war trials and the increasing awareness of the atrocities of the Pacific War, there was still a great deal of hatred and fear of Japanese nationals; however, as the 1950s progressed, attitudes began to change. Gwenda Tavan (2005, 3) emphasises that from the early 1900s there was a general assumption among the Australia populace that 'whiteness, Britishness and Australianness, were crucial elements of Australian nationhood' and that these characteristics should determine entry into and membership of the Australian community, and the war did little to change this. However, the legalisation of Japanese war bride immigration opened the door to understanding and forgiveness, becoming an important step on the path to reconciliation, as Walker and Sobocinska note in *Australia's Asia*; 'Individual encounters [with Japan] precipitated a broader awareness, and the postwar period saw a growing interest in and enthusiasm for what was being seen as Australia's "neighborhood"' (Walker and Sobocinska 2012, 15).

As the twentieth century developed, the Australia-Japan relationship moved into a new phase of trade and mutual diplomatic relations. From the 1950s, the horror of the war ceased to be the dominant narrative in Australia's engagement with Japan. The Australian embassy was re-established in Tokyo in 1952, with the embassy of Japan in Canberra following a year later. Morris Low and Ai Kobayashi both examine the role of sport in re-establishing relations postwar and the role played by the 1956 Melbourne Olympics and the 1954 Baseball Tour of Australia by the Yomiuri Giants in helping to promote a positive connection between Australia and Japan.

Kobayashi examines the Yomiuri Giants' 1954 baseball tour, the first Japanese sporting team to visit Australia after the cessation of WWII hostilities. Kobayashi sets the responses of the individual players against the backdrop of Australian governmental and public responses. Not without problems, this tour was an important step in the lead-up to Japan's involvement in the Melbourne Olympics, which is the focus of Low's chapter. Only four years after the end of the Allied Occupation of Japan, Low argues that the Melbourne Olympics made an important contribution to Australia-Japan relations by reshaping the negative attitudes that had hung on since the end of the war. Through this important sporting event, he examines Australia's changing attitudes towards Japan, just as Japan was struggling to redefine itself on the international stage as an economic success story and repositioning itself as a nation of peace and strength.

Cultural fusion

This section of the book examines Japan in Australia through the lens of cultural fusion, exploring the changing cultural landscape of Australia as more Japanese culture began to filter into the Australian consciousness. While the experience of the war with Japan continued to colour some Australian perceptions of the Japanese people, as memories of the war receded, it again became possible to talk about Japan's long history and traditions.

Japanese media was beginning to participate in the Australia broadcasting landscape, and both at state and national levels, Japan-Australia societies were springing up around the country. Originally established in 1909 with 23 members, the Japan Society of Sydney was reconvened in December 1957, and the first meeting of Australia-Japan Societies was held in Canberra in 1975 (Japanese Society of Sydney Inc 1997, 122). These early postwar interactions were in a context of closer ties between Australia and Japan. A variety of Japan-Australia associations and foundations also grew up in the 1960s, feeding into the boom years of the 1970s. The earliest group was the Australia Japan Society – Victoria Inc established in 1963, with SA in 1967, NSW and Tasmania following suit in 1968; Australia Japan Society of NSW established in 1968 and Canberra in 1972. There are now as many as 16 state and city societies which are members of the Federation of Australia Japan Societies. Although the Federation was not official until 2011, a national meeting of the various Australia-Japan Societies was held as early as 1975 in Canberra with the aim of developing better connections between the groups (National Federation of Australia Japan Societies). There are as many as 108 sister city/state relationships shared between Australia and Japan, the oldest established between Lismore and Yamatotakada city in Nara Prefecture in 1963 (Australian Embassy Tokyo Japan n.d., 38).

The Basic Treaty of Friendship and Cooperation between Australia and Japan was signed by both nations on 22 June 1976 with the express purpose of broadening the bilateral relationship beyond trade and economics, declaring that 'the basis of relations between Australia and Japan shall be enduring peace and friendship between the two countries and their peoples' (Australia Japan Business Co-Operation Committee n.d., 38). The Australian government established the Australia-Japan Foundation in 1976 to facilitate this by providing grants for people-to-people and institutional exchange in arts and culture, sport, science, media and education (Department of Foreign Affairs and Trade 2015, n.p.). The world of media also connected with Japan. Radio Australia commenced Japanese broadcasts from 1960, which proved increasingly popular through the 1970s but ceased in 1990 partly due to increased diversity in broadcasting technologies and the availability of Japanese media through the internet (Taguchi 1998, 122–123). The Sydney-based Nichigo Press first began publication in October 1977 and continues to service the Japanese community in Australia today (Nichigo Press 2017, 45).

Rebecca Hausler focuses on the impact of the Japanese television juggernaut *Monkey*, based on Wu Cheng'en's sixteenth-century Chinese novel *Journey to the West*, which achieved cult status in both Australia and the United Kingdom. Unlike culturally bland shows such as *Astro Boy* and *Kimba the White Lion*, *Monkey*, with its badly dubbed, kung-fu laden, mythological character-filled imagery and catchy theme song, allowed producers to capitalise on both Japanese and Chinese elements.

Lucy Fraser also explores cultural fusion through the literary landscape. Fraser focuses on intertextuality and how Nobel Prize winner Kawabata Yasunari's work has been referenced in the works of two Australian authors, Venero Armanno and Lulia Leigh. Fraser unpicks how Armanno and Leigh engage with Japanese imagery and orientalist stereotypes to question what these works may tell us about the role of Japanese literature in Australia and the place of both cultures in an international creative scene.

In this theme, Laura Emily Clark address the Japan in Australia's literary landscape with a focus on the work of Murakami Haruki. Clark also engages with Murakami Haruki's work through a discussion of his reception in Australia and the role of translated fiction within the Australian literary scene. She examines the tension between this overhyped global marketing and the role of the exotic Japanese 'other' in Australia's popular imagination.

Identity and intercultural relations contacts

Tim Steains provides a fascinating first-hand exploration of experiences transcending the borders of Japan and Australia and their place at the intersections of these borders. He argues that Nikkei identity is uniquely placed to query what it means to work between Japanese and Australian studies and how this relates to, and raises, questions of identity. Steains pays particular attention to the work of Mayu Kanamori and her experiences as a Nikkei artist in Australia. He explores the meaning and significance of notions of white Australian, Asian Australian, Japanese Australian and mixed-race Japanese Australian engagements with Japan and Japanese Australian history.

Koichi Iwabuchi also explores issues of identity and intercultural relations through an examination of academic engagement with trans-Asia approaches. He argues that academic discourse focused on the impact of the globalisation that engenders cross-border flows and connections of capital, people and media culture presumes a dynamic interconnectedness. Iwabuchi proposes an alternative Asia/trans-Asia approach that de-Westernises, de-nationalises and de-compartmentalises analysis of culture flows and connections. He argues for the importance of a Trans-Asia approach to generate more effective cross-border dialogue and reflection on life, society and culture within the Japan in Australia context.

Japanese language education

The development of Japanese language programs at both the secondary and tertiary level began in Sydney and Melbourne in the early 1900s, only to be restricted during the war years to the education of military specialists. Senkichi Inagaki taught Japanese language at Melbourne University from 1919 to 1941. Programs were re-established in the 1950s, which laid the groundwork for the Japanese language boom in of the 1980s (Hayakawa 1990).

Ikuo Kawakami's chapter focuses on the mobility of families in the twenty-first century and how children crossing numerous borders have been impacted and, in turn, how they impact the world around them. Kawakami particularly demonstrates this through an interesting analysis of memory and the way in which children recall their experiences, crossing the many borders they do, and how this influences their lives and the lives of those around them.

Chihiro Thompson focuses on the important topic of Japanese language education in Australia, which she argues has shifted from more policy-driven, instrumentally motivated endeavours to individual consumption of the entertainment aspect of learning Japanese. Thompson expertly guides us through the history of Japanese language education in Australia. She begins with the early days in the context of Japanese imperialism and the White Australia Policy when Japanese language learning was utilitarian in dealing with a nation that was basically seen as a threat to Australian interests. Next, Thompson explores the years of multiculturalism and the very different approach to learning Japanese when the language became the most widely studied foreign language in Australia. Then, on the basis of surveys of tertiary students, she updates us on the motivation behind the Japanese language's continued popularity. Thompson argues that a new type of learner of Japanese has emerged, which she calls 'consumer-learners'. These learners do not fit the traditional mould of 'students of Japanese' but rather often come to Japanese courses not to pursue a committed language learning career at university, but to enjoy socialising in classrooms and absorb some Japan 'cool'. Thompson examines a new perspective of framing Japanese language education that is inclusive of consumer-learners, as opposed to the traditional notion of language learning as future investment.

Conclusion

This edited book aims to bring together diverse perspectives on the impact and influence of Japan on Australia's social, historical and cultural landscape. Moreover, by examining Japan's interwoven presence in the fabric of Australia and moving away from essentialised notions of Japan and Australia, we present a distinct context of intercultural and transcultural connection through a variety of settings, historical periods and circumstances.

Another advantage of this publication is to present Japanese studies in Australia as a field that offers a viewpoint distinct from those in America and Europe. By examining the impact of Japanese culture and society, we can better reflect on the cultural fusion that is contemporary Australia and build the narrative of our shared relationship. This book, although multidisciplinary and contextually varied, is constrained by the usual restrictions of the publication process and the limited size of the research community. It is the work of present and future scholars to add to what will hopefully be a growing body of research in the area of Japan in Australia. There is still much work to be done in this context, and no volume on this topic could claim to be complete. This version is an addition to an endless list of ongoing engagement among people, places and events.

Notes

1 *Sakoku* is the term used for this period and represents Japan's choice to cut itself off from most of the Western world. The concept of *sakoku* is a disputed term, with some, like Toby, arguing that it is in large part a myth; see Ronald Toby, 'Reopening the Question of Sakoku: Diplomacy in the Legitimation of the Tokugawa Bakufu'.

2 Despite living in Australia before coming to Japan, both of the brothers were still US citizens at this time. Alexander Marks naturalised as Australian after returning from Japan to Australia on 9 August 1876.
3 Marks was born in the United States, but he lived in Australia from the age of 6 and, apart from his years in Japan and a brief period in the Philippines, remained in Australia until his death in 1919.
4 For more detail, see McArthur (2013).
5 Although there were some Japanese products (*Japanned Wares*) (Great Exhibition of the Works of Industry of All Nations 1851, 120) at the 1851 Great Exhibition of the Works of Industry of All Nations, these were random and likely collected from merchants at the Treaty Ports in China who had access to Nagasaki in the 1840s (Kornicki 1994, 16). At the International Exhibition of 1862, a greater variety of goods were on display, collected by Sir Rutherford Alcock, Her Majesty's Envoy Extraordinary and Minister Plenipotentiary in Japan (Illustrated London News 1862, 318).
6 Funaki and Iida stayed on until the end of March 1876, leaving with several breeding pairs and breeds of sheep to introduce sheep farming into Japan (Kornicki 1994, 23). Their first names have not been recorded in any documentation recovered so far.
7 In 1892 (Meiji 25), with Barnes and Phillip acting as the agent (intermediary), Yoshisa Imin-gaisha sent 50 Japanese workers to Queensland's cane fields. (1896 archival photo exists in Sisson's archive; Murakami 1998, 30–31). From 1885, a law prohibiting Melanesian workers (referred to as 'Kanakas') was enacted. This led to an increased demand for migrant workers. In 1888 Chinese immigrant workers were similarly banned, which allowed for more Japanese workers to enter, particularly because their reputation as good workers in the Hawaii cane fields preceded them. Yoshisa Imin-gaisha had already sent many workers from Hiroshima prefecture to Hawaii.
8 Also see newspaper *Table Talk* (1893) for a report that the liner *Sagami Maru* stopped at four Queensland ports, Cairns, Townsville, Mackey and Dungeness, to unload these workers.
9 In 1905, 6 zeni would buy you a bowl of curry rice and 20 would get you a ticket into the cinema in Japan ('Mukashi no 1 en wa Ima no nanen?').
10 In 1887 Japanese Consul for Australia Alexander Marks, mentioned above, expressed concern to Tokyo regarding the introduction of Japanese women of 'bad character into Australia' (Mihalopoulos 2011, 43).
11 In 1896 the total population of Queensland was recorded at 57,859, rising to 70,432 by 1901. (Queensland Past and Present: 100 Years of Statistics 1896–1996, 67).
12 Although Alexander Marks, mentioned above, was honourary Consulate for Japan, the Townsville mission involved Japanese nationals as representatives.

References

The Age. 1875. 'Japan', 3 September.
ANZAC Day Commemoration Committee. n.d. 'ANZAC Commemorating 100 Years', accessed 22 December 2018, https://anzacday.org.au/bcof-supplementary-information-and-anecdotes.
The Argus. 1867. 'Impressions of Japan by an Australian Colonist No. IV', 10 September, 7.
Armstrong, J. B. 1973. 'Aspects of Japanese Immigration to Australia Before 1900', *Queensland Heritage*, 2 (9): 3–9.
Australia Japan Business Co-Operation Committee (AJBCC). n.d. 'The Basic Treaty of Friendship Between Australia & Japan', 50th Anniversary Souvenir Book, accessed 7 August 2018, www.ajbcc.asn.au/wp-content/uploads/ajbcc_chapter4_treaty_of_friendship.pdf.

Australian Bureau of Statistics. n.d. 'Year Book Australia', 1940, Canberra, accessed 7 August 2018, www.abs.gov.au/AUSSTATS/abs@.nsf/DetailsPage/1301.01940.

Australian Embassy Tokyo Japan. n.d. 'A Selection of Australia and Japan's 108 Sister-City/Sister-State Relationships', accessed 7 August 2018, http://japan.embassy.gov.au/tkyo/sistercities.html.

Bartley, P. 2018. 'Ambitious Campaign: Japanese Galloper Flies Under the Radar for Australian Cup', *The Sydney Morning Herald*, 19 March, accessed 12 March 2019, www.smh.com.au/sport/racing/ambitious-campaign-japanese-galloper-flies-under-the-radar-for-australian-cup-20180308-p4z3i0.html.

Blair, T. 1991. *Oosutoraia ni idakarete [Embraced by Australia]*. Tokyo: Terebi Asahi.

Bryce, M. 1998. 'Sento-Kiruda bochi ni nemuru nihonjin' [Resting Japanese at St. Kilda Cemetery], in *Ōsutoraria no nihonjin – isseiki o koeru nihonjin no sokuseki [Japanese in Australia: Japanese Footprints Over a Century]*. Tokyo: Kinenshi Henshū Iinkai.

Clark, A. I. and Ely, R. 1888. 'Transcript Inglis Clark's 1888 "Memorandum" on Chinese Immigration Introduction and Commentary by Richard Ely', University of Tasmania Library Special and Rare Materials Collection, Australia, accessed 23 July 2018, https://eprints.utas.edu.au/11912/1/Chinese.pdf.

Commonwealth of Australia. 1901. 'Immigration Restriction Act', accessed 9 August 2018, www.foundingdocs.gov.au/resources/transcripts/cth4ii_doc_1901a.pdf.

Consulate-General of Japan, Sydney. 2012. 'Mission & History of the Consulate-General of Japan, Sydney', accessed 30 January 2018, www.sydney.au.emb-japan.go.jp/english/about_us/history_of_consulate_general.htm.

De Matos, C. and Huggett, N. 2010. *Love Under Occupation: A Personal Journey Through War, Marriage and White Australia*. Glen Waverley, VIC: Sid Harta Publishers.

Department of Foreign Affairs and Trade. 2015. n.p. 'Australia-Japan Foundation: About Us', accessed 30 January 2018, http://dfat.gov.au/people-to-people/foundations-councils-institutes/australia-japan-foundation/Pages/australia-japan-foundation.aspx.

Geelong Advertiser. 1851. 'Loss of the "Eamont" Imprisonment of the Crew', 24 March, 2.

'Great Exhibition of the Works of Industry of All Nations'. 1851. *Official Descriptive and Illustrated Catalogue*. London: Spicer Brothers, Wholesale Stationers, W. Clowes and Sons, Printers, vol. I. Index and Introductory, accessed 26 September 2017, www.e-rara.ch/zut/content/structure/6726810.

Hayakawa, M. 1990. *Moshi Inagaki and Japanese Residents in Australia 1906–1947*, Unpublished BA Honours Thesis, University of Melbourne.

Illustrated London News. 1862. 'The Japanese Court in the International Exhibition', vol. XLI, July–December, 318.

Japan Club of Australia. 1998. 'Nichigō, saisho no sōgū' [Australia and Japan: First Encounter], in *Ōsutoraria no nihonjin – isseiki o koeru nihonjin no sokuseki [Japanese in Australia: Japanese Footprints Over a Century]*. Tokyo: Kinenshi Henshū Iinkai.

Japanese Society of Sydney Inc. n.d. *Shidonii Nihonjinkai 40-nen no ayumi: 1957–1997 [Japanese Society of Sydney: A 40 Year Journey: 1957–1997]*. Sydney: Japanese Society of Sydney.

Jotani, I. 1998. 'Tooresu no umi ni ikita hibi', in *Ōsutoraria no nihonjin – isseiki o koeru nihon jin no sokuseki [Japanese in Australia: Japanese Footprints Over a Century]*. Tokyo: Kinenshi Henshū Iinkai.

Kornicki, P. 1994. 'Japan at the Australian Exhibitions', *Australian Studies*, 8 (1), 15–60.

Kusaka, S. 2017. 'Remarks by Mr Sumio Kusaka, Ambassador of Japan', *Japan Exchange and Teaching (JET) Programme 30th Anniversary and 2017 JET Programme Farewell Reception*, accessed 12 February 2018, www.au.emb-japan.go.jp/files/000272976.pdf.

The Maitland Weekly Mercury. 1905. 'A Japanese Horsebuyer', 28 October, 7.
Matsudaira, M. 2018. *Jō no hitotsubu [Jo's One Grain]*. Tokyo: Shinbunsha.
McArthur, I. 2013. *Henry Black: On Stage in Meiji Japan*. Melbourne: Monash University Publishing.
Meaney, N. 1999. *Towards a New Vision: Australia and Japan — Through A Hundred Years*. East Roseville, NSW: Kangaroo Press.
Melbourne Punch. 1875. 'Our Philadelphian Show', 9 September, 7, 368.
Mihalopoulos, B. 2011. *Sex in Japan's Globalization, 1870–1930*. London: Routledge.
Miyaji-Lawrence, T. 1998. 'Bara to wataru to kiku no hana' [Rose, Wattle and Chrysanthemum], in *Ōsutoraria no nihonjin – isseiki o koeru nihonjin no sokuseki [Japanese in Australia: Japanese Footprints Over a Century]*. Tokyo: Kinenshi Henshū Iinkai.
Mogi, F. 1998. 'Saigo no daibaa: Fujii Tomotaro-san to Nihonjin bochi' [Mr. Tamitaro Fujii the Last Diver and the Japanese Cemetery], in *Ōsutoraria no nihonjin – isseiki o koeru nihonjin no sokuseki [Japanese in Australia: Japanese Footprints Over a Century]*. Tokyo: Kinenshi Henshū Iinkai.
'Mukashi no. 1 en wa Ima no Nanen?' 26 April 2019, http://sirakawa.b.la9.jp/Coin/J050.htm.
Murakami, Y. 1998. 'Nihongjin keiyaku rōdōsha to Kuiinzurando satō-kibi nōba' [Japanese Contract Labourers and Sugar Cane Farms in Queensland], in *Ōsutoraria no nihonjin – isseiki o koeru nihonjin no sokuseki, [Japanese in Australia: Japanese Footprints Over a Century]*. Tokyo: Kinenshi Henshū Iinkai.
Nagata, Y. 1996. *Unwanted Aliens: Japanese Internment in Australia*. St Lucia: The University of Queensland Press.
National Archives of Australia. 2018. 'Internment Camps in World War II', 3 June, www.naa.gov.au/collection/snapshots/internment-camps/WWII/index.aspx.
National Federation of Australia Japan Societies. 'History of the Federation', accessed 3 June 2018, https://austjapanfed.org.au/about/history/.
Nichigo Press. 2017. *Nichigo Puresu 40 nen no ayumi*, vol. 41. Sydney: Nichigo Press, 481.
Parliament of Australia. 2000. 'Australia and Japan – A Trading Tradition', *Japan's Economy Implications for Australia*, accessed 6 June 2018, www.aph.gov.au/Parliamentary_Business/Committees/Senate/Foreign_Affairs_Defence_and_Trade/Completed_inquiries/1999-02/japan/report/c05.
'Queensland Past and Present: 100 Years of Statistics'. 1896–1996. accessed 26 April 2019, www.qgso.qld.gov.au/products/reports/qld-past-present/qld-past-present-1896-1996-ch03-sec-01.pdf.
Robertson, J. 2017. 'Australian Convict Pirates in Japan: Evidence of 1830 Voyage Unearthed', *The Guardian*, 28 May, accessed 12 December 2017, www.theguardian.com/australia-news/2017/may/28/australian-convict-pirates-in-japan-evidence-of-1830-voyage-unearthed#img-1.
Sissons, D. 1972. 'Immigration in Australia – Japanese Relations 1871–1971', in J. A. A. Stockwin (ed.), *Japan and Australia in the Seventies*. Sydney: Angus and Robinson.
———. 1982. 'Australia's First Professor of Japanese: James Murdoch, 1856–1921', unpublished paper, National Library of Australia, MS 3092.
———. 1983. 'Kitamura Toranosuke (1866–1930)', *Australian Dictionary of Biography*, National Centre of Biography, Australian National University, accessed 8 March 2019, http://adb.anu.edu.au/biography/kitamura-toranosuke-6980.
———. 1990. 'Takasuka, Jō (1865–1940)', *Australian Dictionary of Biography*, vol. 12.
———. 1998. 'Selector and His Family', in *Ōsutoraria no nihonjin – isseiki o koeru nihonjin no sokuseki [Japanese in Australia: Japanese Footprints Over a Century]*. Tokyo: Kinenshi Henshū Iinkai.

———. 2016. 'Australian–Japanese Relations: The First Phase 1859–1891', in A. Stockwin and K. Tamura (eds.), *Bridging Australia and Japan: The Writings of David Sisson, Historian and Political Scientist*. Canberra: ANU Press.

Sono, T. 1998. 'Nichigōbōeki no paionia, Kanematsu Fasajirō' [Kanematsu Fasajirō, Pioneer of Australia-Japan Business], in *Ōsutoraria no nihonjin – isseiki o koeru nihonjin no sokuseki [Japanese in Australia: Japanese Footprints Over a Century]*. Tokyo: Kinenshū Henshū Iinkai.

Stockwin, A. 2016. 'Introduction', in A. Stockwin and K. Tamura (eds.), *Bridging Australia and Japan: The Writings of David Sisson, Historian and Political Scientist*. Canberra: ANU Press.

The Sydney Gazette and New South Wales Advertiser. 1831. 'The Brig Haweis', 16 April, 2.

The Sydney Monitor. 1829. 'Domestic Intelligence', 21 November, 3.

Taguchi, A. 1998. 'Rajio Ōsutoraria: Nihongo hōsō 30-nen' [Radio Australia: 30 Years of Japanese Broadcasting], in *Ōsutoraria no nihonjin – isseiki o koeru nihonjin no sokuseki [Japanese in Australia: Japanese Footprints Over a Century]*. Tokyo: Kinenshi Henshū Iinkai.

Tamura, K. 2011. *Michi's Memories: The Story of a Japanese War Bride*. Canberra: Pandanus Books.

Tavan, G. 2005. The Long Slow Death of the White Australia Policy. Melbourne: Scribe.

Toby, Ronald. 1977. 'Reopening the Question of Sakoku: Diplomacy in the Legitimation of the Tokugawa Bakufu', *The Journal of Japanese Studies*, 3 (2) (Summer), 323–363.

Tsurumi, S. 1991. 'Ame no Uzume den' [The Life of Ame no Uzume], in *Tsurumi Shunsuke shū, zoku [Collected Works of Tsurumi Shunsuke, 2nd Series]*, vol. 5. Tokyo: Chikuma Shobō.

Walker, D. and Sobocinska, A. 2012. 'Introduction: Australia's Asia', in D. Walker and A. Sobocinska (eds.), *Australia's Asia: From Yellow Peril to Asian Century*. Crawley, WA: UWA Publishing, 1–23.

Whiley, S. 2018. 'The Experiences of Nikkei-Australian Soldiers During World War II', *New Voices*, (10): 1–28.

Willard, M. 1923. *White Australia Policy to 1920*. Melbourne: Melbourne University Press.

Williams, H. S. 1958. *Tales of the Foreign Settlements in Japan*. Tokyo: Charles E. Tuttle Publishing.

Wood, J. 1998. 'The Australian Military Contribution to the Occupation of Japan 1945–1952', *Australian War Memorial*, www.awm.gov.au/sites/default/files/BCOF_history.pdf.

Yamamoto, T. 2017. 'Japan's Passport System and the Opening of Borders, 1866–1878', *The Historical Journal*, accessed 18 January 2018, https://doi.org/10.1017/S0018246X16000522.

2 Youthful first impressions
Tsurumi Kazuko and Shunsuke in Australia, 1937

Tomoko Aoyama

In the beginning there was Ame no Uzume (*den*)

Sociologist Tsurumi Kazuko (1918–2006) and her brother, philosopher Tsurumi Shunsuke (1922–2015), are without doubt two of the most important and influential liberal thinkers in postwar Japan. Each has produced a vast and varied corpus in multiple fields and disciplines.[1] Some of their publications, such as Kazuko's *Social Change and the Individual: Japan Before and After Defeat in World War II* ([1970] 2015) and Shunsuke's *An Intellectual History of Wartime Japan* ([1986] 2010) and *A Cultural History of Postwar Japan 1945–1980* (1987), became essential references in many fields of Japanese studies and other disciplines. Both studied at prestigious universities in North America from 1938 to 1942. Kazuko completed a master's degree in philosophy at Vassar College and planned to continue her postgraduate studies at Columbia University. After spending a year at the Middlesex School in Concord, Massachusetts, Shunsuke was admitted to Harvard University in 1939 at age 17, and managed to complete his dissertation while in the custody of the Immigration Service in East Boston.[2] After the breakout of the Pacific War, the siblings returned to Japan in 1942 on the exchange and repatriation ship *MS Gripsholm*.[3]

In 1946 the pair teamed up with five other scholars, including Maruyama Masao, to establish a research association and its journal, *Shisō no kagaku* [Science of thought], published continually until 1996.[4] Kazuko returned to the United States in 1962 to study at Princeton University and in 1966 obtained a PhD. She pursued a successful academic career and taught at universities such as Sophia (Jōchi), Toronto and British Columbia. A collection of her essays written in English between 1975 and 1995 was published in 2014 (Tsurumi 2014). Shunsuke, too, had teaching and research positions at Kyōto University, Tokyo Institute of Technology and Dōshisha University, although his academic career was repeatedly interrupted by severe depression and his political opposition to the US-Japan Security Treaty, the Vietnam War and other issues. After he resigned from Dōshisha in 1970 in protest against the university's decision to bring in the riot police to suppress the student movement, Shunsuke never held another full-time academic post at a Japanese university, and instead concentrated on writing, editing, publishing and other intellectual and sociopolitical activities. Although he was unable to take up an invitation from Stanford in 1951 because the United States refused to issue him a visa, Shunsuke spent a year at El Colegio de México as a visiting professor (1972–1973) and several months at McGill University (1979–1980). Both Kazuko and Shunsuke were committed to the social movements for peace, freedom and democracy. Shunsuke was a founding member of the Beheiren, the Citizens' League for Peace in Vietnam (1965–1974). He also founded, together with Oda Makoto, Ōe Kenzaburō and six others, the Article Nine Association (established in 2004), to which Kazuko actively contributed.

While the close yet ambiguous connections of these sibling intellectuals with the United States are well documented both by themselves and their biographers, friends and researchers, their earlier experiences in Australia have attracted little attention, even though Shunsuke's book, *Ame no Uzume den* [The life of Ame no Uzume [1991] 2001],[5] mentions their 1937 visit to Australia. Ame no Uzume is one of the eight million gods in Japanese mythology, whose shamanistic, comic and erotic dance plays a crucial role in one of the most celebrated scenes of Japanese mythology, recorded in the *Kojiki*. Her performance creates laughter, which draws the Sun Goddess Amaterasu out of the cave, rescuing the world from darkness, disease and death. In a later, and less well-known, episode of the *Kojiki*, Uzume confronts a strange giant standing at the crossroads between heaven and earth, and resolves another potential crisis without resorting to violence. Uzume is a carnivalesque trickster who fearlessly crosses geo-cultural boundaries and communicates through her performances. Shunsuke's discussion of Uzume is rich and profound, and it is particularly useful when we consider intercultural exchange and communication in difficult circumstances such as those experienced by the Tsurumis in 1937 and subsequently. Uzume, according to Shunsuke, offers a range of possibilities and strategies for finding democratic and nonviolent solutions to conflicts and crises.

As noted above, at the very beginning of *Ame no Uzume den*, Shunsuke mentions his visit to Adelaide in 1937.[6] There were no Japanese residents in the city at the time, but a group of people with an interest in things Japanese held regular meetings to learn about Japanese language and culture using English-language books and other sources as references. Shunsuke was welcomed to one such meeting as a rare Japanese traveller. They handed him a copy of what turned out to be a rough English summary of the *Kojiki*, which mentioned a *democratic* meeting of gods, including a stripper god, who he gathered was Ame no Uzume. He was struck by the free and liberated depiction of the mythology, which was completely different from the familiar nationalistic discourse propagated in Japanese schools in those oppressive times. As he briefly yet clearly states on the first page of *Ame no Uzume den*,[7] this liberated image of Ame no Uzume that he first encountered in Adelaide grew inside him for more than half a century and culminated in the 1991 book, which he himself regarded as the most important of his numerous publications.[8]

Tracing the Tsurumis' trajectory in 1937

Shunsuke's brief description of this Australian visit in 1937 raises a series of questions about the historical trip. Why was Shunsuke, aged 15, in Adelaide? What was he doing? And how long was he in Australia? Did he write anything more about this trip? Some of these questions are easily answered. Shunsuke's father, Yūsuke (1885–1973), who was a member of the Diet, visited Australia to attend a series of events as a Japanese representative of the international congress on education. This provided two of his four children with the opportunity to travel to Australia. This chapter presents a critical analysis of the historical journey of the Tsurumis and its legacies, with a particular focus on the contrasting experiences of Kazuko and Shunsuke in Australia, although Yūsuke also plays an important role in each. By uncovering neglected or inaccurately reported details, and by contextualizing their own and others' comments and reports at the time as well as in later periods, the research contributes not only to the biographical studies of this illustrious intellectual family but also to our understanding of 'Japan in Australia', especially people-to-people exchange at personal and more public and political levels.

Various newspapers reported the Japanese politician's visit to Australian capital cities, often mentioning his 19-year-old daughter. An Adelaide newspaper, *The Advertiser*, for example, included this photograph of the father and daughter (Figure 2.1) next to an article titled 'Education Conference to Begin Next Week', with the caption:

> Mr. Yusuki [sic] Tsurumi, a Japanese delegate, who will visit Adelaide for the New Education Fellowship Conference, which will begin next Thursday. He is with his daughter, who is in national costume.
> (Education Conference to Begin Next Week 1937, 31)

Brisbane's *The Courier-Mail* introduced the father and daughter in 'Japanese Parliamentarian's Visit' with the caption 'Mr. Ysusuke [sic] Tsurumi and his daughter, Kazuko, who are visiting Brisbane. Mr. Tsurumi is a member of the Japanese Parliament'. Some of the photos showed the photogenic Kazuko by herself, dancing or posing in gorgeous kimono. *The Courier-Mail* published a photograph of Kazuko with the caption, 'Picturesque Dancer', and another Brisbane paper, *The Telegraph*, showed a photograph of 'Miss Kazu-ko Tsurumi in characteristic pose during her display of Japanese dances in the Lord Mayor's reception room last night'. Kazuko was also interviewed by herself without an interpreter. Another Adelaide paper, *News*, reported on 'a rather shy and charming visitor to the conference':

> Speaking with a slight accent, she said that many Japanese girls studied classical dancing as a means to a better understanding of ancient Japanese legends. [. . .] Miss Tsurumi has brought four gay kimonos with her to Adelaide, in case she finds an opportunity to dance. Besides being a dancer, she is a student of English literature at the Tsuda Teachers' Training [sic] in Tokio.
> (Women Educationalists: Experts in Various Arts 1937, 6)

Kazuko was also reported as saying 'Women are not admitted to the Universities in Japan . . . and many of them finish their studies when they leave high school,

Figure 2.1 Mr Yūsuke Tsurumi's visit to Adelaide (1937)

unless, as I have done, they go on to the teachers' colleges' (Women Educationalists: Experts in Various Arts 1937, 6).

Kazuko was clearly an articulate and accomplished young woman from a privileged class. Although described as 'shy' here, from a very early age she was always very confident, as the following delightful episode testifies. When the British newspaper tycoon Viscount Northcliffe visited the Tsurumis, Kazuko, aged three, was not pleased that she was not invited to the welcome gathering. She decided to walk into the room and introduce herself to him, saying 'I am . . . perapera. . .'. The girl thought 'perapera', which is an onomatopoetic expression used for being fluent in a foreign language, was English. Northcliffe was very impressed, and described her as the only female he met in Japan who was not bashful (Tsurumi and Kurokawa 2009, 126).[9]

Kazuko's dancing, which is featured in almost all Australian media reports, was nothing like Ame no Uzume's shamanistic and erotic dance; it was a serious artistic performance supported by more than ten years' training with the leading master, Hanayagi Tokutarō (1878–1963). *The Courier-Mail*'s article 'Golden Age of Culture in Japan: Father Speaks and Daughter Dances' indicates that Yūsuke aimed to promote and introduce traditional and modern Japanese culture to Australians as part of his public, or people's, diplomacy,[10] with the aid of his daughter, who was indeed an ideal collaborator.

> Miss Kazu-Ko Tsurumi danced Japanese classic studies, while her father explained their symbolic meaning before members of the Australian Institute of International Affairs in the Lord Mayor's reception room of the City Hall last night. In a land that has produced male players of female parts for so many centuries that women can never hope in the opinion of cultured Japanese to compete seriously with the artistry of these impersonators, Miss Tsurumi ranks as a notable performer – for a woman! Her father, Mr. Yusuki [sic] Tsurumi, a member of the Japanese Parliament and a distinguished educationalist, explained in choicest English and engaging platform manner that although most of the peoples of the world knew of Japan's industrial expansion – and unfortunately of its wars – few seemed to know that it was now passing through its golden age of culture.
> (Golden Age of Culture in Japan 1937, 16)

Kazuko was introduced as a daughter of 'Yuseke [sic] Tsurumi' and 'granddaughter of the late Count Goto' [i.e., Gotō Shinpei] (Kazuko Tsurumi Has Found Paradise 1937, 4). Although this report, too, has a certain condescending tone, it does state that Kazuko collected volumes about flora and fauna in Australia, including David G. Stead's study, *The Rabbit in Australia*, and cites her comments that even though her father had tried to find books on Australia while he was in London, he could not find anything suitable. In the article, Kazuko also explains that while the kind of education for women that her mother's generation had received aimed at creating *ryōsai kenbo* (good wife, wise mother), girls of her generation are pursuing a much wider variety of subjects: 'At college which I now attend the most important subject is English literature. Then, of course, we learn economics, psychology, Japanese and world history' (Kazuko Tsurumi *Has Found Paradise* 1937, 4).

The young Kazuko's accomplishments did not only include English literature and Japanese traditional dance; she was also studying tanka poetry with none other than Sasaki Nobutsuna (1872–1963), the authority on this genre. In fact, Kazuko wrote a series of tanka in the form of a poetic travel diary recording her thoughts and experiences in Australia. These were included in Kazuko's first collection of poetry, *Niji* [Rainbow], which was published in 1939 with a preface by Sasaki Nobutsuna.[11] The volume is divided into two parts: Occasional Poems and Travel Poems, the latter with three subsections: Australia, North America and Middle China. The 'Ōsutoreeria'[12] subsection is further divided into 16 groups of poems with brief titles such as 'Setting sail from Moji', 'First sight of the Australian continent on the evening of the seventeenth day after leaving Japan' and 'Arriving in Sydney Harbour'. Although undated, this tanka diary tells us the order of places she visited; some important events, including her father's being awarded a Doctor of Laws by Melbourne University and her performing 'Musume Dōjōji' by invitation of Melbourne International Women's Club. The number of poems in each group varies from a single tanka to 12 composed during the three-day journey from Canberra to Melbourne. Melbourne and Adelaide also produced a larger number of tanka than other aspects of the trip. Australian flora and fauna feature frequently, but eucalypts (14 tanka) seem to have impressed and inspired Kazuko by far the most, followed by koalas (4), kookaburras (4), sheep (3), parrots (2), wattle flowers (2), bunya pines (2) and so on. There are also poems about events, conversations and other types of human interactions. The collection provides an interesting range of her youthful impressions, some of which may sound a little naïve, but many others display her intellectual and poetic gifts.

Shunsuke's absence in the records

There is one noticeable absence: Shunsuke is not even mentioned in any of the newspaper articles[13] and announcements, or in Kazuko's Australian tanka. Was the boy not with his father and sister? Arguably he was a rebellious boy and perhaps did not want to be photographed with his father and sister or be interviewed by the local media. This hypothesis is based on the accounts of Shunsuke's turbulent adolescence and his antagonism towards his parents, teachers and authorities apparent in his own talks and writings as well as in those by others. Shindō Ken's critical biography focusing on the young Shunsuke is entitled *Boku wa akunin* [I am a bad person], a phrase Shunsuke coined himself, and quotes the following:

> Since my primary school days, I could not help feeling that I was a bad person, and this self-consciousness separated me from the militarism to which the teachers and elite students subscribed. It was by sheer chance (and if I believed in God, I would call it a divine blessing) that I managed to survive the war without killing anyone. I managed to persevere in isolation among the one hundred million good Japanese people because I was conscious of my badness and used to the loneliness of the wicked.
>
> (Shindō 1994, 60)[14]

One reason for this sense of himself as a bad person seems to have stemmed from his mother Aiko's constant surveillance of Shunsuke, which was accompanied by physical, verbal and psychological abuse from very early on. He understood even as a small child that this was not because she did not love him but, on the contrary, because she loved him excessively and expected far too much of him as the eldest son of the Tsurumi family and the grandson of her father, Gotō Shinpei (Tsurumi 2015, 203–205, 209, 220, 256–260). In one famous episode, when he was about three, Shunsuke stole some cake from the cupboard and was caught red-handed by his mother, who was so shocked by his 'heinous crime' that she told him that she would have no choice but to kill him and then herself in order to apologise to their ancestors (Tsurumi and Kurokawa 2009, 83).[15] The contrast between this three-year-old boy and Kazuko at three is stunning. The situation steadily deteriorated, and by age 15, the 'bad boy' Shunsuke had acquired other 'vices' such as sex and drugs, had attempted suicide and had been admitted to a mental hospital on three occasions.

Given this background, it is not entirely surprising that Shunsuke did not appear in any of the media reports on the Tsurumis' visit to Australia. While archival research allows a reconstruction of the Tsurumis' itinerary – at least for the father and daughter – there is confusion and a lack of evidence about Shunsuke's experience in Australia. For example, American scholar of Japanese history Lawrence Olson states that:

> In 1938, seeking some way to deal with his increasingly recalcitrant son, Yūsuke sent him briefly to Australia. When for whatever reason that experiment failed, the father took advantage of one of his American connections.
> (Olson, *Ambivalent Moderns* 1992, 118)

The date here should clearly be 1937, and whether the trip was a 'failure' is certainly open to debate, but Olson's use of 'for whatever reason' suggests his view that this Australian trip was unworthy of any further discussion. In a recent biography of Shunsuke, there is an even more careless, in fact ridiculous, error: in quoting Yūsuke's reminiscence, which will be discussed later, the word Australia 濠州 is misquoted as Manchuria 満州, not once but twice (Murase 2016, 84–85). Even more puzzling are the seemingly contradictory comments by those who were directly involved, including Shunsuke himself. In 1982, when he returned to Australia to give a lecture at La Trobe University, he told Roger Pulvers, who interviewed him for *The Age*, that he had been sent to Australia by himself after being thrown out of three Japanese schools (Pulvers 1982, 11).[16] It is very strange, if not impossible, that a 'difficult' 15-year-old boy without English skills would be sent *by himself* to a White-Australian Adelaide where there were no Japanese residents. In addition, in Ueshina Kazuma's biography of Yūsuke, there is a photograph of the father and his two children on the deck of a ship (Figure 2.2), with the caption, 'With eldest daughter Kazuko and first son Shunsuke, on the *Canberra-maru* on their way to Australia (July 1937)', which clearly demonstrates that Shunsuke was travelling with his father and sister (Ueshina 2011, n.p.).

Figure 2.2 Father, daughter and son (1937)

Furthermore, in Ueshina's book, this photograph is followed immediately by Shunsuke's preface, in which he writes:

> When my father took my sister and me to Australia, I had a chance to hear him make a speech in English to the English-speaking audience. It was in

1937. [. . .] I was proud that he could make people laugh with his speech. But this may be because my English was quite limited then.

(Shunsuke in Ueshina 2011, 1)

This contradicts his earlier claim that he had been sent on his own. Shunsuke's comment about the pride he felt also raises a few further questions. Throughout his life, Shunsuke was extremely critical of his father's political stance. Yūsuke was a liberal statesman who was well informed on international relations, but from the viewpoint of his young son, who decades later was to write *The Intellectual History of Wartime Japan, 1931–45*, it was unforgivable that his father had defended Japan's position at the time of the Manchurian Incident (1931). For this reason, too, it would be unsurprising if the boy had refused to attend the events organised by the New Education Fellowship Conference and government and diplomatic organisations with his father. However, even if he was absent from these public scenes, the contradiction between Shunsuke being sent 'by himself' but also pictured on deck with his father and Kazuko remains.

Two teens and the father: first impressions of Australia

A resolution can be found in Yūsuke's speech manuscript in English, 'My Australian Impressions', which is kept in the National Diet Library's Modern Japanese Political History Materials Room:

> I brought my two children, a daughter and a son, with me this time. It is their first experience in a foreign country. They are both in their teens and are naturally sensitive and impressionable. Their reaction to the Australian people was most interesting to watch. They immediately felt so much at home with them. An instantaneous fondness was born in their hearts. And the reason was not far to seek. It was the intuitive reaction of youth to kindly hearts. They found Australians genuinely human and humanly kind. There was nothing artificial nor conventional in their manners. They were just nice and kindly. My boy, who is only fifteen, liked this country so much that he wanted to stay behind us to spend months or even years here.
>
> (Tsurumi 1937b, 4)

Later in the speech Yūsuke mentions that he is 'going away in a few days', after outlining his impressions of the cities he had visited: Sydney, Melbourne, Canberra and Adelaide, praising Melbourne and Adelaide especially, noting that they 'stand to the credit of any nation for its foresight and ability' (Tsurumi 1937b, 5–6). Based on the full program of the New Education Fellowship Conference and other documents, including Kazuko's tanka, it is evident that Yūsuke only participated in events in four of the seven capital cities (asterisked below) where the conference was held:

Brisbane (4–6 August)
Sydney (9–16 August)*

Canberra (18–20 August)*
Melbourne (24–31 August)*
Hobart (30 August–1 September)
Adelaide (3–9 September)*
Perth (14–18 September)

According to Kazuko's (undated) poetic diary, after Adelaide they returned to Sydney and then went to Brisbane, but we can see from the conference program that this would not have been as part of the Education Conference. As the speech does not mention Brisbane, and as it provides a more positive evaluation of Melbourne and Adelaide than Sydney and Canberra, we can surmise that the speech was delivered in Adelaide in early September, towards the end of their Australian tour.

If this is the speech Shunsuke heard and mentioned in the passage quoted above, it is possible to identify some mildly humorous elements, including the mention of Shunsuke's wish to stay behind, as quoted above. There are no hearty jokes in the speech manuscript, but there are some that we can imagine would bring polite laughs and amusement, such as: 'And I could go on enumerating the topsy-turvy-ness (if there is such a word in English) of Australia at any length.' Yūsuke then recounts his 'disappointments': starting with Sydney ('I did not like the reddish colour of the houses that crowded all over on the hills'), and he talks about eucalypts that were 'too big to be beautiful to my Japanese eyes':

> Their enormous size was depressing and even menacing. In colours and shape everyone seemed different from another. So irregular, so individualistic. They were so different from the cryptomeria avenue of Nikko, where every towering tree stands in orderly line, similar in height, colour and shape, apparently conforming to the strictest of regimentation. Australian forests seemed to me too wild to be beautiful.
> (Tsurumi 1937b, 2–3)

However, all these 'disappointments' turn out to be a rhetorical device to introduce his greater appreciation, after a month, of what he perceived to be Australian characteristics, inseparable from the Australian natural environment.

> My first and strongest impression of Australians was their handshake. They grasped so firmly and shook so warmly that my hand very often ached for some time afterwards. This seemed to me an index to their characteristics. They are young and vigorous. They are spontaneous and warm-hearted.
> (Tsurumi 1937b, 3–4)

There may be nothing really new or outrageous in his comments, but these impressions are recounted with a civilised light-heartedness that suited the occasion. At the same time, Yūsuke demonstrates in a nonaggressive way his own knowledge, experience and pride. In his praise of Australian people's courtesy and kindness, for example, he remarks, 'I felt as if I were back in Vienna, where you feel yourself a friend of everybody in town' (Tsurumi 1937b, 4).[17]

Shunsuke has commented on his father's English abilities on a number of occasions. Although in 1937 Shunsuke's English was very limited,[18] after their return from America in 1942, Yūsuke asked Kazuko and Shunsuke to correct his English pronunciation. Shunsuke recalls that only then did he realise that his father's English was the result of his elite secondary and tertiary education in Japan, and that even though he spent some time in the United States later in life, his pronunciation had never changed. 'For example, he pronounced words with a double n such as "connection" as "kon-nekushon"' (Ueshina 2011, 2). Even with such a heavy Japanese accent, Yūsuke was able to use humour to get through to his Australian audience. Shunsuke believed that this was due to the oratorical training and experience Yūsuke had received in high school and university debating clubs. In Kazuko's memoirs, too, Yūsuke's humour and eloquence in public and at home are fondly described (e.g., Tsurumi 1998b, vol. VII, 37–38, 40).

Just as Kazuko's dancing was closely tied to Yūsuke's aims of educational and cultural exchange, his speech manuscript shows many parallels with Kazuko's tanka. His comments on eucalypts, for example, remind us of Kazuko's favourite subject. Furthermore, the tanka composed in Adelaide resonate with Yūsuke's remark in his speech that he 'found the open fields around Adelaide much easier to appreciate' than the harsh and menacing forests and valleys. 'They have graceful lines, those undulating hills north of Adelaide! And the velvet green of the wheat on them was peerless under the azure sky' (Tsurumi 1937b, 3). Kazuko wrote a tanka about the conference program:

(Listening to the lecture at the Education Conference)
人等どつと笑ふジョークに唯一人残されしごとし笑ひためらふ
They all laughed at a joke
Somehow left behind
I alone hesitate to laugh
(Tsurumi 1998b *Tsurumi Kazuko mandara*, VIII, 90)

Ironically, here in this tanka, Kazuko, who was fluent in English and from very early childhood had been quite used to communicating with guests from overseas, felt 'left behind' when other people were laughing. The tanka that follows the one above is more comforting:

「ごめんください」とだしぬけに呼ばれ見返れば異国少女ほゝゑみ立てり
'Gomen kudasai' (Excuse me),
called suddenly, I turned
a foreign girl standing with a smile
(Tsurumi 1998b *Tsurumi Kazuko mandara*, VIII, 90)

The 'foreign girl' was probably a member of the Japanese learning group who was eager to practice the language. The tanka is followed by a note: 'After the lecture. In Adelaide dozens of people get together to form a Japanese language association and study the language enthusiastically' (Tsurumi 1998b *Tsurumi Kazuko mandara*, VIII, 90). This fits well with Shunsuke's comment at the beginning of *Ame no Uzume den* about a group of Japanophiles eager to learn Japanese language and culture. Yūsuke, too, reported on the enthusiastic Japanese language learners in his reports and lectures (see Shimazu 2004, 2012). In a brief typewritten note titled 'Japan and Australia', which must have been used for an interview by an Australian reporter after their return to Tokyo, Yūsuke includes the following point:

> Nothing has pleased me so much as the knowledge that many Australians are seriously studying Japanese. Undoubtedly this will go a long way in promoting the real understanding of our two nations.
> (Tsurumi 1937a)

Another point on which all three agree is the kindness and open-mindedness of Australians. Here is Shunsuke in 1982:

> People were very generous to me, and I had no personal experience of discrimination. But I knew that there was an official policy of a White Australia, and for that reason I couldn't stay on. So I went to America and eventually entered Harvard.
> (Pulvers 1982, 11)

There are a few different accounts regarding Shunsuke's wish to stay on in Australia, however. In a 1954 dialogue between Yūsuke and Kazuko, the father recalls the teenage Shunsuke, who, in second grade at middle school, refused to go to school as 'he disagreed with the policies of the Japanese Ministry for Education' (Tsurumi and Tsurumi 1998, 67). As an avid reader, the young Shunsuke had far too much knowledge of, for instance, classical Chinese etymology, to write the simple answers expected in Japanese primary or middle school exams. Consequently, he struggled at school. The father reminisces:

> I realised it was impossible to educate him in Japan. Around then I was asked to give talks in Australia. So, I took him with me, together with Kazuko. Then he said, 'I'd like to spend the remainder of my life here' (laugh). I thought it would be a problem if he spent the rest of his life after the age fourteen [sic] in Australia. That's how I took them both to America. It was a form of guidance through change of environment.
> (Tsurumi and Tsurumi 1998, 67)

Yūsuke believed that his son would not have been able to develop his talents within the Japanese education system and society. Kazuko also suggests elsewhere that the compulsory military drills at school did not suit Shunsuke's personality or physique (Tsurumi 1998b, VII, 118). In any case, while it seems clear that Shunsuke did want to stay in Australia, why did his father not allow him to do so? The White Australia Policy may be just one of the reasons. After all, Yūsuke had sought to give each of his children the best chance to develop her/his potential, and he saw the United States as the best place for this – even in the late 1930s. Had Shunsuke been allowed to stay in Australia, he would soon have been held in one of the internment camps before being sent back to Japan after the war.

Another important factor to consider is that even though the father, daughter and son all mention the kindness and friendliness of Australians, there was growing hostility against Japan – which is not at all surprising since the Second Sino-Japanese War broke out in July 1937, only several weeks before the Tsurumis arrived in Sydney. After visiting Canberra, Melbourne and Adelaide, they returned to Sydney around 16 September and then travelled to Brisbane in late September. Yūsuke's biographer reports that the audiences for his public lectures gradually decreased and the 28 September lecture in Brisbane had such a small audience that a lecturer in the School of Law at the University of Queensland, T. P. Fry, sympathetically explained to Yūsuke that the size of the audience by no means indicated hostility toward him personally but was because many people felt they had to decline the invitation to avoid looking as though they sanctioned Japan's actions in China (Ueshina 2011, 276). Shortly after this, in mid-December, the Nanjin Massacre began. Ueshina also mentions that when Kazuko gave a talk on the radio in Sydney, 14 people rang the radio station in support and 28 rang in protest against broadcasting a talk by a Japanese person (Ueshina 2011, 276). In Kazuko's tanka, we find:

(returned to Sydney. Broadcast a short Q&A)
よき言葉どうしても浮かばぬたまゆらをしいんと電波のおとのみ冴ゆる
Just cannot think of the right expression
that momentary silence
just the buzz of the radio waves sounds clear.
(Tsurumi 1998b, VIII, 92)

She also seems to have given another talk on the radio in Brisbane.
アナウンサーの紹介終わり部屋ぬちはしづまりかへりぬ一人立てり我は
The announcer's introduction over
a dead silence fell over the room
standing by myself.
(Tsurumi 1998b VIII, 95)

As we have seen, by juxtaposing various documents and references, it is possible to identify and reconstruct the family's 1937 travels. However, some questions remain. For instance, even the names of the ships vary: in Ueshina's book, the picture of the three on deck was captioned as 'on the way to Australia on the

Canberra-maru, July 1937', but elsewhere in the book it recounts that 'On 28 July 1937 they left Tokyo, and sailed out from Moji on the 29th by the *Tokyo-maru*' (Ueshina 2011, 268). There are also references to the *Kitano-maru* in some other documents, and it is still not clear whether Shunsuke travelled alone for some of the journey. The key to resolving these remaining questions lies in comments made by Shunsuke in the 2006 interview: *Nichibei kōkansen*. He observes in this interview that while his father travelled with Kazuko to various capital cities, he travelled separately from Sydney to Melbourne and then to Adelaide, where he stayed the longest. As for the questions of his command of English and therefore his ability to travel alone without his family, he explains:

> I learned to speak English while moving around on my own. I was allowed to travel but because of White Australia Policy, I couldn't get residency. [. . .] My father arranged that Mr Inokuchi Ichirō accompany me, and told the Australian officials that he was my tutor. My father asked Mr Inokuchi to write a report on Australia.
> (Tsurumi, Katō and Kurokawa 2006, 194)

Inokuchi was a journalist who had lost his position because of his socialist beliefs. Yūsuke gave him a job as his research assistant. Shunsuke further explains that he had no interest in studying in Australia but just wanted to stay in Adelaide, where, he claims, his father and Kazuko were not planning to visit (Tsurumi, Katō and Kurokawa 2006, 195). He probably meant that the father and daughter spent the first month visiting other cities, rather than that they never went to Adelaide. But then, in response to a question about why he liked it so much in Adelaide, Shunsuke answers:

> There were hardly any Japanese. So, people were curious about the Japanese. Besides, my father didn't give a speech there. So, I lived there, away from my father's umbrella, speaking some English.
> (Tsurumi, Katō and Kurokawa 2006, 195)

Here we have another contradiction – unless the speech by Yūsuke that Shunsuke referred to earlier (Tsurumi, in Ueshina 2011, 1) was delivered in another city, or unless Shunsuke was referring here to a public lecture rather than a six-page speech on a social occasion. In any case, while there are many other puzzles and contradictions, at least the information about Inokuchi provides a key to solving some questions, including the names of the ships.

The National Archives of Australia has a record showing that Inokuchi, aged 37, 'tutor', and Shunsuke, aged 16 in the document, 'student', arrived on the *Kitano-maru* on 13 August. They boarded the ship in Nagasaki. The father and daughter, on the other hand, arrived on the *Sydney-maru* on 15 August. The outgoing passengers' list at the port of Brisbane shows Yūsuke 'MP', 52, and Kazuko 'student', 19, embarking on the *Canberra-maru* for Yokohama on 2 October 1937. There is another male Japanese person on the same list, but he is aged 42 and has a different name. So, it looked as though Shunsuke was travelling separately in both directions. However, I realised that 'Shunsuki' (student) and Inokuchi (professor) embarked on the '*Canberra Maru*' at the port of Sydney, headed for Osaka, on 29 September 1937 (SP1148/2 – Manifests Passenger – Outward Ships – Sydney). To sum up, the photograph does seem to have been taken on the *Canberra-maru*, but on their voyage home in October rather than on their way to Australia. The photographer may perhaps have been Inokuchi.

Significance and legacies of the 1937 travels

What significance did this travel have for each of the three, especially the two children? The father, as a skilled politician, was trying hard to build a good relationship between Japan and Australia in these difficult years. Kazuko also contributed to this aim, though not as a mere mouthpiece of her father but as an independent young individual. After their return to Japan, Yūsuke's comments were published in the *Sydney Morning Herald*:

> Australian [sic] were more friendly to Japan [sic] than was generally supposed in Japan. This, however, excluded some 'ultra-British' politicians and publications. He declared that the Press naturally followed the British lead and gave prominence to reports from China and from London that were unfavourable to Japan. They also, however, published some news from the Japanese side so that intelligent readers could gauge the true situation and not be misled by Chinese fabrications.
> (Friendliness of Australians, Mr. Tsurumi Describes It in Japan 1937, 17)

The visit motivated Yūsuke to continue to get to know Australia better, especially as a trade partner. He published a book on Australian nature and society in 1943 (Ueshina 2011, 277).

For Kazuko, the tour provided an opportunity to experience her first overseas travel and exchange ideas with people from Australia and other countries through conversation; interviews and, importantly, through her dance performances, and to express her impressions in the form of tanka. Even with her talent and privilege, there were some awkward and tense moments, although these would pale in comparison to the difficulties she was to face in America after the outbreak of the war. Apart from the tanka collection, there is no direct tangible outcome of the trip in her work. Interestingly, dance and poetry, which played significant roles during this trip, were gradually to disappear from her busy academic life, but they feature again after many decades in her old age with great power and maturity (Tsurumi 1998a, 2007). It is meaningful, therefore, to examine their importance at this early stage of Kazuko's life.

As for Shunsuke, the Adelaide experience certainly seems to have offered an opportunity for the 'bad' 15-year-old to transform into a serious and dynamic scholar of pragmatism.[19] As mentioned above, Shunsuke returned to Australia in 1982. Before his lecture at La Trobe, he attended an international symposium on the comparative study of Japan held at Noosa Heads in Queensland. As Gavan McCormack explains, he was there as the proxy for Hidaka Rokurō, who had been refused a visa by the Australian government. 'Tsurumi's second Australian visit may be seen as one isolated and incidental happy consequence of the "Hidaka affair" (McCormack's Introduction to Tsurumi 1982, 2).[20] We might recall that Shunsuke himself experienced the rejection of a visa application by the US authority three decades earlier. In his essay on this Noosa Heads Conference, Shunsuke suggests that Japanese studies in Australia can offer a new viewpoint, distinct from those in America, which 'acts almost like a suzerain of Japan', or in Japan, which was then 'an economic giant'. Shunsuke sees that from Australia's position on the globe, Japan is viewed not in isolation but alongside other Asian nations, and he sees hope in this for a new intercultural approach to Japanese studies (Tsurumi 1991, 311). This, together with his *Ame no Uzume den*, may be regarded as the most important legacy of the Tsurumis' 1937 sojourn.

Notes

1 For the sake of convenience, the members of the Tsurumi family will be cited by their personal names in this chapter. The research for this chapter was supported by a Japan Study Grant from the National Library of Australia, which enabled me to spend three weeks at the Library in January 2016. I am grateful to the NLA and its staff for their generous support and assistance.
2 Olson (1992, 118–124) outlines Shunsuke's experience in America during this period. See also Shunsuke's (1995) illustrated storybook, *Watashi ga gaijin datta koro*.
3 See Tsurumi, Katō and Kurokawa (2006) for a series of interviews with Shunsuke about repatriation.
4 For studies of this association, see Bronson (2016), Ward (2017) and Avenell (2008).
5 In this chapter I use the edition included in *Tsurumi Shunsuke shū, zoku*, vol. 5. For a more detailed study of Ame no Uzume and Tsurumi's theory, see Aoyama (2018).
6 The following description of Shunsuke's encounter with Ame no Uzume in Adelaide overlaps with Aoyama (2018, 45–46).
7 Tsurumi ([1991] 2001, 4).
8 In an interview Shunsuke declared that *Ame no Uzume den* was the book he liked best of all his publications and that he would be happy if he were remembered for this single work (Tsurumi 1997, 45). See also (Ueno 2013, 59).
9 Northcliffe visited Japan in November 1921. See O'Connor (2010, 323).
10 See Ueshina 2011 for detailed discussion of Yūsuke as the pioneer of public diplomacy.
11 *Niji* is included in Kazuko (1998b, VIII, 7–191).
12 Kazuko's spelling is slightly different from the standard loan word 'Ōsutoraria' for Australia.
13 See Australia in Japanese Eyes (1937); Dances by Japanese Visitor (1937); Japanese Dances Consul's Reception for Delegates (1937) and Japanese Parliamentarian's Visit (1937).
14 See also Shunsuke, Ueno and Oguma (2004, 23–35); Tsurumi and Kurokawa (2009, 83–86).
15 Similar descriptions are found in Shindō (1994, 23), Olson (1992, 116–117) and many other places. Ishizuka (2010), Chapter 2, offers a useful detailed chronology, especially 181–200. Harada (2001, 39–46) is a study of Shunsuke as, according to Harada, 'an intellectual masochist' and includes a careful analysis of Shunsuke's adolescent 'decadence as a method' of existential freedom.

16 Shunsuke's public lecture at La Trobe University was published as 'Japanese Conception of Asia'.
17 After graduating from Tokyo Imperial University in 1910 with the second highest results, Yūsuke became an elite bureaucrat, and from 1911 he travelled to the United States and other countries many times, initially as the secretary of Nitobe Inazō and Gotō Shinpei.
18 See Olson (1992, 118–121) on Shunsuke's year at Middlesex School, including interesting comments by his former teacher: 'He had enough math to meet college requirements, but his spoken English was limited to some very polite comments, said with a smile. His reading ability was fairly well advanced, but one was never sure at the beginning whether he understood what was said to him. He usually answered, "Yes, sir" to everything', 119.
19 In a sense, it is as if both the wild and disorderly 'bad' brother of Amaterasu, Susano-o, and the hurt and depressed Amaterasu could find an Ame no Uzume who could help to open up the enclosure – both for the trapped and for those around them.
20 Regarding the 'Hidaka incident', see McCormack's afterword in Hidaka (1985). Tsurumi (1991, 308–310), which also explains the incident.

References

Aoyama, T. 2018. 'Ame no Uzume Crosses Boundaries', in L. Miller and R. Copeland (eds.), *Diva Nation: Female Icons in Japanese Cultural History*. Oakland, CA: University of California Press, 34–50.
'Australia in Japanese Eyes: Mr. Tsurumi's Impressions'. 1937. *The Age*, 15 October, Friday.
Avenell, S. 2008. 'From the "People" to the "Citizen": Tsurumi Shunsuke and the Roots of Civic Mythology in Postwar Japan', *Positions: East Asia Cultures Critique*, 16 (3): 711–742.
Bronson, A. 2016. *One Hundred Million Philosophers: Science of Thought and the Culture of Democracy in Postwar Japan*. Honolulu: University of Hawaii Press.
'Dances by Japanese Visitor'. 1937. *The Courier-Mail*, 1 October, 24.
'Education Conference to Begin Next Week'. 1937. *The Advertiser*, 27 August.
'Friendliness of Australians: Mr. Tsurumi Describes It in Japan'. 1937. *The Sydney Morning Herald*, 16 October, 17.
Harada, T. 2001. *Tsurumi Shunsuke to kibō no shakaigaku [Tsurumi Shunsuke and the Sociology of Hope]*. Kyoto: Sekai Shisōsha.
Hidaka, R. 1985. *The Price of Affluence*. Melbourne: Penguin.
Ishizuka, Y. 2010. *Tsurumi Yūsuke shiryō [Research Materials on Tsurumi Yūsuke]*. Tokyo: Kōdansha Shuppan Service Centre.
'Japanese Dances Consul's Reception for Delegates'. 1937. *The Sydney Morning Herald* (NSW: 1842–1954), 17 September, 4.
'Japanese Parliamentarian's Visit'. 1937. *The Courier-Mail* (Brisbane, QLD: 1933–1954), 30 September, 14.
'Kazuko Tsurumi Has Found "Paradise"'. 1937. *The Australian Women's Weekly*, 4 September, Saturday.
'Miss Kazu-ko Tsurumi in Characteristic Pose During Her Display of Japanese Dances in the Lord Mayor's Reception Room Last Night'. 1937. *The Telegraph*, 1 October, 10.
Murase, M. 2016. *Tsurumi Shunsuke*. Tokyo: Genshisha.
New Education Fellowship Conference, Conference Program, 1 August–20 September 1937. National Library of Australia, NLP370.63 NEW.

O'Connor, P. 2010. 'Alfred Harmsworth, 1st Viscount Northcliffe (1865–1922): An Uncomfortable Visitor to Japan', in H. Cortazzi (ed.), *Britain and Japan: Biographical Portraits*, vol. VII. Leiden: Brill, 323–339.

Olson, L. 1992. *Ambivalent Moderns: Portraits of Japanese Cultural Identity*. Savage, MD: Rowman & Littlefield.

Pulvers, R. 1982. 'The Top Scholar Who Failed at School', *The Age* (Melbourne), 11 February.

Shimazu, T. 2004. *Ōsutoraria no nihongo kyōiku to nihon no tai-ōsutoraria nihongo fukyū: Sono 'seisaku' no senkanki ni okeru dōkō [Japanese Language Education in Australia and Japan's Policy for Dissemination of Japanese Language in Australia: Changes in Policies in Interwar Period]*. Tokyo: Hitsuji Shobō.

———. 2012. 'Tsurumi Yūsuke to 1930-nendai no Ōsutoraria ni okeru nihongo kyōiku: "Nihongo netsu" no hakken to sono senchū sengo e no eikyō' [Yusuke Tsurumi and Japanese Language Education in Australia in the 1930s: The Discovery of the Japanese Language Learning "Boom" and Its Influence During and After World War II], *Ōsutoraria kenkyū [Australian Studies]*, 25: 17–28.

Shindō, K. 1994. *Boku wa akunin: Shōnen Tsurumi Shunsuke [I Am a Wicked Person: The Boy Tsurumi Shunsuke]*. Osaka: Tōhō Shuppan.

Stead, D. G. 1935. *The Rabbit in Australia: History, Life Story, Habits, Effect Upon Australian Primary Production, and Best Means of Extermination*. Sydney: Winn & Co.

Tsurumi, K. [1970] 2015. *Social Change and the Individual: Japan Before and After Defeat in World War II*. Princeton, NJ: Princeton University Press.

——— 1998a. *Onna shosei [Woman of Study]*. Tokyo: Haru Shobō, 1997.

———. 1998b. *K. Tsurumi Kazuko mandara [Tsurumi Kazuko Mandala]*, 9 vols. Tokyo: Fujiwara Shoten.

———. 2007. *Yuigon [A Testament]*. Tokyo: Fujiwara Shoten.

———. 2014. *The Adventure of Ideas: A Collection of Essays on Patterns of Creativity and a Theory of Endogenous Development*. Tokyo and San Francisco: Japanime, accessed 4 January 2018, www.japanime.com/turumi/.

Tsurumi, S. 1982. *Japanese Conceptions of Asia*, Papers of the Japanese Studies Centre, 5, Monash University.

———. [1986] 2010. *An Intellectual History of Wartime Japan*. London: Routledge.

———. 1987. *A Cultural History of Postwar Japan 1945–1980*. London: KPI.

———. 1991. 'Nūsahezzu kaigi no teiki shita mono' [What the Noosa Heads Conference Suggests], in *Tsurumi Shunsuke shū*, vol. 9. Tokyo: Chikuma Shobō, 304–311.

———. [1991] 2001. 'Ame no Uzume den' [The Life of Ame no Uzume], in *Tsurumi Shunsuke shū, zoku [Collected Works of Tsurumi Shunsuke, 2nd Series]*, vol. 5. Tokyo: Chikuma Shobō.

———. 1995. *Watashi ga gaijin datta koro [When I Was a Foreigner]*. Tokyo: Fukuinkan Shoten.

———. 1997. *Kitai to kaisō [Expectations and Recollections]*, 2 vols. Tokyo: Shōbunsha.

———. 2004. 'Ueno Chizuko and Oguma Eiji', in *Sensō ga nokoshita mono: Tsurumi Shunsuke ni sengo sedai ga kiku [The Legacies of the War: Post-War Generations Interview Tsurumi Shunsuke]*. Tokyo: Shin'yōsha.

———. 2015. *Manazashi [Gaze]*. Tokyo: Fujiwara Shoten.

Tsurumi, S., Katō, N. and Kurokawa, S. 2006. *Nichibei kōkansen [Japan-America Repatriation Ships]*. Tokyo: Shinchōsha.

Tsurumi, S. and Kurokawa, S. (interviewer). 2009. *Futei rōjin [The Recalcitrant Old Man]*. Tokyo: Kawade Shobō Shinsha.

Tsurumi, Y. 1937a. 'Japan and Australia', typed notes, Tsurumi Yūsuke bunsho, No. 1631, National Diet Library, Parliamentary Documents and Official Publications Room.

———. 1937b. 'My Australian Impressions', typed speech manuscript, Tsurumi Yūsuke bunsho, No. 1631, National Diet Library, Parliamentary Documents and Official Publications Room.

Tsurumi, Y. and Tsurumi, K. 1998. 'Ō mai papa: Oya no kōfuku, musume no kōfuku', in K. Tsurumi (ed.), *Tsurumi Kazuko mandara*, vol. VII. Tokyo: Fujiwara Shoten, 60–69.

Ueno, T. 2013. *Shisō no furyō-tachi [Ideological Delinquents]*. Tokyo: Iwanami Shoten.

Ueshina, K. 2011. *Kōhō gaikō no senkusha, Tsurumi Yūsuke 1885–1973 [Pioneer of Public Diplomacy, Tsurumi Yusuke, 1885–1973]*. Tokyo: Fujiwara Shoten.

Ward, V. B. 2017. 'Rethinking Intellectual Life in Early Postwar Japan: *Shisō no kagaku* and Common Man's Philosophy', *Positions: East Asia Cultures Critique*, 25 (3) (August): 439–468.

'Women Educationalists: Experts in Various Arts'. 1937. *News*, 3 September.

3 Forging an Australian artistic modernity

How Japanese woodblock prints informed Margaret Preston's early paintings and prints

Penny Bailey

Introduction

> *Australia is a fine place in which to think . . .*
> *You do not get bothered with foolish new ideas.*
> *Tradition thinks for you, but Heavens! how dull!*
> *To keep myself from pouring out the selfsame*
> *pictures every year I started to think things out.*
> (Preston 1923, 20)

Margaret Preston (née McPherson 1875–1963) was one of Australia's earliest and most notable modernists. By all accounts, she was an energetic public figure whose uncompromising opinions and irreverent attitude towards the establishment earned her both the admiration and derision of her contemporaries.[1] Preston's boundless energy and creativity led her to experiment with various forms of art, including painting and ceramics, but today she is chiefly remembered as one of Australia's most innovative printmakers. Over the course of her artistic career she became proficient in an array of printing techniques, producing etchings, monotypes, screen and stencil prints, as well as relief prints in the woodcut, linocut and Masonite cut mediums (Riddler, Peel and Edwards 2010, 270). In addition to her impressive *oeuvre*, Preston left behind a substantial body of writing providing insights into her approach and practice, and her visionary aspirations to forge a national category of art. From the early 1920s, growing tired of what she viewed as hackneyed artistic appropriations of European traditions, Preston launched her earliest attempts to capture and define the parameters of a modern national art for Australia. Later in her career Preston's aesthetic interests shifted heavily towards the adaptation of Aboriginal patterns and motifs, but initially this distinctive vision of an Australian artistic modernity was articulated through a synthesis of Eastern and Western idioms, inspired by her discovery of Japanese woodblock prints (*ukiyo-e*), and the works of a growing group of avant-garde artists in Europe who offered radical new pathways to pictorial representation.

As Preston did not travel to Japan until 1934, her direct encounters with *ukiyo-e* prints were a result of both the European and Australian iterations of *Japonisme*.

The term *Japonisme* was coined in the late eighteenth century[2] to describe the Western fascination with Japanese aesthetics, history and culture prompted by the shiploads of Japanese goods entering European markets following the abolition of Japan's *sakoku* ('closed country') policy and its resumption of diplomatic relations with the outside world. Even prior to Japan's first highly acclaimed exhibition space at the Parisian Exposition Universelle in 1867, household wares including ceramics, fans, screens and kimono proved extremely popular among European consumers (Volk 2004, 40). The reach of *Japonisme* also extended to literature and the performing arts, in such works as Edmond and Jules de Goncourt's novel *Manette Salomon* (1867) and Gilbert and Sullivan's opera *The Mikado* (1885). Of all the works arriving from Japan, however, the most favourably received were the *ukiyo-e* (lit. 'pictures of the floating world') woodblock prints which demonstrated how simple and transitory subjects such as daily life in Edo (present-day Tokyo) could be rendered in aesthetically appealing ways (Ives n.p.; Kōdera et al. 2017, 15–16). In the West, these works exerted a pronounced influence among artists experimenting in 'modern' styles; some integrated Japanese subject matters and motifs into their works, while others embraced *ukiyo-e*'s pictorial techniques, including elevated horizon lines, multiple viewpoints, abstracted forms, and flattened spaces (Hickey 2015, 21).

Like many of her contemporaries, Preston admired the aesthetic conventions employed in Japanese *ukiyo-e* prints for their radical departure from the conventional academic methods of true-to-life representation championed by Western art training academies. The move away from this mimetic style to more abstracted forms among many artists was strongly aligned with the ideals and methods driving the modern art movement, which gained ground as new vehicles of expression capable of embracing the complexity and contradictions of life in the early twentieth century (Hartley 2016, 1).[3] This chapter argues that Preston adopted Japanese pictorial conventions in her repertoire as part of her own quest to forge a distinctively Australian modern artistic style. The paintings and prints which evolved from her meeting with *ukiyo-e* prints are invaluable not only because they help to document the development of Australian modernism, but also for the ways that they demonstrate how borrowed elements can be inscribed with new meanings and values when transposed to different cultural settings (Howes 1996, 5). Although such considerations have been widely recognised in a host of academic studies on European artists, they have not been nearly as well documented in the Australian context.[4] One complicating factor is the difficulty of identifying a clear genealogy of Australian *Japonisme*, as many Japanese artistic idioms first reached Australian consumers filtered through products of the Aesthetic movement and the Arts and Crafts movement, which flourished contemporaneously with *Japonisme* in late nineteenth-century Europe. The chapter begins by charting Preston's early career and the gradual changes that evolved in her painting style following two prolonged stints in Europe. It then examines the ways that Preston's paintings and woodblock prints of the 1920s and early 1930s executed 'in the Japanese manner' guided her early contributions towards the establishment of an Australian modernist style.

Preston's early institutional training and first stint in Europe

At age 12, in her hometown of Adelaide, Preston determined that she wanted to become an artist. Recognising her intuitive talent for drawing, her parents arranged for lessons with the seascape painter William Lister Lister (1859–1943). In 1893, when the family moved to Melbourne, Preston enrolled in classes at the prestigious National Gallery of Victoria Art School and took instruction from Frederick McCubbin (1855–1917). After a hiatus due to her father's failing health that required her return to Adelaide (where she attended the School of Design, Painting and Technical Arts), Preston resumed her studies at the Victorian School in 1896 under the tutelage of the director Bernard Hall (1859–1935) (Edwards and Peel 2010, 15). Following his own training at the Royal College of Art in London, Hall offered a thorough education in the Munich style, which espoused 'structured picture-making based on rigorous observation, accurate drawing and tonal realism' (Harding 2016, 18). This approach – which had been handed down from Europe's eighteenth-century academies of art training – taught students various painting conventions dictating the use of linear perspective, foreshortening, colour application and the tonal effects of *chiaroscuro*.[5] It was under Hall's direction that Preston made the propitious decision to focus her efforts on still life painting, despite its marginalised reputation as the domain of hobbyists, or as an occasional diversion for serious painters (Harding 2016, 17). The endemic prestige afforded to the history, portraiture, religious and landscape genres by the academies was of little concern to Preston, who busied herself arranging quotidian domestic scenes to sketch and paint. Before long, it became apparent that she had found her *métier* working with what she described as her 'laboratory tables on which aesthetic problems [could] be isolated'.[6]

After graduating in 1899, Preston set up a studio in Adelaide where she taught art classes and painted in her spare time. Her earliest works demonstrate a kinship with the seventeenth-century *vanitas* works of Dutch and Flemish painters, and the eighteenth-century French artist Jean Baptiste Siméon Chardin (1699–1779) (Harding 2016, 17). *Still Life: Lobsters* (1901), for instance, clearly demonstrates Preston's mastery of the techniques underpinning academic realism. In her famous testimonial about her career trajectory written in the third person, 'From Eggs to Electrolux' (1927), Preston recalled that at this point in her career,

> Against all opposition of friends and relatives she painted eggs, dead rabbits, onions – just everything she liked. It was no use for her to explain to people that the standardised beauty for art of landscapes, sunsets and ladies did not interest her . . . Every week-end found her painting away at her eggs or rabbits; her ideal at this time was to paint them with such fidelity to nature that they could almost be used in the kitchen. . . . If she really painted as well as that, surely she would be the very best painter of still life in the world.
>
> (Preston 1927, 49)

In 1904, curious to gauge her level of expertise against the artists of Europe and to 'get some "finishing" lessons' (Preston 1927, 49), Preston and her artist friend

Bessie Davidson (1879–1965) boarded a ship bound for Genoa. On their first stop in Germany, however, the foundations of Preston's training were greatly tested by her exposure to the works of breakaway modern art groups such as the German Secessionists, whose subversion of 'truth to nature' made her 'feel sick' (Preston 1927, 50). She later recalled her reaction to the

> two very strong elements in Munich at that time, the dead realists and the lively moderns. Naturally, I condemned as mad and vicious the moderns and went willingly with the deads (sic).
>
> (Preston 1923, 20)

Moving on to Paris, Preston's meetings with more examples of the creative ferment unfolding under the banner of modernism further challenged her understanding of the boundaries of pictorial representation. At the 1904 Salon d'Automne[7] – a show which she described as 'exceed[ing] the outrageousness of the Secessionists' (Preston 1927, 50) – Preston viewed the pioneering abstracted works of Paul Cézanne, Odilon Redon and Wassily Kandinsky. The following year, Preston marvelled at the Fauvist methods of Henri Matisse, Albert Marquet and André Derain, whose canvases used radically intense colour in portrayals of space and light as a means to communicate personal experience. Before leaving Europe, retrospectives of Vincent van Gogh and Paul Gauguin rounded out Preston's exposure to new avenues of expression that stimulated her thinking as an artist and would help precipitate her first tentative steps away from academic realism (Edwards and Peel 2010, 23–24).

As Preston was beginning to discover, Western art practice as she encountered it in the museums and galleries of Europe was firmly ensconced in a revolutionary phase that was absorbed in the dismantling of tradition and the experimentation with new pictorial modes (Ives n.p.). Far from a passing interest, the flourishing of this modernist aesthetic was catalysed by a weariness with the strictures of the traditional means and methods associated with the Neoclassical and Gothic revival styles. Preston and her contemporaries had come of age in an era when the goal of painting was no longer didacticism or imitation, but an expression of individuality and creative freedom. Many artists harnessed this newfound freedom to shun the 'narrative' underpinning traditional academic works to create abstracted art based on their direct experiences of life, using traditional techniques and materials in innovative ways (Gombrich 1972, 378–379). Accompanying and encouraging the radical changes in expression, publications outlining revolutionary ideas in art theory spurred modernism's proponents not only to cultivate new ways of seeing, but also to question the very function of art. In many ateliers, copies of publications outlining new art historical approaches such as Arthur Wesley Dow's *Composition* (1899) triggered lively debates and guided a new generation of artists towards a spirit of experimentation (Mimmocchi 2016, 50; Edwards and Peel 2010, 46–47).

Returning to Adelaide in 1906, Preston attempted to apply the lessons she gleaned from European art to her own work. In 'From Eggs to Electrolux', she described the painstaking task of how she 'started off again' by 'tr[ying] to add another quality to her realism' (Preston 1927, 50). In essence, Preston began to concentrate on honing her style by reducing imitation in her work in order to pursue an approach grounded in experimenting more with light and colour (Kastner 2016, 76). Despite this change in practice – which gave her 'bad growing pains' – Preston maintained her resolve to push the limits of her craft: 'I found at last that the eggs and onions as part or whole of a picture could appear different and suggest something more than being merely edible. I could not paint the smell so I needn't paint the species. Realism had its first rebuff' (Preston 1923, 20).

Preston's second stint in Europe and her maturing style

It was not until the mid-1910s, however, that Preston truly began to gain a confidence and maturity in her artistic style. In 1912, she embarked on her second, longer stint in Europe with her artist friend Gladys Reynell (1881–1956). The women first took up residence in Paris, before moving on to various locales including Brittany, London and Bunmahon. In London, Preston was invited to participate in several exhibitions hosted by such groups as the Society of Women Artists. Following a review in the London press maligning her work as 'bringing nothing new into art',[8] Preston began to reorient her approach to painting with a fierce determination to break away from her conservative training. She delved into the principles that underpinned the work of the myriad groups associated with modernism, trying to decipher their methods in the construction of pictorial space (Kastner 2016, 76). Floundering for a precise direction, however, Preston sought counsel from fellow expatriate painter Rupert Bunny (1864–1947), who exhorted her to go and study Japanese prints at the Musée Guimet, where she discovered

> that there is more than one vision in art. That a picture could have more than eye realism. That there was such a thing as aesthetic feeling. That a picture that is meant to fill a certain space should decorate that space. . . . She found she had been hopping about on one rung only of the ladder of art.
> (Preston 1927, 50–51)

Preston's account alludes to her fresh understanding of the subjectivity of artistic vision that was feeding the work of her progressive contemporaries. For many of the artists around her, Japanese woodblock prints provided an exciting source of inspiration that opened the way for a host of new technical possibilities in the representation of perspective and depth, asymmetrical composition and the application of flat areas of colour. However, this move away from the traditional modes of mimetic representation was puzzling to many viewers, as renowned *Japoniste* Edmond de Goncourt explained:

> It is strange, this revolution brought by Japanese art in the taste of a people who, in matters of art, are the slaves of Greek symmetry and who, suddenly, are becoming impassioned over a plate on which the flower is not set dead in

the middle, over a fabric in which harmony is not achieved by a gradation of tints but by a knowledgeable juxtaposition of raw colours.
(Goncourt quoted in Lambourne 2005, 32)

As the introduction noted, this 'revolution brought by Japanese art' was fuelled predominantly by the enthusiastic reception of *ukiyo-e* prints. In 1862, the International Exhibition in London showcased an extensive array of Japanese works, while Paris hosted Japanese delegations at the aforementioned Exposition Universelle in 1867, and again in 1878 (Findling 1990, 51). Then, in 1890, the École Nationale des Beaux-Arts hosted its first-ever show of foreign works in an enormously successful exhibition of 725 Japanese prints which familiarised visitors with (among others) the works of famous masters such as Suzuki Harunobu (1725–1770), Kitagawa Utamaro (1753–1806), Katsushika Hokusai (1760–1849) and Andō Hiroshige (1797–1858) (Kōdera et al. 2017, 1–3, 24, 27). The exhibition was visited by more than 30 well-known artists, including many of whom were already attuned to experimenting with Japanese modes of representation, such as Claude Monet, Mary Cassatt and Edgar Degas (Kōdera et al. 2017, 31–34; Berger 1992, 188).[9] Among the famous Japanese-inspired works postdating the exhibition are Monet's *Waterlilies and the Japanese Bridge* (1897–1899), in which he suppressed detail in favour of rendering atmospheric, light-filled scenes, and Cassatt's series of aquatints influenced by Utamaro's prints, along with other intimate genre scenes such as *Maternal Caress* (1891) (Kōdera et al. 2017, 31–32). A follower of Degas, Henri de Toulouse-Lautrec, also employed sharp outlines, asymmetrical compositions and cropped framing in striking graphic poster works such as *Divan Japonais* (1892–93). Many of the designs of the Art Nouveau movement were also indebted to Japanese woodblock prints, including the work of Aubrey Beardsley, whose boldly simple black-and-white illustrations were instantly recognisable for their Japanese-style lack of modelling (Berger 1992, 188).

As Preston toured the museums and galleries of Europe in the 1910s, she was able to identify that 'in Japanese prints the impressionists had found an expanded space' and that for post-impressionists, '*ukiyo-e* provided a means of eliminating illusionism through simplified structurally based design' (Edwards and Peel 2010, 37). Years later she would lament that she had not 'had the advantages offered by the Slade school in London, where the sculpture of the Greeks and Co. flourish in museums and not in a live school, and where all imitativeness is discouraged' (Preston 1923, 20). In 1913, after moving to London, Preston had the opportunity to view many *ukiyo-e* first hand in the Victoria and Albert Museum's landmark exhibition of Japanese prints (Colton 2010, 22). A letter written that year to artist Norman Carter (1875–1963) indicates that she was becoming increasingly absorbed in her quest to abandon tonal imitation in favour of structuring space in different ways: 'Decorative work – it is the only thing worth aiming for in this our century – it is really the keynote of everything. I am trying all I know to reduce my still-life to decorations and find it awfully difficult' (Preston quoted in Edwards and Peel 2010, 35). In essence, the 'decorative' style that Preston hoped to master was not a turn to pretty ornamentation, as the term implies, but a focus on rhythm and design that would come to characterise much of her later work (Harding 2016, 30; Butler 1993, 40). 'Once design enters', Preston explained, 'every form or shape realised on the canvas alters the nature and character of the original stimulus'.[10] This discovery was revelatory to Preston's method, and also helped her to reconceptualise her works with a stronger dependency on colour and abstraction. In modernism's spirit of experimentation, she recorded how 'From now on she would allow herself full license in colour – only letting her subjects appear as realistic as her aesthetic feelings allowed' (Preston 1927, 52).

The lessons Preston learned from the use of saturated colour, strong lines and shallow space in Japanese woodblock prints and the works of Anglo-American artists are evident in a number of her works from the mid-1910s. One early example is her 1915 work entitled *Still Life with Teapot and Daisies* (Figure 3.1), which features a casual arrangement of objects in a brightly coloured outdoor table scene, painted on a sunny day in Bunmahon, Ireland. Preston's composition, which

Figure 3.1 Margaret Preston (Australia; England; France, b.1875, d.1963) (*Still life with teapot and daisies*) (1915). Oil on cardboard, 44.3 x 51.2 cm. Art Gallery of New South Wales. Gift of the W.G. Preston Estate 1977

Photo: Christopher Snee, AGNSW

Source: © Margaret Rose Preston Estate, licensed by Viscopy, Sydney. 192.1977 features a zig-zagged placement of objects on sharp diagonals anchored towards one corner, clearly signals her challenge to the codes underpinning Western perspectival balance and harmonious composition. These codes are further brought into question by the pink- and white-striped pattern of the tablecloth, which leads the viewer's eye from the foreground behind the objects to the rear left of the composition, where the pattern abruptly changes direction, rendering the creation of perspectival depth impossible. This in turn flattens the pictorial space and adds drama to the abrupt compositional cropping of the jug on the left border of the work (Edwards and Peel 2010, 54–55). By employing these techniques used by *ukiyo-e* artists, Preston not only took the preliminary steps that would become foundational to her mature hallmark style, but also ventured into the broader current of modernist painting which revolutionised the genre by emphasising the medium and the surface of the work rather than the historical method of 'using art to conceal art' (Greenberg n.d.). The incorporation of these techniques also heightens *Still Life*'s visual tension, as their effects are disrupted by the illusionistic shadows cast by the tight composition of the objects, the mimetic depiction of the daisies and the reflection in the teapot playfully revealing a parasol-carrying woman approaching the table.

Nasturtiums (c1916, Figure 3.2) is another work that this chapter argues clearly charts Preston's increasing engagement with Japanese woodblock prints. It appears to be carefully constructed based on a work by Harunobu, *Courtesan of the Motoya Looking at the Face of a Komusō Reflected in Water* (c1769–1770, Figure 3.3). Preston's painting directly transposes Harunobu's figural representations (a courtesan on the left and a komusō monk[11] on the right) as the central objects of her still life study. A close inspection of the two works reveals Preston's meticulous appropriation of their compositional forms and lines and the dynamic interplay of the objects that surround them. In the painting, the two figures become two ceramic vessels holding cream- and orange-toned flowers, their contours closely mimicking the courtesan's *shimada* hair style and shoulder line and the many layers of the komusō's outer garments, respectively. The white vessel sits atop a raised platform in like manner to the courtesan, while the sharp corner angle of the platform emulates the corner angle of the *en* (narrow veranda) outside the courtesan's room (also repeated in the placement of the tatami mats behind her). Preston also faithfully adopted Harunobu's framing devices: the bamboo screen to the left of the courtesan becomes a curtain, the timber doorframe a window casing, the black *noren* curtain an almost void space in dark-toned paint but for the highlights corresponding closely to the *noren*'s script pattern. As in the *ukiyo-e*, viewers of the painting capture a glimpse of garden foliage behind the central composition, and a low table on the left of the composition simulating the *hibachi* brazier. Rendered in burnt oranges, rich browns and dusty creams, the expressive brushwork of *Nasturtiums* also adopts the warm hues of Harunobu's palette, even extending to the refracted light and highlights on the vessels, which echo the bursts of colour in the kimono patterns. At the base of the brown vessel, Preston's juxtaposition of light and shadow seems to take cues from the round dish of water capturing the komusō's face and the forward folds of his gathered garments brushing the ground.

Figure 3.2 Margaret Preston (Australia; England; France, b.1875, d.1963). *Nasturtiums* (circa 1916). Oil on cardboard, 61.2 x 50.7 cm. Art Gallery of New South Wales. Purchased 1920

Photo: AGNSW

Source: © Margaret Rose Preston Estate, licensed by Viscopy, Sydney. 684

Preston's quest for an Australian modernism

Following the World War I armistice, Preston was free to return to Australia with her fiancé, discharged soldier William Preston, whom she had met in 1917. Arriving in mid-1919, the Prestons married at the end of the year before settling in Mosman in 1920 (Harding and Mimmocchi 2016, 168). In spite of her

Figure 3.3 Copyright holder of the image: Museum of Fine Arts, Boston. Suzuki Harunobu, Japanese, 1725–1770. *Courtesan of the Motoya Looking at the Face of a Komusō Reflected in Water*. Japanese, Edo period, about 1769–70 (Meiwa 6–7). Woodblock print (nishiki-e); ink and color on paper. Vertical chūban; 28.6 x 21.8 cm (11 1/4 x 8 9/16 in.). Museum of Fine Arts, Boston. William S. and John T. Spaulding Collection. 21.4989

Source: Photograph ©2019 Museum of Fine Arts, Boston

newfound financial security, Preston faced an impasse in her career due to her feeling that her art was neither in sync with the times nor with the changes in her own artistic vision prompted by her prolonged exposure to many different art currents in Europe (Preston 1927, 52). Adding to her woes, Preston was dismayed to find the Australian art scene in an impoverished state and the nation lacking an innate grasp on its cultural identity. In a radio interview many years later, Preston recalled that at the time 'I saw that things had not changed . . . [the art] was all imitative . . . [and] none of the work had any of the fundamental characteristics . . . of Australia' (Preston quoted in Butler 1987, 41). Never shy to speak her mind, Preston lamented, for example, that the style of the Heidelberg painters was too derivative of the European impressionists, and that a number of artists seeking admission to the Australian Society of Artists were 'all a bunch of copyists' (Preston cited in Grishin 2006, 82). However, her disappointment at the state of Australian art spurred in her a renewed sense of purpose, and in the ensuing years she became an outspoken public commentator on the cultural issues that she identified as pertinent to the shaping of modern Australia. After reading Roger Fry's *Vision and Design* (1920), for instance, Preston began to perceive art as a 'tangible symbol of the spirit of a country' (Preston quoted in Art Gallery of New South Wales n.p.) and identified the need to define the parameters of a communal and democratic national art as a pressing concern. Australians, she chided, must 'hurry then and use [their] own material in an Australian spirit before other nations step in and we are left without even having tried' (Preston 1924, 31).

Preston's commentary on the cultural aspects relevant to the forging of modern Australia resonated with other progressives in Sydney. Among them was the entrepreneur and publisher Sydney Ure Smith (1887–1949), who became one of Preston's greatest supporters. By his estimation, Preston had not only earned a place at 'the very front rank of present-day still-life painters' (Ure Smith quoted in North 1980, 6) for her exceptional body of work but also for her ingenuity in highlighting the need to capture a distinctively Australian aesthetic 'more urgently and single-mindedly than any other artist' (Long 1935, 18). Ure Smith shared Preston's passionate advocacy to modernise Australian designs, driven by her loathing of 'those wretched kookaburra, gum leaves, and wattle blossoms done on cushions in a Kensington school-of-art manner' (Preston 1930, 22). He frequently reproduced her art and printed her ideas and opinions in the pages of his journals *Art in Australia* and *The Home: An Australian Quarterly*. In 'Why I Became a Convert to Modern Art', for example, Preston laid out her reoriented nationalist vision for her own work: 'And now I want to think and think and try and get those onions, etc., without any remembrance of the Greek, German, French brand, and portray them as a purely Australian product' (Preston 1923, 20). In the early 1920s, Preston made great strides towards this vision with her success in making Japanese-style woodblock prints. In combination with her understanding of the techniques and principles of underlying modern Western art, these works helped her to hone a syncretic, abstracted style encapsulating a modern Australian vernacular (Riddler, Peel and Edwards 2010, 275; Edwards and Peel 2010, 62). Her practice of incorporating disparate traditions into her modern style rested partly on her romanticised vision of Australia as a logical crossroads between East and West (Edwards and Peel 2010, 75).

The hundreds of decorative woodblock prints Preston made throughout the 1920s and 1930s greatly contributed to a revival of the medium in Australia (Butler 2007, 165). In a number of works Preston experimented with designs closely emulating Japanese prototypes (for example, *Rocks and Waves, Balmoral, NSW*, c1929 and *Black Swans, Wallis Lake NSW*, 1923), but generally she maintained a determination that the persistent influence of the Japanese techniques in her repertoire would not obscure her artistic independence or hinder the search for a distinctly Australian idiom. In fact, it was the medium of the woodcut that she believed pushed her to find new forms of expression: 'In my search for forms which will suggest Australia I prefer wood blocking to painting, for the wood hinders facility and compels the worker to keep the forms in his composition severe' (Preston quoted in Long 1935, 18). Preston's approach was more concerned with extracting and interpreting than appropriating – a lesson she learned from Pablo Picasso, whom she admired because he 'never imitated but always created' (Preston quoted in Edwards and Peel 2010, 38). Thus, despite their indebtedness to the simplified shapes and lines, intense pure colour and bold patterning found in *ukiyo-e* prints, the rhythmic designs, spatial voids and geometrical forms of Preston's woodcuts became instantly recognisable as familiar motifs and landscapes embodying her nationalist aims. She explained the regional nuances of her approach:

> Australia is a country that gives the impression of size and neutral colour. To give this impression on canvas or woodblocks I find it necessary to eliminate 'dancing' colour and to heap my light and shadows. I have abandoned the regulation yellow-colour sunlight and made form explain light. . . . In my effort to give a feeling of sharp flatness I force my compositions with as much solid light as possible . . . I am eliminating distracting detail.
>
> (Long 1935, 18)

Preston's series of prints capitalising on the views of the growing Sydney metropolis and the harbour views around her Mosman home shored up her reputation as a successful artist. In the popular press, the *Evening News* reported that Preston believed that 'there is a great future for [woodblock prints] for the decoration of flats' (*Evening News* quoted in Lebovic 1987, 100). Ure Smith also took to the pages of *Art in Australia* to encourage his readers to invest in the burgeoning field of decorative art, noting that 'the prints reproduced here are now being issued for sale in strictly limited editions, signed and numbered. The prices are moderate, and already there is a considerable demand for Australian woodcuts' (Ure Smith 1923, 37). In 1923, a number of Preston's prints attained broad public exposure when they were displayed with prints by Lionel Lindsay and Ethyl Spowers alongside 24 works by Utamaro, Hiroshige and Hokusai at the *Woodcuts Exhibition* hosted by Tyrell's Gallery. Preston followed the success of this exhibition with an intense, sustained period of work which produced some of her most acclaimed landscape woodcuts, including *Circular Quay* (1925) and *Sydney Bridge* (c1932, Figure 3.4), and her exuberant, flat and asymmetrical depictions of Australian wildflowers such as *Red Bow* (1925) and *Wheel Flower* (c1929). The positive reception of these works not only credited Preston with introducing a new genre of stylised decorative art into Australia, but also with making a resoundingly original contribution to Australian modernism (Edwards and Peel 2010, 79).

In 1926 and 1930, Preston communicated her knowledge of Japanese printing in her articles 'Coloured Woodprints' and 'Wood-Blocking as a Craft'. Designed as practical guides, they outlined the Japanese methods of cutting the cherry woodblock for the black outlines (and subsequent blocks for each additional colour) and applying pressure from a pad covered in bamboo leaf (*baren*) to print the paint onto finely textured mulberry paper. Preston was aware that in Japan, the production of woodcuts was divided into the roles of artist, carver and printer, but naturally she undertook all three roles herself. 'Coloured Woodprints' also introduced Preston's preferred 'primitive' method, in which she cut one block for outlines and then hand-coloured each of the spaces 'in simple crude masses' with

Figure 3.4 Margaret Preston (Australia; England; France, b.1875, d.1963). *Sydney Bridge* (circa 1932). Woodcut, printed in black ink, hand coloured with gouache on cream Japanese laid paper, 19 x 23.2 cm. Art Gallery of New South Wales. Purchased 1964

Photo: Christopher Snee, AGNSW

Source: © Margaret Rose Preston Estate, licensed by Viscopy, Sydney. DA30.1964

gouache (Preston quoted in Riddler, Peel and Edwards 2010, 276). In some prints, she appears to have used a stencil, presumably to aid in the consistent application of the ink, and for *Wheel Flower*, she commissioned a block formed from nine Huon pine panels. These approaches illustrate Preston's innovative adaptations of Japanese techniques, which she explained as methods 'from a western point of view' (Peel 2010, 259–262). Although in 1934 Preston was fortunate to take instruction on the art of *ukiyo-e* printing with the son of Hiroshige in Kyoto (Harding and Mimmocchi 2016, 173), at this point in her career, her knowledge hinged on her study of woodblock printing at London's Camberwell School of Arts and Crafts in 1916 (Edwards and Peel 2010, 58), and possibly at the School of Design in Adelaide, which had a strong allegiance with the Arts and Crafts movement in England. She also learned some aspects of the art from the myriad publications circulating in Australia at the time that dealt with Japanese art and printing (Edwards and Peel 2010, 46–48).

From 1894, for example, the English journal *The Studio* carried many articles detailing technical aspects of Japanese woodcuts (Butler 1987, 68), and classic studies such as William Anderson's *Pictorial Arts of Japan* (1886) were widely available. A number of books from Preston's extensive collection contain her own sketches in the margins, confirming her reliance on them as reference works (Butler 1987, 40–41). They include many texts released in the early years of the twentieth century, including Heinrich Wölfflin's *The Principles of Art History* (1915), Clive Bell's *Art* (1914), Ernest Fenollosa's *Epochs of Chinese and Japanese Art* (1912) and Seiichi Taki's *Three Essays on Oriental Painting* (1910). For practical advice, she turned to Dow's work *Composition* (1899), which put forth his theory that painting is 'essentially a rhythmic harmony of coloured spaces' (Dow 1997, 4). She would have appreciated his insistence on the modernist parity of arts and crafts, as well as his exhortation to modern painters to simplify and abstract, paying heed to the harmonic relations between line and colour, as well as tonal rendering based on Japanese ideas of *notan* (systems of dark and light) (Butler 1987, 40). It also seems likely that Preston followed his recommendation to make tracings of Japanese prints to uncover their underlying structure for *Nasturtiums*.

Such lessons from Japan are reiterated in Preston's series of banksia and eucalyptus paintings executed in 1927 and 1928, as she refined the pictorial strategies of painting she learned in Europe to meet local conditions. In *Western Australian Gum Blossom* (1928, Figure 3.5), for instance, Preston expressed her modernist interpretation of the national flora made iconic by the academic pastoralist landscapes of painters such as Hans Heysen (1877–1968) and Arthur Streeton. The stark black-and-white geometric planes in the background and the assured dark outlines of the arrangement work together to intensify the effect of the floating ground on which the arrangement sits. Preston's incorporation of large, flat areas of dark paint serves to highlight the vibrancy of the gum flowers and the pronounced lack of tonal modulation in their forms. Such applications of paint, which Preston also used with success in *Nasturtiums* and *Gum Blossom (or Eucalyptus)* (1928), indicate her knowledge of the techniques used in a number of European modernist works such as *French Window at Collioure* (1914) and *The Black Table* (1919) by

58 *Penny Bailey*

Figure 3.5 Margaret Preston (Australia; England; France, b.1875, d.1963). *Western Australian gum blossom* 1928. Oil on canvas, 55.3 x 46 cm. Art Gallery of New South Wales. Purchased 1978

Photo: Diana Panuccio, AGNSW

Source: ©Margaret Preston Licensed by Viscopy, 2018

Henri Matisse, which were themselves indebted to Japanese pictorial representation. Other aspects of *Gum Blossom* such as its architectonic forms, asymmetrical composition and vertical cropping are also clearly indebted to woodblock techniques. By compressing the spatial plane and simplifying the work's abstracted forms, Preston reconceptualised the familiar subject of native Australian flora into a dramatic composition, prompting Somerset Maugham to declare it her most accomplished work (Riddler, Peel and Edwards 2010, 278).

Conclusion

Preston's encounters with Japanese woodblock prints in Europe and Australia early in her career and later in Japan played a significant role in her contributions to the transmission and birth of an Australian modernism. Freed from the constraints of mimetic representation, Preston used her creative spirit and exposure to new artistic idioms to develop a body of work including paintings and prints that synthesised the principles, techniques and motifs of Asian and Western, and later Aboriginal, art. The decorative explorations in form, line and colour in Preston's paintings and the clarity and exuberance of her remarkable prints are testament to her sustained and thorough efforts to find a new and dynamically modern aesthetic. Preston's most iconic works – the still lifes, bustling cityscapes and serene landscapes created in 1920s Sydney – became symbolic markers of place in her broader vision of creating authentic expressions of Australian nationhood. Many of these works remain among the most beloved examples of Preston's abstracted modernist style today.

The Prestons spent much of the 1930s living in Berowra, north of Sydney, on a rural property bordering a national park. In a radical departure from her brightly coloured works of the 1920s and early 1930s, Preston's continued search for a framework of national art led her to harness the properties of Aboriginal art and design to reimagine Australian wildflowers and scenery with an emphasis on content and symbol. However, Preston remained fond of the art of woodblock printing, remarking that 'a lover of art cannot do better than study Japanese woodcuts if he wants to know something about design. They are famous for this quality and yet they are never "empty"' (Preston quoted in Edwards and Peel 2010, 44). However, in 1941 (at age 66), Preston wrote to a friend that she was 'not doing any more wood blocks as they are very trying on the hands – pulling the thumbs quite out of shape – and being very painful' (Preston quoted in Edwards and Peel 2010, 67). In a career marked by continual innovation and change, many of Preston's most recognised works would be unthinkable without her encounters with Japanese woodcuts in the waves of *Japonisme* that reached Australian and European shores. Her continued incorporation of Japanese pictorial conventions into her aesthetic practice throughout her career helped to secure Preston's place as an outstanding champion of Australia's modern visual culture, underscoring the dynamism, creativity and complexity that can spring from intercultural exchange.

Notes

1 For example, Preston's protégé Thea Proctor (1879–1966) described her as 'a distinguished and original artist in Australia – an artist with abundant vitality', while fellow artist Lionel Lindsay (1874–1961) portrayed her as 'a raging jealous creature who burns her work when it doesn't sell [and] Hasn't one ounce of gratitude in her carcase' (Edwards and Peel 2010, 9).
2 Art critic Philippe Burty (1830–1890) and literary critic Jules Claretie (1840–1913) both used the term *Japonisme* in print in 1872 (Clarke and Clarke 2010, n.p.).

60 Penny Bailey

3 As modern art (c1850s–1960s) encapsulates an evolving and sometimes conflicting set of ideas that were bound by their impulse to reject traditional methods and produce works in original and innovative ways, it is not always appropriate or accurate to classify artists and their works into movements or schools. In many cases, the diversity in modes of representation resists categorisation.
4 Two notable exceptions are the research associated with the impressive exhibitions *Making Modernism: O'Keeffe, Preston, Cossington-Smith* in 2016–2017, and *In the Japanese Manner: Australian Prints 1900–1940* in 2011.
5 For example, students of academicism were trained to use bright colours and pure black sparingly, by building up their canvases with dark tones and shading before overlaying them with lighter tones and impasto highlights. Acclaimed artists of the academic style include Jacques-Louis David (1748–1825), J.A.D. Ingres (1780–1867), Jean-Leon Gerome (1824–1904).
6 This is Aphorism 46 of 92 'by Margaret Preston and others' printed in Preston (1929, n.p.).
7 The Salon d'Automne (Autumn Salon) is an art exhibition that has been held annually in Paris since 1903. Founded in reaction to the conservative policies underpinning the Paris Salon (established in 1667 under the auspices of the Académie des Beaux-Arts), it quickly became a showcase for innovative twentieth-century works in painting, sculpture, architecture and the decorative arts. (Clarke and Clarke 2010, n.p.).
8 *Athenaeum* (20 February 1915) quoted in Butler (1993, 41).
9 For example, famous works predating the exhibition include *Flowering Plum Tree* (1887), by Vincent van Gogh, which faithfully replicates in oil Hiroshige's *Kameido umeyashiki* (Plum Garden in Kameido 1857), and Edgar Degas's *Dancers Practising at the Barre* (1887), one of many ballet-themed canvases employing intricate foreshortening, elongated pictorial formats and unusual vantage points. (Edwards and Peel 2010, 26–28).
10 Aphorism 25 of 92 'by Margaret Preston and others' printed in Preston (1929, n.p.).
11 Komusō (lit. monk of nothingness) were mendicant monks belonging to the Fuke sect of Zen Buddhism which flourished during the Edo period (1603–1868). They wore *tengai* (reed hoods) over their heads in order to annihilate the ego, and played meditative *honkyoku* (lit. original music) on the *shakuhachi* (bamboo flute) when collecting alms (see Blomberg 1995, 101–104).

References

Art Gallery of New South Wales. n.d. 'Margaret Preston: Art and Life', accessed 15 December 2018, www.artgallery.nsw.gov.au/sub/preston/artist_1920.html.
Berger, K. 1992. *Japonisme in Western Painting from Whistler to Matisse*. Cambridge: Cambridge University Press.
Blomberg, C. 1995. *The Heart of the Warrior: Origins and Religious Background of the Samurai System in Feudal Japan*. Sandgate, Folkestone: Kent Japan Library.
Butler, R. 1987. *The Prints of Margaret Preston: A Catalogue Raisonné*. Melbourne: Oxford University Press.
———. 1993. *Poster Art in Australia: The Streets as Art Galleries – Walls Sometimes Speak*. Canberra: National Gallery of Australia.
———. 2007. *Printed: Images by Australian Artists 1885–1955*. Canberra: National Gallery of Australia.
Clarke, M. and Clarke, D. 2010. *The Concise Oxford Dictionary of Art Terms*, 2nd edition. Oxford: Oxford University Press.
Colton, E. 2010. 'In the Japanese Manner: Australian Prints 1900–1940', *Artonview*, 62 (Winter): 22–25.

Dow, A. W. 1997. *Composition: A Series of Exercises in Art Structure for the Use of Students and Teachers*. Berkeley: University of California Press.

Edwards, D. and Peel, R. (eds.). 2010. *Margaret Preston*. Fishermans Bend, VIC: Thames and Hudson.

Findling, J. E. (ed). 1990. *Historical Dictionary of World's Fairs and Expositions: 1851–1988*. New York: Greenwood Press.

Gombrich, E. H. 1972. *The Story of Art*. London: Phaidon Press.

Greenberg, C. n.d. 'Modernist Painting', in *Forum Lectures 1960*. Washington, DC: Voice of America, accessed 15 December 2018, www.yorku.ca/yamlau/readings/greenberg_modernistPainting.pdf.

Grishin, S. 2006. 'Margaret Preston: Art and Life – A Major Touring Exhibition of One of Australia's Most Celebrated Artists', *Craft Arts International*, 66: 81–83.

Harding, L. 2016. 'The Modern Art of Painting Flowers: Reinventing the Still Life', in L. Harding and D. Mimmocchi (eds.), *O'Keeffe, Preston, Cossington-Smith: Making Modernism*. Sydney and Bulleen: Art Gallery of New South Wales and Heide Museum of Modern Art, 1–7.

Harding, L. and Mimmocchi, D. (eds.). 2016. *O'Keeffe, Preston, Cossington-Smith: Making Modernism*. Sydney and Bulleen: Art Gallery of New South Wales and Heide Museum of Modern Art.

Hartley, C. 2016. 'Introduction', in L. Harding and D. Mimmocchi (eds.), *O'Keeffe, Preston, Cossington-Smith: Making Modernism*. Sydney and Bulleen: Art Gallery of New South Wales and Heide Museum of Modern Art, 16–35.

Hickey, G. 2015. 'Cultural Divide: Japanese Art in Australia (1868–2012)', *Japan Review*, 28: 191–223.

Howes, D. (ed.). 1996. *Cross Cultural Consumption: Global Markets, Local Realities*. London: Routledge.

Ives, C. n.d. 'Japonisme', in *Heilbrunn Timeline of Art History*. New York: The Metropolitan Museum of Art, accessed 15 December 2018, www.metmuseum.org/toah/hd/jpon/hd_jpon.htm.

Kastner, C. 2016. 'Abstraction and the Creation of National Identity', in L. Harding and D. Mimmocchi (eds.), *O'Keeffe, Preston, Cossington-Smith: Making Modernism*. Sydney and Bulleen: Art Gallery of New South Wales and Heide Museum of Modern Art, 75–89.

Kōdera, T., Saito, T., Soda, M. and Aitkin, G. 2017. 'Reconstructing Bing's Legendary 1890 Exhibition of Japanese Prints at the École des Beaux-Arts', *Journal of Japonisme*, 2 (1): 1–37.

Lambourne, L. 2005. *Japonisme: Cultural Crossings Between Japan and the West*. London and New York: Phaidon Press.

Lebovic, J. 1987. *Masterpieces of Australian Printmaking*. Sydney: Josef Lebovic Gallery.

Long, G. 1935. 'Some Recent Paintings by Margaret Preston', *Art in Australia*, 3 (59): 18–23.

Mimmocchi, D. 2016. 'Unveiling Nature: Landscape in the "Epoch of the Spiritual"', in L. Harding and D. Mimmocchi (eds.), *O'Keeffe, Preston, Cossington-Smith: Making Modernism*. Sydney and Bulleen: Art Gallery of New South Wales and Heide Museum of Modern Art, 43–63.

North, I. 1980. *The Art of Margaret Preston*. Adelaide: Art Gallery Board of South Australia.

Peel, R. 2010. 'Drawing Connections', in D. Edwards and R. Peel (eds.), *Margaret Preston*. Fishermans Bend, VIC: Thames and Hudson, 252–269.

Preston, M. 1923. 'Why I Became a Convert to Modern Art', *The Home: An Australian Quarterly*, 4 (2) (June): 20.

———. 1924. 'Art for Crafts: Aboriginal Art Artfully Applied', *The Home: An Australian Quarterly*, 5 (5) (December): 30–31.

———. 1927. 'From Eggs to Electrolux', *Art in Australia (Margaret Preston Number)*, 3 (22). (December): 45–52.

———. 1929. *Recent Paintings, 1929*. Sydney: Art in Australia.

———. 1930. 'Away with the Poker Worked Kookaburra and Gumleaves', *Sunday Pictorial* (Sydney), 6 April, 22.

Riddler, E., Peel, R. and Edwards, D. 2010. 'Biographical Notes', in D. Edwards and R. Peel (eds.), *Margaret Preston*. Fishermans Bend, VIC: Thames and Hudson, 270–281.

Ure Smith, S. 1923. 'The Revival of the Woodcut', *Art in Australia*, 3 (4) (May): 35–37.

Volk, A. 2004. 'A Unified Rhythm: Past and Present in Japanese Modern Art', in C. M. E. Guth, A. Volk and E. Yamanashi (eds.), *Japan & Paris: Impressionism, Post-Impressionism, and the Modern Era*. Honolulu: Honolulu Academy of Arts, 38–55.

4 Japan-Australia friendship through bat and ball

The Yomiuri Giants' baseball tour of Australia in 1954

Ai Kobayashi

In Brisbane on the evening of 12 November 1954, the first baseball match of the Yomiuri Giants' Australian tour was played at the Exhibition Ground. The Yomiuri Giants beat a combined Brisbane side easily. Reporting on the contest, the *Courier-Mail* praised the Giants highly, saying that the team 'showed world class form to beat Brisbane 22–3'. 'The Japanese, who play baseball in a big way in their own country, were outstanding in all departments' (Japs Too Strong 1954, 30).

The Yomiuri Giants was (and is) a leading Japanese professional baseball team. It was also the first Japanese professional baseball team to visit Australia, and the first Japanese sporting team to do so after World War II. Over ten days, the Giants played eight matches against local teams in Brisbane, Sydney and Canberra. The original schedule included several matches in Melbourne and Perth, but the tour was cut short due to a number of factors, including bad weather conditions in Melbourne.

Drawing on both Japanese and Australian source material, including various reports, personal accounts, archival documents and newspaper articles, this chapter illustrates the Yomiuri Giants' baseball visit to Australia and provides an insight into the complex process of rebuilding relations between the two countries in the early postwar period. One and half years had passed since the Peace Treaty came into force and the two countries had resumed a diplomatic relationship, but the timing of the tour was still delicate in light of popular ill-feeling in Australia towards the Japanese. The visit of the top Japanese professional baseball team to Australia was not treated simply as a sporting event: the Yomiuri Giants was keen to promote it as a goodwill mission 'through bat and ball' to improve Japan-Australia relations, while the occasion raised the question of how prepared the Australian public was to accept new and friendly relations with the Japanese. This chapter assesses the outcome of the baseball contact.

Background

Baseball was introduced to Japan in the late nineteenth century and was the most popular participant sport by the early 1910s (Guttmann and Thompson 2001, 82). The Yomiuri Giants was at the centre of the Japanese baseball industry. Founded in 1934, it was one of the original teams of the Japan Professional Baseball League established in 1936. The Australian tour was the Giants' sixth overseas trip; previous tours took place in the United States three times and the Philippines twice (Gōshū ensei o maeni 1954, 5; Guthrie-Shimizu 2012, 130–134, 155, 192). The team owner was (and still is) *Yomiuri Shinbun*, one of the major newspapers in Japan, so the novelty of the Australian tour was reported eagerly in the newspaper. As the Australian tour coincided with exhibition games for the *Yomiuri Shinbun*'s 80th anniversary, only a minimum number of members were sent to Australia. However, the team included star players such as Takumi Otomo, who was the best pitcher of 1953, and Kaname Yonamine, a regular outfielder, who had the most hits in the Central League in 1952 and became the top hitter in 1954 (*Giants' 80nenshi* 2014, 107). Most of them had played in the pennant competition, so it was a strong team.

Baseball had also been introduced to Australia in the latter half of the nineteenth century. The sport was played by American residents in Australia and cricket players who took up baseball during winter months as 'fitness training' before the cricket season. Encouraged by American team visits, such as the exhibition tours of two Major League teams, the New York Giants and the Chicago White Sox, in 1914 and Stanford University teams in 1928, as well as numerous games played against visiting US ships, baseball grew popular steadily in the early decades of the twentieth century, though it remained in the shadow of cricket (Clark 2003, 41–59). A national governing body, the Australian Baseball Council, was formed in 1912 and began operating with real influence from 1926.

There had been occasional interaction between Japanese and Australian baseball players before World War II. As with visiting US ships, there were many baseball players on board Japanese ships, and local baseballers took advantage of the opportunity to play games against them. Sydney, Melbourne and Adelaide benefitted most. Joe Clark, a historian of Australian baseball, notes these Japanese visitors were 'an invigorating influence on Australian baseball' (Clark 2003, 50). Japanese residents in Australia also played. A Japanese team entered the New South Wales Baseball Association's competition in 1924, and some Australian teams recruited resident Japanese players. Australians regarded Japan highly as 'the other leading baseball nation' after the United States (Clark 2003, 50–53). The Japanese Consul General in Sydney supported the game by sponsoring the Sydney first-grade competition, which played for the Nippon Cup. However, the outbreak of the Pacific War ended this friendly interaction.

Soon after World War II, the number of baseball clubs in Australia increased noticeably. Clark observes that the increase was stimulated by the 'baseball interest inspired by American servicemen', 'the return of "keep-fit-for-cricket" participants' and 'newcomers who had seen the game during the war and now wanted to play too' (Clark 2003, 60–61). Local teams had many opportunities to play with American servicemen stationed in Australia, and some games were said to have attracted as many as 7,000 spectators (Clark 2003, 56–59). At the time of the Giants' visit, it was reported that there were over 350 teams in Australia. Their breakdown was about 20 in Queensland, about 100 in New South Wales and

Victoria, 120 in South Australia and about 40 in Western Australia (Zendo ni 350 chīmu 1954, 4).

When the Peace Treaty came into force in April 1952, the Japanese and Australian governments resumed diplomatic relations. Efforts were made on both sides to normalise the bilateral relationship. However, ill-feeling in Australia towards the Japanese was a significant obstacle, and the Australian government's cautious consideration of public opinion in its dealing with Japanese matters impeded political and economic co-operation. Nevertheless, in August 1954 the Australian government made a major decision to adopt a more liberal policy towards Japan. The Japanese government was aware of the ill-feeling towards Japan in Australia, so it sent one of its best diplomats, Haruhiko Nishi, as the first Japanese Ambassador to Australia (Kobayashi 2014b, 531–533). Nishi's perceptive reports informed the Japanese government of Australian conditions and attitudes. However, as the Japanese government initially sought to regain international status and rebuild its own economy, it appears that little effort was made to devise goodwill activities to encourage change in local sentiment in Australia. The Yomiuri Giants' visit to Australia in 1954 took place, therefore, as the Australian government's basic attitude to Japanese relations was changing but in the absence of any Japanese government initiative to more actively seek positive Australian public opinion.

Arranging the Yomiuri Giants' visit to Australia

Two American men were involved in arranging the tour of the Japanese team. Initially, Mike Castor, an American sports promoter based in Melbourne, noticed a growing interest in baseball in Australia. With the hope of developing Australian baseball, he negotiated with the American Major League to bring an all-star team to Australia, but was unable to organise a tour. Frank O'Doul, whom Castor had hoped would lead the all-star team to Australia, suggested that Castor consider inviting the Yomiuri Giants instead (Gōshū e yuku kyojingun 1954, 69). Castor took up O'Doul's suggestion, and with the agreement of the Australian Baseball Council, arranged for a Yomiuri Giants team to visit five Australian cities over a period of two weeks. It was agreed that O'Doul join the Giants' tour in Australia.

O'Doul was a former Major Leaguer and the coach of the Auckland Oaks in the Pacific Coast League. He had strong connections with the Japanese baseball industry, particularly with the Yomiuri Giants. Since 1931 he had often visited Japan as part of the Major League combined team, helping to improve Japanese baseball techniques by coaching student baseball, and contributing to the establishment of the Japanese Professional League. After the war, he brought the San Francisco Seals to Japan in 1949 and restored the Japan-US baseball exchange, which had lapsed for over a decade.[1] O'Doul was now keen to lend a hand to the development of Australian baseball, and was hopeful of a positive effect on Japan-Australia relations.

Hosting a Japanese team was not a problem for the majority of the Australian baseball community. Reg Darling, the secretary of the Australian Baseball Council, said 'We will play any team irrespective of what country they come from'

(15 Giants Players Slated to Make Australian Tour 1954, n.p.). However, the South Australian league, which had nearly one-third of the baseball teams in Australia, decided not to play with the Giants 'because of the possibility of "incidents" ' (Jap Tour in Doubt 1954, 6). This demonstrates that although the pursuit of sporting interest and ill-feeling towards the Japanese might have operated at different levels, they could not be separated.

Whether the Giants team should be allowed to come to Australia was discussed in the Federal Cabinet. The ban on the entry of Japanese nationals into Australia was gradually relaxed after the Peace Treaty, but the government continued to pay careful attention to Japanese entry. Initially there was a 'division of opinion' in the Cabinet, but the committee formed to advise the Prime Minister 'decided to take no action to prevent' the Japanese baseball players from visiting Australia (Record of Conversation by Shaw 1954). It appears that the view of the Department of External Affairs that Australia 'should not discriminate against Japanese amongst non-Europeans in such matters' carried weight with the Minister for Immigration (Record of Conversation by Shaw 1954). In making the final decision there was still 'doubt whether too early a reception of such visits by Japanese might not cause a reaction in Australia', but since a delegation of the Japanese wool industry was expected to come later in November and an official delegation to discuss trade might also come in a few months, a visit by sportsmen was regarded as a useful 'test of public opinion' (Record of Conversation by Shaw 1954). The fact that baseball was a minor sport in Australia was also a factor. Considering the impact of sporting exchange on the public mind, one official could not help wishing the team were 'tennis players, in which sport we could probably beat them and in which there was probably more interest than in baseball' (Record of Conversation by Shaw 1954).

The Japanese government was not involved in the tour's organisation, but its support was evident by permitting a foreign exchange allocation for the Giants' visit to Australia. Until the mid-1960s the Japanese government limited travelling overseas to those whose purpose was in the national interest, such as official business, commerce and research. This restriction was designed to prevent a deficit in the balance of payments. It can therefore be inferred that the government judged the tour to be beneficial for Japan. While the initiative was left to commercial interests, any positive effect would be a welcome development for the bilateral relationship.

Australian reactions

Notable criticism came from the Returned and Services League (RSL). Following the public announcement of the Giants tour, the RSL annual congress decided to protest to the government 'against commercial interests bringing a Japanese baseball team in Australia' (RSL Protests at Baseball Tour by Japs 1954, 5). William Yeo, the president of the New South Wales branch of the RSL, expressed fierce opposition, saying 'the RSL did not oppose Japanese coming for the Davis Cup or the Olympic Games, but it opposed commercial interests being allowed to sponsor the visit of these people, who would be taking money from Australia' (RSL Protests at Baseball Tour by Japs 1954, 5). The federal president of the RSL, Sir George Holland, warned the delegates not to let their emotions overcome their judgment. He had already protested to the tour organisers about the first match being played on 11 November, Armistice Day (No Ban on Japanese Players 1954, 2). That consideration was readily appreciated by the promoter, and the date of the first match was changed to 12 November. In response to Holland's reminder that at some point the RSL had to accept the entry of Japanese people into Australia, Yeo remained uncompromising, stating that it should only be 'after the deaths of the last living relatives of Australian servicemen who were "butchered" during the last war' (No Ban on Japanese Players 1954, 2). The meeting carried a resolution, moved by N.D. Wilson of Victoria, that the congress should 'define its policy on the admission into Australia of Japanese sportsmen or other persons sponsored by commercial interests, or nationally organised' (Jap Team "Out to Win Friends" 1954, 5). On 4 November, Menzies stated the official policy in the Parliament: 'the Government had decided for "a variety of reasons" that it would not be proper to stop the team visiting Australia' (PM on Jap Athletes 1954, 8).

The Australian press responded swiftly to the RSL's protest. An editorial in the Melbourne *Age* on 27 October criticised 'the perpetuation of enmities':

> There are some indications that the natural tide in international relationship is taking charge. . . . It cannot be checked and it will not be smoothed by fanning smouldering hatreds best left to extinguish themselves in the passage of time.
> (Accepting Japanese Relationships 1954, 2)

Similarly, an editorial in the *Sydney Morning Herald* on 28 October described the objections raised at the RSL congress as 'exaggerated and unrealistic', commenting that 'it is time we ceased nourishing its antagonisms' and that the RSL 'should encourage a more adult attitude' (No Ban on Japanese Players 1954, 2). The editorial in the *Argus* on 28 October was supportive of sporting exchanges, particularly in light of the Melbourne Olympics, saying that 'Australians do not hate sportsmen', while expressing a conditional acceptance of the Japanese: 'Nor do we hate Japanese who are trying to redeem the faults of an unpleasant past' (You Can't Hate a (Not Even a Japanese) Baseball Team 1954, 4). A letter to the editor from B. Morris of Carlton, which appeared in the *Age*, emphasised the importance of future, not past, relations with the Japanese (Morris 1954, 2). Leading clergymen were also reported as supporting the tour and appealing for better relations between the two countries (15 Giant Players Slated to Make Australian Tour 1954, n.p.).

Some viewed the Giants visit with great interest as a sporting event. The prominent cricket player Ian Johnson wrote in his column, 'On the Spot', in the *Argus* that the Giants would give 'Australian fans an idea of the standard of the game out here', explaining that the Yomiuri Giants had exchanged visits with the New York Giants and therefore would be 'the toughest opposition our boys have ever encountered'. In the previous year the Yomiuri Giants had beaten the New York Giants twice. Johnson even speculated that, 'If this tour proves a financial success, there is a possibility that next year will see a visit from a Major League American team' (Johnson 1954, 29). Australian interest in baseball was going to be tested.

Absence of criticism of the RSL congress and the positive press in Brisbane is noteworthy. It might have been simply a sign of lesser interest in the Giants' tour in Brisbane as compared to Melbourne and Sydney, but it could also be read as an indication of lack of support.

Tokyo was not unduly concerned by the RSL's protest. The Giants' spokesman was reported as saying 'The opposition to the tour is quite understandable. But I do not believe this view represents the true attitude of all Australians.' The spokesman added that 'The team was not going just as a commercial proposition', but rather aimed to foster friendship between Australia and Japan through baseball (Jap Team "Out to Win Friends" 1954, 5).

Friendship through bat and ball

'Japan-Australia friendship through bat and ball' became the slogan of the Giants' Australian tour. When the tour was confirmed, Shoji Yasuda, the president of *Yomiuri Shinbun*, expressed a hope by referring to the recent visit of Frank Sedgman, who before turning professional in 1953 had won all the Grand Slam tennis titles:

> Mr Sedgman, a professional tennis player, who we had invited recently, is an Australian and his play and manner gave a very good impression. I hope the Giants tour will also be like that. Given that in baseball Japan is a developed country, I expect the tour will have a great impact on Australian techniques. It will be great if these things can be a boost for the bilateral friendship.
> (Kyojingun no gōshū ensei hongimari 1954, 4)

The representative of the Yomiuri Giants, Hashimoto, said: 'There is nothing that can deepen goodwill between countries more than international sporting matches. Especially, baseball because it is a lively and fun sport that can be liked by anybody, so it should be even more effective' (Kyojingun no gōshū ensei hongimari 1954, 4). Tsuneo Harada, who was appointed as the team manager, remarked that 'Australia's baseball fever is rising tremendously, I believe the Giants' visit at this time will play a great role in goodwill between Australia and Japan' (Gōshū e shinzen yakyū 1954, 7). He had led the Yomiuri Giants to the United States in the previous year,

> Born in 1921 in California, Harada was a Japanese American who played an important role in developing Japanese baseball during and after the American Occupation in Japan. (Guthrie-Shimizu 2012, 174–176, 181, 189, 192). During the Pacific War he was an intelligence officer in the US Army and in 1942 on General MacArthur's staff in Brisbane. He was now a sports promoter and

president of Tokyu Airline in Japan. His wartime connection with Australia was reassuring to the organisers.

At a Giants' send-off party attended by about 100 people, including representatives of the Australian Embassy, the Giants' Australia tour was presented as a goodwill mission. It is not known whether any representative of the Japanese government attended this party. Yasuda concluded his speech of encouragement by saying: 'Please work to improve the relationship of Japan and Australia by showing your full sportsmanship and making sport a tie that binds these two countries' (Supōtsu de nichigō shinzen hakare 1954, 7). Shigeru Chiba, the coach of the touring team, said: 'We hear Australian baseball is not strong, but without underestimating them, we would like to accomplish our mission of Japan-Australia friendship by playing games with all our might' (Ganbare!! Kyojingun 1954, 7). David Beattie, who represented the Australian Ambassador, expressed the hope that the Giants would ensure good games, but also remarked jokingly that he 'wanted Australia to win' (Supōtsu de nichigō shinzen hakare 1954, 7). *Yomiuri Shinbun* summed up the atmosphere of the party: 'The send-off party . . . was not only to say "go and win", but was also a reflection of the nation's expectation of the diplomatic goodwill mission, hoping that they will blow the stagnant air between Japan and Australia away through baseball' (Ganbare!! Kyojingun 1954, 7). On the eve of the departure, the Australian Ambassador, Ronald Walker, held a farewell party at the Australian Embassy in Tokyo, which further demonstrates the diplomatic significance of this tour. It suggests that Walker was keenly aware of its potential as a goodwill activity between the two countries and hoped to encourage them to make their best endeavours. Arriving in Australia, Harada declared that, 'We are emissaries of goodwill' ('Friendship', Slogan of Jap. Team 1954, 8). All the members were wearing red Remembrance Day Poppies bought at the Australian Embassy.

Before leaving the United States for Australia, O'Doul also emphasised this goodwill aspect. He said that 'the Tokyo Giants' tour would help to establish friendly relations between the nations' (Japanese Baseball Tour Hopes 1954, 14). He noted that the Giants' team manager, Tsuneo 'Cappy' Harada, was 'a native of California', who had 'fought with the American troops out of Australia through the South Pacific Campaigns', and that four other Giants members visiting Australia were born in the United States (Japanese Baseball Tour Hopes 1954, 14). They were Hawaiian-born with Japanese parents, who had joined the Yomiuri Giants in recent years. It was possible that their American background had been considered in the selection of the team members. Their language skills would prove useful in communicating with Australian players and fans.

For the players, going to Australia meant various things: the warm climate in November would be favourable compared to cold weather in Japan; finding out how Australians played baseball would be interesting; conditioning themselves for the following pennant race while away was necessary but could be challenging; ill-feeling towards the Japanese was a concern. Before leaving Japan, the team had been warned 'to be careful' because Australian sentiments towards the

Japanese were still quite negative (Shinzen ryokō o oete 1954, 4). However, it appears that the excitement of going abroad outweighed any nervous feelings about the Australian reception. Australia was new to all except Harada. Some had never been on an airplane. For 24-year-old Onpei Minami, this was a first overseas trip. The young men were open for new adventure.

On the day that the Giants' tour started, Castor announced that the entire profits of the Giants tour would be donated to the United RSL Poppy Day Appeal 'as a gesture of goodwill and peace' to 'restore pre-war relations' (Wreath-Laying by Japanese 1954, 3). Clearly the promoter wanted to clear the air by responding to the RSL's protest with grace, knowing that public support was essential. The Giants' willingness to act as a goodwill mission must have encouraged the decision. In the sense that the Giants were privately owned, the tour was commercial, but once the announcement was made that any profits would be donated, its commercial purpose was very restricted. However, this announcement attracted little media attention. The RSL's response to it is not known. The lack of publicity might have been an indication of an absence of support or interest.

The matches in Australia

Between 12 and 21 November 1954, the Giants played eight exhibition matches: two in Brisbane, four in Sydney and two in Canberra. All except the games in Canberra were held at night. Except for the NSW champion, 'the Marrickville', local combined teams challenged the Giants. The Giants won all the matches, most of them comfortably. The score in the first match against the Brisbane combined team was 22–3, the second against a Queensland team 10–1, the third against a Sydney team 14–4, the fourth against a New South Wales team 20–1, the fifth against the Australian team 14–8, the sixth against Marrickville 16–0, the seventh against a Canberra team 21–6, the eighth against the Australian team 13–1.

The fifth match was classed as the first 'test' match. Unlike the other games, it was very close and heated. The Australian team was winning until the Giants tied the score, 8–8, in the ninth inning. The game then went into extra innings. The Australian Baseball Council proudly recorded that 'This game was of a high standard and it was only after extra innings that the visitors ran out winners' (The Australian Baseball Council 1955, 6). Of the second 'test' match, which became the last game of the tour, the Australian Baseball Council recorded that 'the visitors were far too good, winning 13 runs to 1' (The Australian Baseball Council 1955, 6).

The number of spectators at each match was small. It was reported that 'only 400 people' watched the first game at the Brisbane Exhibition Ground (Wreath-Laying by Japanese 1954, 3). This included a few dozen Japanese men who were crew members of *Kashima Maru*, a Japanese government fishing training vessel. They happened to be stranded in Brisbane due to engine troubles (The City's Surprise Arrivals 1954, 1; Jap Cheer Squad for Baseballers 1954, 3). For the second game, the *Courier-Mail* reported that the attendance was 500 (Japs Too Strong 1954, 30). In Sydney, all four matches took place at the Sydney Sports Ground. There was reportedly a crowd of 437 people at the first game, and 333 on the following day (Giants Win 1954a, 13, 1954b, 15; Giants Crush NSW 20–1 1954, 7). About ten Japanese war brides were among them (Sensō hanayome mo seien 1954, 4). While the numbers for the following two days are not known, the *Argus* reported that in total 'no more than 2,000' people saw the baseball matches in Sydney (Too Wet 1954, 5). In Canberra, about 250 to 300 spectators attended the Manuka Oval on 19 November. Among them were 'members of the Diplomatic Corps, youths and children who hunted autographs from the visitors' (Baseball 1954, 12; Japanese Baseball Team in Exciting Match at Manuka 1954, 4). Two days later, the Sunday afternoon 'test' match attracted the biggest crowd in the whole tour, between 700 and 900 spectators (Baseballers Cancel Australian Tour 1954, 1; Too Wet 1954, 5). Having the game on a Sunday afternoon would have helped boost the attendance compared to night games.

Yomiuri Shinbun sent a special correspondent, Roy Saeki, to accompany the baseballers. Saeki was a Hawaiian-born sports writer with *Yomiuri Shinbun* who had covered the Yomiuri Giants' tour in the United States in 1953, the Helsinki Olympics and the last Asian Games (News of the Day 1954, 2). *Hōchi Shinbun*, a sports daily owned by *Yomiuri Shinbun*, also drew on Saeki's reports. Feature articles, including interviews with the Giants players, appeared in these newspapers. Few reports appeared in other major Japanese newspapers.

It is noticeable that *Yomiuri Shinbun* and *Hōchi Shinbun* did not report the attendance at each game. A passing reference was made that 'over 4000' spectators attended the first match in Sydney, but this number seems unlikely given the Australian press reports (Kyojin mitabi rakushō 1954, 4). Hironoshin Furuhashi, who had accompanied the Giants' tour as a local guide, wrote at the end of the tour that 'the audience was much smaller than expected, but it was a fact that the players' friendly actions were definitely well accepted by the local people' (Kyōjingun no ninki 1954, 4). Furuhashi was a former Japanese swimming star who had first come to Australia in early 1953 to study wool-classing as an employee of a Japanese wool spinning company, staying for one year. This time he was back in Australia as a wool buyer. The enthusiasm of spectators compensated for the low attendance, and the Japanese accounts focused on that aspect.

The Yomiuri Giants' experience

Australian spectators appeared to be very appreciative of the Japanese baseballers. The correspondent Saeki as well as the Giants players were impressed with the fair attitude displayed by spectators; they would give 'a round of applause' to fine play by the Giants and 'boo' umpires for unfair decisions against the Giants. Reporting the result of the second match in Brisbane, Saeki noted that 'none of the spectators left the stadium until the game was finished', and many sought to shake hands with the Japanese players, and apologised for the umpires' unfair judgments. Some said that 'Without flattering, the attitude of the Giants at the game was magnificent'. Saeki reported confidently that 'Giants were totally popular and accepted by spectators', and that all the Giants members were 'very pleased' (Otomo no sokkyū ni odoroku 1954, 4).

Minamimura spoke of the spectators' attitude at a *Yomiuri Shinbun*'s international telephone interview: 'They are so keen to study the Japanese full-fledged baseball, and are very sophisticated because Australians have a high sporting standard. . . . They hoot if the Australian team are lazy and if the umpire gives a lazy judgment, they also relentlessly put him down.' To his surprise, this attitude was maintained even at the first 'test' match in which Australia was almost winning: 'I thought we were going to be hooted down when we scored the tie run at the bottom of the ninth inning, but they were happy and said that it was a good game' ("Zengō" ga daigaku teido 1954, 1). Hideo Fujimoto, the coach of the team, compared Japanese and Australian spectators. In both countries, spectators would applaud fine play and flock to players for autographs, but the composition of the audience was different. In Australia, 'there were more adults than children and about half of them were women, which was different from Japan' (Kyojingun gōshū o yuku 1954, 6).

Contrary to their expectations, the Japanese players felt welcome, even outside the stadium. Harada was 'nervous' when they touched down in Darwin, but Australian journalists and returned servicemen welcomed them at the airport and the Customs officers let them go through without examination. This smooth process at the first airport in Australia left the Giants with 'a very good impression' (Shinzen ryokō o oete 1954, 4). Team members had been advised not to walk alone, but once they became accustomed to the hotel and the city, they wandered around freely. In Brisbane, to Fujimoto's great surprise, when he walked out from the hotel, he saw 'a conductor waving when the tram stopped'; 'I could not believe that he was waving to me but there was nobody around me, so I realised it was for me and I waved back. Then he smiled and started the tram' (Kyojingun gōshū o yuku 1954, 6). Similarly, Minami said that, 'some people waved to us in the city when they noticed we were the Giants players' (Ōsutoraria mitamama 1954, 4). Morimichi Iwashita said he found no animosity, and that 'As individuals they were very nice people' (Ōsutoraria mitamama 1954, 4). Furuhashi observed that 'Australian sentiment towards the Japanese has become much better than last year' when he first came, though he admitted that he still occasionally encountered people with ill-feelings ("Zengō" ga daigaku teido 1954, 1). There was no direct protest made against the Giants. Some ex-servicemen were among Australian players. Minami said he did not feel 'enmity', but found everyone loved the sport and demonstrated sportsmanship (Ōsutoraria mitamama 1954, 4).

The visiting team made gestures of goodwill. In Brisbane, the players laid a wreath of fresh-cut flowers at the Shrine of Remembrance and the Australian-American War Memorial. Before the first match, Harada gave Alderman Dower, the chairman of the Brisbane City Council's transport and electricity department, who represented the Lord Mayor of Brisbane, 'a heavily embroidered scarf with the team's name worked in silk'. Having led the Giants onto the ground, Harada spoke through the ground amplifier: 'I am no stranger to Brisbane. I am happy to be able to return here with the Tokyo Giants' (Jap Cheer Squad for Baseballers 1954, 3). In Sydney, the team visited the Sydney City Hall and greeted Kevin Dwyer, the Deputy Lord Mayor, as the Lord Mayor was absent. Dwyer gave a speech to acknowledge the Giants' visit in which he emphasised future Japan-Australia relations:

> As the Giants are very strong, I have mixed feelings of happiness and sadness. But the war has ended and from now on Japan and Australia must hold hands to fight against communism through an international sport like baseball. I hope your visit in Australia will remain as a good memory forever.
> (Sidonī shiyakusho hōmon 1954, 1)

Before the 'test' match in Canberra, Harada presented Allen Brown, the head of the Prime Minister's Department who represented Menzies, with a pigeon blood-red cloisonné vase 'as a token of goodwill from the people of Japan' (Baseballers Cancel Australian Tour 1954, 1).

Japanese residents in Australia were pleased to see their fellow countrymen showing their sporting prowess. A number of war brides in Brisbane entertained the Giants with a Japanese meal at their homes (Sensō hanayome ga gochisō 1954, 7). In Sydney, about a dozen war brides as well as a number of wool buyers and the Japanese Consulate staff watched the Giants' games. Ryuta Kawasaki, the Japanese Consul in Sydney, entertained the team with a Japanese dinner (Matsuda 1955, 132). The Japanese Ambassador, Haruhiko Nishi, welcomed the Japanese players at Canberra airport and threw a cocktail party for them to which ambassadors and ministers of other countries, including the US Ambassador, as well as Australian baseball players and officials, were invited. Nishi was said to have supported the baseball tour by buying tickets to give to other diplomatic missions. He probably did so as part of his duty of entertaining other diplomats as well as introducing Japanese sporting culture, while showing support to the Japanese visitors. The Yomiuri Giants was the top Japanese baseball team, and their exhibition matches were a rare spectacle in Canberra.

Australian baseball

The standard of the Australian all-star team was roughly estimated at about that of top-level Japanese university baseball teams. While Australian baseball was behind in technique, the consensus of Japanese opinion was that given the good climate, vast space and the fact that players had great physical strength, Australian baseball would improve remarkably if there were coaches from the United States or Japan. Above all, the Giants were impressed with the enthusiasm and the serious attitude of Australian players ("Zengō" ga daigaku teido 1954, 1).

There was some confusion because the Australian rules did not comply with the conventional rules. For example, a walk and a dead ball were counted locally as at-bats and base umpires squatted down in the batter's way. To the Japanese players' greatest surprise, once an umpire said 'play ball', a pitcher would throw the ball even if the batter was not in the box. It would then be counted as a strike. Takumi Otomo experienced this when he was looking for a bat. When he protested, he was told there could be no complaint during the match, but he would be heard after the game ("Zengō" ga daigaku teido 1954, 1).

There were also some lighter moments. In a Brisbane match, the pitcher Otomo's ball was so fast that the local side were shouting from the first base coach's box: 'Swing the bat when Otomo raises his leg!' Both the spectators and the Giants side laughed loudly (Otomo no sokkyū ni odoroku 1954, 4; Gōshū Dayori 1954, 3). The Australian coach said he 'had never seen such a fast ball' (Otomo no sokkyū ni odoroku 1954, 4). Another source of laughter was that the decision which team would bat first was made by tossing a coin, a practice used in Australia for football and cricket. The Japanese found this strange, and 'laughed a lot' (Gōshū miyage zadankai 1954, 4). Some field announcers used nicknames, such as 'Sunday' and 'koala bear', because of their difficulty in pronouncing Japanese names ("Zengō" ga daigaku teido 1954, 1).

The main problem was poor lighting. At the Sports Ground in Sydney, there were only four lighting poles, which were apparently inadequate to illuminate the whole ground. Both sides had a hard time dealing with strong grounders and fly balls. Not being able to see where the ball went after hitting it was a shock to the Japanese players (Gōshū miyage zadankai 1954, 4). O'Doul commented after the first match in Sydney that 'lighting seemed a little too dark', but he praised both sides for the game and Australians for absorbing techniques very quickly (Shōmei fubi, goro ni kushin 1954, 4). Looking back, Otomo said that 'lighting should be five times brighter for a baseball match' (Gōshū miyage zadankai 1954, 4). As no grounds were devoted to baseball in Australia, such inconvenience was inevitable. Poor facilities were a telling indication that baseball was only a minor sport.

Another problem was the equipment. There was no standard ball like the one used in the United States or Japan, and teams could use any ball as long as the league approved it (Sakan na ōsutoraria no yakyūnetsu 1954, 4). There were big balls and small balls of varying weight. The Japanese found it hard to use these balls, which could also warp easily. Australian bats and gloves were again different from the standard ones used in the United States or Japan; the tip of their bats was fat and heavy, like a 'primitive weapon', and their gloves were smaller, just four fingers, and 'did not have cores and were like those for warming hands' (Gōshū Dayori 1954, 3). Some thought the bat seemed to hit well, while the glove was considered unfit for a hard ball. Australian players were surprised at the size of the Japanese gloves and 'impressed' when they were told that the one used by the Japanese players were standard there (Matsuda 1955, 132).

The Japanese and Australian players interacted with each other before and after the game, teaching and learning baseball techniques. Language was a problem for many of the Japanese players, but they seemed to communicate adequately through gestures and broken English. O'Doul, who had joined the Giants in Sydney, offered lessons to Australian players during the tour. He was so impressed with how quickly Australian players picked up the techniques, he hoped to organise an international baseball competition among the United States, Japan and Australia in the near future (Otomo, 20 sanshin ubau 1954, 4). The Giants also offered lessons to fans, including female softball players and boys. Darling said 'It was fortunate not only that Australian players were able to meet them at the stadium, but also that besides the matches, they gave us all their baseball knowledge. We have gained a deeper knowledge of baseball' (Togō kyojin no sokuseki tatau 1954, 4).

Social occasions were limited. They would have been difficult to organise since the matches were held at night and many local players were working or studying during the day. However, the Japanese and Australian players mingled at Nishi's party at the Japanese Embassy in Canberra. This time the Giants taught Australians how to use chopsticks (Matsuda 1955, 132). The diplomatic event allowed the players to mix off the field, which supported the goodwill aspect of the tour.

The abrupt end of the tour

The Giants tour ended in Canberra. The original plan had been to have three matches in Melbourne, including another 'test' match, and two in Perth. However, instead of flying to Melbourne, the team left Australia for Manila, where it had been invited for further exhibition matches. The stated reason for the cancellation was heavy rain in Melbourne and the prospect of continuing wet weather. Because of the upset to the team's itinerary, the Western Australian leg of the tour was also cancelled. The announcement was made soon after the last match in Canberra finished. It was 'an unfortunate happening', recorded the Australian Baseball Council, for 'Victoria and Western Australia missed seeing the visitors in action' (The Australian Baseball Council 1955, 7). Before leaving Australia, Harada stated that 'We are very sorry not to be going to Melbourne and Perth', adding, 'All the boys were looking forward to it' (Abrupt End to Jap Tour 1954, 1).

The abrupt ending was reported in Australia with strong speculation that the tour was 'a failure financially' after a series of poorly attended matches and that this had contributed to the cancellation of the rest of the tour (Japanese Ball Team Ends Tour 1954, 3; Abrupt End to Jap Tour 1954, 1; Baseballers Cancel Australian Tour 1954, 1; Too Wet 1954, 5). The *Argus* even suggested that rain was a cover-up for ending the tour earlier by quoting the secretary of the Royal Agricultural Society, Colin Woodfull, saying on the Sunday before they were due to leave for Melbourne that 'there was nothing wrong' with the Melbourne Showground, where the matches were to take place (Too Wet 1954, 5). The weather report was true. Melbourne had record 'rainfall of almost five inches' between Friday night and Monday morning (News of the Day 1954, 2). However, the annual report of the Australian Baseball Council noted that 'the poor support afforded to the games forced the promoter to cancel visits to Melbourne and Perth' (The Australian Baseball Council 1955, 6). The wet weather would have been an important contributing factor, but the likelihood that the gate takings would not cover tour expenses must have been decisive in the promoter's decision to give up on the tour.

The cancellation was a great disappointment to the Australian Baseball Council, and its annual report recorded that

> A great deal of adverse publicity in Queensland and practically no publicity at all in Sydney doomed the venture to failure, which was a pity as the Japanese team was possibly the best baseball team ever to play in Australia, and the

players were a fine bunch of young men when they were guests of the Ambassador for Japan at a reception of the visiting Japanese players.

(The Australian Baseball Council 1955, 6–7)

Darling believed that the lack of publicity and high ticket prices contributed to the poor attendance. Prices for the matches in Melbourne were 17/6, 12/6 and 7/6, well above the cost for attending other sporting events (Japanese Ball Team Ends Tour 1954, 3). Saeki was also reported as saying, 'It was the bad publicity that killed the baseball tour' (Moses 1954, 30). He thought the tour should have started in Canberra, where 'everything was friendly', and moved backwards, finishing in Brisbane.

The less favourable atmosphere in Brisbane can be inferred by considering newspaper responses to the objections raised at the RSL congress to the Giants' visit. In Sydney the *Sydney Morning Herald*, and in Melbourne the *Age* and the *Argus* responded to the RSL's protest swiftly by editorialising about it. In essence, all these editorials shared the view that except for the organiser's blunder of setting the opening day on the Armistice Day, the intolerance displayed by the RSL to the visit of Japanese baseballers was unacceptable (Accepting Japanese Relationships 1954, 2; No Ban on Japanese Players 1954, 2; You Can't Hate a (Not Even a Japanese) Baseball Team 1954, 4). The *Argus* reported the enthusiasm of the Australian Baseball Council as well as the dissent of leading ex-servicemen from the RSL's objections (RSL Protests at Baseball Tour by Japs 1954, 5; Bury Hatchet, Say War Leaders 1954, 5). However, the *Courier-Mail*, the major newspaper in Brisbane, made no criticism of the RSL congress; at best, a columnist urged readers to keep an open mind: 'Let's suspend judgment on the Japanese baseball team due here tomorrow morning' (Vine 1954, 12).

Advertising for the baseball matches in Melbourne, scheduled for 22, 23 and 24 November, appeared daily in the *Age* in the preceding week, but no such advertisements appeared in the *Courier-Mail* or *Sydney Morning Herald*. A report of the Giants laying a wreath in Brisbane appeared with a photograph in the *Sydney Morning Herald*'s world news page, and a small notice of the team's arrival and the first game in Sydney appeared in its sports page (Wreath-Laying by Japanese 1954, 3; Japanese Side Here 1954, 6). However, no further reports appeared in the *Sydney Morning Herald* until the tour's cancellation was announced.

The Australian Baseball Council did not speculate on the reasons for the 'lack of support afforded to the games', which disadvantaged the venture. There were two apparent reasons, a general lack of interest in baseball and the fact that the team was from Japan, though it is difficult to determine which played the greater role. Even so, attention to the Japanese factor stood out in the Australian press.

In response to the news of the cancellation, William Yeo declared that the Japanese tour was 'ill-considered and ill-timed', emphasising Australian feeling against the Japanese. He said 'The time is not yet opportune for any Japanese commercial sporting club to come here on a money-making tour' (Abrupt End to Jap Tour 1954, 1). From the beginning, RSL critics took the professional nature of baseball as an argument against it. They were appealing to amateurism, which back then had much greater legitimacy in Australia than playing for monetary gain. Once the promoter said all profits would be donated, it ceased to be a 'money-making tour', yet Yeo continued to play on this Australian attitude.

An editorial in the *Argus* also attributed the unexpected ending of the tour primarily to Australian public sentiment, though it pointed out in passing that baseball was a minor sport. The editorial declared that the 'hurried departure' of the Giants was 'sharp proof that Australia is not yet ready to welcome the Japanese with open arms'. It blamed the promoter for bringing the 'unlucky young players to Australia without proper assessment of the Australian mind toward them. That mind is not turned against them as sportsmen, but as representatives of a nation that brought untold misery to thousands of Australians' (The Japs and Us 1954, 4).' Ken Moses of the *Argus* summarised the Australian reception of the Giants visit aptly: 'From the time it arrived in Brisbane until its final appearance in Canberra last Sunday, there was never a sign of a welcoming red carpet being laid out for it' (Moses 1954, 30).

Evaluation

At a sporting level, the tour helped Australian baseballers to improve their techniques and interpretation of the rules, as had the tours of United States teams before World War II. Some formed a personal bond with the Japanese players. A number of Australians who had played in several exhibition matches saw them off at the Canberra airport and shook hands firmly in farewell. Matsuda wrote in his published diary that: 'Again, I felt poignantly the significance of bilateral friendship through sport' (Matsuda 1955, 132).

As a promotion of baseball to a wider audience, the Giants tour fell short of expectations. No doubt the lack of promotion and expensive ticket prices handicapped interest and attendance, but in light of the greater interest in baseball at the time, the poor attendance was notable. Overt expressions of antagonism were few, except for a section of the RSL, but the lack of support in publicity and attendance could well be read as a silent resistance to the Japanese team. Menzies worried that this might be seen to be the case by the Japanese. In the following year, when a group of Japanese journalists visited Australia, he did his best to reassure them that 'Australians are not familiar with baseball and the timing was not the best' (Ogi 1955, 51).

The Giants formed a very favourable impression of Australia. The country was clean and beautiful with numerous big parks, the land was vast, the people were laid-back and friendly, there were no beggars or shoe-cleaners on the streets. Hirai, who had visited the United States in the previous year, found Australians were dressed in plainer clothes than Americans, which he found agreeable, and he had an affinity for Australians. Minami even said 'I would like to live here in the future' (Ōsutoraria mitamama 1954, 4). The cancellation of the tour was disappointing, but the team left with a sense of achievement. Upon return to Japan, Harada declared that 'the purpose of Japan-Australia goodwill was accomplished' (Shinzen ryokō o oete 1954, 4).

The Japanese evaluation of the tour focused on the positive aspects. Harada revealed that he was told by the Consul in Sydney, Kawasaki, that the RSL was sorry for the attitude of Yeo, which was said to be motivated by his political ambition (Shinzen ryokō o oete 1954, 4). *Yomiuri Shinbun* had a feature article of interviews with the Giants players, highlighting that 'The Giants played a good pilot role for the Olympic delegation' (Shinzen ryokō o oete 1954, 4). Furuhashi regarded the Giants tour as an achievement, even though the attendance was small. He commented: 'I have also visited Australia several times but I had never been so favourably welcomed at each location as this time. From the viewpoint of improvement of baseball techniques and as a goodwill tour, it was a great success' (Kyojingun gōshū o yuku 1954, 6). No mention was made about the tour as a financial failure for the promoters.

Conclusion

The Giants' tour was a limited success, but a step forward in the bilateral relationship. The Australian government made a conscious decision not to discriminate against Japanese in a sporting visit, and the Japanese players were aware of the positive influence they could exercise through baseball. However, the Giants' visit turned out to be a poor medium for testing public opinion. The fact that baseball was only a minor sport in Australia was clearly a problem. Had the visiting Japanese team been tennis players or rugby players, there would have been greater interest and the Australian teams would have had a competitive advantage. Under these circumstances, the Australian reception might have been different. As baseball was Japan's strength, the Japanese side could afford to emphasise the goodwill value of the tour.

In any case, the Japanese experience of Australia was positive and the Australian impression of the Giants team was favourable. Although the direct impact of the event might have been small, its part in a chain of events cannot be ignored in rebuilding relations between the two countries. During the Giants' Australian tour, Japan received an official invitation to the Melbourne Olympics. The Giants' visit reminded the Australian Olympics Organising Committee of the need to prepare Australians for warmly accepting all nationalities, including Japanese visitors, to avoid 'irreparable harm to Australia's prestige and future standing in the world' (Ill Will to Olympic Guests Could Harm Nation'. 1954. *Age*, 7 December, 1). The baseball contact provided an important stepping stone for both Japan and Australia to prepare for a friendly meeting at the Melbourne Olympics.

Note: This research was made possible by the Australian Research Council's Discovery Early Career Researcher Award (DE120102132). The author thanks Stuart Macintyre for his valuable comments and suggestions.

Note

[1] Frank O'Doul was entered into the Baseball Hall of Fame in Japan in 2002 (15 Players Slated to Make Australian Tour 1954).

References

'15 Giants Players Slated to Make Australian Tour'. 1954. *Nippon Times*, 28 October.
'Abrupt End to Jap Tour'. 1954. *Sydney Morning Herald*, 22 November.
'Accepting Japanese Relationships'. 1954. *Age*, 27 October.
The Australian Baseball Council. 1955. 'Annual Report 1954–1955', in the possession of Douglas Corker, Perth, Western Australia.
'Baseball'. 1954. *Sydney Morning Herald*, 20 November.
'Baseballers Cancel Australian Tour'. 1954. *Canberra Times*, 22 November.
'Bury Hatchet, Say War Leaders'. 1954. *Argus*, 28 October.
'The City's Surprise Arrivals: 43 Japs Land in Brisbane'. 1954. *Courier-Mail*, 11 November.
Clark, J. 2003. *A History of Australian Baseball: Time and Game*. Lincoln and London: University of Nebraska Press.
'"Friendship", Slogan of Jap. Team'. 1954. *Courier-Mail*, 12 November.
'Ganbare!! Kyojingun: Kokusai gekijō de togō sōkōkai' [Break a Leg!! Giants]. 1954. *Yomiuri shimbun*, 8 November.
Giants' 80nenshi: Kanzen hozonban, Part 4 [80 Years History of the Giants]. 2014. Tokyo: Bēsubōru Magajinsha.
'Giants Crush NSW 20–1'. 1954. *Sydney Morning Herald*.
'Giants Win'. 1954a. *Courier-Mail*, 16 November.
'Giants Win'. 1954b. *Courier-Mail*, 17 November.
'Gōshū dayori' [News from Australia]. 1954. *Shūkan Giants*, 30 November.
'Gōshū e shinzen yakyū' [A Friendly Baseball Visit to Australia]. 1954. *Yomiuri Shinbun*, 26 October.
'Gōshū e yuku kyojingun: Kitai o motte matsu fan' [Giants Goes to Australia]. 1954. *Shūkan Yomiuri*, 13 (November): 47.
'Gōshū ensei o maeni' [Before a Trip to Australia]. 1954. *Shūkan Giants*, 9 November.
'Gōshū miyage zadankai' [Round-Table Talk on Australian Trip Stories]. 1954. *Shūkan Giants*, 7 December.
Guthrie-Shimizu, S. 2012. *Transpacific Field of Dreams: How Baseball Linked the United States and Japan in Peace and War*. Chapel Hill: The University of North Carolina Press.
Guttmann, A. and Thompson, L. 2001. *Japanese Sports: A History*. Honolulu: The University of Hawaii Press.
'Ill Will to Olympic Guests Could Harm Nation'. 1954. *Age*, 7 December.
'Japanese Ball Team Ends Tour'. 1954. *Age*, 22 November.
'Japanese Baseball Team in Exciting Match at Manuka'. 1954. *Canberra Times*, 20 November.
'Japanese Baseball Tour Hopes'. 1954. *Age*, 6 November.
'Japanese Cheer Squad for Baseballers'. 1954. *Courier-Mail*, 13 November.
'Japanese Side Here'. 1954. *Sydney Morning Herald*, 15 November.
'Japanese Team "Out to Win Friends"'. 1954. *Argus*, 28 October.
'Japanese Tour in Doubt'. 1954. *Sporting Globe*, 3 November.
'The Japs and Us'. 1954. *Argus*, 23 November.
'Japs Too Strong'. 1954. *Courier-Mail*, 14 November.
———. 2014b. 'Australia and Japan's Admission into the Colombo Plan', *Australian Journal of Politics and History*, 60 (4): 518–533. doi.org/10.1111/ajph.12073.

80   Ai Kobayashi

'Kyojingun gōshū o yuku' [Giants Visits Australia]. 1954. *Yomiuri Shinbun*, 19 November.
'Kyojingun no gōshū ensei hongimari' [Giants' Visit to Australia Confirmed]. 1954. *Yomiuri Shinbun*, 29 October.
'Kyojingun no ninki: Furuhashi Hironoshin dōkōki' [The Giants' Popularity]. 1954. *Yomiuri Shinbun*, 26 November.
'Kyojin mitabi rakushō' [Giants' Easy Victory Third Time]. 1954. *Yomiuri Shinbun*, 16 November.
Matsuda, K. 1955. 'Gōshū chindōchū' [Road to Australia], *Yakyūkai*, 45 (1): 131–132.
Morris, B. 1954. 'Hostility to Japanese', *Age*, 29 October.
Moses, K. 1954. 'Jap Team "Made a Mistake"', *Argus*, 24 November.
'News of the Day'. 1954. *Age*, 23 November.
'No Ban on Japanese Players'. 1954. *Sydney Morning Herald*, 28 October.
O'Doul, F. *List of the Hall of Fame*. Tokyo: The Baseball Hall of Fame and Museum, accessed 25 January 2018, www.baseball-museum.or.jp/baseball_hallo/detail/detail_143.html.
Ogi, T. 1955. 'Ōsutoraria kengaku' [A Study Tour to Australia], *Sekai Shūhō*, 36 (20): 50–51.
'Ōsutoraria mitamama' [Australia As We Saw It]. 1954. *Yomiuri Shinbun*, 26 November.
'Otomo, 20 sanshin ubau' [Otomo Got 20 Strikeouts]. 1954. *Yomiuri Shinbun*, 17 November.
'Otomo no sokkyū ni odoroku' [Amazed with Otomo's Fast Balls]. 1954. *Yomiuri Shinbun*, 15 November.
'PM on Jap Athletes: "Giants Won't Be Last"'. 1954. *Argus*, 5 November.
Record of Conversation by Patrick Shaw with Heyes, Secretary, Department of Immigration, 14 October 1954, NAA A1838, 759/1/6.
'RSL Protests at Baseball Tour by Japs'. 1954. *Argus*, 27 October.
'Sakan na ōsutoraia no yakyūnetsu' [Australian Enthusiasm for Baseball]. 1954. *Yomiuri Shinbun*, 13 November.
'Sensō hanayome ga gochisō' [Feast at War Brides' Home]. 1954. *Yomiuri Shinbun*, 14 November.
'Sensō Hanayome mo seien' [War Brides Cheering Too]. 1954. *Yomiuri Shinbun*, 18 November. 'Shidonī shiyakusho hōmon' [Visiting the Sydney City Hall]. 1954. *Hōchi Shinbun*, 19 November.
'Shinzen ryokō o oete' [After the Friendly Tour]. 1954. *Yomiuri Shinbun*, 30 November.
'Shōmei fubi, goro ni kushin' [Poor Lighting]. 1954. *Yomiuri Shinbun*, 17 November.
'Supōtsu de nichigō shinzen hakare' [Sport for Friendly Relations Between Japan and Australia]. 1954. *Yomiuri Shinbun*, 5 November.
'Togō kyojin no sokuseki tatau' [The Giants' Contributions Acclaimed]. 1954. *Yomiuri Shinbun*, 14 December.
'"Too Wet" – They Said Jap "Ball" Team Makes a Home Run'. 1954. *Argus*, 22 November.
Vine, Jim, 'Japs – Some of Whom "Played Ball"'. 1954. *Courier-Mail*, 10 November.
'Wreath-Laying by Japanese'. 1954. *Sydney Morning Herald*, 13 November.
'You Can't Hate A (Not Even a Japanese) Baseball Team'. 1954. *Argus*, 28 October.
'Zendo ni 350 chīmu: Sakan na ōsutoraria no yakyūnetsu' [350 Teams Throughout the Country]. 1954. *Yomiuri Shinbun*, 13 November.
'"Zengō" ga daigaku teido' ['All-Australia' University Level]. 1954. *Hōchi Shinbun*, 19 November.

5 Japan at the 1956 Melbourne Olympics[1]

Morris Low

Introduction

In an episode of the television series *The Australian Story* (18 August 2016) on 'The Olympic Spirit', Australian swimmer Murray Rose said the following:

> When I was growing up I was a part of a propaganda campaign for the Australian war effort. Fast forward a few years and I'm swimming at the Olympic Games and my main rival and competitor is Tsuyoshi Yamanaka-san. We embraced across the lane line and a photograph of that moment was taken and was picked up by newspapers all over the world, for one main reason: the date was the 7th of December 1956, the fifteenth anniversary of the Japanese attack on Pearl Harbor. So it became symbolic of two kids that'd grown up on opposite sides of the war, had come together in the friendship of the Olympic arena.
>
> (ABC 2016)

Rose's friendship with a Japanese swimmer was emblematic of how many Australians had put memories of the war behind them and welcomed Japanese participation at the 1956 Melbourne Olympics that were held from 22 November through 8 December. This chapter throws light on an important stage in the history of Australia-Japan relations. Major sporting events facilitated not only interactions between athletes but can also be regarded as a form of cultural diplomacy. Historians tend to focus on Australian participation in the 1964 Tokyo Olympics, but the 1956 Melbourne Olympics occurred at a formative stage in relations between Australia and Japan when there was still considerable anti-Japanese sentiment and the Japanese economy was being rebuilt. The effort, endurance and discipline that were associated with sports were also seen as being conducive to winning in business. Japanese success promoted a greater sense of confidence in themselves, redefining a national cultural identity that was focussed on winning at sport more than at war.

This chapter first examines how it was that Japan was readmitted into the Olympic 'family' despite resistance to the idea by some Australians. The next section notes the welcome they received and the media coverage of their arrival and competition. But it was not only the athletes who were at work. Officials used social events as a strategy to lobby for and ultimately secure the 1964 Olympics for Tokyo.

Japan rejoins the Olympic family

An important figure in Japan's readmission into the Olympic 'family' after the war was Avery Brundage, who served as the fifth president of the International Olympic Committee (IOC) from 1952 to 1972. He was first elected to the IOC in 1936. As such, he was privy to the Japanese arrangements and preparations for the cancelled 1940 Summer Olympics, which were to have been held in Tokyo. After the war, Occupied Japan was effectively excluded from the London Olympics held in 1948. Brundage explained in a letter that he wrote on 13 August 1947 to Sawada Ichirō (Mitsui Bussan), an active figure in the world of amateur sport who had worked for Mitsui in New York City prior to the Pacific War and been involved in preparations for the 1940 Olympics, that neither Germany nor Japan had been invited. There were a number of reasons for Japan's exclusion. Japan could not be considered an independent country, and the war had left unhealed scars and generated much hatred and bitterness (Brundage to Sawada 13 August 1947). *The Nippon Times* reported on 10 December 1948 that future participation in the Olympics would depend on General Douglas MacArthur (Japan's Olympics Entry Depends on MacArthur 1948, 1). Three months later, MacArthur wrote to John Jewett Garland, a US IOC member based in Los Angeles, to put on the record that it was his personal hope that Japan would be a competitor at Helsinki in 1952. He noted that strong Japanese performances in swimming during the Allied Occupation suggested that the Japanese might do well. Participation would help the Japanese rejoin other nations in peaceful, cultural pursuits (MacArthur to Garland 10 March 1949).

On Remembrance Day, 11 November 1948, the day of the year which marks the Armistice that ended World War I and the day on which Australian veterans and members of the public remember the loss of lives from all wars and conflicts, the Federal Congress of the Returned Soldiers' League in Sydney adopted a resolution opposing the participation of Japanese athletes at the Olympics in Melbourne in 1956. In response to a question at the meeting, Minister for Immigration Arthur Calwell reassured the crowd that if it depended on him, he would never grant permission for them to come to Australia. What is more, he related how he had been asked for permission for two Japanese businessmen to enter Australia to help develop the trade relationship and how he had refused as 'we should not so much concern ourselves with trade as with the feelings of mothers, wives, and sisters of the victims of Japanese atrocities' (We don't want Japs in Olympics – RSL 1949, 5).

Despite Calwell's utterances, Japanese amateur sporting officials continued their preparations for participation at the Olympics. Asano Kinichi, chairman of the Japanese Track and Field Association, pointed to how the Melbourne Olympic Invitation Committee had, as a gesture of the Australian sporting world's goodwill, sent a case of wine to each of the three Japanese International Olympic

Committee delegates: Takaishi Shingorō (former president of the national newspaper *Mainichi Shinbun*), the late Count Soejima Masamichi and Japanese diplomat Nagai Matuzō. The wine was accompanied by an official brochure and invitation book. In an attempt to discredit these three men, the Australian Associated Press, in its article in *The Sun* on 13 November 1949, pointed to how Takaishi had been purged by General Douglas MacArthur's GHQ, that Soejima had recently died, and how the diplomat Nagai had voted in Rome for Melbourne as the host of the 1956 Olympic Games (Australian Associated Press 1949b, 1).

The Sunday Mail in Brisbane added that Japan was planning on sending a team of around 50 members to the Helsinki Olympics in 1952 but were hoping to use the Melbourne Olympics to make a large-scale comeback into world sport with a team of some 300 athletes. As part of their long-term, six-year plan for Melbourne, Asano Kinichi related how they had already earmarked young men at high schools throughout Japan who would, by that time, be 25 or 26 and in their prime for Olympic competition. Two coaches had already been appointed and recently sent to the United States to study the latest training techniques (Australian Associated Press 1949a, 1).

The following day, *The Argus* drew attention to Asano's comment that 'we believe Australian sportsmen will join together to have us down there, but they are unlikely to make a move until the time is ready. They are keeping silent at the moment for political reasons' (Japs say they will be running here at Olympics 1949, 1). Sir Frank Beaurepaire, chairman of the Olympics Games Organising Committee, stated that a case of Australian wine had been sent to the full list of the International Olympic Committee delegates, and not only to the Japanese. He acknowledged that a Japanese delegate had attended the Rome meeting thanks to General Douglas MacArthur but added that the delegate had taken 'no part in the proceedings' (Japs say they will be running here at Olympics 1949, 1). The Olympic Federation secretary, Edgar S. Tanner, commented that neither the Australian Olympic Federation nor the Organising Committee had actually discussed the question of Japanese participation.

On 20 November 1949, the Australian academic and diplomat W. Macmahon Ball, on his ABC radio news commentary program 'Australia in the Pacific', which was broadcast on 3LO and 3AR in Melbourne, addressed the question 'Should We Accept Japanese Visitors?' not least during the proposed Melbourne Olympic Games. He acknowledged that 'of all the nations that fought Japan, Australia seems clearly the one most reluctant to resume any of the normal peacetime contacts' (National Archives of Australia, W. Macmahon Ball – Sunday (News) Commentary, 148). Trade with Japan had been growing rapidly, yet Japanese businessmen were not permitted to visit Australia to negotiate. There was, he noted, an inconsistency between political policy towards Japan and Australian attitudes to Japanese visitors. In Tokyo, Asano welcomed Macmahon Ball's broadcast and comments, saying that 'we believed and hoped Australian sportsmen would come to our support. Mr. Ball's statement is an example of the tendency we knew would come to the surface in Australia, despite the official opposition' (Australian Associated Press-Reuter 1949, 1).

In the following weeks there was further heated debate. Just a week after Macmahon Ball's broadcast, *The Queensland Times* (Ipswich) reported that Sir Eugen Millington Drake, who had been chairman of the Reception Committee of the 1948 London Olympics, suggested that consideration of Japan's entry for the 1956 Melbourne Olympics had been postponed for a couple of years (Decision on Japan and Olympics Postponed 1949, 1). On 10 December 1949, an Australian Federal election was held. Immigration Minister Arthur Calwell (Labor Party) used the controversy as part of his political campaign. He had declared in the lead-up to the election that no Japanese would enter Australia while he was minister for Immigration. He was quoted as saying that 'No athletic body, local or international, will dissuade me from that policy' (Calwell Bans Japanese for Olympics 1949, 1). However, he would not remain minister for long. The Labor Party which had been led by Prime Minister Ben Chifley, was defeated by a Liberal Party-Country Party coalition led by former Prime Minister Robert Menzies. This helped bring about a change in government attitude to the question of Japanese participation in the Melbourne Olympics (Japs. More Hopeful on Olympics 1949, 1).

By 21 December, *The Townsville Daily Bulletin* in Queensland was complaining in an editorial that Australia had been told 'that Nippon's athletes will compete at the Melbourne Olympic Games, whether Australia likes it or not' (Japan's Rehabilitation Too Fast for Australia's Comfort 1949, 2). In 1950 MacArthur justified Japanese participation in the Olympics by saying that

> If the Japanese were no longer to be allowed near the battlefield, it would be wise at least to let them back onto the playing field. To restore morale and instil hope for a new Japan, the defeated nation needed to learn about winning again.
>
> (Collins, The Imperial Sportive 2012, 1736)

In order to understand Australian resistance to the idea of Japanese participation, we need to appreciate that this was a time when the Australian-led British Commonwealth Occupation Force was still in Japan and there were prominent Australians such as the politician W.S. Kent Hughes who were still coming to terms with their ill treatment as POWs under the Japanese. Kent Hughes had published *Slaves of the Samurai* in 1946 with Oxford University Press in Melbourne and went on to serve as chairman of the Melbourne Olympic Games Organising Committee from 1951. Apparently, there was animosity between Kent Hughes and Brundage in regard to the tardiness of Australian preparations for the games. Both Kent Hughes and Brundage appear to have supported Japanese involvement.

Tabata Masaji, honorary secretary of the Japan Olympic Committee, hoped in late 1949 that the opportunity for Australian athletes to actually meet Japanese competitors at the 1952 Summer Olympics in Helsinki (19 July–3 August) would reinforce the perception that young Japanese were different from the 'old timers' who had been responsible for the war (Japs. More Hopeful on Olympics 1949, 1). But veterans in Australia would continue to oppose Japanese participation. On 14

January 1950, the NSW state secretary of the RSL, J.B. Lewis, warned of potential trouble if the Japanese were to come, viewing the athletes as being 'in the same category as wartime suicide troops' ('Blood-bath' if Japs in Olympics 1950, 2). *The Truth* (Brisbane) used the sensational headline ' "Blood-bath" if Japs in Olympics'. That same article reported that the IOC would meet in Copenhagen in May 1951 to discuss Japanese participation in the Helsinki Olympics. It soberly explained that if Australians competed against Japanese in Helsinki, it would be difficult to object to competing against them in Australia. And if objections were made and the Australian team decided not to compete in Helsinki, 'then it is certain that the International Committee would decline to stage the 1956 games here' ('Blood-bath' if Japs in Olympics 1950, 2). Thus, the question of Japanese participation in Melbourne was key to holding the games in Australia.

On 29 August 1950, the six-member executive of the IOC unanimously voted in favour of permitting West Germany and Japan to compete at Helsinki. A subsequent meeting of the full IOC would be held in May 1951 in Vienna to make the final decision (Return of West Germany, Japan to Olympics Voted by Committee 1950, 35). On 18 April 1952, Ōshima Kenkichi, sports writer at the *Mainichi Shinbun* newspaper, wrote to Brundage, soon to be the new IOC president, thanking him for facilitating their participation later that year at Helsinki. It would be the first time in 16 years that the Japanese were able to participate in an Olympics, and he expressed how the people of Japan were deeply grateful for helping to reinstate Japan into the family of the sporting world (Ōshima to Brundage 18 April 1952). He did express some concern about the participation of the USSR and foresaw how problems might arise, especially at the IOC meetings, but he was hopeful that all would go well (Ōshima to Brundage 18 April 1952). These cold war tensions that Ōshima referred to would ultimately rear their head in Melbourne, but balancing such concerns were more optimistic messages of the positive role of the Olympics amongst young people.

Ultimately, Japan sent its first postwar delegation to the Helsinki Olympics with a small, young team of 62 men and 10 women. They were hopeful of doing well in swimming but only won one gold, when Ishii Shōhachi won the bantamweight medal in wrestling (Japan's 44 Years in Olympics 1956, 5–6). The Japanese organizers hoped to do better in Melbourne. In December 1952, after the Helsinki Summer Olympics had ended, the editor-in-chief of *Shōnen* boys' magazine, Kanei Takeshi, wrote to Brundage asking him to complete a questionnaire about his own childhood, his life motto and which leader in the past or present he admired most. Kanei's motivation was to teach sound morals to Japanese boys and provide them with advice and knowledge that would provide them with a compass to lead satisfactory lives (Kanei to Brundage 20 December 1952). In this way, the Olympics, and indeed sports, were seen as providing valuable lessons for Japan's young people that went beyond physical competition.

One of the members of the men's gymnastics team at Helsinki was Ono Takashi (b. 1931), who won a bronze medal for the men's horse vault. He was the right age and on track to perform well in Melbourne. Despite anti-Japanese feeling in Australia, all carried photographs of Ono balancing on one hand or back-somersaulting with his fellow Japanese gymnasts.[2] Such positive representations of Japanese men in the Australian press were unusual, to say the least.

That same month, *The Courier Mail* (Brisbane) reported on its front page that Japan was proposing to send a team of at least 200 members to the Melbourne Olympics. Abe Kitarō, Japan's Olympic team manager, was reported as saying that

> We know there has been a tremendous feeling against Japan since the war but we are hoping it will have disappeared by the next Olympics. From information I received I know that 99.9 per cent of Australians hate Japanese. I do not blame the Australians. It is quite understandable when you think of the treatment Australian soldiers received when they were prisoners of the Japanese. Still we are hoping to get a good reception out there. We feel the anti-Japanese feeling will have decreased a great deal.
> (200 Japs for Aust. 1952, 1)

Abe was overstating Australian dislike and opposition to Japanese participation in the Melbourne Olympics. In an Australia-wide Gallup Poll of 2,000 men and women which was reported on in *The Sun* (Sydney) on 2 February 1950, one-third of Australians interviewed were actually in favour of Japanese participation. A large 56 percent were opposed and 11 percent polled were noncommittal. The article noted that women were particularly hostile, with 60 percent in Queensland and Tasmania being opposed and 57 percent of women in Victoria being against Japanese participation. Arthur Calwell had been politically astute in appealing to women in his Remembrance Day comments the previous year. The main reason given by those who were opposed to Japanese participation was Japan's treatment of prisoners of war and fear that the Japanese would again threaten world peace. There was a common belief among those supporting Japanese participation that 'as sportsmen, we should forgive and forget' (Japs not wanted at Melbourne Olympics 1950, 20).

On 10 May 1954, the IOC cleared the way for the 1956 Summer Olympics to be held in Melbourne when it voted in favour of finding a new site, outside Australia, for the equestrian events. Australia's strict quarantine rules required imported horses to be held in quarantine for six months, making equestrian events impractical. The last obstacle to Melbourne hosting the games was thus removed, and Melbourne proceeded with full preparations for the games (Aussies Assured Games 1954, 5). The equestrian events would be held in Stockholm.

Arrival of athletes

At the Australian Olympic trials held at the new Olympic Swimming and Diving Stadium in Melbourne on 30 October 1956, Murray Rose, the Australian 1,500-metre freestyle swimming champion, broke the world record that had been held by the American George Breen since April that year. Breen had in turn broken the record held by the Japanese swimmer Furuhashi Hironoshin since 1949. Furuhashi was among the swimmers whom MacArthur had admired. *The Canberra Times* noted how Furuhashi, Japan's swimming team manager, was one of the first to congratulate Rose (World 1500-Metre Record Smashed by Murray Rose 1956, 14). *The Japan Times* carried a photograph showing a be-suited Furuhashi shaking Rose's hand (*The Japan Times* 1956a, 5). The friendly rivalry in swimming between Japan, Australia and the United States, and between the Soviet Union and Japan in gymnastics (Hopes Running High for Several Medals 1956, 5), would be among the great stories of the Melbourne Olympics.

The Olympic Village at Heidelberg, Melbourne, was officially opened on 29 October, but in a comedy of errors, the People's Republic of China flag was raised instead of that of Nationalist China, and the Hungarian flag was raised upside down. So, when the Japanese flag was raised the following day by the Australian corporal R.G. Farmer, a veteran of World War II, Australian officials were careful to check with a Japanese delegate that the correct flag went up! Japanese officials, including the manager of the swimming team Furuhashi Hironoshin, took up residence at the village.

The press noted the arrival of Japanese team contingents. On 6 November, the first group of 41 Japanese athletes were greeted by a crowd of 200 flag-waving Japanese, including businessmen, journalists and officials. It was said to have been the most impressive team arrival so far due to the organized nature of the welcome and size of the crowd (Associated Press 1956c, 5). When the third group of Japanese athletes arrived at Melbourne's Essendon Airport on 15 November, a crowd of 2,000 people greeted them, including W.S. Kent Hughes, chairman of the Australian Olympic Organising Committee, who, as *The Japan Times* noted, had been a Japanese prisoner of war during World War II (Japan Athletes Get Big Welcome 1956, 5). In all, a total of 158 Japanese delegates participated in the Melbourne Olympics (Japanese Flag Raised at '56 Olympic Village' 1956, 5; for the list of officials and athletes, see Roster of Japan's Olympic Delegation 1956, 5, 8; Nakashima 1956d, 5). The Japanese team was one of the largest there and competed in all events except field hockey. Despite the size of the team, there was a recognition that there might only be five or six athletes who would win gold medals (Japan's Olympic Team 1956, 8). This would nevertheless be a considerable improvement on the one gold medal won at Helsinki.

Despite the Japanese athletes being at a disadvantage when compared to Australians in terms of having to travel from the northern hemisphere and competing when they would not normally be in peak condition, they would perform well for a nation that was rebuilding its international sporting profile. They were buoyed by a flood of fan letters and telegrams of encouragement from well-wishers back home every day. General team manager Asano Kinichi noted that the bulk of the letters came from high-school girls and boys. Sometimes, *senbazuru* origami paper cranes were included as good-luck charms. There were also requests for Australian souvenirs and stamps (Associated Press 1956d, 5).

W.S. Kent Hughes urged competitors and spectators to make the games 'an occasion for the improvement of international relations' (Olympic Preparations Pushed Despite Tension 1956, 5). This statement was prompted by the withdrawal of seven nations from the Olympics. Spain and the Netherlands had quit in protest at Soviet aggression in Hungary. Switzerland had initially decided to join them but then reconsidered due to nationwide protests from the Swiss people. However, they had left it too late and the Swiss were unable to make last-minute transport arrangements to send their team to Australia (16th Olympiad Opens Today at Melbourne 1956, 1, 9). The People's Republic of China withdrew from the games due to the participation of Nationalist China. Egypt, Iraq and Lebanon also did due to tensions in the Middle East. Norway and Denmark had, at one stage, also considered doing so due to the situation in Hungary, but having already sent teams, it was difficult to change plans (Olympic Preparations Pushed Despite Tension 1956, 5; Switzerland 6th Country to Quit Olympic Games 1956, 5; Politics and the Olympics 1956, 12). This left a total of 68 countries to compete in Melbourne. Sixty-nine countries had competed in Helsinki in 1952 and an impressive 83 nations in Rome in 1960.

Media coverage

Due to the small time difference, there were only two countries, Japan and New Zealand, which received live radio broadcasts. The Japanese people were thus able to share in the excitement of Japan's success in Melbourne and know that it was happening as they heard it, courtesy of the vast radio network of Kokusai Denshin Denwa (KDD), which promised to provide all the 'hot' Olympic news from Melbourne (Hot News of Olympic Games at Melbourne 1956, 5), whereas European and North American radio stations broadcast prerecorded transmissions (Keys 2006, 304). Likewise, evening editions of the big three newspapers, *Asahi Shinbun*, *Mainichi Shinbun* and *Yomiuri Shinbun*, were able to take advantage of the lack of time difference to report same-day news, especially the opening of the Olympic Games (Japanese Papers Play Up Opening 1956, 5).

Among the international journalists who covered the Melbourne Olympics was the Hawaii-born, Japanese-American Leslie Nakashima, who had lived in Japan since 1934 and written for both United Press International and *The Japan Times* (Inoshita 1998, 10). He represented the Tokyo Bureau of United Press at Melbourne. Famous for having written the first inside story of Hiroshima in 1945, Nakashima would cover the Melbourne, Rome and Tokyo Olympics. His stories with the UP byline and those of other sports writers were carried by *The Japan Times*. They were among some 500 accredited journalists and photographers from throughout the world who gathered in Melbourne to write stories and capture images to distribute to millions of readers (Rowland 1956, 7).

Competing at the games

To Australian audiences at the Olympics, the Japanese team sometimes stood out for cultural reasons. In pre-Olympic warm-up matches, its basketball team became the 'darlings' of Australian fans when they trotted out onto the floor in single file, formed a large circle in the middle of the court and bowed deeply to the audience, who responded with cheers and loud applause (Games Sidelights 1956, 9). Lingering memories of the Japanese treatment of Australian prisoners of war were also not far from the minds of those in the stands who watched the Japanese team enter the Olympic stadium (the Melbourne Cricket Ground) at the opening ceremony on 22 November. Wrestler Sasahara Shōzō led the team, carrying the 'Rising Sun' flag before some 110,000 people (for a photograph, see 16th Olympic Games Opened 1956, 1). The Japanese team received an initially lukewarm reception, but Australian audiences would warm to the young Japanese athletes over the course of the games.

Japan's team did not do well on the track and field. Tabata Masaji, chief of the Japanese delegation and president of the Japan Swimming Federation, told Leslie Nakashima that he had spent some sleepless nights worrying about Japan's poor showing in athletics, rowing, basketball and soccer. Tabata wept with joy on 1 December when, midway through the games, Ikeda Mitsuo, captain of the wrestling team, won Japan's first gold medal at Melbourne in welterweight class freestyle wrestling. Sasahara won Japan's second gold medal in featherweight class freestyle wrestling (Kyodo-United Press 1956, 1; Nakashima 1956a, 5), and their fellow team member Kasahara Shigeru won a silver medal in the featherweight division (all three are pictured in Medal Winners 1956, 5).

Japan's Olympic team included six male and six female gymnasts but press coverage focussed on the men. It was hoped that the men's team would win first place all-round, and the women third place. An individual silver medal for all-round performance was seen as a fairly certain possibility for Ono Takashi, with coach Kondō Takashi hoping for gold. Even US and Soviet commentators thought that in gymnastics, it would be a race between Japan and the Soviet Union (Good Showing Seen in Gymnastic Events 1956, 6). Kondō's hopes were realised when Ono became the first Japanese to win an individual Olympic gold medal for gymnastics at the Glaciarium, the skating rink in South Melbourne, which was converted to the venue for basketball and gymnastics. But rather than for all-round performance, Ono's gold medal was won on the men's horizontal bar, one of five medals that he accumulated there. He featured in both Japanese and Australian representations of Japan at the Olympics in 1956. On 5 December 1956, *The Japan Times* showed a photograph of him winning the horizontal bar compulsory exercises (Scores Highest Point 1956, 5). The Melbourne *Argus* that same day described the six-member men's gymnastics team of 'smooth-working Japanese' with 'perfect muscle control and co-ordination of movement' (Japanese Bid for Russia's Title 1956, 24). *The Argus* reported that they would bring the best out of the Soviets. It noted in particular that the 'stockily built' Ono was a potential gold medallist. A couple of days later, the newspaper gleefully reported Ono's gold medal on the horizontal bar in terms of 'Jap. Stops Russian Clean-Up' (Japanese Stops Russian Clean-Up 1956, 24). The article lamented that no Australian competitors won medals in the men's gymnastics events and that Ono had 'stopped the Russians from making a clean sweep'. After Ono's gold-medal–winning performance, *The Japan Times* reported how a crowd of people came onto the floor to congratulate him and the Japanese team. One of the judges, American Tom

Maloney from West Point Military Academy and coach of the 1952 US Helsinki team, was quoted as saying that the Japanese team had made the greatest improvement of any team in the world since the last Olympic games. He had no doubt seen Ono perform in Helsinki (Ono Clinches Gold Medal in Gymnastics 1956, 7).

Victor Tchukarin (USSR)[3] beat Ono for the men's individual all-round gold medal, with Ono winning the silver. On Friday, 7 December, the Duke of Edinburgh visited the West Melbourne Stadium for the presentation of 11 gold medals won by Soviet gymnasts the previous day. *The Argus* reported that Ono received the biggest acclamation that afternoon, not only for allowing a break in the playing of the Soviet national anthem but because after receiving his gold medal, he spontaneously did a demonstration on the horizontal bar (Duke Saw Russia's Golden Hour 1956, 14).

Although Ono's gold medal performance attracted the most press attention, he also won a bronze medal on the parallel bars, a silver on the pommel horse, a silver for the individual men's all-round competition and yet another silver in the men's all-round team competition. The Japanese gymnastics team, with Ono as a member, would have to wait until Rome in 1960 to obtain gold, showing their dominance in competition again in Tokyo in 1964 (Takashi Ono 2018). In this way, the spotlight on the Japanese was seen relative to other competitors and as part of a carefully planned journey to national glory in Tokyo.

On 4 December, Charles Roeser, manager of the US swimming team, expressed his disappointment with the performance of the Japanese swimming team. He suggested that they were the best swimming team in the world 'but when they can qualify only one man for the 100-meter freestyle and when they lose to the Russians in the relay something is wrong' (Associated Press 1956e, 5). He thought that both the Americans and the Japanese had suffered from having to reach their peaks in performance too many times in a season. Also, these warm-water swimmers may have had difficulty adapting to the cold weather they had been experiencing. Perhaps Roeser spoke too soon. That same day, Japanese swimmer Yamanaka Tsuyoshi beat American George Breen to the silver medal in one of the feature races of the swimming program, the 400-metre men's freestyle event (Associated Press 1956a, 5). While Yamanaka Tsuyoshi would win two silver medals (rather than gold) at Melbourne for the men's 400-metre freestyle and 1,500-metre freestyle events, he lost to Australia's Murray Rose in both events and was thrown into the spotlight. The 1,500-metre freestyle swimming event had been expected to be a battle between the United States (George Breen) and Australia (Murray Rose), but in a thrilling race, Rose won, Yamanaka came second and Breen was well behind in third place (Rose Takes 1,500 M.; Yamanaka Second 1956, 1).

There clearly was a friendship between Rose and Yamanaka, the two 17-year-old swimmers. Its cultural significance was apparent to all. The day before the 1,500-metre freestyle swimming event, Japan belatedly won its first swimming gold medal in two Olympic Games when 20-year-old Furukawa Masaru won the gold medal in the men's 200-metre breaststroke event. His teammate and fellow Nihon University student Yoshimura Masahiro won the silver medal, beating the Soviet swimmer Kharis Iounitchev. Furukawa had swum underwater for the first 40 metres using a submarine stroke, which would be banned in future competition. In front-page news in *The Japan Times*, Leslie Nakashima reported how Furukawa and Yoshimura were proudly presented with their medals by Azuma Ryōtarō, president of the Japan Amateur Athletic Association and IOC member, and Takaishi Shingorō, another IOC member (Nakashima 1956b, 1).

But, interestingly, it was the photograph of Murray Rose hugging Yamanaka in the 400-metre freestyle swimming final that was chosen for the one page of highlights in *The Japan Times*. The caption began with the slightly cryptic words 'Top Tankmen', which had the double meaning of two men in a swimming tank and two men thrown together in a military tank. But any association with the war was quickly dispensed with when it described how Yamanaka got a hug from Rose, who won first place in a new Olympic record time. A smiling Yamanaka recorded a personal-best time and beat the American George Breen, who was placed third. The photograph complemented one of the British athlete Gordon Pirie and the Soviet long-distance runner Vladimir Kuts hugging at the finish of their 5,000-metre race despite Cold War tensions. Both photographs spoke to the text in the centre of the page, which made the point that:

> Above all, the Melbourne Games, held at a time when world tension is at its highest, has proved as never before that sportsmen can rise above national rivalries and hatreds in international competition
> (Associated Press 1956b, 6).

Other Japanese athletes were also shown on the page: Ono on the horizontal bar with body outstretched like a starfish, Sasahara Shōzō in a featherweight freestyle wrestling bout, boxer Ishimaru Toshikazu in a boxing bout and the Japanese team marching past the Royal Box with pride at the opening ceremony (Associated Press 1956b, 6).

In a listing of the Olympic gold medal winners, the sole photograph was that of Ono in team uniform. The article noted that he had won a total of five medals ('Olympic Gold Medal Winners 1956, 5). All in all, Leslie Nakashima reported that the Japanese coaches were generally satisfied with their athletes' performances, the chief reason being that they had won four gold medals, three more than in Helsinki (Nakashima 1956d, 5). In Asano Kinichi's opinion, Japan had done better than expected. He considered that Japan's main strength was in gymnastics, but they had done quite well in wrestling, with two gold medals and one silver medal. The three young swimmers Furukawa, Yoshimura and Yamanaka had all won medals, 'done wonders and give us great hope for the future' in terms of success in sport (Nippon Athletes Perform Better Than Expected 1956, 5).

Towards the 1964 Tokyo Olympics

In the weekend prior to the opening of the Congress of the International Olympic Committee at Melbourne Town Hall, which in turn preceded the opening of the

Olympics Games, the governor of Tokyo, Yasui Seiichirō, held evening cocktail parties in honour of the IOC at the Menzies Hotel. Although the venue for the 1964 Games would not be decided in Melbourne, the cities of Tokyo, Mexico City and Buenos Aires were waging active campaigns (Olympic Briefs 1956, 5). It was at the Congress that the site for the 1958 meeting would be decided. And it would be at the 1958 meeting that the host of the 1964 Olympics would be determined. IOC President Avery Brundage had mentioned that he favoured Tokyo as the location of the 1958 Congress (The Japan Times 1956b, 5). This would enable the IOC to inspect existing facilities during the Third Asian Games in Tokyo that year.

On 26 November, after the games had opened, the consul for Japan held a short reception at the Federal Hotel in Collins Street followed by an evening reception by the ambassador of Japan and the governor of Tokyo at the Menzies Hotel for Olympics officials and their guests. The following evening, President Tsushima, of the Organising Committee for the 1958 Asian Games to be held in Tokyo, held a reception for Asian Games Federation councillors at the prestigious Hotel Windsor (Melbourne City Council, Olympic Civic Committee n.d.). In this way, the Melbourne Olympics provided an opportunity for quiet diplomacy as it prepared the way for the 1964 Tokyo Olympics.

At a banquet on 14 December, Governor Yasui honoured two US officials who were visiting Tokyo briefly on their way home from Melbourne. The officials, Carl H. Hansen, president of the American Amateur Athletic Union, and Harold A. Berliner, vice-chairman of the US Track and Field Committee, met with leading Japanese officials and athletes. Hansen and Berliner agreed that the general feeling among officials from various nations at Melbourne 'was pretty good for the staging of the 1964 Games in Tokyo'. They noted that the Olympics had never been held in an Asian city, but they were quick to point out that their comments were not a complete endorsement of Tokyo and that a decision would be made by the IOC in 1958. Detroit was also bidding for the games (Miike 1956, 8).

By going to Melbourne, the Japanese were also able to see what was entailed in hosting the Olympics. In Leslie Nakashima's opinion, 'it took so much money and effort that visitors from Asia wonder if any Asian city can ever equal the spectacular standard set by the Australians'. He described Governor Yasui of Tokyo as being 'amazed at the superb facilities prepared by the people of Melbourne' (Nakashima, Holding of Olympics was Stupendous Job 1956c, 5). In a way, the governor could benchmark his own city's plans with what he saw in Melbourne.

Japanese officials certainly viewed Japan's participation in Melbourne as part of a sporting trajectory beyond 1956, to the Third Asian Games in 1958, which Tokyo would host, and to the 1964 Olympics in Tokyo where Ono would also compete. Ono's success and that of his fellow gymnasts was seen by some Japanese as evidence of the nation's spiritual background, the Olympic spirit and the Japanese yearning for 'beauty, peace and strength' (Yasui 1964, 363). Japan would go on to dominate Olympic team titles in gymnastics in the 1960s, and their success would also mirror Japan's growing confidence at a time of rapid economic growth.

In early 1968, Brundage himself wondered about the connection. Writing to his Japanese friend Azuma Ryōtarō, he asked to what extent Olympic principles, *bushidō* and physical education were taught in Japanese schools. In July, he was sent a signed copy of *Industrial Japan and Industrious Japanese* by Takahata Seiichi, who was the former chairman of the board of the Nisshō Corporation in Osaka. The book outlines Japan's postwar reconstruction, discusses world politics and the economy, Japan's politics, world trade and then each of Japan's major industries. There is the implication that this was all the result of industrious Japanese. '[A] young active industrial nation like Japan can be aggressive, but [the] Japanese must behave themselves by self-restraint' (Takahata 1968, 422). Through discipline and hard work, Japan would become an advanced, industrial nation. Brundage replied a month later, thanking Azuma and acknowledging that he had drawn on the contents in a speech which he gave about Japan's postwar economic miracle, which he attributed to application of Olympic principles. He suggested that the transmission of the concept of Bushido, loyalty, justice and self-discipline through many generations had also helped (Brundage to Takahata 7 August 1968). He was struck by how the same qualities that had resulted in Japanese sporting success were being channelled into industry and that Japan was reaping the benefits.

Notes

1 Due to space limits, this chapter focuses on reporting in Australian newspapers, and the Japanese English-language newspaper *Nippon Times*, which was renamed *The Japan Times*. I would like to thank the editors and the anonymous reviewers for their constructive comments and gratefully acknowledge the Nippon Foundation and the Queensland Program for Japanese Education for a Japanese Studies Travel Grant in 2015, which enabled me to travel to Japan to conduct research for this chapter.
2 See *The Age* (Melbourne) (12 July 1952), (Gymnasts Show Their Skill 1952, 8), *The Examiner* (Launceston) (17 July 1952), (Gymnasts Show Their Skill 1952, 8), (The Newcastle Sun 1952, 7), *The Chronicle* (Adelaide) (24 July 1952) and (Sidelights on the Games 1952, 22).
3 Also spelt Viktor Chukarin and Victor Tchoukarine.

References

'16th Olympiad Opens Today at Melbourne'. 1956. *The Japan Times*, 22 November.
'16th Olympic Games Opened'. 1956. *The Japan Times*, 23 November.
'200 Japs for Aust.'. 1952. *The Courier Mail*, 28 July.
ABC. 2016. 'The Olympic Story', *Australian Story*, August, accessed 28 January 2019, www.abc.net.au/austory/the-olympic-spirit/7698920.
Associated Press. 1956a. 'Australia's Rose Wins 400 Freestyle', *The Japan Times*, 5 December.
———. 1956b. 'Highlights Through the Camera of Melbourne Olympic Games', *The Japan Times*, 7 December.
———. 1956c. 'Olympic Briefs', *The Japan Times*, 23 November.
———. 1956d. 'Japanese Athletes Reach Melbourne', *The Japan Times*, 7 November.
———. 1956e. 'Poor Japanese Tank Showing Major Surprise', *The Japan Times*, 5 December.
'Aussies Assured Games: Horse Event Switch Gains Approval of IOC'. 1954. *The Nippon Times*, 13 May.

Australian Associated Press. 1949a. 'Japs Train for Our Olympics', *The Sunday Mail*, 13 November.
———. 1949b. 'Japs Won't Take No: Plans for Olympics', *The Sun* (Sydney), 13 November.
Australian Associated Press-Reuter. 1949. 'Japan to Train Silently for 1956 Olympics', *Canberra Times*, 23 November.
'"Blood-Bath" if Japs in Olympics'. 1950. *The Truth* (Brisbane), 15 January.
Brundage, Avery to Sawada, Ichirō, 13 August 1947, Avery Brundage Collection, Reel 76.
Brundage, Avery to Seiichi Takahata, 7 August 1968, Avery Brundage Collection, Reel 76.
'Calwell Bans Japanese for Olympics'. 1949. *Sydney Morning Herald*, 14 November.
Collins, S. 2012. 'The Imperial Sportive: Sporting Lives in the Service of Modern Japan', *The International Journal of the History of Sport*, 29 (12): 1729–1743.
'Decision on Japan and Olympics Postponed'. 1949. *Queensland Times* (Ipswich), 28 November.
'Duke Saw Russia's Golden Hour'. 1956. *The Argus*, 8 December.
'Games Sidelights'. 1956. *The Japan Times*, 22 November.
'Good Showing Seen in Gymnastic Events'. 1956. *The Japan Times*, 8 November.
'Gymnast'. 1952. *The Examiner* (Launceston, Tasmania), 17 July.
'Gymnasts Show Their Skill'. 1952. *The Age* (Melbourne), 12 July.
'Hopes Running High for Several Medals'. 1956. *The Japan Times*, 8 November.
'Hot News of Olympic Games at Melbourne'. 1956. 'Advertisement', *The Japan Times*, 8 November.
Inoshita, Day (Hiroshi). 1998. 'Part One: 1945–1954, the Occupation and the Korean War Years', in C. Pomeroy (ed.), *Foreign Correspondents in Japan: Reporting a Half Century of Upheavals – From 1945 to the Present*. Tokyo: Charles E. Tuttle Publishing, 2–91.
'Japan Athletes Get Big Welcome'. 1956. *The Japan Times*, 17 November.
Japan Times. 1956a. 1 November.
———. 1956b. 18 November.
'Japanese Bid for Russia's Title'. 1956. *The Argus*, 5 December.
'Japanese Flag Raised at '56 Olympic Village'. 1956. *The Japan Times*, 1 November.
'Japanese Papers Play Up Opening'. 1956. *The Japan Times*, 23 November.
'Japanese Stops Russian Clean-Up'. 1956. *The Argus*, 7 December.
'Japan's 44 Years in Olympics'. 1956. *The Japan Times*, 8 November.
'Japan's Olympic Team'. 1956. *The Japan Times*, 5 November.
'Japan's Olympics Entry Depends on MacArthur'. 1948. *Nippon Times*, 10 December. Avery Brundage Collection, Reel 76.
'Japan's Rehabilitation Too Fast for Australia's Comfort'. 1949. *The Townsville Daily Bulletin*, 21 December.
'Japs More Hopeful on Olympics'. 1949. *Warwick Daily News* (Queensland), 16 December.
'Japs Not Wanted at Melbourne Olympics'. 1950. *The Sun* (Sydney), 2 February.
'Japs Say They Will Be Running Here at Olympics'. 1949. *The Argus* (Melbourne), 14 November.
Kanei, Takeshi to Avery Brundage, 20 December 1952, Avery Brundage Collection, Reel 76.
Keys, B. 2006. 'The 1956 Melbourne Olympic Games and the Postwar International Order', in C. Fink, F. Hadler and T. Schramm (eds.), *1956: European and Global Perspectives*. Leipzig: Leipziger Universitatsverlag, 283–307.
Kyodo-United Press. 1956. 'Japan Captures Two Gold Medals', *The Japan Times*, 2 December.

MacArthur, Douglas to John Jewett Garland, 10 March 1949, Avery Brundage Collection, Reel 42, Box 76.
'Medal Winners'. 1956. *The Japan Times*, 3 December.
Melbourne City Council, Olympic Civic Committee. n.d. 'The Olympics Games: Details of Functions, Official and Otherwise', 13 November 1956, Prime Minister's Department, National Archives of Australia, series no. A463, 1956/1379, barcode 757638.
Miike, P. N. 1956. 'Two American Officials to Olympics Stop Over', *The Japan Times*, 14 December.
Nakashima, L. 1956a. 'Aussies "Really Strong" Olympic Chief Admits', *The Japan Times*, 4 December.
———. 1956b. 'Furukawa Wins First in Breast', *The Japan Times*, 7 December.
———. 1956c. 'Holding of Olympics Was Stupendous Job', *The Japan Times*, 10 December.
———. 1956d. 'Japan Leads 16 Nations of Asia at Melbourne', *The Japan Times*, 9 December.
National Archives of Australia. 'W. Macmahon Ball – Sunday (News) Commentary', Series SP369/2, W. Macmahon Ball, 426151, 147–150, esp. 148.
The Newcastle *Sun*. 1952. 22 July.
'Nippon Athletes Perform Better Than Expected'. 1956. *The Japan Times*, 9 December.
'Olympic Briefs'. 1956. *The Japan Times*, 21 November.
'Olympic Gold Medal Winners'. 1956. *The Japan Times*, 9 December.
'Olympic Preparations Pushed Despite Tension'. 1956. *The Japan Times*, 9 November.
'Ono Clinches Gold Medal in Gymnastics'. 1956. *The Japan Times*, 7 December.
Ôshima, Kenkichi to Avery Brundage, 18 April 1952, Avery Brundage Collection, Reel 76.
'Politics and the Olympics'. 1956. *The Japan Times*, 16 November.
'Return of West Germany, Japan to Olympics Voted by Committee'. 1950. *The New York Times*, 30 August.
'Rose Takes 1,500 M.; Yamanaka Second'. 1956. *The Japan Times*, 8 December.
'Roster of Japan's Olympic Delegation'. 1956. *The Japan Times*, 8 November.
Rowland, N. 1956. 'They'll Tell the World: International Press Turns Melbourne Into Vast Newspaper Office', *The Australian Women's Weekly*, 5 December.
'Scores Highest Point'. 1956. *The Japan Times*, 5 December.
'Sidelights on the Games'. 1952. *The Chronicle*, 24 July.
'Switzerland 6th Country to Quit Olympic Games'. 1956. *The Japan Times*, 10 November.
Takahata, S. 1968. *Industrial Japan and Industrious Japanese*. Osaka: Nissho Co. Ltd.
'Takashi Ono'. 7 January 2018, www.olympic.org/takashi-ono.
'Want Jap Team in Olympics'. 1950. *The Sun* (Sydney), 12 February.
'We Don't Want Japs in Olympics – RSL'. 1949. *The Argus* (Melbourne), 12 November.
'World 1500-Metre Record Smashed by Murray Rose'. 1956. *The Canberra Times*, 31 October.
Yasui, S. 1964. 'Speech by Representative of Tokyo Metropolis, to Invite the Games of the XVIIth Olympiad, at the 50th Session of the IOC', 1964 Tokyo Olympic Games Dossier, 1, IOC Archives, Lausanne.

6 Japanese sleeping beauties abroad

Australian retellings of Kawabata Yasunari's fairy-tale novella

Lucy Fraser

Introduction

> A small book. About the privilege of an old man to sleep next to someone beautiful. Maybe for the simple moment of recapturing youth. Or beauty. Very passé. No one will believe this story today.
>
> (Armanno 2006, 186)

This pithy description of Kawabata Yasunari's [1961] 1967 novella *House of the Sleeping Beauties* is proffered by a young French woman named Emilie, one of the central characters in Australian author Venero Armanno's 2006 novel *Candle Life*. Emilie's review might resonate with some readers, especially feminists. However, her dismissal of the book is somewhat ironically belied by her own knowledge and discussion of it, and indeed by the major role Kawabata's scenario plays in *Candle Life* itself.

In fact, Armanno is not the only storyteller to have taken up Kawabata's novella in recent decades; others, including several Australians, incorporate *House of the Sleeping Beauties* into their own creative pieces. Here, I discuss Armanno's *Candle Life* as well as another major Australian retelling, the 2011 film *Sleeping Beauty*, written and directed by Julia Leigh. These works are evidence of the complex ways in which Australian creators are engaging with Japanese literature. I question what these works might tell us about the role of Japanese literature in Australia, and the place of both cultures in an international creative scene. Armanno and Leigh seem to be both troubled and stimulated by Kawabata's 'small book' and by the fairy tale at its heart. I argue that where direct representations of Japanese people and places in fiction can become mired in stereotype, instances of cross-cultural literary intertextuality such as these can uncover more nuanced and challenging Australian relationships with, and ideas of, Japan.

Reading Kawabata Yasunari's 'Fairy Tale for Old Men' in foreign countries

Kawabata's novella tells the story of old Eguchi, who visits an inn that provides a special service: the chance for elderly men such as himself to share a bed with a naked young woman in a drugged sleep. Eguchi is asked not to 'do anything in bad taste' (Kawabata 1968, 13), implying that he should not have sex with the women or hurt them. Instead he touches and explores their inert bodies, which inspires him to reminisce about the women in his life. At sixty-seven years old, Eguchi's advancing age is the main concern of his musing; however, the story closes not with Eguchi's life ending but rather with the death of one of the young sleeping women.

House of the Sleeping Beauties was first published in *Shinchō* magazine in 1960–1961, then as a book in 1961. It was around this time that Kawabata (1899–1972) was receiving the highest accolades in his career, including the Japanese Order of Culture in 1961. Within the same decade, in 1968, Kawabata became the first Japanese author to be awarded the Nobel Prize for Literature. This was after some of his major works had been translated into English, many by the renowned translator, scholar, and advocate of Japanese literature Edward Seidensticker. Seidensticker's translation of *House of the Sleeping Beauties* was released in 1969, the year after the Nobel Prize was awarded. In other words, it was published in English at a point where recognition of Kawabata's name and interest in his work were very high. Seidensticker's English translation also included an introduction by Mishima Yukio, another prominent Japanese author. Thus, the combination of Kawabata's Nobel Prize and the literary authority of Mishima and Seidensticker established the novella as 'foreign'/Japanese work worth reading in English, gaining it a place within a canon of international literature. Kawabata has certainly maintained a strong presence in Japanese, English, and other languages. The coeditors of a 2018 special issue of *Japan Forum* journal on 'Kawabata Yasunari in the Twenty-First Century' attest to this, noting in their introduction that data shows that Kawabata remains Japan's most translated writer. He is, they write, a figure 'for the changing position of contemporary Japanese culture since the 1970s, as it shifted from minor to (relatively) major status within the Eurocentric and US-centric global cultural system' (Bourdaghs, Sakai and Toeda 2018, 4).

The House of the Sleeping Beauties – originally titled in Japanese simply as *Nemureru bijo* (Sleeping beauty/beauties) is, of course, named after a famous European fairy tale. Part of the novella's appeal may be the way in which this familiar source text is juxtaposed against the 'exotic' setting of a traditional Japanese inn. Armanno's young French woman, Emilie, cited in the epigraph, also describes Kawabata's novella as 'a fairy tale for old men' (Armanno 2006, 185). She is probably referring to the elements of fantasy and wish fulfilment that fairy tales are known for. However, when examining Kawabata's work outside of Japan, it is worth further pursuing the fairy tale context his title implies. Any 'classic' fairy tale has a long, mixed ancestry of oral folk tale, literary text, and more, and Kawabata was likely to have encountered a variety of 'Sleeping Beauty' stories. The story known in English today as 'Sleeping Beauty' finds its immediate sources in several fairy tale publications, the most important being Charles Perrault's *La belle au bois dormant* (The sleeping beauty of the wood, in *Histoires ou contes du temps passé* 1697). The first known Japanese translation appeared in a collection of Western tales in 1896, just before Kawabata was born, followed by translations in 1926 and then one in 1928 by a patron of Kawabata, Kikuchi Kan ('Perō hen' 2007, 705–706). Another significant version of the tale is the English retelling of Perrault's story 'Sleeping Beauty' collected by folklorist Andrew Lang in *The Blue Fairy Book* in 1889. Notably, Kawabata is attributed as the supervising editor of one set of Japanese translations of Andrew Lang's *Fairy Books* series, published in Japan 1958–1959, though 'Sleeping Beauty' is omitted from the collection (these were not the first nor the only Japanese translations). Another connection to 'Sleeping Beauty' of note here is the Walt Disney animation *Sleeping Beauty* (dir. Clyde Geronimi 1959), released in Japan as *Nemureru mori no bijo* – the same title as Perrault's story – in 1960, the year Kawabata was writing his novella (Matsugu 2011, 494).

Any interest of Kawabata's in foreign fairy tales is not a focus of the scholarship on his writing. Yet beyond the title, *House of the Sleeping Beauties* harks back to earlier moments in the 'Sleeping Beauty' narrative tradition in its sexualisation of inert female bodies. Imagery hinting at penetration, interdiction, and violation exudes from the first words of Kawabata's novella, which begins: 'He was not to do anything in bad taste, the woman of the inn warned old Eguchi. He was not to put his finger into the mouth of the sleeping girl, or try anything else of that sort' (Kawabata 1969, 13). Much of the work deals in minute descriptions of the bodies of the unconscious girls; as Mishima Yukio puts it, 'the sleeping beauties themselves are fragments of human beings, quite without subjectivity' (Mishima 1969, 8). This type of obsession with beautiful sleeping (or dead) women has a long history in the visual and literary arts.[1] 'Sleeping Beauty' and related fairy tales are emblems of this tradition, as is made clear in one early iteration, 'Sun, Moon, and Talia', in Giambattista Basile's 1634 collection of Neapolitan tales, *The Pentamerone*. Here the sleeping heroine Talia is not only kissed but raped and impregnated by her royal admirer, finally awakened by her own suckling children, whom she birthed while she slept (Basile [1634] 1993). 'Sun, Moon, and Talia' is viewed as a precursor to Perrault's 1697 sleeping princess story and the Grimm's 'Briar Rose' (1812). 'Snow White', also made famous by the Grimm brothers' 1812 version (see Ashliman n.d., 709), very similarly ends with the sleeping princess, thought to be dead, awakened by the prince's kiss. As we shall see, the more explicit sexual and physical elements that form the heritage of the modern-day 'Sleeping Beauty' seep into many retellings of Kawabata's novella, but are especially taken up by Julia Leigh's Australian film adaptation.

Kawabata's novella transforms characters, events, and themes of 'Sleeping Beauty' stories. On a character level, the sleeping girls appear to play the role of the princess. The sleeping beauty service is run by a woman in her forties; as the older figure who puts the girls to sleep, she doubles in the role of the bad fairy who curses the princess to die at sixteen, and the good fairy who mitigates the curse into a hundred-year sleep. The client Old Eguchi might fancy himself as the prince, though he cannot wake the drugged girls; conversely, he is even involved in the death of one of them. This is one of the many direct reversals of the fairy tale that the novella enacts: another is that rather than having a princess awakened by a prince's kiss, the presence of each sleeping woman somehow works to emotionally 'awaken' and enliven the man who lies beside her (see Harries 2011, 367). The fairy tale motif of the young woman whose virginal purity is preserved by her sleep finds its match in Kawabata's writing, in which one important theme, as Mishima notes, is 'the worship of virgins' (Mishima 1969, 8).[2]

The House of the Sleeping Beauties, as noted, has a confirmed position within a global literary canon, and Kawabata's use of the shared imagery and narrative of 'Sleeping Beauty' has been reimagined in turn by diverse authors. For some, Kawabata's novella offers an opportunity to explore some of the woes of ageing, which are treated by authors and critics as 'universal', or at least widely appealing. This offers an interesting counterpoint to the presentation speech for Kawabata's Nobel Prize in Literature. The speech represents so-called *Nihonjinron* attitudes (See Mouer and Sugimoto 1995) that emphasise the uniqueness of a homogenised, stereotyped ideal of Japan. It praises Kawabata for his 'narrative mastery, which, with great sensibility, expresses the essence of the Japanese mind', and connects Kawabata's style to seemingly as many Japanese cultural traditions as possible, including 'classical literature', particularly the work of Murasaki Shikibu, as well as 'Japanese painting', haiku, and so on (Österling 1968). Kawabata's Nobel lecture, 'Japan, the Beautiful and Myself', a meandering contemplation of Zen Buddhism, poetry, calligraphy, and tea ceremony, perhaps worked to perpetuate such impressions of Japan and his work. However, contemporary Australian responses to Kawabata's novella do not limit their understanding of Japan to its 'representative' traditional literature and arts.

In the last two decades, storytellers from Australia and elsewhere have responded to Kawabata's novella in creative ways. One significant retelling of Kawabata's novella comes from a fellow Nobel Prize winner, Colombian author Gabriel García Márquez (1927–2014). Márquez's *Memoria de mis putas tristes* (Memories of My Melancholy Whores 2004), which cites Kawabata's novella in the epigraph, tells of an elderly man who regains pleasure in life through sleeping next to a drugged fourteen-year-old girl that a brothel madam has procured for him. This story forms part of an extended engagement with Kawabata's novella on the part of Márquez, who had already discussed *House of the Sleeping Beauties* in an earlier essay and short story.[3] In 'Old Men and Comatose Virgins: Nobel Prize Winners Rewrite "Sleeping Beauty"', scholar of French fairy tales Elizabeth Wanning Harries places Kawabata and Márquez within an international literary history of stories about old men and young sleeping women, discussing another Nobel Prize winner, South African-Australian author J. M. Coetzee, as well as the famed author of the paedophilic tale *Lolita*, Russian-American Vladimir Nabokov. Harries identifies similarities rather than cross-cultural differences in these authors' fairy tale engagements. She argues that the stories by Kawabata and Márquez commodify the sleeping girl, as well as the 'sleeping, "frozen" fairy tale' itself (Harries 2011, 368), largely perpetuating rather than reimagining its confining structures: 'their revisions have, if anything, intensified the dominant male perspective and the misogyny that lie embedded in the stereotype' (Harries 2011, 368).

Australian works feature prominently among retellings of *House of the Sleeping Beauties*. One example that responds to the sensuality of Kawabata's story is

100　Lucy Fraser

Krissy Kneen's *The Adventures of Holly White and the Incredible Sex Machine* (2015). In this erotic novel, Kawabata's novella is named among a number of existing works of erotic literature, connected with a 'Sex Book Club' that the eponymous protagonist Holly White joins in suburban Brisbane. In each chapter Holly experiences scenarios from the books she reads; in the *House of the Sleeping Beauties* chapter, Kawabata's gender roles are reversed and Holly becomes aroused by the body of her sleeping boyfriend (Kneen 2015). In this way, whereas other works treat *House of the Sleeping Beauties* as 'serious' literature, Kneen lines it up with more controversial – if well recognised – erotic literary classics, ranging from Leopold von Sacher-Masoch's *Venus in Furs* (1870) to Angela Carter's *The Infernal Desire Machines of Doctor Hoffman* (1972) and Erica Jong's feminist favourite *Fear of Flying* (1973). Another mention of Kawabata's novella in an Australian work is William Yang's piece, 'Japan', included in *Fruit: A New Anthology of Contemporary Australian Gay Writing*. Yang also emphasises the erotic element, using Kawabata's novella as a (somewhat tired, orientalist) frame to muse on his experience of gay men's sexual practices in Japan (Yang 1994). In this chapter, I focus on the more extended responses to *House of the Sleeping Beauties* found in the aforementioned novel *Candle Life* by Venero Armanno, and the film *Sleeping Beauty*, written and directed by Julia Leigh. These two Australian works represent complex intertextual engagements with Japanese literature that offer an alternative view of Japan-Australia cultural relationships.

　A few scholarly works analyse the 'neglected category' of representations of Japan in the Australian literary and visual arts (Kato 2008, 9). Megumi Kato, in *Narrating the Other: Australian Literary Perceptions of Japan* (2008), and Alison Broinowski, in several publications (1992, 2011), offer insightful accounts of Australia's creative dealings with Japan. Their investigations, however, focus on quite literal depictions: how Australian works view and discuss Japanese characters and Japan itself. Such an approach cannot sufficiently address Armanno's and Leigh's works, which instead adapt the scenario of Kawabata's novella into situations outside Japan. These stories should be treated as intertextual interactions, that is, conversations between texts across cultures, more than 'representations' of Japan. This is particularly important because both the novel and the film play with not only Kawabata's *House of the Sleeping Beauties*, but also with the 'Sleeping Beauty' fairy tale tradition and other texts from different cultures, in many different ways. The novel and film construct a Japan-Australia relationship within the cultural realm where famous foreign works are available for dialogue, critique, and adaptation to (highly literate) Australian authors and their characters.

Re-writers and world literature in Venero Armanno's *Candle Life*

Venero Armanno's 2006 novel *Candle Life* is narrated by a young Australian man. At the beginning of the novel, he is living in special accommodation for visiting artists, the Communes des Arts in Paris. He suffers from writer's block as he grieves the recent death of his Japanese-Australian girlfriend, Yukiko, who embodies (in a ghostly way) a Japan-Australia connection. Written in English and published in Australia, the novel nevertheless 'participates' in 'world literature', as Damrosch puts it, because 'the author reaches out to foreign literary traditions' as well as 'sending [his] characters abroad' (Damrosch 2017, 107). *Candle Life* reimagines Kawabata's Japanese novella and the fairy tales on several levels: firstly, characters such as the young French woman Emilie discuss and critique *House of the Sleeping Beauties* as a literary work. Secondly, Emilie and several other characters may be read as 'sleeping beauty' figures themselves. Thirdly, Armanno restages a 'house of sleeping beauties' business; at the climax of the story, the narrator experiences his own drugged sleep and emotional re-awakening. This multilevel engagement takes place among endless reference to world literature, art, music, and historical events from the setting of a chaotic, cosmopolitan Paris as seen by a narrator from Brisbane. As such, *Candle Life* offers a means to question the place of Australia within a global literary scene.

Armanno's works often explore cross-cultural connections, particularly relating to his own heritage as the child of Sicilian migrants to Brisbane. *Candle Life* features a huge cast of international characters and texts from across cultures. As well as several 'sleeping beauty' figures which will be discussed further, some important characters include the Black Cuban-American Jackson Lee, also known as Carlos Juan-Luis Cemi, a former academic and author and now a beggar in Paris; another beggar, 'Harry', thought to be the Jewish assassin Herschel Grynszpan[4] but revealed to be a man who came to Paris to escape his Nazi German past; Andre, the narrator's Parisian friend whom he met in Brisbane; and Roman Zielinski, a Ukrainian-born chemical scientist and artist. Intertextuality is one of the major features of the novel: that is, direct quotes and descriptions, indirect allusions, and other such relationships with creative artists and creative works abound. The more obvious examples are mentions that range from writers such as Ernest Hemmingway and D.H. Lawrence (Armanno 2006, 111–112), artists such as Andy Warhol (123), and productions and characters such as *The Phantom of the Opera* and Quasimodo (243), to musical acts such as George Harrison (132), R.E.M. (211), Radiohead (212), and more. The work overlaps at some points with other Australian novels that retell Kawabata's *House of the Sleeping Beauties*: Armanno's narrator brings up a few works and authors of erotic fiction which were later to be retold by Krissy Kneen, namely Leopold Ritter von Sacher-Masoch's *Venus in Furs* (149) and Erica Jong (273).

It is against this international intertextual backdrop that *Candle Life* plays with Kawabata's novella and the fairy tale it draws from. In the acknowledgements, Armanno writes, 'I was assisted in the writing of this book by historical texts and articles as well as works of fiction' (Armanno 2006, 350). *House of the Sleeping Beauties* is the first and only novel in the short list that follows (350–351). Armanno's novel thus sits firmly within the multicultural artistic tradition that developed in the 1980s and 1990s: from this period, in line with accelerating globalisation, government policies promoting multiculturalism, and economic and cultural exchange, as well as travel between Australia and Japan, more diverse perspectives of Japan flourished in Australian literature (Kato 2008, 165–187), and Australian-Asian hybridisation became prominent in the Australian arts (Broinowski 1992, 216–231). As we shall see, through multiple, multicultural engagements with Kawabata's work, Armanno's novel connects with and seeks ways to expand and transform the novella. In examining ideas about Japan in Australian literature, Kato convincingly argues for the analysis of distinctions and 'othering', stating that 'by looking at how Australians have differentiated themselves from Japan and the Japanese in their writings, it may be possible to capture glimpses of the transient meanings of "identity", "culture", and "nation" for Australians' (Kato 2008, 4). However, in Armanno's work, the meanings of these same notions might equally become apparent in repetitions, similarities, and fusions of Japanese, Australian, and other texts.

Like old Eguchi in Kawabata's novella, the narrator of *Candle Life* is enlivened by a sleeping beauty experience. Armanno, however, renders this a more dramatic inner change through reversing gender roles and de-aestheticising the sleeping experience. Initially, the sleeping beauty service that Armanno's narrator encounters is very similar to the one that Kawabata's depicts. The business is named Les Belles Endormies (The Sleeping Beauties); this name, notably, refers not to fairy tale titles 'The Sleeping Beauty of the Wood' (Perrault 1697) or 'Sleeping Beauty' but rather the translated French title of Kawabata's novella (Kawabata 1970). Les Belles Endormies, like Kawabata's inn, is a business that provides opportunities for elderly men to sleep next to attractive young women. However, Armanno's novel rewrites both the women and their customers. Firstly, where Kawabata's sleeping beauties remain in their sleeping, objectified state, in *Candle Life* they are given agency through the character of Zoya, a Russian former sex worker who is now employed by Les Belles Endormies, she says, to provide sympathy rather than sex (Armanno 2006, 169). Through Zoya we learn that the sleep-inducing drug used in the service has a different effect on each user. Zoya loses her voice temporarily, a quite literal reflection on the voiceless girls of Kawabata's work. But Zoya's voice does return and even when she is mute she can laugh, sing, and communicate by writing. That is, Zoya gives a voice and a story to the empty canvasses of the girls in Kawabata's novella. Interestingly, this might be described as a return to the current fairy tale trends, as most standard versions of 'Sleeping Beauty' in circulation today focus more on the princess than the prince.

Kawabata's Eguchi requests several times to take the sleeping drug that the girls are given, but the female inn-proprietor refuses him. Armanno's book explores a plot where the narrator does take the drug, himself becoming a 'sleeping beauty'. This plot change sets off a series of twists to the gender roles of Kawabata's novella and depicts a more chaotic, ugly, and lively sleeping experience. When Armanno's narrator takes the drug, he, a young man, sleeps next to one older man and then another, both of them beggars he has encountered in Paris. One of these men, the Cuban-American former author Jackson Lee, tells the narrator:

> I'm not one of the naked girls Roman used as window-dressing and sugar to attract us flies when he promised enlightenment. No pretty girls here, but the truth is we don't need them and never did. Like I said, window-dressing

and sugar, that's all they were. Titillation. Titillation to add some spice to the search for wisdom – how very twenty-first century. Only proves we're creatures of the dark and always will be.

(Armanno 2006, 274)

The narrator's drugged state enables him to dream of his dead girlfriend Yukiko, but also to enter the memories and experience the lives of the men who lie beside him. This insight into the lives of others, the book implies, will give him fodder for his writing to overcome his creative impasse. *Candle Life* quite literally drags Kawabata's novella into the sewer as the narrator enters the Parisian underground catacombs and, on awakening, must find his way out in a scene of re-birth and revival.

A few other characters in *Candle Life* can be identified as 'sleeping beauty' figures. The first is the narrator's girlfriend Yukiko. Yukiko has died some months before the events of the story; however, she does not rest peacefully within the novel, as the narrator is haunted by her memory and her loss. The Yukiko of the narrator's memories is by no means the stereotypical 'submissive' or 'passive' Japanese wife; she is outspoken, artistic, and dynamic. However, as an eternally sleeping Japanese woman, Yukiko may recall the English-speaking reader to Kawabata's Japanese novella. As a mixed-race character she also embodies a bridge between Australia and Japan that is not always a comfortable combination of cultures. With an Australian mother and Japanese father, she feels alienated from Japan (Armanno 2006, 255). Yukiko's early attempts to remember her own dead parents begin with reaching for more traditional, typical Japanese arts. She says,

All the time I was growing up I thought I'd make their life story a beautiful book. Very Japanese. Very short, elegant and poignant. I'd do ink drawings on rice paper to flesh it out. Now I just prefer to paint them.

(Armanno 2006, 257)

Yukiko died in Brisbane and it seems that as a result, the city of this tragedy, and even all of Australia, has become a dead end for the narrator. In order to allow her to rest, and in order for him to take up a new life, the cosmopolitan and creative centre of Paris, as well as its people, becomes essential.

Part of the enlivening world of Paris is Emilie, a young French woman who becomes the narrator's new girlfriend. Emilie is the other side to Yukiko's coin. Where Yukiko's 'sleep' is that of death, Emilie's represents life: she becomes pregnant, which makes her tired, but as another sleeping beauty, her rest is wholesome; a healthy, radiant exhaustion that heralds new life. Unlike the mute Zoya and the dead Yukiko, Emilie's voice is unrestricted; her confident critique of Kawabata's 'fairy tale for old men' signals her escape from the confining sleeping beauty character mould of the fairy tales, and of the stories by Kawabata and later Gabriel García Márquez. In this way Armanno's novel itself likewise escapes the confines of its ancestor *House of the Sleeping Beauties*. In the final pages, after the narrator is transformed by his drugged sleep, he fights to escape the catacombs that represent his own gloomy grief and artistic emptiness, and the novel closes on him emerging into the vibrant Parisian streets with the thought that he will make his way back to Emilie.

Despite Kawabata's novella framing the plot, and the important Japanese character Yukiko, Japanese literature is not featured very heavily among the myriad of quotations, allusions, and reworkings of other texts in *Candle Life*. As the narrator says, musing on his knowledge of Japanese authors: '[there is] Mishima, of course, and I can name several others, but I'm no expert' (Armanno 2006, 186). This clarifies the particular Japanese literary scene that informs the global canon here: not the more recent bestseller, Murakami Haruki, but rather the mid-twentieth-century translation successes, Kawabata and Mishima Yukio (1925–1970). Though Mishima is only mentioned in this brief way by Armanno, and his work is quite different from Kawabata's, both Mishima's and Kawabata's writings inform the image of Japanese literature that is invoked in Armanno's novel: erotic, keenly aesthetic, and highly literary, preoccupied with the interiority of a masculine self.

Likewise, among the huge number of creative artists and works cited in *Candle Life*, there are few references to Australian authors, musicians, or public figures. Moreover, the creative arts in Asian countries outside of Japan are hardly mentioned in the novel. This is not a personal bias on Armanno's part but rather reflects the shape of the established canon of world arts and literature for English speakers. That is, the seemingly international cultural centre of Paris that is depicted in the novel, as well as the intertextual scope of *Candle Life*, functions within the borders of what Bourdaghs, Sakai, and Toeda describe as 'the Eurocentric and US-centric global cultural system' (Bourdaghs, Sakai and Toeda 2018, 4), where Kawabata has an established place as a prize-winning, translated author of 'high' literature.

A fairy tale adventure often begins when the protagonist leaves home and sets off into a mysterious new world. *Candle Life* is about the character's need to build a new life away from Brisbane; he is awakened from his darkness in the cultural home of 'Sleeping Beauty', encountering a motley assortment of mostly European and North American characters, themselves often concerned with creative endeavours such as writing or painting. The novel reimagines and reshapes Kawabata's novella. There is little 'othering' of Japan and little unease about Australian cultural identity, but certainly some imbalance in the small number of Australian and Japanese works that form this identity, in relation to the huge number of Anglo-American and Western European creative achievements. Yet the novel's structural appropriation of Kawabata's Japanese novella and the European fairy tale intertext into the plot, as well as its incorporation of foreign characters and stories, envisions a global literary scene where translated Japanese texts are equally open to appropriation by Australian authors and other well-read characters.

Japan slumbering in Julia Leigh's *Sleeping Beauty*

Sleeping Beauty (2011) was written and directed by the Australian Julia Leigh. Her first feature film, it was nominated for respected prizes, including the Cannes

Film Festival 'Caméra d'Or' and 'Palme d'Or' (Festival de Cannes 2011). Like Armanno's *Candle Life*, the film depicts a sleeping beauty–style business modelled on Kawabata's depiction. However, Armanno's characters actually discuss Kawabata's novella, whereas in Leigh's film, the name Kawabata and the title *House of the Sleeping Beauties* are at no point mentioned, nor is any Japanese character, nor even the country Japan. Neither is the 'Sleeping Beauty' fairy tale directly discussed. That is, instead of representing Japan through Japanese characters or locales, the film builds yet another kind of relationship with Japanese literature and arts. It uses Kawabata's scenario to frame the plot and revisits Kawabata's themes, as well as employing visual intertextuality: a certain Japonisme and broader orientalism inform its sometime fairy tale aesthetic.

Filmed and set in Sydney, Leigh's *Sleeping Beauty* follows the life of Lucy (played by Emily Browning), a young woman who juggles university study with several part-time jobs, seemingly providing some financial support to her bad-tempered, alcoholic mother (only appearing via a telephone conversation and mentions) and emotional support to a depressed and sometimes difficult friend Birdmann (Ewen Leslie), who eventually takes his own life with Lucy lying beside him. Lucy has few qualms in taking work with an upmarket organisation, where she begins as a semi-nude waitress to dinner parties of the wealthy. The film's connection with *House of the Sleeping Beauties* becomes clear to any reader of Kawabata's novella, as Lucy's next role is in a service that very closely replicates Kawabata's inn: old men pay for the privilege of sharing a bed with drugged, naked young women such as Lucy, and the business transaction is facilitated by an immaculately groomed middle-aged woman, Clara.

As Leigh herself explains, the film grew from her own unease with sleep as a vulnerable state (Leigh 2012). The sources for the story include, as with Armanno's novel, many texts and traditions from different cultures. Leigh has widely acknowledged the classic 'Sleeping Beauty' fairy tale, Kawabata's and Gabriel García Márquez's retellings, and other stories, from the biblical story of the ageing, cold, King Solomon having warm young virgins brought in sleep next to him, to more contemporary depictions online in the 'sleeping girls' genre of pornography (for example, see Leigh 2011, 2012). However, Kawabata's work is the focus; with its fairy tale intertext, it seems to have proved especially suitable for Leigh to explore a discomfort with sleep and critique some of the problems with stories depicting young women sleeping.

Orientalist visual references to Japan and to fairy tales underscore the film's retelling of Kawabata's story. If the touchpoint of Armanno's novel is the modern Japanese literature of 1960s, Leigh's film is perhaps inspired in part by Kawabata's nostalgia for 'old' Japan, or by Anglo-European romanticising of Japanese arts, as discernible in the Nobel Prize presentation speech (Österling 1968) and Kawabata's lecture (1968). In the film, the nude waitressing and sleeping beauty businesses, as well as their clients, are aligned with traditional Japanese arts which then are associated with a realm of wealth, self-indulgence, and cruelty. The scene of the dinner party where Lucy waitresses in lingerie recalls Tanizaki Jun'ichirō's 'The Gourmet Club' (Tanizaki 2001) and his other early, decadent tales: naked or scantily clad women pose and serve in a house decorated with marble, antique Japanese gold-leaf screens, ornate oriental mirrors, Chinese paintings, Persian carpets, and brocade armchairs. Later the proprietor of the sleeping beauty business, Clara, gives the sleeping drug to Lucy in an elegant Japanese tea ceremony-based ritual, pouring from an antique Worcester Porcelain-style teapot decorated with Japanese maple leaves, and even stirring with a bamboo *chashaku*.

Leigh's film is simply titled *Sleeping Beauty*, thus making a more direct reference to the fairy tale source text than is drawn in Armanno's novel. This reference is substantiated by imagery, particularly the iconic scene used in a promotional poster that features Lucy sleeping in a wide gilt-framed upholstered bed with an opulent matching bedspread, set against a plain, almost starkly decorated room. Lucy's white skin and red hair recall iconic paintings of sleeping women, particularly those in the pre-Raphaelite style (see also Dijkstra 1986). The stillness of her body and the room, the frozen-in-time moment, is reminiscent of picture-book illustrations for the fairy tale. The film's engagement with an aesthetic obsession with sleeping beauties is intertwined with its use of Japonisme: famous fairy tale illustrations and other images of sleeping women often employ gorgeous orientalist motifs and accoutrements of the Near, Middle, and Far East (see examples by Edmund Dulac, Warwick Goble, and others in Heiner 1999; see also Dijkstra 1986). Throughout the film, orientalist décor is often presented in static, wide, illustration-like shots.

Orientalist and fairytale imagery is contrasted with other scenes of mundane houses, pubs, offices, and a university lecture theatre, as well as a bright white laboratory setting where Lucy participates in a clinical trial for money. This medical trial, the opening scene of the film, is another reference to the shocking first lines of Kawabata's story, warning Eguchi not to put his finger into the mouth of the sleeping girls: Lucy sits still for a young male researcher to painfully feed a tube down her throat as she retches. As such, Leigh's film exposes the visceral and disturbing nature of the 'sleeping beauty' business, which exemplifies the many ways in which young women's bodies are exploited by others.

However, Leigh's stated intent to revise 'Sleeping Beauty' and *House of the Sleeping Beauties* from the young woman's perspective (Leigh 2011) is not fully achieved. The oriental objects themselves are so beautiful, and presented in such fairy tale tableaux, that they invite aesthetic admiration on the part of the camera and the viewer. In the same way, the visuals are so carefully crafted and the camera is so focused on Lucy's (Browning's) slender, porcelain-white body, the film cannot help but perpetuate the tradition that Harries identifies of 'freezing' the sleeping princess in time and commodifying both the girl and the classic story of her passive state. In the same way that human women are hired for decoration at the dinner parties of the wealthy, so Lucy herself seems a part of the gorgeous décor. In a film history context, the titillating objectification is, one reviewer says, 'a throwback to the artporn and chateau-erotica of the 1970s' (Bradshaw 2011).

Fairy tale intertexts equally shape the gaze. In a book section titled 'Sleep as Spectacle; Sleep and the Undecaying Corpse' (Katagi 1996, 102), scholar of French literature and fairy tales Katagi Tomotoshi traces a history of 'Sleeping

Beauty' stories, highlighting the way the princess's sleeping body is set up on display, as Snow White is in her glass coffin. The 'surface' portrayal finds its home in Kawabata's writing. Novelist Takahashi Takako critiques women's 'exteriors, as perceived through men's eyes' in his work: 'Kawabata Yasunari's women seem to be wearing masks, and it's as if those masks are being observed through a man's eyes. But what's behind the mask isn't described at all' (Takahashi and Tsushima 2006, 120). In Leigh's film retelling, the screen acts as the surface of the glass coffin, displaying the beautiful body of the sleeping (and waking) woman behind it, preserving her life but veiling her inner life. It can be an uncomfortable experience for the viewer: Lucy's smooth exterior hardly cracks and the viewer is given little insight into her seeming indifference to what happens to herself and her body, making it difficult to sympathise with or understand her.

In Leigh's *Sleeping Beauty*, film critic Genevieve Yue sees 'no conventional feminist rewriting of the fairy tale' (2012, 36) but she does argue that Lucy is presented as having agency, which she conceals with a mask-like opacity. Yue claims that 'Lucy's extreme passivity is . . . disruptive and resisting' because she refuses to make her interior available to viewers (2012, 37). This resistance may be difficult for many viewers to perceive. However, Leigh makes one noticeable revision to the ending of her tale: where the fairytale princess wakes and happily submits to marriage, and Kawabata's female beauties are only ever shown as sleeping or dead, Leigh's film closes on Lucy awakening both literally and emotionally. As with Armanno's novel, the film hooks into the *House of the Sleeping Beauties* intertext by retelling Eguchi's desire to take the sleeping drug used by the girls. Armanno's narrator is permitted to take the drug where Eguchi was not; likewise in *Sleeping Beauty* an elderly client takes a lethal dose of the drugged tea in a suicide assisted by Clara. When Clara checks on the man in the morning, Lucy, who had recklessly used recreational drugs the previous night, has trouble waking and the madam proves herself to be both a good fairy and a prince when she desperately uses mouth-to-mouth resuscitation to kiss her back to life. This hint at a supportive connection between women contrasts to the pragmatic, indifferent response of the inn-keeper to a girl's death in Kawabata's novella. Leigh's film ends with Lucy screaming in horror when she wakes to see the dead man beside her. We finally witness an emotional reaction from underneath the seemingly indifferent surface of her beautiful body.

Sleeping Beauty received mixed reviews; some mention the Japanese source text but most are more concerned with its disquieting eroticism. Film critic and researcher Sarinah Masukor ties Australian responses in particular to anxieties about the international reception of national screen culture. Masukor prefers to highlight what she sees as the film's universal themes, arguing that it is not suitable for examining particular ideas of Australian-ness (nor, we might thus infer, the creative relationship between Australia and Japan):

> This anxiety over how we, as a nation, might be perceived via our on-screen images of sex remains. While *Sleeping Beauty*'s true themes are ageing and the waning of one's passion for life, the film's Australian origins, combined

with its plainly shot nudity and the erotic nature of Lucy's job, have dominated discussions in the media. *Sleeping Beauty* is neither actively un-Australian, nor actively Australian. Despite its Sydney setting, most of the film takes place indoors or in banally unrecognisable urban areas. Prostitution, sex and getting old are human themes pondered by all nations, and the characters here are distinguished by their class and social standing rather than by their nationality. [. . .] *Sleeping Beauty* has nothing at all to say about being Australian, but a lot to say about being human.

(Masukor 2011, 27)

Masukor's take certainly highlights the way that both the 'Sleeping Beauty' fairy tale and Kawabata's novella adapt flexibly into new settings. However, it is possible to ascribe the very class distinctions she mentions as characteristically Australian. In the film, where Lucy and her friends speak Standard Australian English, the affluent, corrupt elite use some approximation of Standard British English accents. Sinister wealthy characters with refined accents is more of a film cliché than a realistic representation. The (versions of) Standard British Accents become particularly apparent in a dialogue between Clara (played by Rachel Blake) and one of her elderly clients (played by Peter Carroll). Ostensibly speaking to Clara, the man performs an almost Shakespearean monologue directly to the camera.[5] Rob Pensalfini, in his research on contemporary theatre productions of Shakespeare in Australia, finds that 'Standard British English accents are still defaulted to as the norm for non-comic characters' and argues that this 'represents the persistence of the – probably unconscious – colonial attitude that Australians are not worthy of heightened dramatic language' (Pensalfini 2009, 142). The accent differences in *Sleeping Beauty* may similarly point to some anxiety about the right of 'ordinary' Australians to engage with foreign artistic 'culture'. That is, the wealthy characters with more 'refined' accents are the ones with the authority to appreciate the arts and literature: they re-enact a business depicted in a Japanese novella by an internationally distinguished author, unselfconsciously staging Japanese-style tea ceremonies or decadent dinners against backdrops of oriental arts and antiques. In this way the film implies that refined Japanese décor and arts are available to a few privileged Australians.

The elderly man's monologue reiterates the 'universal' themes of Kawabata's novella, of ageing and the longing for youthful bodies. In the vein of Eguchi, the man reminisces about his youth and his wife – 'I did not cherish her', he says – by citing not Japanese literature, but a short story that he identifies as 'The Thirtieth Year' by Austrian woman writer Ingeborg Bachmann. In other words, this is another instance of 'world' storytelling that reaches out to a huge range of tradition and texts. Leigh as writer and the director of the film cites Kawabata's novella and several other works as sources, demonstrating that, like Armanno, she plays freely and creatively with foreign literature and arts. Rather than explicitly naming Kawabata, the film appropriates the premise of *House of Sleeping Beauties*, complicating its narrative perspective. It provides, if not insight into the sleeping girl's inner world, then at least the story of her waking life outside of the oppressive house, and her final awakening to its horrors. The film's intertextual sources and its international release signal that, like *Candle Life*, it enters into dialogue with Kawabata's novella in a context of the multiple possibilities and scenarios of a 'world' literature and storytelling stage.

Conclusion

Alison Broinowski notes a decline in interest in language study and international relationships between Japan and Australia in the 2000s, and finds little excitement in Japanese-Australian literary interactions during this period:

> In the last decade, each country appears to have lost the capacity to stimulate the imagination of the other as a site of fiction or memoir. The decline may be explained by a loss of novelty and a sense of sameness, even an absence of sexiness in the relationship.
>
> (Broinowski 2011, 40)

The textual interactions discussed in this chapter, however, are neither inspired by difference nor numbed by sameness. They link in different ways to a fairy tale that has French/European origins but is familiar to Australian and Japanese readers. They adapt from Kawabata's *House of the Sleeping Beauties* seemingly (but questionably) 'universal' themes of ageing and desire for youth and youthful bodies; of quests for agency and selfhood against disobedient bodies, against the loss of others.

Such intertextual conversations between stories continue the life of Kawabata's novella, which seems to have sparked a flame of 'sexiness' in some Australian literary responses. Krissy Kneen's erotic interpretation in *The Adventures of Holly White and the Incredible Sex Machine* is, again, an example of a textual interaction with one particular Japanese work positioned among a varied list of international works, rather than a literary representation of Japanese people or the nation of Japan.

Armanno's novel and Leigh's film could not be straightforwardly labelled as sexy; their relationship with *House of the Sleeping Beauties* is more complex. Both works are troubled and invigorated by the premise of Kawabata's novella, and they take the desires of his protagonist Eguchi in new directions and offer other characters' perspectives. Armanno's novel rejects the 'window dressing' of the beautiful girls and focuses on the transformative force of the drugged, dream-filled sleep for its narrator. Leigh's film delves into the life of the 'window dressing', the character of Lucy who is herself presented as a kind of opaque surface. However, the film revels in its own beautiful surfaces, visually representing Japonisme, as well as dwelling on Lucy's beautiful body, which creates contradictions for Leigh's feminist goals. Interestingly, Leigh's film was subtitled and released in Japan under the title *Suriipingu Byūtii: Kindan no yorokobi* (Sleeping Beauty: The Pleasure of the Forbidden 2011). Though Japanese commentators of course recognise Kawabata's novella as a source text, the distribution company,

KlockWorx, do not mention it (KlockWorx 2018), indicating with their English loanword title and seductive subheading their choice to market the film's sex and nudity rather than its venerated local literary sources.

For Leigh, using Kawabata's novella seems to provide the opportunity to manipulate a gorgeous orientalist aesthetic, but the stories of the Australian novel and film are not stimulated by Japan as a country. Rather, Armanno and Leigh position Kawabata's novella as one text among a raft of stories and ideas available to Australian writers and film-makers, even though in some ways 'high' literature and refined Japanese art are only enjoyed by a wealthy or educated few. Regardless, as retellings in themselves, the works keep Kawabata's novella alive and point to creative interactions between texts and cultures beyond portrayals of places and characters: they suggest a different Japan-Australia relation, one of ongoing conversations that take place within networks of world film and literature.

Acknowledgements

I would like to acknowledge the research work conducted for this project by several students taking part in the UQ Summer Research Program: Anthony Morgan, Shimada Ken'ichiro, and especially Rebecca Hausler, whose detective work uncovered Kneen's and Yang's stories.

It was Cory Taylor's passionate and articulate response to Leigh's film that inspired me to write about it.

Notes

1 See, for example, Bram Dijkstra (1986) on 'Dead Ladies and the Fetish of Sleep'.
2 Literary criticism has traditionally admired Kawabata's ability to write female characters, an attitude that has unsurprisingly been much critiqued by feminists in Japan and elsewhere. Natsuo Kirino's 1995 gritty crime novel *Mizu no nemuri hai no yume* (Sleep in water, dream in ashes) has been identified as a retelling of the novella that is oriented to the female perspective (Matsugu 2011, 494).
3 For a close comparison of Kawabata's and Márquez's novellas, see Hanagata (2006).
4 A Polish Jewish refugee who assassinated a German diplomat in 1938 and later disappeared.
5 It is unclear whether these accents were used at directorial request or by the actors themselves. Blake plays up her own semi-English accent into refined, confident pronunciation; Carroll speaks in interviews with a refined Australian accent and has performed in a number of Shakespeare productions, which may inform his performance.

References

Armanno, V. 2006. *Candle Life*. Sydney: Vintage.
Ashliman, D. L. n.d. 'Snow-White and Other Tales of Aarne-Thompson-Uther Type 709', *Folklore and Mythology Electronic Texts, 1998–2013*, accessed 25 April 2018, www.pitt.edu/~dash/type0709.html.
Basile, G. [1634] 1993. *The Pentameron*, Richard Francis Burton, trans. London: Spring Books.

Bourdaghs, M. K., Sakai, C. and Hirokazu, T. 2018. 'Introduction: Kawabata Yasunari in the Twenty-First Century'. *Japan Forum*, 30 (1): 2–11.
Bradshaw, P. 2011. '*Sleeping Beauty* – Review', *The Guardian* – *Australia*, 14 October, accessed 25 April 2018, www.theguardian.com/film/2011/oct/13/sleeping-beauty-film-review.
Broinowski, A. 1992. *The Yellow Lady: Australian Impressions of Asia*. Melbourne: Oxford University Press.
———. 2011. 'Contesting Civilizations: Literature of Australia in Japan and Singapore', *Antipodes*, 25 (1): 37–43.
Damrosch, D. 2017. *How to Read World Literature*, 2nd edition. Hoboken: Wiley-Blackwell.
Dijkstra, B. 1986. *Idols of Perversity: Fantasies of Feminine Evil in Fin-de-Siècle Culture*. Oxford: Oxford University Press.
Festival de Cannes. 2011. '"Sleeping Beauty", a Writer Behind the Camera', *Festival de Cannes 64th Edition 2011*, accessed 25 April 2018, www.festival-cannes.com/en/69-editions/retrospective/2011/actualites/articles/sleeping-beauty-a-writer-behind-the-camera.
Hanagata, K. 2006. 'Gaburieru Garushia Marukesu *Waga kanashiki shōfutachi no omoide* to Kawabata Yasunari *Nemureru bijo*: koraaju to hensō' [Collage and Variation: Gabriel Garcia Marquez 2004, 'Memoria de mis putas tristes' and Yasunari Kawabata, 'The Sleeping Beauties'], *Hon'yaku no bunka/bunka no hon'yaku*, 1: 21–43.
Harries, E. W. 2011. 'Old Men and Comatose Virgins: Nobel Prize Winners Rewrite "Sleeping Beauty"', *Études de lettres*, 34: 359–378.
Heiner, H. A. 1999. 'Sleeping Beauty', *Sur La Lune Fairy Tales*, accessed 25 April 2018, www.surlalunefairytales.com/sleepingbeauty/index.html.
Katagi, T. 1996. *Perō dōwa no hirointachi [The Heroin's of Perrault's Tales]*. Tokyo: Serika shobō.
Kato, M. 2008. *Narrating the Other: Australian Literary Perceptions of Japan*. Clayton, VIC: Monash Asia Institute.
Kawabata, Y. [1961] 1967. *Nemureru bijo [Sleeping Beauty]*. Tokyo: Shinchō bunko.
———. 1968. 'Japan, the Beautiful and Myself', E. Seidensticker, trans., in *Nobel Media*, 12 December, accessed 25 April 2018, www.nobelprize.org/nobel_prizes/literature/laureates/1968/kawabata-lecture.html.
———. 1969. *House of the Sleeping Beauties and Other Stories*, Edward Seidensticker, trans. Tokyo: Kodansha International.
———. 1970. *Les Belles Endormies*, René Sieffert, trans. Paris: Éditions Albin Michel.
KlockWorx. 2018. 'Suriipingu Byūtii' [Sleeping Beauty], 24 April, http://klockworx.com/movie/m-400049/.
Kneen, K. 2015. *The Adventures of Holly White and the Incredible Sex Machine*. Melbourne: Text Publishing.
Leigh, J. 2011. 'Julia Leigh Interview – *Sleeping Beauty*', *Empire Magazine*, accessed 24 April 2018, www.youtube.com/watch?v=jFOsZNwoiNQ.
———. 2012. 'Julia Leigh Discussed *Sleeping Beauty*', *SydFilmFest*, accessed 30 January 2019, www.youtube.com/watch?v=Dwc-IM9oKoc.
Masukor, S. 2011. 'Sleep Like Death: Julia Leigh's *Sleeping Beauty*', *Metro Magazine: Media & Education Magazine*, 170: 24–28.
Matsugu, M. 2011. 'Kawabata Yasunari's *House of the Sleeping Beauties*, Retold: Kirino Natsuo's *Sleep in Water, Dream in Ashes*', *Japan Forum*, 23 (4): 485–504.
Mishima, Y. 1969. 'Introduction', in E. Seidensticker (ed. and trans.), *House of the Sleeping Beauties and Other Stories*. Tokyo: Kodansha International, 7–10.
Mouer, R. and Sugimoto, Y. 1995. *Nihonjinron at the End of the Twentieth Century: A Multicultural Perspective*. Bundoora: School of Asian Studies, Latrobe University.

Österling, A. 1968. 'Award Ceremony Speech', *Nobel Media*, accessed 25 April 2018, www.nobelprize.org/nobel_prizes/literature/laureates/1968/press.html.

Pensalfini, R. 2009. 'Not in Our Own Voices: Accent and Identity in Contemporary Australian Shakespeare Performance', *Australasian Drama Studies*, 54: 142–168.

'Perō hen' [Perrault chapter]. 2007, in Jidōbungaku hon'yaku daijiten henshū iinkai (ed.), *Zusetsu jidōbungaku hon'yaku daijiten* [Illustrated Encyclopedia of Translated Children's Literature], vol. 3. Tokyo: Ōzorasha, 685–709.

Perrault, C. [1697] 2003. *The Sleeping Beauty in the Wood*, A. E. Johnson and S. R. Littlewood, trans., D. L. Ashliman, revised, accessed 24 April 2018, www.pitt.edu/~dash/perrault01.html.

Sleeping Beauty. 2011. Dir. Julia Leigh. Magic Films.

Takahashi, T. and Yūko, T. 2006. 'Female Sexuality and the Male Gaze', Maryellen Toman Mori, trans., in R. Copeland (ed.), *Woman Critiqued: Translated Essays on Japanese Women's Writing*. Honolulu: University of Hawai'i Press, 119–134.

Tanizaki, J. 2001. *The Gourmet Club: A Sextet*, Anthony H. Chambers and Paul McCarthy, trans. Tokyo: Kodansha.

Yang, W. 1994. 'Japan', in G. Dunne (ed.), *Fruit: A New Anthology of Contemporary Australian Gay Writing*. Sydney: Blackwattle Press, 55–64.

Yue, G. 2012. 'Two Sleeping Beauties', *Film Quarterly*, 65 (3): 33–37.

7 The irrepressible magic of Monkey

How a Japanese television drama depicting an ancient Chinese tale became compulsory after-school viewing in Australia

Rebecca Hausler

Introduction

Born from an egg on a mountain top, *Monkey* became an irrepressible force that would exert its magical influence on an ancient Chinese tale again and yet again. The Japanese television show *Saiyūki*, known as *Monkey* to its English language viewers, was a retelling of the classic Chinese tale *The Journey to the West* and became the unlikely hero of children's television during the 1980s, with a cult following whose popularity endures even today. Unlike other Japanese television shows such as *Astro Boy* or *Kimba the White Lion* that were not easily identifiable as Asian and were in a sense 'culturally odourless' (Iwabuchi 2002, 24–28; Chapman 2015, 356–357), *Monkey* aligned itself more with the similarly popular and 'culturally odour-ful' 1960s black-and-white series *The Samurai* (*Shintarō*) (Chapman 2015, 356–357). However, unlike *The Samurai*, the English language–dubbed *Monkey* was wildly popular in Australia, with the series screening and repeating several times over from its original air date in 1980 through to the early 2000s. Its ongoing appeal meant that the show and its characters have remained a quirky mainstay in popular culture and have inspired a myriad of reinterpretations in film, theatre, and television both in Australia and overseas.

So, what was it about this Japanese television drama that captured the imagination of Australian viewers and made *Monkey* a cult classic whose popularity persists even today? *Monkey*'s appeal lay not only in its distinctive oriental aesthetic, but in the way that the Japanese production took a somewhat comical yet deeply religious and philosophical Chinese folktale, hammed up the visual gags and visual effects, and set it to a popular funk music soundtrack. It was then exported to Britain where it metamorphosed into a cheeky slapstick comedy filled with slang, jokes, and sexual innuendo, thus making it entirely unique and utterly appealing to a wide range of young viewers. Furthermore, I suggest that *Monkey*'s popularity has endured, not only through viewers' nostalgia for the series' iconic imagery and catchy theme song, but due to the way that both Japanese and Chinese elements were encapsulated into the show, ensuring that it stays relevant in an ever-changing global environment.

114 *Rebecca Hausler*

These elements reflect both a notion of 'oriental cool' and how we can view this through a transcultural lens. In this chapter I will examine Chapman's (2015) notion of 'oriental cool' through a transcultural lens, arguing that, unlike *The Samurai*, which was distinctly Japanese in its content and aesthetics, *Monkey* fed into an increasing interest in what was generally a leaky notion of Asian or Oriental culture as exhibited or mimicked in Western productions or re-productions. *Monkey*'s eclectic incorporation of cultural input takes a Chinese folktale, re-enacted through a Japanese production company, which was rewritten and dubbed by Worldwide Sound London on behalf of the BBC to maximise its palatability to an English-speaking audience, while maintaining distinctly Japanese aspects and Chinese foundations. Despite the often essentialist ways in which British reworking of this tale depicted these Asian characters, I argue that it was precisely this combination of Chinese, Japanese, and British elements that allowed *Monkey* to rise to the cult classic status it enjoys today in Australia.

Utilising theories of transculturality employed by Berry and Epstein (1999, 3), as well as a working model proposed by Dagnino (2015, 1–2), I will assert that the artistic output of any one culture was insufficient to create such a phenomenon, and it was this cultural dislocation and creative openness that allowed the show to highlight to audiences the overlapping of our disparate cultures, rather than our oppositions. I will then briefly summarise the journey of this series, starting from its Chinese folktale roots, through its journey into Japan, and eventually into Britain as a translated and abridged novel. This background is important for situating the story's importance and history in China, Japan, Britain, and by extension Australia. I will then provide historical context to the series itself, with its production in Japan as well as in its English reworking and dubbing. Finally, I will explore its initial and subsequent reception, examining how fans in 1980s Australia fought back against initial critics of the show, establishing its popularity for decades to come.

Border crossings: the transcultural effects behind 'oriental cool'

The concept of 'oriental cool' was conceived by Chapman (2015, 357) who suggests that the initial wave of interest towards Japanese popular culture in Australia began with the 1960s Japanese period drama *The Samurai*, with its 'exotic and esoteric nature' the driving force behind the popularity of the show (Chapman 2015, 357). Consumption of 'oriental cool' continued long after *The Samurai* disappeared from the airwaves, with interest in Japanese television productions growing in popularity over the following decades, as seen in the enduring popularity of *Monkey*. International interest in productions such as these ultimately led to Japan's foray into pop-culture diplomacy and expansion of soft power (Iwabuchi 2015, 422–423).

Chapman's use of the term 'oriental cool' rather than 'Japanese cool' suggests an interesting nuance in the consumption of such 'exotic' cultural imports. Unlike the 'Cool Japan' and 'Japan's Gross National Cool' concepts that gained traction in the early 2000s as public relation strategies that were heavily promoted by Japan's Ministry of Economy, Trade, and Industry (METI) (Chapman 2015, 356–357), 'oriental cool' is not necessarily associated with one particular culture or country. Instead, the use of the word 'oriental' implies a general association with Asia. According to Edward Said, the term 'oriental', which is steeped in subtext of historical knowledge and power, 'designated Asia or the East, geographically, morally, [and] culturally'. He notes that the word could be used to describe anything from an atmosphere, to a tale, or a mode of production, and the meaning would be entirely understood as pertaining to a 'foreign and distant' outside of the heteronormative collective consciousness of European descent (Said 2003, 31–32).

Chapman (2015, 357) states that, either intentionally or unintentionally, descriptions and depictions of *The Samurai* were often 'essentialist and orientalist', highlighting the audience's over-simplified understanding of Asian pop-culture productions. I suggest that Chapman's use of 'oriental cool' in relation to *The Samurai* describes a scenario in which Australian audiences were acutely aware of the 'culturally odour-ful' and exotic nature of the media they were consuming, but that they did not necessarily associate that odour with Japan. Rather, such cultural depictions may have been viewed as part of a wider concept of 'Asia' or 'the Orient' or even more vaguely as 'foreign'. With the Second World War still in recent memory, and Australia still subsisting under White Australia Policy, it is not unreasonable to suggest that many Australians in the 1960s would have had, at best, a rudimentary understanding of Asian traditions and cultures. Media imports and localised depictions of the exotic East will have contributed to both positive and negative orientalist views of shows such as *The Samurai* at the time.

I suggest that terms such as 'oriental cool' would be ideal for describing the popularity of transcultural productions that are not limited to one particular culture, such as *Monkey*. Despite the fact the term has been in use since the 1940s, there is still no universal consensus defining the term 'transcultural'; however, it has been generally used in relation to the cultural change and exchange in colonial and postcolonial contexts (Berry and Epstein 1999, 3–4). In recent years, technological advancements have amplified the ease and speed of the globalisation process, making terms such as 'transcultural' increasingly relevant and useful. Its use also recognises that countries are not necessarily monocultural, and that productions even from a single nation may be composed of a variety of cultural inputs including ethnic, professional, racial, sexual, and linguistic, among many others. As such, transculturalism can be defined as 'an open system of symbolic alternatives to existing cultures and their established sign system' (Berry and Epstein 1999, 24).

The difference of utilising a transcultural model lies in what Berry and Epstein describe as the expansion of the limitations of a singular cultural identity. Unlike the homogenisation of the 'melting pot' metaphor, or the cultural specificity of the multicultural model, transculturalism recognises the importance of one's cultural origins, but also that one is not bound to remain within the confines of such borders. Instead, it 'stresses the power of confluences, overlappings, and interactions'

116 *Rebecca Hausler*

that can and often do transcend the border of any one single culture (Dagnino 2015, 1). When a transcultural lens is applied to literary and cultural productions, it has the effect of making 'all cultures look decentered in relation to all other cultures, including one's own' (Berry and Epstein 1999, 312). Considering the impact of globalisation on the modern world, such a lens is needed to 'connect works which are no longer identifiable with only one culture or one national landscape' (Dagnino 2015, 8). I argue that a production such as *Monkey*, which derives its spiritual origins from India, its literary origins from China, before being further influenced and altered by translations and adaptations in both Japan and Britain, constitutes a transcultural work that has expanded (and continues to expand) beyond any one cultural or national background.

From China to Japan: Monkey's journey through the East

The 1978 Japanese television series *Saiyūki* was exported to a number of countries, including New Zealand, India, and Mexico, and dubbed into a number of languages, including English and Spanish (Sun 2018, 119). Despite this worldwide distribution, the series attracted the most widespread attention and longevity in the United Kingdom and Australia. In order to understand the background of this television series, I will first briefly explore the history of *The Journey to the West*, before discussing the history of the Japanese television production itself.

Based on an actual religious pilgrimage by a monk named Xuanzang, the Chinese oral folktale *Xiyouji* or *The Journey to the West* appeared as a written novel of one hundred chapters in the late 16th century (Chen 2009, 26–27). While there has been some disagreement regarding the original author of the written text, contemporary scholars have generally attributed its authorship to Wu Cheng'en, a respected writer from the Qing dynasty (Yu 2012a, 21–23). *The Journey to the West* recalls the pilgrimage of the monk Xuanzang from China to India to obtain Buddhist scriptures, accompanied by Sun Wukong the supernatural monkey, Zhu Bajie the pig monster, and Sha Wujing the river monster. Needless to say, the actual Xuanzang was unlikely accompanied by such a colourful and magical troupe. The monkey king, who almost usurps the monk as the hero of the story, has been attributed by several scholars as part of a shared motif between China and India of monkey lore (Yu 2012a, 10). These shared motifs, originating from India's Spirit Vulture Mountain and China's Lingyin Monastery, focus on depictions of various species of simians "as beings capable of responding to Buddhist evangelistic speech and action" (Yu 2012a, 10–11). Early Indian references to a great monkey leader date back even further, to around the 1st century. In the tale of *Mahākapi Jātaka*, as illustrated in the Buddhist complex of Sāñchī, the leader of a great monkey tribe is depicted as a preincarnation of Buddha, as evidenced by his enlightened state (Marshall 1918, 70). Further evidence of this shared motif is seen in the Sanskrit name the protagonist monk is gifted in *The Journey to the West*, which refers to the 'three baskets' in which the holy scriptures from the West were kept (Miller 2015, 64; Wu 2012, 128). As such, we can see that even in the story's very early origins, there has been a sharing between cultures in order to elevate this tale to something much greater than simply the tale of a pious monk.

Written records of the story appearing in Japan have been traced back to the 13th century through the Kōzanji monastery in Kyoto. The two texts *Xindiao Da Tang Sanzang Fashi Qujingji* ('*The Newly Printed Record of the Procurement of Scriptures by the Master of the Law, Tripitaka, of the Great Tang*') and *Da Tang Sanzang qujing shihua* ('*The Poetic Tale of the Procurement of Scriptures by Tripitaka of the Great Tang*') feature minor linguistic differences but essentially depict the Chinese story faithfully (Yu 2012a, 7). In the Tokugawa period (1603–1868), at least two versions were rewritten into Japanese and became popular books read for entertainment, rather than for religious purposes. According to Kameda-Madar, *Tsūzokusaiyūki* ('*Popular Journey to the West*') was translated and disseminated in 1758 using a combination of kanji and katakana, followed by an illustrated version in 1806, *Ehonsaiyūki* ('*Illustrated Journey to the West*'), which used both kanji and hiragana, providing a text that was presented in a more reader-friendly format. He notes that *Ehonsaiyūki*'s illustrations were in the style of *ukiyo-e*, with contributions made by the likes of famed woodblock artist Hokusai Katsushika (Kameda-Madar 2011, 156). Considering issues of translation and simplification, as well as the accompaniment of pictorial representation to the text, the story had already likely changed to incorporate Japanese cultural nuance in these later editions.

Undergoing a process of metamorphosis from oral folktale to written text in a number of languages and dialects, versions of the Chinese story had been a literary and entertainment mainstay in Japan for at least several hundred years before its foray into the relatively new medium of television and film. Japan released several filmic interpretations, such as Toho Studio's *Songoku* in 1940, which was remade again in 1959 (Galbraith 2008, 43, 155–156), as well as an animated version by Toei Studios in 1960 (Clements 2013, 214). In the late 1970s, as part of its 25th anniversary celebrations, Nippon Television commissioned a dramatisation of the popular story entitled *Saiyūki*, which they were hoping would be popular with adults and children alike (Clements and Tamamuro 2003, 199). The characters of the monkey Son Gokū, pig-man Cho Hakkai, ex-cannibal kappa Sa Gojō, and a transformative dragon/horse Gyoku Ryū accompany the monk Sanzō Hōshi on his journey west, defeating a plethora of miscreants and demons and making for compelling television. Unfortunately, as only two seasons were made, the group never made it to India to obtain the holy scriptures, much to the chagrin of fans.

While several aspects of *The Journey to the West* lent themselves well to the television production, *Saiyūki* differed in several ways. Daniel Kane has noted that while the series was 'based on the original characters . . . and brought out their characteristics very well: the monk with a mission, the restless, rebellious monkey, the easy going, gluttonous, lustful pig, and the mournful, pessimistic sand spirit', he held reservations about other aspects of *Saiyūki*'s adaptation, stating that overall the series had 'little reference to the original book' (Kane 2008, xxix). One aspect of the series that Kane took issue with was the casting of women in several male roles. While the original story was dominated by male characters, the Japanese production included a number of actors in roles that did not match their assigned gender. For example, the role of Buddha was played by the prolific actress Takamine Mieko ('Mieko Takamine' 2018), while the Bodhisattva Guanyin/Kannon, a deity depicted in female form since China's early Ming dynasty (1368–1644) (Yuhang 2012, 76), was depicted as a male. Perhaps the most famous gender swap involved the boy monk Sanzō Hōshi, who was played by actress and model Natsume Masako. While Japan has a history of women playing beautiful male roles, for example in Japan's Takarazuka all-female theatre troupe, according to an interview with actor Sakai Masāki, who played Son Gokū, the reason for casting Natsume came down to ratings. He supposed that 'if only men were used it would not be interesting, so the thought of using beautiful Natsume Masako for the role of the priest . . . added to the buzz that was generated by the programme' (Divola 2001, 121). Such changes led Kane to note that the Japanese series as an interpretation of *The Journey to the West* was 'truly weird' (Kane 2008, xxvii).

Nippon Television not only cast beautiful and famous female roles to enhance audience interest, but they also cast a number of well-known personalities as well. The role of the monkey king was played by actor and singer Sakai Masāki. Sakai was credited as introducing the 'Monkey Dance' craze to Japan, which was similar in style to other fad-style dances of the 1960s such as the 'Twist' (Clements and Tamamuro 2003, 199). Thus, his casting as the monkey character Son Gokū playfully highlights the use of celebrities to appeal to older parental audiences. Also enjoying musical success as part of the 'Group Sounds' movement which swept Japan in the 1960s was Kishibe Shiro, who before being cast as river-dwelling kappa Sa Gojō, enjoyed success both in Japan and internationally with his band The Tigers (Carter 2000, 13). Other notable celebrity cast members included Nakamura Atsuo and Inoue Takao, who had both starred in a number of high-profile shows prior to their guest roles in *Saiyūki*.

Furthermore, unlike previous live-action incarnations of the martial arts drama, *Saiyūki* capitalised on advancements in special effects allowing the monkey king's magical abilities to come to life. Key effects included Son Gōku's cloud flying (activated by his trademark finger-blowing gesture) and his transformation into creatures and objects, as well as the representations of his magical staff. All were executed with greater finesse than was possible in previous filmic adaptations, such as the 1959 film *Son Gokū*, which relied upon animation and substitution splices. Although laughable by today's standards, at the time the special effects were more fluid and were able to more closely mimic the magical visuals achieved in animated productions such as the 1960 anime production of *Saiyūki*.

Don't let translation get in the way of a good story: Monkey's journey to the West

In order to understand the success behind this television series, I will first explore the translational history of *The Journey to the West* in Britain, before tracing instances of 'oriental cool' during the 1960s and 1970s which paved the way for shows such as *Saiyūki* to be introduced into the cultural consciousness of Britain and Australia. Finally, I will discuss the BBCs alterations to *Saiyūki* and the show's impact on Australia, which would reverberate for decades to come.

The Journey to the West was initially adapted for the English-speaking world in 1913 as *A Mission to Heaven* by Timothy Richard, with another version appearing in 1930 by Helen M. Hayes entitled *The Buddhist Pilgrim's Progress*. Both versions were merely brief paraphrases of the original tale; Richard's text was heavily abridged, and Hayes's text, though readily accessible, was criticised for inaccuracies (Yu 2012b, xiii; Waley 1984, 8).

In 1942 English academic Arthur Waley released *The Journey to the West* as a translated novel entitled *Monkey* (Wu 1984). Unlike other scholars of the period who merely 'dabbled in Orientalia', Waley possessed a vast knowledge of both European and Asian culture and language (De Gruchy 2003, 14). According to John Walter de Gruchy, Waley possessed a great aptitude for foreign languages and was familiar with eleven languages before embarking upon his studies of both Chinese and Japanese. Waley had also previously worked in the British Museum cataloguing Chinese and Japanese art and translating Chinese and Japanese poetry (De Gruchy 2003, 55). He had received praise and acclaim for his translation of the Japanese novel *The Tale of Genji*, which had taken him some twelve years to complete, 'securing his reputation as one of the most successful and influential translators of the twentieth century' (De Gruchy 2003, 118).

Due to the immense length of Wu Cheng'en's *The Journey to the West*, Waley's translation was an abridged form of the text with only approximately one-third of the original included and many chapters, portions of chapters, and poems omitted entirely (Yu 2012b, xiii). Waley's introduction addresses these omissions. Unlike other translations and abridgements of the tale which sought to tell the full one hundred chapters in a very condensed format that often removed characters' dialogue altogether, Waley chose an almost polar approach, omitting many chapters or 'episodes' but translating the retained chapters 'almost in full'. He does, however, note that he deliberately excluded many of the poetic verses that feature in *The Journey to the West*, due to the fact that in his opinion they could not be adequately translated into suitable English prose (Waley 1984, 7). Perhaps due to the novel's shortened nature (a mere 336 pages compared to other translations such as Anthony Yu's approximately 1,900-page work), Waley's very readable translation still remains one of the most famous and widely read versions of the tale in English (Yu 2012b, xiii).

As part of Waley's translation, the character's names were anglicised to convey a sense of the allegorical nature of the travellers. Waley's interpretation of these characters was that Monkey 'stands for the restless instability of genius'; Pigsy 'symbolises the physical appetites, brute strength, and a kind of cumbrous patience'; Sandy 'is more mysterious . . . [and] in some inexplicable way essential to the story . . .' (Waley 1984, 8). Finally, for Waley, the monk 'Tripitaka stands for the ordinary man, blundering anxiously through the difficulties of life' (Waley 1984, 8). These anglicised names were retained for the BBC's dubbed series, also entitled *Monkey*, as well as for subsequent productions of the tale in English.

Kane notes that Waley's translation 'reflects the taste of the urbane British reader of the thirties' (Kane 2008, xxviii), with *Monkey* exhibiting a distinct British quality. As noted by Waley in his introduction, '*Monkey* is unique in its combination of beauty with absurdity, of profundity with nonsense' (Waley 1984, 7). Perhaps it is this combination of elements which makes this story so attractive to the British reader. As Agata Figiel notes, '[h]umour in most British comedies is based mainly on absurdity, irony, sarcasm, situational humour, surprise and unpredictability, together with humiliation' (Figiel 2015, 44). Therefore, a television production such as *Saiyūki* which provided such a comedic and whimsical reinterpretation of *The Journey to the West* was sure to appeal to British, and later Australian, television audiences.

The timing of the BBC's interest in this Japanese martial arts drama tied in with a general interest in 'oriental cool' during the 1960s and 1970s. It was during these decades when media such as books, magazines, and major motion pictures 'brought Asian martial arts – and especially karate – into the daily lexicon of popular culture' (Miracle 2016, 94). Unlike the traditional heroes of Hollywood Westerns, who needed guns and horses to outmanoeuvre their enemies, masters of the oriental martial arts could take down an army with nothing but their bare hands. Several popular American productions helped propel this 'oriental cool' into the spotlight, including the Billy Jack series of action films 'The Born Losers', as well as the television series 'Kung Fu', which starred David Carradine. This period also saw an increase in Asian faces on screen, such as in the James Bond film *You Only Live Twice*, and more authentically in Bruce Lee's *Enter the Dragon* or Jackie Chan's *Drunken Master*. In Australia, the Japanese series *The Samurai* was incredibly popular during this time.[1] These years also saw in increase in martial arts schools and instructional guides with a focus on the masculine sporting prowess, rather than the philosophical and esoteric practices of the arts (Miracle 2016, 94). However, despite this increased interest towards oriental exports, as one BBC commentator put it, 'if it's to be a success at all, there is no choice but [to present it in] English' (BBC Archive 2016). Like many imported films and series at the time, subtitles were not popular among English-speaking viewers, so rewriting and dubbing was deemed necessary.

The 1978 Japanese drama *Saiyūki* was thus rewritten into English and given the new title *Monkey*, not only making it more palatable to an English audience, but also acknowledging Waley's well-known translation of the Chinese source text on which the television series was based. The task of rewriting *Monkey* for an English-speaking audience was performed by well-known television writer David Weir, who had success with yet another Nippon Television series entitled *The Water Margin*, which began screening on the BBC in 1976 (BBC Archive 2016; Household 1979, 15). As a predecessor to *Monkey*, for many children in the United Kingdom, *The Water Margin* was their first encounter with the Far East and was presented in an easily accessible television format. Weir was enlisted to convert and rewrite *The Water Margin* into English, despite the fact he had never undertaken this sort of work before, nor did he understand any Japanese.

The irrepressible magic of Monkey 121

According to a BBC interview, 'David Weir is the man who's got the job of putting English words, into Japanese mouths, in this the film of a Chinese legend'. According to Weir, his process involved watching each episode many times over, in order to get a feel for what he needed to convey. He would then write two versions of the script: an ideal version where they would say what he would most like them to say, and then a version where their words fitted closely with the actors' lip movements. Weir felt no pressure to ensure his scripts correlated with the original dialogue, noting that far from being a translation of the original, he could make them say 'anything at all, of course' (BBC Archive 2016).

Also working with Weir was Michael Bakewell, who was the dubbing editor and director. He worked with the voice actors to ensure that the dialogue fitted the visuals as closely as possible, to help avoid the cheap and often ridiculous visuals that accompany films with poorly synchronised dubbing. These substandard offerings were usually dubbed haphazardly in English, creating a disconnect between the movement of the mouths and the spoken dialogue. This was further heightened when accents did not match the audience's presumption of the speaker's native tone. In some cases, this was done with such reckless disregard that it became a trope of the genre and a source of comedy for the befuddled viewer, as was the case with the English rendition of *The Samurai*.

Bakewell stated 'at first [we thought it] was undubbable because of the vast Japanese performances we didn't think we could get any kind of English equivalent to those at all . . . We therefore decided that the only way to get at it was to do it in what I can only describe as kind of English-Oriental tradition. It's somewhere in-between Fu Man Chu and the Goon show' (BBC Archive 2016). The behind-the-scenes footage shows Bakewell's 'English-Oriental tradition' in action, with him directing the voice actors to 'make it a bit more Chinese-y' when he felt their acting sounded 'a bit [too] English' (BBC Archive 2016).

In the three years following his work on *The Water Margin*, Weir developed a strong interest in Asia, researching and travelling to China, Japan, and India.[2] It was during this time that he also took an active interest in the teachings of Buddhism and Taoism (Household 1979, 15–16), which likely influenced his writing style on the English dub of *Monkey*.

Weir and Bakewell's team stripped *Monkey* down to 39 episodes from the original 52 shown in Japan due to time constraints necessary for the work provided in rewriting and dubbing the show. This gave Weir the freedom to create dialogue that would more closely fit the mouths of the actors, but also let him inject idiomatic British humour into the show. While the lip movements were far from a perfect match, the vocal disparities were noticeable enough for it to provide an element of comedy without being too distracting. The voice actors' quasi-oriental accents clearly mismatched the visual cues of an ancient Asian legend, which was then overlaid with localised British-style humour. The combination of these effects took the humour to a whole new level bordering on gag-dubbing. While it would be difficult to create such an effect today without causing racial offense, a similar gag-dub style can be seen in videos featured on the popular YouTube channel 'Bad Lip Reading' (2018).

Weir's British humour often meant that the dialogue was imbued with subtle sexual overtones, enough to keep older audiences amused, but to fly straight over the heads of younger viewers, much like Monkey on his magic cloud. Take for example a scene in the opening episode where Monkey is trying to capture one of the heavenly figures named Star Vega. As she is saved by one of her male servants (the yet-to-be-banished Pigsy), in the original Japanese she mutters '*kimochi wa warui wa*', suggesting that she feels 'disgusted' by the situation. In the English version, however, the meaning is totally inverted when Pigsy threatens to report Monkey to the Emperor of Heaven for his attack on Star Vega, and she mutters they are 'just good friends', insinuating a kind of hidden sexual or romantic relationship. Such cheeky lines and common speech allowed the dialogue to become reconceptualised into an ironic, playful, and postmodern take on the classic Chinese story, as well as the martial arts genre. There is also a plethora of contemporary slang which is knowingly out of place with the context of the show, as best exemplified by the insults characters used towards each other. For example, insults such as 'poofter' or 'sissy' were bantered about during over-the-top flight scenes between Monkey and the various demons he battled against. These slurs, while more commonplace in both Britain and Australia in the 1970s, make for uncomfortable viewing in later decades, in light of their derogatory and homophobic connotations.

The writers also sought to include humour through the pseudo-philosophical musings of the omnipresent narrator. Due to the nature of the Buddhist pilgrimage story, philosophical teachings of the way of the Buddha such as the cultivation of good and moral restraint gave the show an air of seriousness, which was juxtaposed by the silliness of the dialogue and playful acting. These teachings were seamlessly interwoven with nonsensical kōans, which could easily be missed if you were not paying attention. Lines such as 'when what is indestructible meets what is irresistible, the female all too often wins' or 'if goodness is like a mountain, sometimes it is equally hard to achieve' were constantly sprinkled through the show's narration. Much of this wordplay would have been aimed at older audiences who could detect such slips and provided humorous appropriations of the genre's philosophical tropes.

The rewritten dialogue and narration often played into the slapstick physical humour of the series. Aside from the fight scenes, visual humour such as Monkey enduring debilitating physical pain as punishment for his misdeeds or petty quarrels resulting in scuffles between the monstrous travellers were not uncommon. These types of visually humorous scenes were not dissimilar from the slapstick humour portrayed in English speaking comedies such as Fawlty Towers, and differed from the more serious fight scenes seen in other martial arts film and television exports. These visual gags, even without the aid of the altered script, were able to transcend cultures and age brackets, providing something that all audiences could recognise and enjoy.

The final element that set this show apart from other traditional Sino-Japanese dramas, and arguably the one that helped drive the success of the series, was the choice of soundtrack. Unlike other martial arts series or period dramas, which used oriental styles of music to purvey a sense of traditionalism or exoticism to the shows, the Japanese producers of *Saiyūki* chose to opt for contemporary pop music sung in English, which was also retained and used in the BBC production. Japanese band Godiego created the soundtrack for the series, with synth keyboards, guitars, and drums creating a funky beat that could not be more far removed from the traditional flutes and percussions that audiences may have expected. Godiego's sound channelled a funk quality which originated in African American culture and was popular during the 1960s and 70s. These contemporary sounds accompanying martial arts fight scenes certainly made the scenes feel more comedic and imbued them with a sense of contemporary coolness. The title track, 'Monkey Magic', featured a lyrical opening hook followed by a quirky summary of the legend of *Monkey*:

> Born from an egg on a mountain top
> The punkiest monkey that ever popped
> He knew every magic trick under the sun
> To tease the gods
> And everyone, and have some fun
> Monkey magic, monkey magic, monkey magic, monkey magic, ooooooh.

While Godiego was a Japanese band, its members were composed of both Japanese and non-Japanese members, including Mickie Yoshino, Yukihide Takekawa, Steve Fox, Takami Asano, and Tommy Snyder. According to Billboard magazine, Godiego had previously worked with Nippon Television and sought to tap into international success by singing in English rather than Japanese. Godiego's single of 'Ghandhara/Monkey Magic' was a number-one hit in Japan, selling over 1 million copies, with the full album *Magic Monkey* selling 600,000 copies (Fukatsu 1979, J14). While the soundtrack did not chart as well overseas, the catchy title song is still well known in Australia today.[3]

From BBC to ABC: Monkey works his magic down under

Weir's British humour was popular in Australia, and *Monkey* was an unexpected hit with audiences. The shared nuances between the two countries' wit is evidenced by the number of British comedies that enjoyed successful runs on Australian television, such as *Grim Tales*, which shared the same after-school time slot as *Monkey* on the ABC's *The Afternoon Show*. In reflecting on *Monkey*'s popularity, both with adult and child-aged viewers, I will explore the popular reception the series received through *Monkey*'s original and repeated television appearances and reportage of the series in the media, as well as noting how the cultural specificity of the show became further distorted, with *Monkey* being interpreted as more Japanese than British or Chinese.

The program originally aired in Australia daily for several months in 1981, before a number of repeat airings were screened in 1983, 1984, 1988, 1990, and 1992 in the late after-school time slot of around 6 pm. For most children, this meant they could enjoy a temporary escape into the fantasy of heroic journeys in faraway lands, away from their suburban realities.

When the series initially hit Australian shores in the early 1980s, several articles were run in the influential *Australian Women's Weekly* magazine. In 1981, several short articles written by the abrasive Ian Rolph (the 'TV critic who writes without fear or favour') criticised *Monkey*'s appearance on Australian airwaves. In Rolph's first article, under the subheading '*Monkey* . . . for peanut brains', he begins with a xenophobic and woeful pun in pidgin-style English; 'Confucius say: He (or she) who watch new ABC programme called *Monkey* must have gone bananas'. He asserts his prophetic power as a television critic by asserting that there 'is no chance that the population at large will go ape over *Monkey*', describing the series as 'madness [which defies] description'. Rolph wondered if the fact that the series was Japanese 'could explain its different slant on entertainment' before proceeding to describe lead actor Sakai Masāki as 'an actor with an unpronounceable name and a totally forgettable face' (Rolph 1981a, 115).

Several weeks later, in July 1981, Rolph wrote a second column about the series after receiving a large number of letters from '*Monkey* minions all around the country'. His opinion piece dominated the page with the bold headline '*Monkey* nuts show no sign of cracking!' Holding fast to his disastrous puns and negative initial review, he stated that after watching three episodes of the show, he 'was almost driven to commit Hara-Kiri. Or even chop-suey-cide!' conflating both Japanese and Chinese terms in equally poor taste. He continued his tirade by claiming that the (previously unpronounceable) names of the Japanese actors had become 'etched into [his] cerebral hemisphere for ever and a day. They even disturb my sleep like a terrifying Oriental nightmare' (Rolph 1981b, 114). While the prickly tone of his criticisms was not dissimilar to other television offerings that he found unpalatable, his criticisms seem to be expressed primarily in discriminatory and often racist comments about the show's cast, storyline, or background. While Rolph may have embodied the sentiments of an older generation who were unhappy to see Asian faces on Australian screens given Japan and Australia's wartime history, the younger generation of fans who inundated Rolph's mailbox with letters of protestation were no doubt the ones actually keeping him up at night.

Apparently, the magazine's 'letterbox ran hot' with a 'torrent of abusive mail' following Rolph's comments (Flynn 1981, 165). Several letters to the editor were published over a number of weeks from both adult and younger viewers of the show, critical of Rolph's reception and eager to defend the series. Viewers pointed out erroneous facts in his articles, his inability to understand a show that children can easily grasp, and the fact that there are thousands of viewers – both adult and children – who like the show and regularly tune in. One letter in particular perhaps encapsulates Australian audiences' reaction to the series best: 'Your criticism of *Monkey* displays a distinct lack of sensitivity, or perhaps you did not bother to watch the series beyond the first episode? I, too, was startled initially because the presentation is alien to our western senses. But *Monkey* grows on you!' (Rolph 1981c, 115). As with *The Samurai* that came before it, audiences with 'western' perspectives seemed unsure of how to receive *Monkey*. Not only was the show seen as foreign, it was outright 'alien', despite (or perhaps because of) the familiar injection of British humour and English dialogue. Suffice to say that while 1980s Australian audiences did not really know what it was that they were watching, they certainly liked it.

Australian Women's Weekly quickly realised that Rolph's opinions were unpopular among readers and ran a full-colour double-page spread on the series some weeks later. In a more even-toned piece, Greg Flynn, after 'scurrying back to [his] TV set for another look at *Monkey*', provides a more adequate plot summary of the show, noting that it is a 'Japanese made series' about a 'fivesome' composed of a 'youthful Buddhist priest, a monkey-man, a smallish gentleman who fell into the body of a pig, an artistic type who lived under water, and a dragon-turned-horse' and their journey 'across 16th century China to India to retrieve some holy scriptures'. Upon revisiting the series, Flynn saw the humour in *Monkey*, noting that it was 'good for a laugh' due to its 'creaky visuals, second-hand philosophy, choreographed kung-fooey, and plenty of puns'. Flynn also wonders whether the humour injected into the BBC version is retained in the original Japanese series, judging the dubbed version as a 'combination of the absurd and the profound' (Flynn 1981, 165).

While Flynn's article coincided with the re-running of the series on the ABC after its initial success, it was also clearly an attempt to subdue fans angered by Rolph's previous comments. However, unlike other British-based programs that were equally 'absurd' if not more so, *Monkey* was continually mocked even while it was being praised, seemingly due to its Asian origins. The language that both Flynn and Rolph use shows their casual and overt racism towards the show, which also extended to viewers who enjoyed the series. In these articles, fans are referred to in derogatory terms such as 'cultists',[4] 'nuts', and 'freaks' (Flynn 1981, 164). By insulting not only the show, but also the fans, it seems these commentators tried, and failed, to intimidate readers into abandoning the show. The written responses to Rolph and the longevity of the show prove as much.

After several years of hiatus off air in the mid-1990s, *Monkey* made a resurgence in 1999 and 2000 to appeal to a new audience, targeting older teenage and young adult viewers. *Monkey* was aired on Saturday mornings, replacing the alternative music and pop culture show *Recovery* hosted by Dylan Lewis. *Monkey* would have been familiar viewing to audiences who remembered the show from their childhoods and sought to relive that nostalgia.

A number of magazines and newspapers, including *Rolling Stone Australia* and *The Age*, among others, ran stories and interviews on the series when VHS copies were released in the early 2000s (Divola 2001, 121; Maunder 2000). Even though times had changed, there was still a focus on the 'strange, bizarre, absurd, silly and [yet] wildly entertaining' pull of the show (Divola 2001, 121), although thankfully its fans were no longer referred to as 'freaks'. Critics in the new millennium held *Monkey* in high esteem, rather than berating it with racist taunts like 1980s commentators such as Rolph did, highlighting the vast change in critical reception of the show and, arguably, of Japanese cultural productions on a whole. Trish Maunder's article and interview with Sakai was touted as 'an attempt to understand the enduring appeal of a TV show that combines hokiness and Buddhism', indicating that despite the passing of several decades, the show, while loved by many, was still incomprehensible to some. Maunder suggests that *Monkey* 'sounded a little too eloquent, if not philosophical, for success' in the 1980s, as Australian audiences were not used to being asked to 'consider concepts such as [the] "essences of heaven" and metaphysical musings such as "with our thoughts we make the world"' (Maunder 2000). However, despite any reservations Maunder may have had about *Monkey*'s impact on audiences down under, it seems that the popularity of, and nostalgia for, the series has continued to grow, as evidenced by the number of reinterpretations of *Monkey* in theatre, music, and television that have proliferated in Australia over recent years.[5]

Conclusion

While the series has remained popular in Australia, its history and relevance as a Japanese imported series has been given little academic attention. The history of *Monkey* highlights the diversity of the folktale from its origins hundreds of years ago, through to the contemporary interpretations and continued interest by Australian audiences. I suggest that for most Australians, it is not the classic Chinese tale they connect with, but a comical Japanese appropriation of a 16th-century Ming dynasty novel, which was in turn bastardised by British writers and voice actors to create something incredibly unique. While interest in Japanese and Asian popular culture grew exponentially from the 1980s onward, *Monkey*, much like *The Samurai*, was a trailblazer in introducing Australian audiences to Japanese cultural productions. Admittedly *Monkey* is problematic in its transcultural representation of Asia, as it failed to clearly delineate itself as either Japanese or Chinese to early audiences, playing into public perceptions of a generic 'orientalness'. However, to its credit, *Monkey* gave valuable screen time to a diversity of stories and nations onscreen, while offscreen, it highlighted changing public opinions towards racial diversity onscreen and the public's interest in exploring alternative forms of popular culture outside the Anglosphere.

In my brief exploration of the story's origins and histories, it is apparent that while the story may have been originally developed and written in China several hundred years ago, *The Journey to the West* has been added to, appropriated, and reimagined for almost as long. The Japanese television drama *Saiyūki* provided a transcultural medium for the show to reach a much wider audience outside of Asia, and its reworking into a distinctly British piece of humour allowed it to become overwhelmingly successful both in the United Kingdom and Australia.

While initial media response to the program in 1981 highlighted continued averseness to Asian cultural imports, the success of the show and audience feedback showed that younger generations of Australians were ready to move past the consternations of the Second World War and embrace 'oriental cool'. While perhaps audiences were left feeling confused or alienated over religious, historical, or mystical elements that they had not seen on their television screens before, it certainly was not enough to put them off. In fact, this state of ecstatic confusion made an indelible mark on the public, building upon an increasing global interest in Asian cultures and inducing a powerful nostalgia that would be felt for decades to come.

Given Australia's relationship with Japan, and more recently with the rise of China, it is perhaps unsurprising that the show has remained a cult classic here. Ongoing interest in and reinterpretations of the show in Australia continue to absorb audiences and attract media attention, and while the style of reproductions may be moving away from the 1980s *Monkey* we all know and love, its continued relevance in our globalised world highlights the increasing awareness of due care when exploring literature, history, and cultural offerings of countries and cultures other than our own. In considering the show's history, which has enjoyed such long-running success and was created from such disparate cultural elements, recreating something as unique as *Monkey* seems impossible. However, perhaps this transcultural phenomenon is best summarised by a quote from the show itself: 'The harp does not play music if its strings are too tight or too loose. The music comes only when the strings are stretched just right'.

Notes

1 See Chapman 'Suburban Samurai and Neighbourhood Ninja: Shintarō and Postwar Australia'.
2 Weir also travelled throughout Thailand and Nepal. See Household, 'Monkey Business'.
3 Katori Shingo, the lead actor in a 2006 *Saiyūki* remake, was surprised to learn that Australians knew not only of the story but knew Godeigo's title track by heart. See McLeod, 'Cult TV series Monkey is being remade in Japan'.
4 The term "cult" was also used in media reports on the popularity of the 1960s Japanese television series *The Samurai*. See Chapman, 'Suburban Samurai and Neighbourhood Ninja: Shintarō and Postwar Australia'.
5 The most recent example being the 2018 television series *The New Legends of Monkey*. See Hausler 'Far from white-washing, ABC's Monkey Magic remake takes us back to its cross-cultural roots'.

References

'Bad Lip Reading'. n.d. Accessed 15 January 2018, www.youtube.com/user/BadLipReading.
'BBC Archive', 21 September 2016, accessed 15 November 2016, www.facebook.com/BBCArchive/videos/292232651149772/.
Berry, E. E. and Epstein, M. N. 1999. *Transcultural Experiments: Russian and American Models of Creative Communication*. New York: St. Martin's Press.
Carter, Y. 2000. 'Irrepressible!', *The Guardian: The Guide*, 31 March.
Chapman, D. 2015. 'Suburban Samurai and Neighbourhood Ninja: Shintarō and Postwar Australia', *Japanese Studies*, 35 (3): 355–371.
Chen, I. 2009. 'Monkey King's Journey to the West: Transmission of a Chinese Folktale to Anglophone Children', *Bookbird*, 47 (1): 26–33.
Clements, J. 2013. 'Tezuka's Anime Revolution in Context', *Mechademia*, 8: 214–226.
Clements, J. and Tamamuro, M. 2003. *The Dorama Encyclopedia: A Guide to Japanese TV Drama Since 1953*. Berkeley: Stone Bridge Press.

Dagnino, A. 2015. *Transcultural Writers and Novels in the Age of Global Mobility*. West Lafayette: Purdue University Press.

De Gruchy, J. W. 2003. *Orienting Arthur Waley: Japonism, Orientalism, and the Creation of Japanese Literature in English*. Honolulu: University of Hawai'i Press.

Divola, B. 2001. 'Hey, Hey, He's the Monkey', *Rolling Stone Australia*, 582.

Figiel, A. 2015. 'British Humour as Part of Contemporary *Homo Ridens:* Based on an Exploration of the Comedy Series *Fawlty Towers*', *Styles of Communication*, 7 (1): 39–58.

Flynn, G. 1981. 'Twisting Monkey's Tale', *Australian Women's Weekly*, 22 July, 134–135.

Fukatsu, K. 1979. 'Artists and Producers Strive for Inroads Overseas', *Billboard*, 26 May.

Galbraith, S. 2008. *The Toho Studios Story: A History and Complete Filmography*. Plymouth: Scarecrow Press.

Hausler, R. 2018. 'Far from White-Washing, ABC's Monkey Magic Remake Takes Us Back to Its Cross-Cultural Roots', *The Conversation*, 31 January, https://theconversation.com/far-from-white-washing-abcs-monkey-magic-remake-takes-us-back-to-its-cross-cultural-roots-90853.

Household, N. 1979. 'Monkey Business', *Radio Times*, 2922.

Iwabuchi, K. 2002. *Recentering Globalization: Popular Culture and Japanese Transnationalism*. Durham: Duke University Press.

———. 2015. 'Pop Culture Diplomacy in Japan: Soft Power, Nation Branding and the Question of "International Cultural Exchange"', *International Journal of Cultural Policy*, 21 (4): 419–432.

Kameda-Madar, K. 2011. 'Transmission of Meanings: A Study of Shen Wai Shen (Body Outside Body) by Xu Bing', in R. T. Ames and T. Hsingyuan (eds.), *Xu Bing and Contemporary Chinese Art*. Albany: State University of New York Press.

Kane, D. A. 2008. 'Introduction', in T. Richards (ed.), *The Monkey King's Amazing Adventures: A Journey to the West in Search of Enlightenment*. North Clarendon: Tuttle Publishing.

Marshall, Sir John. 1918. *A Guide to Sanchi*. Calcutta: Calcutta Superintendent Printing.

Maunder, T. 2000. 'Monkey Grips the World', *The Age*, 15 September.

McLeod, S. 2006. 'Cult TV Series Monkey Is Being Remade in Japan', *ABC News*, 18 February, accessed 15 November 2016, www.abc.net.au/radio/programs/am/cult-tv-series-monkey-is-being-remade-in-japan/802690.

'Mieko Takamine'. n.d. *IMDB*, accessed 15 January 2018, www.imdb.com/name/nm0847302/?ref_=nmbio_bio_nm.

Miller, S. 2015. *A Strange Kind of Paradise: India Through Foreign Eyes*. London: Penguin.

Miracle, J. 2016. *Now With Kung Fu Grip! How Bodybuilders, Soldiers and a Hairdresser Reinvented Martial Arts for America*. Jefferson: McFarland and Company.

Rolph, I. 1981a. 'Monkey . . . for Peanut Brains', *Australian Women's Weekly*, 10 June.

———. 1981b. 'Monkey Nuts Show Signs of Cracking!', *Australian Women's Weekly*, 8 July.

———. 1981c. 'Your Say', *Australian Women's Weekly*, 1 July.

Said, E. 2003. *Orientalism*. London: Penguin.

Sun, H. 2018. *Transforming Monkey: Adaptation and Representation of a Chinese Epic*. Seattle: University of Washington Press.

Waley, A. 1984. 'Introduction', in A. Waley (ed.), *Monkey*. London: Unwin.

Wu, C. 1984. *Monkey*, A. Waley, trans. London: Unwin.

———. 2012. *The Journey to the West: Revised Edition*, A. C. Yu, trans. Chicago: University of Chicago Press.

Yu, A. C. 2012a. 'Introduction', in A. C. Yu (ed.), *The Journey to the West: Revised Edition*. Chicago: University of Chicago Press.

———. 2012b. 'Preface to the First Edition', in A. C. Yu (ed.), *The Journey to the West: Revised Edition*. Chicago: University of Chicago Press.

Yuhang, L. 2012. 'Oneself as a Female Deity: Representations of Empress Dowager Cixi as Guanyin', *Nan nü*, 14: 75–118.

8 Nikkei Australian identity and the work of Mayu Kanamori

Timothy Kazuo Steains[1]

Introduction

> When people like Murakami, myself and all of us who have left our ancestral home lands go on holiday, we often go back to where our loved ones live to reconnect and rekindle that love. And then we go back to another life in another place with others to love.
> – Mayu Kanamori, *Yasukichi Murakami*

In the passage above, Mayu Kanamori meditates on Japanese Australian experiences of moving and belonging between Japan and Australia. She highlights a sense of distance between the two countries, combined with the feelings of love and attachment associated with each place mingling together within the self. Rather than simply envisioning a separateness between Japan and Australia, she shows how Nikkei Australian (Japanese Australian) experience involves an internal conversation between the two. This is a conversation of diverse emotional pulls, social ties, and senses of belonging. By rethinking boundaries between Japan and Australia, I bring this conversation to our own understanding of the idea of 'Japan in Australia'.

Is 'Japan in Australia' intended to bring a Japanese studies lens to the historical and contemporary flows of Japanese people and cultures into Australia? Or does it also consider how Australian studies might inform such approaches? Where does Nikkei identity fit within these frameworks? Of course, these frameworks do not necessarily stand in opposition to each other, and in this chapter I explore the linkages and spaces between them. In fact, I argue that Nikkei identity is uniquely positioned to ask productive questions about identity and what it means to work between Japanese and Australian studies (especially Asian Australian studies). To that end, I explore Japanese Australian artist Mayu Kanamori's body of work to examine the similarities and differences in conceptualising 'Japan in Australia' and 'Nikkei Australia'.

Questions of national identity in contemporary academic studies often centre on the hybrid and transnational character of such identities. In *Resilient Borders and Cultural Diversity: Internationalism, Brand Nationalism, and Multiculturalism in Japan*, Koichi Iwabuchi examines the transnational flows that disrupt bordered, self-contained understandings of nation: 'notions such as hybridisation, deterritorialisation and transnationalism have drawn our attention to cross-border interaction, fusion, and mobility, which seriously put the clearly demarcated national cultural borders into question' (Iwabuchi 2015, 1). Iwabuchi tempers this now-familiar form of analysis with an awareness of the 'resilient borders' that are incited by the push towards internationalism. David Chapman's work on the *koseki* family registry highlights this resilience through a focus on the barriers that multinational individuals and families face in claiming Japanese nationality. His suggested changes to the system attempt to 'adequately and appropriately address the increasingly diverse and multifaceted population of residents living in Japan today' (Chapman 2016, 64).

Studies of Australia's interconnectedness with Asia also draw attention to the diverse cross-cultural realities within the nation. Fran Martin et al. explore how public discourse on 'Asia', as well as the lived realities of migrants and international students, reveal the cultural and national mixedness of Australian life: 'the recognition that the translocal, inter-cultural experience that I argue is a defining feature of contemporary Australian life must profoundly (re)shape our understanding of both the nation, and our selves' (Martin et al. 2015). Asian Australian studies highlights how diasporic Asian Australian identities also trouble the boundaries of nationhood: '[A] diasporic framework foregrounding tropes of hybridity and mobility decentres the nation as the ultimate signifier by emphasising the multiple and heterogeneous forms of belonging to, and traveling within and beyond, the nation' (Lo 2006a, 17).

Are Nikkei Australian people evidence of the transnationalisation of Japan or Australia – or both? If both, how do we account for this position between Japanese and Australian frameworks that Nikkei Australians fall into? Jacqueline Lo's contention that diasporic identities garner multiple senses of belonging may offer a way forward in thinking through this problem. The test of the modern multicultural nation often appears to be its ability to allow a sense of 'belonging' to its marginalised and racialised groups. Iwabuchi stresses the importance of 'ensuring neglected voices are expressed and heard in the public space and giving due recognition to marginalised subjects as full members of the national society' (Iwabuchi 2015, 5). Writing on Australian multiculturalism, Ghassan Hage examines the 'mis-interpellation' that happens when migrants are ostensibly included into a multicultural identity while at the same time suffering from exclusion from true senses of national belonging:

> When the nation hails you as 'hey you citizen' everything in you leads you to recognize that it is you who are being hailed: but you reply 'yes it is me' you experience the shock of rejection where the very ideological grid that is inviting you in the nation expels you through the petty and not so petty acts of exclusion that racists engage in in their everyday life.
>
> (Hage 2010, 245)

Exclusion from national belonging represents a key point of contention for racialised minorities. The desired outcome for these minorities is apparently a full, authentic, and unambiguous sense of belonging to the nation. However, does this desire for total belonging represent the persistence of national frameworks in our thinking about identity? Are we not simply reproducing the logic of nationalism by demanding inclusion in Australia or Japan? A similar critique can be lobbed at racial identities, such as Asian Australian or Japanese Australian identity. Paul Gilroy criticises 'the ethnic absolutisms that have offered quick ethnic fixes and cheap pseudo-solidarities', which reproduce the fiction of race: 'Too often in this century those folk have found only that shallow comfort and short term distraction in the same repertory of power that produced their sufferings in the first place' (Gilroy 2000, 6).

Thus, Lo's version of 'multiple and heterogeneous forms of belonging' within the Asian Australian subject appears to offer a more disruptive version of identity than in many ethnic identity models. Japanese people exhibit significant ambiguities in their senses of belonging to Australia. As Kanamori and Masako Fukui note, most Japanese migrants to Australia do not identify as Japanese Australian or as Nikkei, but as 'Japanese living in Australia' (Fukui and Kanamori 2017, 8). For some Japanese migrants to Australia, 'belonging' does not seem to be a high priority. 'Belonging' to Australia and Japan can of course take many forms and include many contradictory and ambivalent feelings.

'Nikkei Australian' as a category contains within it feelings of belonging, desires for belonging, feelings of unbelonging, and feelings of being in between. Kanamori's art project *In Repose*, for instance, raises the question of whether a migrant to Australia can belong in Aboriginal country. What does it mean to desire belonging when that belonging is predicated on colonial theft? Thus, the precarious and still unformed term 'Nikkei Australian' draws out the deep ambivalence around belonging embedded not only in Japanese Australian experience but in any experience of national identity. In drawing Japan and Australia together under a shared sign, 'Nikkei Australia' delinks us from national frameworks and offers new possibilities for identity. In this sense, 'Nikkei Australia' does not secure a rigid identity category so much as it attempts to reveal a productive and creative tension between Japanese and Australian culture.

Each of Kanamori's works offers a different way of questioning, critiquing, and re-evaluating belonging in Japanese and Australian contexts. In this way, her body of work draws attention to the varied manifestations of Nikkei Australian experience, and offers innovative ways of connecting Japanese and Australian cultural identity. Her works ask questions about how to belong in Australia or in Japan; they highlight gaps in belonging; they examine feelings of intergenerational migrant affiliation, or a lack of such affiliation; they consider feelings of cross-ethnic migrant solidarity. In this chapter, I show how each work showcases a creative interpretation of the shifting boundaries between Japan and Australia.

Nikkei Australia

In order to show how Kanamori's work sheds light on the particularities of Nikkei Australian identity, I provide a brief history of the Nikkei Australia research group, outline the identity questions that arise out of the group's initiatives, and further elaborate on the differences I see between the concepts of 'Japan in Australia' and 'Nikkei Australia'.

Nikkei Australia activities involve a varied group of people and projects. These projects include community engagement related to Japanese Australian history, academic and journalistic work related to Japanese Australian history, academic and journalistic work on contemporary Japanese Australian cultural products and questions of identity, and art projects that explore Japanese Australian experience.

As Kanamori and Fukui highlight in 'The Creation of Nikkei Australia: Rediscovering the Japanese Diaspora in Australia', Nikkei Australia was founded during the Civilian Internee Project. This project included the erection of the Civilian Internment Interpretive Board at the Cowra Japanese War Cemetery (CJWC) and a two-day international symposium entitled 'Civilian Internment in Australia During World War II: History, Memories and Community heritage' – both events took place in 2014. CJWC is an important landmark in Nikkei Australian history; it does, of course, hold the bodies of many of the Japanese soldiers that perished during the Cowra Breakout. But 189 of the 524 graves there are those of Japanese civilian internees who died in the Australian internment camps during the war (this number also includes 10 sea merchants) (National Archives of Australia, n.p.). There was no existing information at the cemetery to explain the civilian graves that visitors encounter. The history of not only Japanese internment but Japanese residence in Australia was not properly acknowledged. Kanamori, Lorna Kaino, Keiko Tamura, and Yuriko Nagata collaborated to create the interpretive board in order to provide information about the graves and the history that they are attached to. This board represents 'the first public acknowledgement of the history of Japanese civilian internees in Australia' (National Archives of Australia, n.p.). The symposium also included an arts program co-ordinated by Kanamori that will be explored later in this chapter. The Nikkei Australia website includes information on the current projects and existing work of its members (Nikkei Australia, n.p.).

Nikkei are Japanese diasporic people; the term is often associated with poor Japanese migrants who left Japan in the nineteenth century in search of work and livelihood. In the Americas there are large groups of people who identify as Nikkei, and there are Pan American Nikkei events where Nikkei groups bond over their shared Japanese diasporic heritage. Ayumi Tekanaka writes of such an event: 'Even though participants spoke different languages (Spanish, Portuguese or English), many claimed "something common", or, as Ricardo Hirota put it, "some affinity that we naturally feel toward Nikkei from other countries"' (Ayumi Takenaka 2009, 1326). Part of the desire for Nikkei Australian identity is of course to be part of this larger global community of Japanese diasporic peoples. But the local connections are important, too. In the United States, Japanese Americans constitute a historically significant place within the larger Asian American community. As Rey Chow observes (albeit in a rather critical way), internment in the US context created a memory of marginalisation and exclusion that offers a rallying point for Japanese American identity (Rey Chow 2002). This experience of marginalisation connects them to the broader feelings of marginalisation shared by the Asian American community. However, because the Australian government forcibly repatriated the Japanese that they interned (Nagata 1996, 212), this history of marginalisation is not part of the identities of the many Japanese who immigrated to Australia after the Second World War. As Fukui and Kanamori note, many Japanese Australians are not even aware of this history (Fukui and Kanamori 2017, 7). Thus Japanese Australian identities are severed from this Nikkei history; the Nikkei Australia project is, in some part, an attempt to reconnect Japanese Australian identity to this history. This is not an attempt at rallying around feelings of marginalisation but rather a desire to acknowledge the individuals and events that have shaped Japanese residence in Australia. While some of us may not have direct family ties to this history (although some in the group certainly do) (Andrew Hasegawa 2014, n.p.), seeing ourselves as part of this history ties us to a Japanese Australian heritage that unsettles the tendency to separate out Japan and Australia, and it opens up the possibility of building a sense of community that is sorely lacking amongst Japanese Australians.

Nikkei Australia is indebted to the community and identity work created by the Asian Australian Studies Research Network. In many ways, I mirror the Nikkei identity I tentatively propose on the Asian Australian identity (or identities) modelled by the network. Lo writes of the network's use of ethnic and racial identity: 'the concept of race is not deployed as biological "fact" but rather used strategically to unite people of various Asian ethnicities thereby enabling a degree of political solidarity and critical purchase' (Lo 2006a, 15). Recent writing on ethnic identity has attempted to steer clear of the essentialist connotations of labels such as Asian American or Asian Australian. Vincent Cheng, for instance, argues that, 'as a functional (albeit patently artificial) category, "Asian American" is an inherently – and functionally – "mixed-race" identity and category' (Vincent John Cheng 2004, 143). The category itself contains an extremely heterogeneous mix of ethnic and racial groups – including many mixed race people – and can therefore be said to be 'mixed race'. The same could be said of Nikkei Australian: the term does not attempt to police an essentialist definition of Japanese Australian race or ethnicity, but rather contains ethnic mixedness (as we will see in Kanamori's work) and the possibilities of very different migration histories.

Nikkei Australian, as a tentative identity category, is not an existing identity so much as it is a project that the writers of this article are involved in, along with several others. I do not use this category with the belief that all Japanese living in Australia should adopt it. However, Nikkei Australian is roughly analogous to 'Japanese Australian' as opposed to 'Japanese in Australia'. Drawing hard distinctions between Japanese Australian and Japanese in Australia is redundant, and one could argue that Japanese in Australia disrupt national boundaries just as much as Japanese Australians. Therefore, Nikkei Australian constitutes more of an explicit or outward commitment to the enmeshment of Japanese and Australian cultures and identities. It is a hybrid position that intentionally disrupts the borders between Japan and Australia in self and practice. This is not to say that less intentional practices of hybridisation are less important or significant – or that I am not interested in those practices. The 'term' Nikkei speaks to the specificity of diasporic experience, as opposed to simply Japanese experience, and it is in this domain that our loosely formed category offers a space for self-conscious mixing between Japan and Australia.

The Heart of the Journey

The Heart of the Journey is a slideshow of hundreds of photographs that are accompanied by a soundtrack which includes Kanamori and Lucy Dann's voiceovers (Kanamori and Dann 2000). It explores the life and identity of Lucy Dann, a mixed race Japanese Aboriginal woman from Broome, Western Australia. Dann was not aware of her Japanese heritage until later in life, but, growing up, she had feelings of being different due to the comments of those around her: people called her 'round face' and 'moon face' and some would misrecognise her as Hawaiian. When Dann is told, in her adult life, that her biological father is Japanese, her identity as an Aboriginal woman goes through a process of change. She begins to see herself as Asian or Japanese, as well as Aboriginal, and goes on a journey, with Kanamori, to find her biological father in Japan. She feels affinity with her family due to their welcoming attitude and because of similarities in their physical appearance. As Lo argues, 'Dann and her Japanese relatives connect at the level of the body; each perceives the Other through the embodied Self, and vice versa' (Lo 2006b, 181). At the end of the slideshow, Dann's reunion with her father and his family lead her to a sense of wholeness: 'This confirmed me as a human being and where I stand in this world and who I am'.

While *The Heart of the Journey* is ostensibly about mixed race identity, it also highlights the fact of Aboriginality and its place within conceptualisations of Australian identity. In thinking about the connections between Australia and Japan, this slideshow raises the question of how to understand Australia in light of Australian Indigenous experiences. Can we draw a seamless connection between Indigeneity and Australianness, or do we need more sensitive and complex methods? Ikyo Day's study of this work places it within a transcolonial history of Japanese internment: Dann's father was interned. In addition, Dann's Aboriginal family's silence about her heritage was most likely because of the removal of mixed race children from Aboriginal homes: a part of Australian history known as the Stolen Generations (some argue that this process is still taking place today). However, Day rightly points out that *The Heart of the Journey* does not draw equivalence between Aboriginal and Japanese experiences of dispossession (Day 2010, 119). So the triangulated connections among Aboriginal, Japanese, and Australian identities are fraught just as they are lived and real.

Dann's story also draws attention to the culturally and racially mixed history of Australia during the nineteenth and twentieth centuries. Even during the white Australia policy, Japanese and other Asian individuals coexisted and commingled with white and Aboriginal people. Once aware of her heritage, Dann sees herself in the mixed population of Broome:

> I looked around and I see all the other kids. [I thought] hey I look something like that kid, oh I've got long black hair like this kid, I've got that chocolate colour and slanty eyes.
>
> (Kanamori and Dann 2000)

While colonial Australia attempted to separate itself geographically and racially from Asia, as David Walker and Agnieszka Sobocinska point out:

> Asia was never simply an external force to be resisted, placated or engaged. Even during the high point of the White Australia Policy several communities, particularly the northern port towns of Broome, Darwin and Cairns, had large Asian–Australian populations that sometimes outnumbered white residents.
> (Walker and Sobocinska 2012, 13)

Dann's discovery of the Asianness inscribed on her body and in her family history, for the audience, also serves as a discovery of the centuries-old history of racial and cultural mixture between 'Australians' and Japanese.

While Dann's Aboriginal identity is deeply rooted and secure, the discovery of her Japanese heritage creates a gap inside that Dann feels the need to fill. But as she travels to Japan to meet her family, she begins to feel insecure about whether her family will accept her: 'In terms of the colour of my skin, for me . . . in the back of my mind . . . [I worried that the Japanese relatives] might think I'm too black to be their sister'. There is a pull towards Japanese identity for Dann, but an uncertainty about whether she belongs in that identity. This feeling is typical of mixed race experience, and Gloria Anzaldúa describes it thusly,

> The ambivalence from the clash of voices results in mental and emotional states of perplexity. Internal strife results in insecurity and indecisiveness. The mestiza's dual or multiple personality is plagued by psychic restlessness.
> (Anzaldúa 2007, 78)

Dann's story shows how mixed race people can have an ambivalent sense of belonging to their cultural and racial heritages. It shows how belonging can take multiplicitous forms even within a single individual. These feelings can change with time and through interactions with others. The mixed race experience is an excellent metaphor for what Lo calls the diaspora's 'multiple and heterogeneous forms of belonging'.

Dann's acceptance by her family, and her feelings of affinity with the bodies of her relatives, seems to fill the gap that had been left by the secret of her Japanese roots. Despite her insecurities about what her family would think of her skin colour, 'their body language said it all . . . it didn't matter and like I said, stepsister or half-sister – [it] didn't matter'. The sense of wholeness that Dann feels shows how kinship can play a large role in enabling and/or disenabling feelings of belonging. The simple fact of one's race is not enough to secure clear-cut feelings of belonging to racial, national, or cultural identities. Dann's positive experience of reconnecting with her Japanese roots highlights an internal mixing of her Aboriginal Australian and Japanese selves. Anzaldúa, writing about mixed race Mexican American experience, says,

> The new *mestiza* copes by developing a tolerance for contradictions, a tolerance for ambiguity. She learns to be an Indian in Mexican culture, to be

Mexican from an Anglo point of view. She learns to juggle cultures. She has a plural personality, she operates in a pluralistic mode – nothing is thrust out, the good the bad and the ugly, nothing rejected, nothing abandoned. Not only does she sustain contradictions, she turns the ambivalence into something else.

(Anzaldúa 2007, 79)

The mixed race person's ability to draw together apparently opposing or contradictory cultural identities and perspectives speaks to the diasporic experience of negotiating overlapping cultural frames. Dann's ability to introduce her Japanese roots into her sense of self marks an internal shift in the borders between Japan and Australia (as contested a version of Australia her experience might represent). Likewise, Kanamori's creative role in *The Heart of Journey* presents us with a complex picture of belonging as well as unique possibilities for the mixing of Japanese and Australian cultures and identities.

In Repose and the Cowra Japanese War Cemetery Ceremonial Performance

In Repose (Kanamori 2007) and the Ceremonial Performance at the Cowra Japanese War Cemetery (Kanamori 2014) are performance works conducted at different grave sites housing Japanese people from different periods of Australian history. *In Repose* was performed at gravesites in Townsville, Broome, and Thursday Island – where Japanese civilians, mostly from the pre-WWII era, are buried. The Ceremonial Performance was of course performed at the Japanese War Cemetery in Cowra and commemorated the unveiling of the Civilian Internment Interpretative Board.

In Repose uses video, sound, and performance art at specific sites and represents *kuyo*: 'an act of ceremonial prayer or offering to respect, honour and calm the spirits of the deceased' (Kanamori 2008, 493). The work is a collaboration between Japanese Australian artists Wakako Asano (dance/choreography), Satsuki Odamura (*koto*/sound), Kanamori (visual art), and the Scottish Australian artist Vic McEwan (sound). The *kuyo* that these artists offer does not represent a traditional Japanese version of paying respect to the deceased. While traditional elements are included – such as the burning of incense and the ritual of pouring water on the graves (so that the spirits do not go thirsty) – the use of contemporary dance and modern *koto* music (commissioned by Odamura especially for this project, and composed by three different contemporary Australian composers) signifies a break from tradition and a process of adapting Japanese practices to fit new temporalities and geographies. In some performances Odamura collaborated with Indigenous musicians, creating cultural crossovers through music.

The *In Repose* ceremonies involved significant collaborations with local communities, including Indigenous ones. Part of the reason for this was because some of the cemeteries included the bodies of mixed Japanese Indigenous people. As Dann's story shows us, sometimes this mixed heritage is hidden from individuals and communities. At the Broome ceremony, Yawuru Elder Dorris Edgar gave a welcome to country and revealed that she had only recently learnt of her own Japanese heritage. One of her ancestors was in fact buried at the cemetery where the *kuyo* took place. As Lo writes, the *In Repose* ceremonies draw attention to the silent histories which continue to haunt Australia and its contemporary life. Lo quotes Avery, who describes haunting as 'when things are not in their assigned places [. . .] when disturbed feelings cannot be put away, when something else, something different from before, seems like it must be done' (quoted in Lo and Kanamori 2013, 68). For Kanamori, one of the things that had to be done was to illuminate and pay respect to Japanese Aboriginal ancestries as well as the history of Japanese residence in Australia.

In addition to this, *In Repose* creates a conversation between culturally different ways of understanding the dead. Japanese traditions maintain that if deceased persons do not have descendants to tend to their graves, the spirits become disconnected or homeless. The *kuyo* is an attempt to appease the souls and allow them to settle into the land and 'become part of the Australian landscape' (Kanamori 2008, 497). When discussing this idea with Yawuru elder Pat Dodson, Kanamori was told that his people believed that one's spirit returns to one's country upon death. Dodson believed that the Japanese people's spirits had already returned to Japan. Kanamori made the point that some of these people had made a life and a family on Australian land and that their spirits may have remained on country. These different conceptions of death reveal a significant ambivalence around who belongs to what country. *In Repose* does not propose a hard answer to this question; rather it presents an open-ended tension that complicates simplistic understandings of belonging.

The question of which spirits belong where informs the question of who amongst the living belong on what country. This performance work is partly a response to Kanamori's contemplation of *hone o uzumeru kakugo* – one's preparedness to bury one's bones. Kanamori's preparedness to bury her bones in Australia signifies her feelings of belonging to that country. One Japanese elder in Broome was particularly moved by Kanamori's contemplation of *hone o uzumeru kakugo* in her artwork, as he had also been thinking about becoming part of the landscape in death. Thus, *In Repose* serves as a meditation on belonging that draws Aboriginal, 'Australian', and Japanese identities into productive tension. It reminds us that any sense of migrant or settler belonging to Australia requires negotiation with Indigenous cultures and peoples. In this sense, it puts forward a nuanced and sometimes unsettling meditation on the unresolved questions that haunt not only Japanese Australian but also broadly Australian feelings of belonging on country.

The Ceremonial Performance at the Cowra Japanese War Cemetery also folds unresolved questions about the past into the present. There has been no formal apology by the Australian government for the internment of innocent Japanese civilians during the war – despite the fact that such apologies have taken place in the United States and in Canada. In addition to this, complicated questions of Japanese conduct during the Pacific War are raised alongside the injustice of internment. Japanese wrongdoing in this war remains a deeply divisive and contested issue in the Asian region, but local experiences of internment in Australia mean that questions of responsibility require reconciliatory work that must be informed by different cultural and community perspectives.

The arts program attached to the internment symposium and the unveiling of the interpretive board in Cowra extends the work of offering *kuyo* to Japanese spirits buried on Australian land. But it also creates cross-ethnic migrant connections in contemplating similar questions to those in *In Repose*. Kanamori included a contemporary Indonesian puppet show about the Indonesian political prisoners buried in the Cowra General Cemetery; this was created and performed by Indonesian Australian artists Jumaadi (puppeteer) and Ria Soemardjo (musician) together with local musicians and school children. Kanamori also collaborated with Malaysian Australian voice artist Weizen Ho and Jewish Australian movement artist Alan Schacher. Ho had an interest in working on appeasing the spirits of the dead, and Schacher had a personal interest in civilian internment because some of his family members are Holocaust survivors. Ho and Schacher created a performance with youths from Cowra and a local Japanese farmer and Shinto Sho player, Shigeki Sano. They directed and walked their audience from the Indonesian graves to the Japanese graves through music and dance. They merged with Buddhist priests who were chanting and ended their performance by guiding the commemorators to give water to the graves as is done in Japan.

The various artists contributed their different cultural, ethnic, and personal perspectives in the process of appeasing Japanese spirits at the cemetery. By moving the audience from the Indonesian graves to the Japanese ones, they establish a dialogue between cultural positions and show how the issues of exclusion and belonging raised by the graves are not isolated to individual racial and cultural groups. This performance makes a statement about how we cannot resolve these issues of belonging in the Australian national space unless we collaborate and cross racial and cultural borders. The creative mixing of cultural traditions and perspectives opens up a space of possibility for re-evaluating the rules of belonging and forming new futures for the nation. In this way, the ceremony rethinks the Japan Australia relationship by extending it into intercultural territory and versions of identity and cultural production that draw on multiple points of reference.

Yasukichi Murakami: through a distant lens

Yasukichi Murakami: Through a Distant Lens (Kanamori 2015) is a documentary theatre piece that takes the audience through Kanamori's journey of discovering the lost photographs of Yasukichi Murakami (played by Kuni Hashimoto), a photographer and inventor who moved to Australia from Japan in 1897 and died in Tatura Internment Camp in 1944. Kanamori (played as 'Mayu' by Arisa Yura) discovers details about Murakami's life, interviews his descendants, and converses with his ghost. She eventually finds many of Murakami's photographs in his home town of Tanami: he had them sent back to his family during his life in Australia. As in the previous works we have looked at, this play uncovers the history of pre-war Japanese residence in Australia.

Murakami's story speaks to the particularities of Japanese diasporic experience in Australia. The stage becomes a space for exploring this experience and realising the convergence of Japanese and Australian cultures. In Avtar Brah's influential book *Cartographies of Diaspora* (1996), she draws attention to the complicated multiplicities of what she calls 'diaspora space':

> Diaspora space is the intersectionality of diaspora, border, and dis/location as a point of confluence of economic, political, cultural, and psychic processes. It is where multiple subject positions are juxtaposed, contested, proclaimed or disavowed; where the permitted and the prohibited perpetually interrogate; and where the accepted and the transgressive imperceptibly mingle even while these syncretic forms may be disclaimed in the name of purity and tradition.
>
> (Brah 1996, 208)

The multiplicitous and contradictory influences on diaspora space are reflected in the play's complex understanding of belonging. Murakami's ghostly presence in Australia suggests that he belongs to Australia – especially in light of *In Repose*'s contention that Japanese ghosts have not returned to Japan, but haunt that Australian national space. However, towards the end of the play – when Mayu travels to Tanami, Japan – she muses on diasporic feelings of longing and belonging:

> When people like Murakami, myself and all of us who have left our ancestral home lands go on holiday, we often go back to where our loved ones live to reconnect and rekindle that love. And then we go back to another life in another place with others to love.
>
> (Kanamori 2015)

These mixed feelings about place and the networks that we have in different diasporic spaces highlight what Lo and Gilbert called the seminal motif of displacement in diasporic stories: these stories register 'the loss of place and belonging that migrancy entails' (Lo and Gilbert 2010, 152). Here, ambivalent feelings about space and place highlight the varied forms of personal and cultural investment that national spaces can have – and also how individuals can have multiple sources of such investment. As Thomas Hammar observes, 'national identity is not a zero-sum game, which means that individuals do not have a limited number of "identification units" that they have to divide between different groups and that, therefore, the increase in identification with one country proportionately reduces ties to the other' (Naujoks 2010, 13). The Australia that we see in this play represents a diaspora space mixed with various practices, identities, and feelings of belonging.

The search for Murakami's photographs animates the plot of the play; however, the photographs themselves stand in for the lived realities of Japanese Australian experience. They are physical, conceptual, and emotional evidence of Nikkei Australian life. Thus, the search for the photographs can in many ways be a search for the reality of Nikkei identity. *In Repose* attempts to 'connect the living to the dead so that the departed may find peace away from the natal land. . . . By putting the dead to rest, the work offers an opportunity for the present generation of immigrant Japanese to create a sense of ethical belonging' (Lo and Kanamori 2013, 70). Similarly, *Yasukichi Murakami* connects past Nikkei Australians to present-day Nikkei Australians and attempts to create coherence around that identity. This is especially so given that internment is such a formative part of North American versions of Nikkei identity.

However, Mayu (the character who represents Kanamori in the play) finds it quite difficult to uncover all the details of Murakami's life. Not only is the location of the photographs a mystery, but the ghost of Murakami shields his personal life – especially his marriage to his first wife Eki – from Mayu. In this way, part of Mayu's journey is a realisation that she cannot know all the truth about Murakami's existence. Murakami parallels the difficulties of attaining truth in history to the difficulty of capturing truth in photography:

> Photographs – they reveal, and at the same time, conceal the truth. In that split second when the shutter falls, we grasp all that is real, all that is hidden and all that may be forgotten. A great photographer leaves in the photograph, a trace of what we thought we had grasped. Mayu san, sometimes, you have to listen to see. Sometimes we have to learn to know there are things we cannot photograph.
>
> (Kanamori 2015)

The impossibility of any hard truth that can be captured and contained reflects the impossibility of truly attaining a perfect, authentic ethnic identity. Vincent J. Cheng highlights the anxiety in our contemporary world around needing to claim an authentic, distinctive cultural subjectivity, saying, 'previously distinct cultures suffer an anxiety about the perceived loss of identity and subjectivity, thus requiring the continuing construction and maintenance of fantasmatic identities and authenticities so as to continue to be able to assert difference and superiority' (Cheng 2004, 6).

If the whole truth cannot be captured in the photograph, what can be, according to Murakami? He says to Mayu,

> Go and get your tripod, and set it up.
> Put it on a slow shutter speed.
> See what you find.
> You may see something deeper. Beyond.
> Maybe you will capture a movement of spirit, where all seems set in stone.
>
> These graves are not going anywhere.
> The perfect subject matter on a morning like this.
> Beautiful soft light . . .
> Still, silent, with history.

142 *Timothy Kazuo Steains*

Look at all these people buried here.
Not only them. Forgotten, forgotten people.
Far away from their home, their families,
they came here, lived once,
and contributed to the history of this country,
to our history.

You owe it to them, Mayu san,
To take the time to listen.
Breathe, see, and listen.
                    (Kanamori 2015)

What is the 'movement of spirit' that Mayu can capture when she breathes, listens, and sees? This moment comes at the end of the play when Mayu is taking a photograph of one of Murakami's photographs that were sent to Tanami (Kanamori 2012). This is the last image projected onto the back of the stage.[2]

Photographing Murakami's images inspires an uncanny moment of ghostliness. Kanamori sees beyond the image, as if channelling Murakami's call to 'breathe, see, and listen' (see Figure 8.1). As Kanamori writes in her blog:

As I looked through the viewfinder onto this photograph to photograph it, I intuitively knew the exact spot Yasukichi had focused on – the eyes of young Kathleen. I too focused on her eyes, and she was returning my gaze. Or was it Yasukichi's gaze? [In] the viewfinder, for a moment, I thought was Yasukichi. Or was it Yasukichi's ghost photographing through me?[3]

Figure 8.1 Kathleen and Y on buggy

In this moment of possession, the audience becomes another. As they look at this image on the stage, the audience feels Mayu's and Murakami's presences in their own gaze. For a moment they feel a heightened sense of being more than one person: they are multiple persons. This moment holds the revelatory truth of the play. It passes the audience beyond the threshold of being one/self: they identify with the other in themselves. The non-Japanese audience, especially, becomes the cultural and racial other and experiences an expanded sense of cultural identity. They discover the Asianness imbedded inside the Australian self and open to what Julia Kristeva calls 'the foreigner within' (Kristeva 1991, 191). This process of identifying with the other reflects what Kuan-Hsing Chen calls 'becoming others', a form of identification that attempts to do away with essentialist versions of identity (that is, identity politics) that perpetuate the lie of race (Chen 2010, 99). By destabilising bounded identities and becoming others, we open to new possibilities in cultural, racial, and national identification. The ending of *Yasukichi Murakami* asks us to imagine, within ourselves, a thoroughly mixed version of self that goes beyond an exclusive Australian or Japanese Australian identity. The Australian audience interfaces with Nikkei Australian experience and internalises that difference in the self, and Nikkei Australian identity opens out and interfaces with the multiplicitous identities present in the audience. The play relinquishes restrictive identities that garner closed forms of belonging and gestures towards new and unprecedented forms of personal and cultural exchange between Japan and Australia.

You've Mistaken Me for a Butterfly

The final work to be explored in this chapter is a work in progress. It has been performed at the University of Wollongong, The University of Western Australia, and the National Portrait Gallery. For this work, Kanamori collaborated with composer and musician Terumi Narushima. Like *The Heart of the Journey*, it is a slideshow work that contains music and voiceover. It is the first performance work associated with Kanamori's research of the story of Okin, a Japanese woman who came to live in Australia in the late nineteenth century. Kanamori found Okin's story looking through historical archives at the National Library of Australia. She found information regarding a court case where two white men (Gleeson and Frances) were accused of raping Okin with the help of another man (Edwards). This took place in the town of Malcolm, not far from the town of Butterfly. The men claimed that Okin was a sex worker and that they had paid for sex with her. The contrasting testimonies eventually led to the acquittal of the men. *You've Mistaken Me For a Butterfly* explores Kanamori's own reactions to, and meditations on, this historical material.

The use of the word butterfly, of course, references the famous trope of the Madame Butterfly which continues to structure representations of Asian women in the West today (Degabriele 1996). By drawing on this stereotype, Kanamori leads the audience into a re-evaluation of gendered attitudes towards Japanese women. Okin may have been a *karayuki-san* – that is, one of the many Japanese women who travelled out of Japan to do sex work around the time of Okin's story. As Bill Mihalopoulis writes,

> the movement of young Japanese women into sex work occupations abroad was one spontaneous reaction by the rural poor to the radical social restructuring unfolding in Japan from the 1850s onwards, coeval with the increase in mobility offered to them by their incorporation into a money economy that transgressed national boundaries and borders.
>
> (Mihalopoulos 2001, 170)

As such, their history represents the unique struggles and innovations of Japanese women during a period when Japanese identity was undergoing significant change. Their adaptations to transnational environments are emblematic of Nikkei women's experiences around the globe.

Of course, the trope of the Madame Butterfly brings with its familiar Orientalist images of the helpless and hyper-sexualised Asian woman yearning for a white saviour. Kanamori hints at this narrative structure through the white police officer (Donovan) who 'saved' Okin from her alleged rapists. At the same time, she is not willing to accept such a characterisation of the relationship between Okin and the police officer – 'Don't tell me this is yet another story about our hero rescuing a princess'. Kanamori draws the audience in by inviting something of an Orientalist gaze and then staging a reimagining of that gaze. This becomes possible through the central problem of the impossibility of determining what really happened to Okin. Kanamori does not want to shy away from the possibility that Okin may have been a *karayuki-san*; she wants to speak back to the shame surrounding Japanese women's sex work. As Mihalopolous writes,

> as a way of life, the existence of the karayuki-san, young Japanese women with all their imaginings, and wantings, trying informally to seek work abroad, was just as valid and inseparable from other forms of life exploding into existence in Meiji Japan
>
> (Mihalopoulos 2001, 170)

In addition, Kanamori does not want to dismiss the possibility that Okin was raped, despite the fact that it is impossible to confirm this possibility today. By that same token, Kanamori does not wish to assign guilt to the white men who were accused of raping Okin either – there is no way of determining whether they were her rapists or not. Kanamori challenges the preconceived notion that,

> Because I am Japanese and a woman . . .
> I would tell Okin's story in a certain way
> Perhaps that of sympathy, and talk of the men that raped her as evil . . .'
>
> (Kanamori 2017)

Interpreting the historical records becomes a process of reading and interpreting female Japanese identity. What history does Kanamori want to tell? How will this story reflect her own views about gendered Japanese diasporic experience?

> How I tell Okin's story can change not only Okin's
> But my own past and my future
> Just like in quantum physics
> The here and now can change the past and the future
> How I make my art
> How you view my art can change the past and the future for us all
> (Kanamori 2017)

Telling Okin's story is in part about how we tell our story, and, by extension, how we understand the place of Nikkei in Australia. The narrative constructed by the identity politics that followed postcolonial scholarship is one that can sometimes result in a narrow conception of victimised people of colour and victimising white people and their cultures. Characterising our narratives of belonging or unbelonging to a nation in this limited way does not allow for a hopeful politics of identity and community. We need more than simply narratives of oppression and victimisation. At this present time, we also need narratives of survival, change, and creativity.

Kanamori's ruminations on Okin's story lead her to the surprising determination to forgive those accused of raping Okin and focus on that which draws all in this story together.

> There is a temple for Karayuki-san
> Here, Karayuki-san who left home to work all over the world
> Have set their own names and their donations for their local temple in stone
> Here I prayed I prayed for Okin
> For Enaba [a man Okin lived with], for Donovan,
> And for Gleeson, Francis and Edwards too
> I prayed for you, and for me
> And for all wounded souls
> I prayed that our wounds be healed
> And that I may love
> We may love
> Compassionate love
> That heals all wounds in time (Kanamori 2017)

As Vera Mackie writes, 'Kanamori refuses to work with simple binaries of white/non-white, male/female, good/evil, victim/agent, preferring an openness to the complexities of historical interpretation' (Kanamori and Mackie 2017, 393). By letting go of the old dominator/dominated hierarchies that we often use to make sense of racial relations in Australia, Kanamori opens us to new possibilities in constructing diasporic narratives – and new possibilities for understanding Australian social life.

Kanamori could not initially find any other information on Okin, so she assumed that Okin had left the country at some point after the trial. However, new evidence suggests that Okin may have been interned. If this is the case, and if this project develops further, Okin's story will no doubt move beyond an inversion of the Orientalist frames of Japanese female experience and shed light on the tactics, practices, and ways of loving that characterise female Nikkei experience. The story that remains to be told would give life to the creative and innovative practices that Nikkei women employ in drawing together their Japanese and Australian cultural perspectives.

Conclusion

Nikkei Australian experience allows us to think through the similarities and differences between the concepts of 'Japan in Australia' and 'Japanese Australian'. The productive questions to be drawn from this discussion allow us to add subtlety and complexity to the interactions and cross-sections between Japanese and Australian peoples and culture. I argue for the importance of conscious and creative practices of mixing and hybridising Japanese and Australian identities and cultures. Mayu Kanamori's work exemplifies just such a commitment to creative intercultural engagement. As I have shown, Nikkei feelings of belonging can take many different forms and can raise many different questions in relation to national identity. Each of the works explored in this chapter illuminates its own important preoccupations with the nature of belonging for Japanese Australian people. Kanamori's work calls for a passionate scrutiny of diasporic histories in and between Australia and Japan, it calls for inclusive and evolving forms of Nikkei Australian identity, and it anticipates Nikkei Australians' future contributions to new ways of understanding the relationship between Japanese and Australian lives.

Funding disclosures

In Repose was funded by the Australian government through the Australia Council for the Arts and the Regional Arts Fund; the Queensland government through Arts Queensland; Japan Foundation, Sydney; and supported by Canon Australia, Kumon Australia & New Zealand, and Akira.

Civilian Internment Arts Program/Cowra Japanese War Cemetery Ceremonial Performance was funded by the Australian government through the Regional Arts Fund; the NSW government through the Regional Arts NSW and Arts NSW; Japan Foundation, Sydney; and was supported by Cowra Shire Council, Japanese Gardens and Cultural Centre, Arts OutWest, Aircalin and Rosnay Organic.

Yasukichi Murakami: Through a Distant Lens was funded by the Australian government through the Australia Council for the Arts; the Northern Territory government through the NT Heritage Grants; Japan Foundation, Sydney; Playwriting Australia; and supported by Macquarie University Faculty of Arts, Department of Media, Music, Communication and Cultural Studies.

You've Mistaken Me For a Butterfly was funded by the National Library of Australia through its Japan Studies Grant program; and Institute of Advanced Studies, University of Western Australia.

The Heart of the Journey was funded by the Australian government through the Australia Council for the Arts; ABC Radio National; Japan Foundation, Sydney; and supported by the Australian Embassy, Tokyo.

Nikkei Australia's website was funded by Japan Foundation, Sydney.

Notes

1 This chapter was created in conversation with Mayu Kanamori and is inspired by her keynote address at the 2016 'Japan in Australia' conference. My interview with her took place on December 15, 2017.
2 Image taken from Mayu Kanamori, 'About Murakami'.
3 Ibid.

References

Anzaldúa, G. 2007. *Borderlands: The New Mestiza = La Frontera*. San Francisco: Aunt Lute Books.
Brah, A. 1996. *Cartographies of Diaspora: Contesting Identities*. New York: Routledge.
Chapman, D. 2016. 'Identifying and Defining Self in a Changing Japan', in S. R. Nagy (ed.), *Japan's Demographic Revival: Rethinking Migration, Identity and Sociocultural Norms*. Singapore: World Scientific Publishers, 63–80.
Chen, K. H. 2010. *Asia as Method: Toward Deimperialization*. Durham, NC: Duke University Press.
Cheng, V. J. 2004. *Inauthentic: The Anxiety Over Culture and Identity/Vincent J. Cheng*. New Brunswick, NJ: Rutgers University Press.
Chow, R. 2002. 'The Secrets of Ethnic Objection', in *The Protestant Ethnic and the Spirit of Capitalism*. New York: Columbia University Press, 128–152.
Day, I. 2010. 'Alien Intimacies: The Coloniality of Japanese Internment in Australia, Canada, and the U.S.', *Amerasia Journal*, 36 (2): 107–124.
Degabriele, M. 1996. 'From Madame Butterfly to Miss Saigon: One Hundred Years of Popular Orientalism', *Critical Arts: A Journal of Cultural Studies*, 10 (2): 105.
Fukui, M. and Kanamori, M. 2017. 'The Creation of Nikkei Australia: Rediscovering the Japanese Diaspora in Australia', *Journal of Australian Studies*, 41 (3): 388.
Gilroy, P. 2000. *Against Race: Imagining Political Culture Beyond the Color Line*. Cambridge, MA: Belknap Press of Harvard University Press.
Hage, G. 2010. 'Intercultural Relations at the Limits of Multicultural Governmentality', in D. Ivison (ed.), *The Ashgate Research Companion to Multiculturalism*. Farnham: Ashgate, 235–253.
Hasegawa, A. 2014. 'Story of Hasegawa Family by Andrew Hasegawa', 6 October, accessed 15 January 2018, www.nikkeiaustralia.com/story-hasegawa-family/.
Iwabuchi, K. 2015. *Resilient Borders and Cultural Diversity: Internationalism, Brand Nationalism, and Multiculturalism in Japan*. Washington, DC: Lexington Books.
Kanamori, M. 2007. *In Repose*. Performed at various sites in 2007 and 2008, accessed 15 January 2018, www.youtube.com/watch?v=TtnVX25f7og.
———. 2008. '"In Repose": A Photo-Essay', *Journal of Australian Studies*, 32 (4): 493–497.

———. 2012 'About Murakami', accessed 15 January 2018, https://aboutmurakami.wordpress.com/2012/05/10/the-family-photo-album-2/.

———. 2014. *Ceremonial Performance*. Performed at Cowra Japanese War Cemetery, 9 March, accessed 15 January 2018, www.youtube.com/watch?v=38rjafIV_1M.

———. 2015. *Yasukichi Murakami Through a Distant Lens*. Performed at Griffin Theatre Company, 10–21 February.

———. 2017. *You've Mistaken Me for a Butterfly*. Performed at University of Western Australia, 25 September.

Kanamori, M. and Dann, L. 2000. 'Heart of the Journey', *Radio Eye*, ABC Radio National, 12 August.

Kanamori, M. and Mackie, V. 2017. 'You've Mistaken Me for a Butterfly', *Japanese Studies*, 37, (3): 387.

Kristeva, J. 1991. *Strangers to Ourselves*. New York: Columbia University Press.

Lo, J. 2006a. 'Disciplining Asian Australian Studies: Projections and Introjections', *Journal of Intercultural Studies*, 27 (1): 11–27.

———. 2006b. '"Queer Magic": Performing Mixed-Race on the Australian Stage', *Contemporary Theatre Review: An International Journal*, 16 (2): 171–188.

Lo, J. and Gilbert, H. 2010. 'Diasporas and Performance', in K. Knott and S. McLoughlin (eds.), *Diasporas: Concepts, Intersections, Identities*. New York and London: Zed Books, 151–156.

Lo, J. and Kanamori, M. 2013. 'Returning Memory to Earth: Towards Asian-Aboriginal Reconciliation', *Crossings: Journal of Migration & Culture*, 4 (1): 67–78.

Martin, F., Healy, C., Iwabuchi, K., Khoo, O., Maree, C., Yi, K. and Yue, A. 2015. 'Australia's "Asian Century": Time, Space and Public Culture', *Japan Focus: An Asia Pacific E-Journal*, 13 (6): 1–7.

Mihalopoulos, B. 2001. 'Ousting the "Prostitute": Retelling the Story of the Karayuki-San', *Postcolonial Studies*, 4 (2): 169–187.

Nagata, Y. 1996. *Unwanted Aliens: Japanese Internment in Australia*. St Lucia, QLD: University of Queensland Press.

National Archives of Australia. 'Japanese POWs and Internees Buried or Cremated in Australia', A8234, 13B, Cowra Japanese Military Cemetery.

Naujoks, D. 2010. 'Diasporic Identities – Reflections on Transnational Belonging', *Diaspora Studies*, 3 (1).

'Nikkei Australia', 15 January 2018, www.nikkeiaustralia.com/.

Takenaka, A. 2009. 'How Diasporic Ties Emerge: Pan-American Nikkei Communities and the Japanese State', *Ethnic and Racial Studies*, 32 (8): 1325–1345.

Walker, D. and Sobocinska, A. (eds.). 2012. *Australia's Asia: From Yellow Peril to Asian Century*. Crawley, WA: UWA Publishing.

9 Trans-Asian engagement with Japan in/and Australia

Koichi Iwabuchi

Introduction

In a globalised world, a comprehensive study of any country or region requires us to take into consideration cross-border mobility, connections and exchange and understand how transnationally shared issues are specifically and interrelatedly articulated in a particular country or region. A growing trend of trans-Asia approaches is indicative of the imperativeness of such examination. This chapter will consider the significance of trans-Asia approaches and their potential to further advance the study of Japan in Australia with a particular focus on the ways in which such approaches productively situate 'Japan', 'Australia' and researchers in trans-Asian mobilities and connections. I will first discuss how trans-Asia approaches to human mobilities and cultural connections are beneficial to develop 'the study of Japan' in Australia. Trans-Asia approaches, it will be argued, fruitfully engage with globally shared issues that Japan faces through intra-regional comparison, referencing and interaction. Then I will discuss their implications for the advancement of the study of 'Japan in Australia' and the reimagination of the Japan-Australia relationship, referring to my research projects. Trans-Asia approaches also urge researchers to situate the study of Japan in the intricate relationship between Australia and Asia – Australia as part of Asia and Asia as part of Australia. Furthermore, it will be suggested that a trans-Asia perspective urges researchers engaging with human mobilities and cultural connections between Japan (and Asia) and Australia to cultivate a bird's-eye view and foster collaboration across divides and beyond academia to tackle transnationally shared issues.

Trans-Asia approaches to media cultural connections and human mobilities

In the last 20 years, we have observed the rise of trans-Asia or inter-Asia approaches to the study of sociocultural issues across Asian regions. This trend reflects on two related academic concerns. One is the advancement of globalisation processes that engender cross-border flows and connections of capital, people and media culture, which make many issues transnationally linked beyond national borders. For example, the Social Science Research Council in the United

States has developed Inter-Asia programs since 2008. It aims to 'reconceptualize Asia as a dynamic and interconnected formation' and 'move beyond the territorial fixities of area-studies research'. New journals such as the *Transnational Asia: An Online Interdisciplinary Journal* (Rice University) and *TRaNS: Trans-Regional and -National Studies of Southeast Asia* also focus on inter-Asia or trans-Asia approaches. They aim to 'challenge traditional understandings of Asia, moving beyond the confines of area studies and nation-state focus', as it 'posits that these boundaries are unnecessarily limiting, and attempt to examine issues on the supra-national level'. The National University of Singapore has launched a new PhD program of comparative Asian studies (CAS) and its 'distinctive feature is its attention to inter-Asian connections across regional boundaries and cultural zones'. These developments reflect on the escalation of cross-border flows and connections and the fact that many issues have become transnationally shared and linked in Asian regions, so much so that transcending a conception of fixed borders and areas is required to conduct a comprehensive investigation into them.

In relation to this trend, the rise of inter-Asia/trans-Asia approaches also engages with the promotion of cross-regional dialogue that facilitates de-Westernised knowledge production. In this respect, the successful development of Inter-Asia cultural studies is most relevant. Organising academic activities in terms of journals, bi-annual conferences, consortiums and postgraduate student camps since 2000, it aims to 'build a platform for "Inter-Asia" intellectual community by creating links between and across local circles'. More specifically, one objective is to 'link and facilitate dialogues between the disconnected critical circles within Asia and beyond'. While not being exclusive to researchers located outside Asian regions and being 'conscious that there is no unity to the imaginary entity called "Asia", hence the term "Inter-Asia"', it still has some emphasis on the promotion of hitherto unrealised conversations and alliance among 'local' academics and their works (in local languages). Chen (2010, xv) proposes in his book that it is a project of 'Asia as method' that generates a de-imperialisation of knowledge production: 'using Asia as an imaginary anchoring point can allow societies in Asia to become one another's reference points, so that the understanding of the self can be transformed, and subjectivity rebuilt' and this will lead to the construction of 'an alternative horizon, perspective, or method for posing a different set of questions about world history'.

Trans-Asia approaches are beneficial to the study of the rise of East and Southeast Asian media culture and their trans-Asian flows and connections, in which Japan has been playing a significant role. Since the middle of the 1990s, production capacity of media cultures such as TV dramas, films and popular music has considerably developed in East Asia. Furthermore, inter-Asian promotion and co-production of media cultures have become commonplace through partnerships among the media and cultural industries. There has emerged a loose cultural geography as most of East Asian media cultures except some cultures are capitalised, circulated and consumed predominantly, if not exclusively, in East Asia (including those migrants and diasporas from the region living outside it). Examining socio-historically contextualised experiences that intersect East Asia as region, many researchers, including myself, have been seriously examining cultural dynamics of production, circulation and consumption that have been engendered under globalisation processes. The intensification of cross-border cultural flows and human mobilities have been newly engendering trans-local exchanges, connections, associations, rivalry and antagonism in East Asian contexts. Such study of cross-regional flows and connections of capital, people and media culture in Asia contributes to advancing de-Westernised knowledge production and going beyond the yet compartmentalised boundaries of the nation and region.

Comparison of the Asian modern experience and the construction of modern subjectivity under Western domination would generate new perspectives and knowledge, and inter-Asian referencing is meaningful to understand modern experiences of Asian countries and East Asian cultural exchange in a new critical light. Based on shared experiences of 'forced' modernisation and less hierarchical relationships than a prevailing West–Asia comparison, which tends to assume temporal distance between them (See Iwabuchi 2002), inter-Asia referencing enables us to have a new perspective and understanding of the issues regarding cultural globalisation processes from similar and different East Asian experiences and facilitates localised (re-)conceptualisation and theorisation through comparison and mutual referencing of (post)modern experiences in East Asia.

Trans-Asian media culture flows have engendered mutual media consumption, which evokes fresh senses of finding resonance with modern experiences of other Asian societies (Wilk 1995). Such resonance is articulated in a mixed feeling of the sense of proximity and distance, which is quite different from the one derived from an Asia–West comparison. Spatiotemporal comparisons with other East Asian media cultures and the examination of inter-Asian influences also productively elucidate the process of cultural mixing and adaptation in terms of two associated approaches: East Asian media culture's negotiation with American counterparts and the interchange between East Asian media cultures. East Asian media cultures have long dexterously hybridised in local elements while absorbing American cultural influences. The analysis of this process is crucial to evade both an essentialist view of Asian values and traditions and a simplified view of American cultural domination. It shows at once the operation of global power configurations in which Euro-American culture has played a central role and the active cultural translation practices in the non-West. Comparative examination of how similar and different experiences of negotiation with American media culture in Hong Kong, Japan and South Korea, for example, would lead to the theorisation of the modes of cultural mixing and adaptation from East Asian experiences. Cultural mixing and adaptation have also been occurring among East Asian media cultures and this has also become a conspicuous constituent of the production of media culture in East Asia as media culture markets in East Asia have become synchronised and producers, directors and actors as well as capital from around the region have been working across national borders.

Remakes of successful TV dramas and films of other parts of East Asia are frequently made, especially between Japanese, South Korean, Hong Kong and Taiwanese media texts, and Japanese comic series are often adapted for TV dramas and films outside Japan, a prominent example being Meteor Garden (*Liuxing Huayuan*), a Taiwanese TV drama series that adopts Japanese comic series. The analysis of the dynamic processes of inter-textual reworking as well as inter-Asian cultural adaptation intriguingly exposes both commonality and difference in the constitution and representation of 'East Asian modernity'. Looking into experiences of various Asian societies also encourages us to make theorisation and conceptualisation from Asian experiences. For example, I discussed the notion of '*mukokuseki*' and 'cultural odour' that I conceptualised in the Japanese context. I used the Japanese concept to discuss how some Japanese animations and video games such as Super Mario Brothers that did not much represent tangible ethno-cultural characteristics of Japan had become well received in many parts of the world. Jung (2011) in turn makes conceptualisation of '*mugukjeok*' in her analysis of the rise of South Korean media culture by referring to my argument. As Chua (2011) points out, Jung's inter-Asian referencing expands the notion of '*mukokuseki*' in two inter-related senses. It makes the conceptualisation trans-locally relevant and applicable to wider ranges of media culture. It also shows how attending to a similar and different experience in East Asia generates a sophisticated understanding of the interaction between transculturation and cross-border mobility of media cultures, which is in turn applied and further developed outside South Korea (not limited to Asian regions). It is this mutual learning process that makes inter-Asian referencing contribute to the innovative production of knowledge.

Migration and multicultural engagement are other fascinating issues for trans-Asia approaches. The first decade of the twenty-first century has witnessed the profusion of multicultural policies and discourses in East Asian countries such as Japan, South Korea and Taiwan, which were historically self-identified as 'ethnically homogenous' societies. In addition to the legacy of the Japanese imperial project, Japan, South Korea and Taiwan share an experience of inter-Asian migration in the process of ethno-cultural globalisation since the late 1980s. In these three countries – in addition to their own indigenous or long-term racial and ethnic minorities – the number of foreign national residents, migrants and people of mixed heritage has risen notably in the last two to three decades. Although none of the governments welcomed migrants with open arms, the influx of labourers and international marriage migrants has been observed, primarily from China and Southeast Asia. More recently, due to the sharply declining birth rates and the rapidly aging populations, with a strong push from domestic industrial sectors, governments in Japan, South Korea and Taiwan have begun to discuss under what conditions migrants should be accepted and what policies should be implemented. In this context, there has been a growing focus on increased multicultural interactions within their borders and the impacts of cultural diversity on the fabric of their nations in the three countries. The trend has attracted academic concern (for example, see Kymlicka and He 2005; Eng, Collins and Yeoh 2013). While the contextualisation of the situation in each of the countries is imperative, a trans-East-Asian comparative and collaborative approach to examining emergent multicultural situations in Japan, South Korea and Taiwan opens up an innovative perspective (see Iwabuchi, Kim and Hsia 2016). By denationalising the discussion of multiculturalism as a policy for managing cultural diversity within the nation-state by consciously comparing domestic situations with other East Asian cases as well as to situate their cases in a wider, transnational context, it adds new horizons from East Asia to our understanding of multiculturalism as a set of policies, discourses and practices that manage, negotiate with and embrace growing human mobility and accompanying cultural diversity – a field that has developed primarily in Euro-American and Australian contexts. A trans-East-Asian perspective is also significant as it elucidates the shared-ness and the 'similarity-in-difference' when examining multicultural issues in Japan, South Korea and Taiwan, as it endows us with fresh insights into the multicultural issues in a more transnationally informed sense. A full understanding of both the possibilities and limitations of multicultural policies, discourses and practices as they have been addressed by national policy-makers, local communities, NGOs, NPOs, civic organisations and the migrant subjects themselves in the three societies will contribute to a renewed discussion of how one might advance a more multicultural future in domestic contexts as well as through transnational cooperation, dialogue and mutual empowerment.

Advancing trans-Asia approaches to Japan in/and Australia

Trans-Asian approaches promote de-Westernisation of knowledge production through de-nationalised perspective over cross-border mobilities and connections in Asian regions. Trans-Asia approaches and inter-Asian referencing contribute to expand and deepen 'the study of Japan' by situating Japan in trans-Asia cultural connections and mobilities. Inter-Asia referencing underlies hitherto underexplored issues and perspectives for the study of Japan through the consideration of comparison, connections and shared-ness with other parts of Asia. Trans-Asia approaches have not yet fully developed, and much more needs to be done. It would be desirable for researchers on Japan in Australia to more consciously and strategically focus on trans-Asia approaches to take the initiative of further developing trans-Asia approaches from Australia. Likewise, trans-Asia approaches enrich the study of 'Japan in Australia'. In relation to inter-Asia referencing and de-Westernised knowledge production, any studies of the presence, connection and mobility of culture and people of Japanese backgrounds within Australia would have much merit by looking at other Asian counterparts in Australia. The analysis of the circulation and consumption of Japanese culture and associated issues of Japan's soft power promotion and cultural diplomacy in Australia would merit taking a trans-Asia approach. Comparison of the circulation and consumption of media culture, food and cultural exchange of Japan with those of China, South Korea or Thailand would encourage us to assess similarities and differences among those cultures, thus deepening our understanding in a wider perspective and context. Also relevant is the study of Japanese migration and community in Australia. As demonstrated in Steains's chapter, migration from Japan has long been attracting much academic attention among Japanese studies in Australia (see also a series of studies by Keiko Tamura and Yuriko Nagata). In addition to the development of historical investigation of early settlers and wartime brides, more recently younger-generation scholars have conducted productive studies on the contemporary migrants from Japan such as women married to Australian men, the situation of Japanese communities in Australia and working holiday youth and their labour conditions (Nagatomo 2014; Hamano 2010; Kawashima 2010). While these studies have significant standalone scholarly value within and beyond Japanese studies, I would suggest that a trans-Asia approach would enhance them even more by adding further perspectives and insights through referencing the experiences of migrants from other Asian countries to Australia. This would open up deeper and fresher understandings of the Japanese migrant situation vis-á-vis those from China, Korea or Singapore beyond the confinement of the Japan-Australia relationship. Such comparative investigation would also urge Japanese studies researchers to consider the experiences of Japanese migrants in more theoretically and conceptually attuned ways in terms of diaspora, cultural diversity and social cohesion that have been developed in migration and mobility studies in the 'Western' (including Australia) contexts. Needless to say, many researchers of Japanese studies have worked closely with researchers of other regions and disciplines such as sociology, anthropology, cultural studies, geography and migration studies, but trans-Asia approaches would further encourage interdisciplinary and inter-regional scholarly exchange.

Furthermore, trans-Asia approaches to Japan in Australia encourage us to rethink 'Australia' by placing it within trans-Asian mobilities and connections. The study of Japan or Asia has tended to be compartmentalised in Australia like other Western countries. It is a study of 'over there' and is apt to be dissociated from the local context of Australia and have no substantial dialogue with general theoretical and conceptual issues from various disciplines. However, we are living in a globalised world in which many issues have been shared. While they are differently articulated in diverse local contexts, such articulation is founded on common forces and structures under globalisation processes, and many issues are required to be transnationally dealt with. Thus, the study of Japanese and other Asian sociocultural issues would benefit greatly from consideration by Australian counterparts. This point is especially pertinent to the study of Japan and Asia in Australia since Australia is geographically part of a wider Asian region and trans-Asian human mobilities and cultural connections are even more seriously constitutive of Australian society than other Euro-American societies.

Trans-Asia approaches situate Australia in trans-Asian human mobilities and cultural flows and connections reconceptualise 'Australia' in terms of its relation to Asia and Asian presence and linkage as constitutive of Australian society. It will productively and innovatively advance Asia literacy and capability discourse in Australia. 'Asia literacy' has attracted renewed attention in Australia since late 2012, when the then government published the 'Australia in the Asian Century' white paper. It emphasised the significance of enhancing 'Asia literacy' to 'seize the opportunities that will flow from the Asian century' and proposed to implement the cross-curriculum priority of 'Asia and Australia's engagement with Asia' as well as Asian languages education at Australian schools (see Halse 2015). An apparent problem with the notion of Asia literacy is an underlining assumption that dichotomises Asia and Australia, and it has been subject to much criticism.

Asia literacy represents a lingering Orientalist desire to know and control the Asian other, which has been historically constituted in Australia. The discussion for the advancement of Asian literacy itself functions to presume and reproduce the totalised view of 'Asia'. Conceived both as menace and opportunity, 'Asia' has been the implicit significant Other in the construction of Australian national identity. Currently the overt rise of economic power of many Asian countries has foregrounded an instrumentalist rationale to exploit the opportunity of the Asian century to maximise opportunities for Australia, unlike other Western countries, fortuitously located within Asia.

The previously dominant conception of Australia's relationship to Asia can be explicated in terms of 'in but not of' in the same sense as Japan (Iwabuchi 2002). On the one hand, Australia is regarded as geographically located in the periphery of the Asian (and Pacific) region, which provides Australia an advantage, but also a sense of threat. However, the social and cultural legacy of the United Kingdom and the durable identification with the West hinders the development of a sense of belonging to the region, and Asia has been clearly demarcated as other. The governmental pursuit of Australia's engagement with Asia is accompanied with a reminder that 'Australia is not, and can never be, an Asian nation' (a statement made by then prime minister, Paul Keating, in 1993) and 'Australia does not need to choose between its history [and culture] and its geography' (1997 foreign policy white paper under John Howard's prime-ministership).

This conception of 'Australia being in but not of Asia' works closely in tandem with the concept of 'Asia being in but not of Australia'. Apart from economic partnerships, cultural influences of Asian countries and the noticeable presence of migrants and diaspora from the region constitute significant parts of Australian society. However, such 'Asian' presence is not generally conceived as part of Australian society. The interplay of the two 'in but not of' imaginations is requisite for the construction of an Asia-Australia binary by disregarding sociocultural diversity and complexity both within Asia and Australia. A clearly demarcated dichotomy of Australia and Asia is not just conceptually and epistemologically problematic, it does not match the material realities and mundane experiences in contemporary Australian society either. And this has become even more prominent with intensifying cross-border mobility and interconnections under globalisation processes. In this context, the Asia literacy discourse in the second decade of the twenty-first century has the radical potential to displace the 'in but not of' imagination that has deeply haunted the discourse of Asia literacy. Mundane experiences testify to how 'Asia' has been inseparably composing everyday life in Australia through people's border-crossing practices – physically, imaginatively and virtually. Already extant interconnection and mutual cross-fertilisation between Asian countries and Australia indicate that Australia has been substantially situated as part of trans-Asian flows, networks and commons, and necessitates the promotion of cross-regional conversation over global issues that include environmental risk, the violence of global capital, the rise of various kinds of cultural nationalisms and jingoisms, questions on migration and multiculturalism.

Trans-Asia approaches also encourage us to pay critical attention to the engagement with the multicultural question within Australia. It is often pointed out that, being a multicultural society, the Australian populace is already Asia literate due to the presence of many migrants from Asian regions, but this view tends to perceive people with the heritage of other Asian regions as a useful human resource to enhance Asia literacy in Australia. This is another example of instrumentalism in the recognition of 'Asia' within Australia, which retains the dichotomised notion of 'us' and 'them' intact. To make Asia literacy a cosmopolitan project, researchers engaging with the study of Japan and other Asian areas need to aspire to promote the rethinking of dominant conceptions of self and the (Asian) other, located both inside and outside of Australia, and the entangled relationship between them. This does not just mean the expansion of knowledge of Asian histories, cultures and societies or the acknowledgement of the presence of people with Asian backgrounds and their contribution to Australia. We need to go beyond a predefined framework of knowing about 'us' and 'them' and reflexively rethink why and how 'us' has been perceived in a particular way that does not embrace 'them' as being with and part of 'us'. Through critical examination of the history of Australia's involvement with 'Asia', trans-Asia approaches will elucidate what is yet unknown about 'us' as well as about 'them' and show that Asia literacy is inevitably a matter of Australia literacy.

'Migrant Diplomacy' is a project funded by the Australia-Japan Foundation, which aims to promote exchange and dialogue between the Immigration Museum in Melbourne and related museums and projects in Japan such as the Immigration Museum Tokyo (pilot project) and Tokyo Metropolitan Museum of Arts over a significant role of museum and cultural/artistic activities in fostering diversity and inclusion in the age of hyper-mobility. While various kinds of Australia-Japan bilateral relationships have been developed, this project innovatively enhances them in terms of the presence and experience of Asian migrants in both countries. It will contribute to increased awareness and dialogue between the two countries through common ground related to Asian migration and its accompanying cultural diversity. The Japanese counterparts have much to learn from Australia's rich experience, but Australian participants are also inspired to learn from the practices of Japanese museums and artists. Furthermore, the project's trans-Asia perspective is significant in the Australian context to blur the hitherto dominant conception of Australia's relationship to Asia. The Project's underlining of the commonality between Japan and Australia as part of trans-Asian human mobilities urges us to reconceptualise and reimagine 'Australia' in terms of its geographical positioning in Asia and its relation to Asia's presence and linkage as constitutive of Australian society by way of generating cross-regional conversation over shared issues of migration and inclusive embracement of cultural diversity.

A bird's-eye view: researchers in trans-Asia mobilities and connections

Last but not least, trans-Asia approaches also urge researchers engaging with the dynamic mobilities and connections of Japan (and Asia) and Australia to place themselves with the context of trans-Asia mobilities and connections to cultivate a bird's-eye view and foster collaboration across divides and beyond academia to tackle transnationally shared issues. Here let me refer to my research projects to consider this point. My trans-Asia projects, which I call 'trans-Asia as method', have been developed through my own academic projects and experiences of relocation. Moving back and forth between Japan and Australia and frequent contacts with other East Asian cities and researchers have much to do with the shaping of my own trans-Asia approach. Located in Australia, I could develop a bird's-eye view of trans-Asia cultural dynamics while conducting Ph.D. field research in various parts of East and Southeast Asia. After completing a Ph.D., I worked in Tokyo for more than 12 years. The first part of the period coincided with the rise of inter-Asia cultural studies and a growing academic interest in trans-Asia media culture flows and connections. Collaboration with researchers in Japan and other Asian countries as well as Australia, the United States and Europe, moving back and forth between Japan, Australia and other Asian countries has helped me nurture this kind of comprehensive view. The most common understanding of a bird's-eye view is a view from a high place enabling us to see the wider context in which things exist, giving us a perspective that we cannot get on the ground. As birds move from one place to another, a fresh perspective can be obtained by seeing things from a distant place. The mobility of birds also forges connections between different places. But birds do not actually live in the sky. For most birds, the ground is the source of life where they find food. So, while a bird's-eye view tends to be closely associated with a view from the sky or afar, they are also closely anchored to the ground. A bird's-eye view thus indicates four ways of innovatively observing. Considering a wider socio-historical context, it helps us debunk preconceptions and seemingly self-evident ideas. Looking at a similar thing in another place (and another time) enables us to relativise our viewpoint about it through comparisons. Mobility also gives us insights into how things in two (or more) places are not separated but interconnected and shared. It also makes one sensitive to the emerging trends across borders. A birds-eye view is not a detached observation from afar, but a grounded one. Combined with mobility, groundedness encourages us to conduct multi-sited, engaged research on an issue. It is often said that a smart person should have an insect's eye (being grounded and micro-focused) and a fish's eye (grasping the tide) in addition to a bird's eye, but the bird's eye actually covers the other two as well. Having a bird's eye seems an ideal intellectual posture!

This is especially pertinent to the trans-Asian approaches that I have been undertaking. My research activities have been founded on the move between Japan (Tokyo), Australia (Sydney, Perth and Melbourne) and various Asian cities (such as Taipei, Hong Kong, Seoul). Being mobile between the locations of research has pros and cons. It often gives us an innovative perspective somewhat freed from the centripetal force of the local. Being located in Australia was really productive for my Ph.D. research on Japan's renewed cultural connections with other parts of Asia, for I could relativise my understanding of the relationship between 'Japan' and 'Asia' that had been deeply instilled throughout my life in

Japan. And, for the first time, I was forced to know my 'Asianness' through the dominant gaze of Australian society and mundane encounters with other Asians in Australia. That sense of awakening to being both Japanese and Asian has become a significant base for my multi-sited research activities on trans-Asian connections. After I moved back to Tokyo, I further engaged with trans-Asian cultural connections by working together with scholars in East Asian countries to conduct comparative studies and inter-Asian referencing about shared sociocultural issues. Yet, I gradually found it more and more difficult to develop these approaches in Japan, not least because the East Asian political climate was getting worse and nationalism was on the rise, which made research on trans-Asian connections less vibrant. So, I moved back to Melbourne. My current position and location enable me to actively and freely engage with the advancement of trans-Asian approaches and collaborative projects by closely working with scholars inside and outside Asia, including Australia.

Not being located in an East Asian city, however, I cannot get a nuanced sense of the social atmosphere there (though I can feel another kind of trans-Asian connection in Australia). I do my best to grasp what is going on by collecting data, reading articles, looking at Internet sites and talking to people living there. But nothing can beat mundane experiences. So, I fly to the places we research as often as possible and collaborate with researchers there. Unlike birds, which consume local inhabitants, I need to more eagerly learn from and work with locally grounded knowledge, perspectives and practices of people situated in East Asian cities. Such trans-locally grounded collaborations force me to always remember that there is a thin line between engaged, responsible wanderers and capricious vagabonds and that any hope to tackle intricate issues could be found only through conscientious investigation into how people live with them. Embracing the limitations of a bird's-eye view is indispensable to make the best of its potential.

Thinking and acting trans-Asian-ly

'Japan in Australia' is a fascinating academic topic. It highlights the potential of fruitfully expanding the studies of Japan in the Australian context by going beyond a conventional area study approach that tends to be based on a fixed notion of a particular foreign country and/or region afar. Such investigation urges us to not study 'Japan over there' but look at cross-border mutuality, interaction and exchange to re-think 'Japan', 'Australia' and researchers in a dynamic way. This chapter considers how such potential would be further enhanced by the growing trend of trans-Asia approaches in area studies and other disciplines' investigation in the context of Asia. The consideration of 'Japan in Australia' requires us to look at wider contexts of cross-border flows and connections that have been ever intensifying. It will thus urge us to rethink and reconceptualise 'Japan' by engaging with the entangled relationship of 'here' and 'there' in the consideration of 'Japan' as a fluid and multidimensional object of study. Furthermore, such an approach to Japan, and Asia, also urges us to reconceptualize 'Australia' in terms of its engagement and embracing of Japan or Asia within. The former is concerned with the potential of the study of 'Japan in Australia' for the study of Japan, while the latter raises the potential of 'the study of Japan' complicating the understanding of Australia through rethinking its relationship with the supposed object of study.

Trans-Asian approaches can be defined by three 'de-' terms – 'de-' as productive and innovative advancement of existing situations by critically interrogating them: de-Westernisation via inter-Asian referencing; a de-nationalised perspective, exchange, engagement; and a de-compartmentalising of 'Asia' and 'Australia' beyond a West-Asia binary and beyond clearly separated national-cultural entities to reconceptualising Australia as part of trans-Asia flows/connections. We should also add the de-academicised role of researchers to promote collaboration since trans-East-Asia as method aims to transnationally extend our commitment to the local by taking the trans-Asian connection as a strategic focal point. As such, with a cosmopolitan scope and relevance, it collaboratively aspires to the enhancement of a sense of shared-ness and together-ness to facilitate cross-border dialogue over and above mutual engagement with transnationally shared issues by promoting collaboration with diverse social actors. This is to take perspectives and approaches that 'trans' implies seriously – critical engagement with transnational circulation of capital, people and culture and the uneven connections it engenders ('across/through'), going beyond a mutually exclusively demarcated understanding of region and nation ('beyond') and striving to conceptualise and materialise an open and dialogic social relation ('into another state of things'). The last point is reminiscent of how inter-Asia referencing and associated cross-border dialogue have become people's mundane experiences. Trans-Asia cultural connections have generated cross-border dialogue, which encouraged people in various East Asian countries to self-reflexively reconsider one's own life, society and culture, as well as socio-historically constituted relations with and perceptions of others through the awareness of the spatial-temporal distance and closeness of other East Asian modernities (Iwabuchi 2002). Just as Takeuchi Yoshimi's (2005) experience of a pleasurable surprise when he first visited China that people's thinking, feeling and experiences in China looked both very familiar and very different triggered the formulation of the idea of 'Asia as method', trans-Asia approaches also productively inspire researchers of Japan in Australia to expand the scope, refresh perspectives and collaboratively engage with trans-Asian-ly shared issues with researchers of other regions and disciplines. This drives us in new directions.

References

Chen, K. H. 2010. *Asia as Method: Toward Deimperialization*. Durham: Duke University Press.

Chua, B. H. 2011. 'Conceptualization and Inter-Referencing', Paper presented at ELLAK (English Language and Literature Association of Korea) International Conference, 18 December, Onyang, Korea.

Eng, L. A., Collins, F. L. and Yeoh, B. S. A. 2013. *Migration and Diversity in Asian Contexts*. Singapore: ISEAS Publishing.

Halse, C. (ed.). 2015. *Asia Literate Schooling in the Asian Century*. London: Routledge.
Hamano, T. 2010. *Searching Better Lifestyle in Migration: The Case of Contemporary Japanese Migrants in Australia*. Saarbrücken: Lambert Academic Publishing.
Iwabuchi, K. 2002. *Recentering Globalization: Popular Culture and Japanese Transnationalism*. Durham: Duke University Press.
Iwabuchi, K., Mee, K. H. and Chuan, H. H. (eds.). 2016. *Multiculturalism in East Asia: A Transnational Exploration of Japan, South Korea and Taiwan*. London: Rowman & Littlefield International.
Jung, S. 2011. *Korean Masculinities and Transcultural Consumption*. Hong Kong: Hong Kong University Press.
Kawashima, K. 2010. 'Japanese Working Holiday Makers in Australia and Their Relationship to the Japanese Labour Market: Before and After', *Asian Studies Review*, 34 (3): 267–286.
Kymlicka, W. and He, B. (eds.). 2005. *Multiculturalism in Asia*. New York: Oxford University Press.
Nagatomo, J. 2014. *Migration as Transnational Leisure: The Japanese Lifestyle Migrants in Australia (Social Sciences in Asia)*. Leiden and Boston: Brill.
Takeuchi, Y. 2005. '"Asia as Method": In What Is Modernity?' in R. F. Calichman (ed. and trans.), *Writings of Takeuchi Yoshimi*. New York: Columbia University Press, 149–166.
Wilk, R. 1995. 'Learning to Be Local in Belize: Global Systems of Common Difference', in D. Miller (ed.), *Worlds Apart: Modernity Through the Prism of the Local*. London: Routledge, 110–133.

10 The Australian literary scene and Murakami Haruki
Nobel laureate heir apparent or marketing overhype?

Laura Emily Clark

Introduction

As we face our globalised world, with significant migrant populations, seamless international communication systems, and international companies driving local consumer markets, the Australian literary scene is facing a challenge. On the one hand, national paradigms are falling out of popularity and relevance; on the other, fundamental values and the marketing of literature in Australia are premised on the importance of location and unique 'difference'. This situation holds significance not only for the construction of an Australian literary identity, but also in the reception of foreign authors and works in the Australian context. Damrosch (2003, 6, 11) has argued that when a text enters world literature, it does not necessarily lose its authenticity, but can actually gain it, as it is reinterpreted as *like-but-unlike*. Thus, when an international novel enters the Australian market, it is reinterpreted through our national literary paradigms. However, I will also argue that this is by no means a direct relationship: how Australia receives these foreign works is profoundly shaped by how the rest of the (Western) world already has. This chapter will demonstrate this through the analysis of a series of Australian book reviews of two of Murakami Haruki's (2010, 2013) recent translated novels. What emerges within the corpus of texts is a complex and challenging set of portraits. Although I will argue that many aspects of these constructions reflect Murakami himself as a literary figure, he is also being interpreted through Australian literary discourses. This discussion will pivot around two key themes: 'Murakami as Japanese' and the 'Murakami brand'. Whilst the 'Murakami as Japanese' discourses demonstrate the ongoing strength of national literary paradigms, the 'Murakami brand' discourses are fundamentally engaged with how the world at large has engaged with Murakami.

But first, it is worth answering the question: why is Murakami the subject of this research? Figure 10.1 is an indexed Google trends graph from 2004 to early 2019, displaying Australian IP searches. The consistently highest spiking line is Murakami Haruki, whereas the others signify Yoshimoto Banana, Ogawa Yōko, Tawada Yōko, and Murata Sayaka – all contemporary authors who have received notable scholarly and media attention.

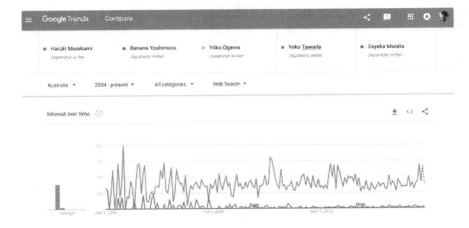

Figure 10.1 Google trends graph
Source: Author's own

What we can clearly see here is that other than a broader burst of interest over the 2004–2006 period, there is consistently and significantly more engagement with Murakami Haruki than any of the other authors. It is also worth noting that the spikes in interest in Murakami coincide with international prizes – whether he wins them or not – and the release of new works. What I conclude from this graph is that Australians are more engaged with Murakami than any other contemporary Japanese literary author. It therefore follows that Murakami is not only subject to significant attention but is potentially being constructed as a representative of Japanese literature overall. So, the question then becomes, who is 'Murakami' when he is being interpreted outside of Japan and into the Australian context?

Conceptualising 'Literatures' in a global context

There are of course a number of approaches to understanding the concept of 'literature' and re-interpreting it within both national and global paradigms. As demonstrated by Dixon and Rooney (2013, xi, xiii), there have been two significant trends in world literature theory: centre-periphery world-system theories such as those developed by Casanova and Moretti, and circulation models such as Damrosch and Apter. For this chapter's discussion, Damrosch's (2003) approach seems most useful. Damrosch rejects the idea of world literature as a list of canonical internationally recognised texts, instead postulating that world literature must be seen as a 'mode of circulation' (2003, 5), as a way to understand how literary works are absorbed and reconstructed in recipient cultures. Damrosch creates space for exploring a global literary-consumerism system, but which is still at a practical level immersed in local, national contexts. Therefore, when a work is received in Australia it is always subject to local knowledge, values, and assumptions. In my discussion below, I will also be drawing into Damrosch's theory the idea that these texts do not arrive in Australia directly, but rather via the rest of the world's reception and construction of the work.

Particular to the Australian context is also a tense history with the concept of a 'national literature'. More specifically, it would seem that for as long as there has been an 'Australia', there has been a search for an 'Australian literature'. Dixon (2007) has pointed out that the quest to define and delineate an Australian canon has been a consistent concern. Of course it is also a matter of what is *not* Australian literature; as Dixon (2012, 71) puts it, 'national literary traditions are defined both by acts of inclusion and acts of exclusion'. In the contemporary context, this historical focus continues to shape discussions and form a fundamental assumption: texts are first and foremost understood from their national literary context. Da Silva (2014, 2) highlights the tension this creates, as Australian literary discussions will often 'refute as much as they reaffirm the importance of national points of origin'. So, on the one hand, national paradigms are out of favour, but on the other, they continue to underpin how literature is received and interpreted within Australia. This particular tension is something we will see reflected within the book reviews of Murakami Haruki's works. Historically, there has been some variation in the reception of foreign works; for example, Halford (2018) notes that Latin American author Jorge Luis Borges had a massive impact on the Australian writing community, yet was separated from his cultural context, with the focus being on his reception in the Global North. The reception of Murakami appears to be more complex as he is 'Japanised' within these reviews, though once again the focus is on his reception in Europe and America.

More generally, translated fiction in Australia is on the rise. As recently as 2007, less than 2% of the fiction available on the Australian market was translated, and had typically been dominated by the 'canon'. This has changed over the past decade, with a significant increase in translated texts from a wide range of countries – particularly from small, independent publishing houses (Mostafa 2011; Whitmore 2018). This being said, most translated novels are not reviewed, and no other contemporary Japanese author was reviewed across all the platforms included in the corpus used for this chapter. There has also been limited critical attention on Australian book reviews, so it is not currently clear what the common trends in reviews have been. In this way, this chapter is part of a burgeoning discussion in how Australian book reviewers approach translated texts more generally.

Murakami as a figure in critical discussions

Murakami Haruki (b. 1949) exploded on the Japanese literary scene in 1979 with his first work *Kaze no uta o kike [Hear the wind sing]*, winning the Gunzo Prize for New Writers as well as being nominated for the prestigious Akutagawa Prize and Noma Literary Newcomer's Prize in the same year. Murakami has been a controversial figure ever since: in tension with the literary establishment (*bundan*) for his unliterary writing style; and, apparently, in spats with major literary figures. Somewhat unusually for Japanese fiction, Murakami's early works were translated and released into the American market relatively quickly by American publishers looking to capitalise on a manga and anime boom (Hirabayashi 2011, 50–51). However, his global takeover has been more staggered: with a boom in Taiwan, Korea, and China in 1990; then a big boom in France, Germany, and Russia in the early 2000s (Kawamura 2006, 14). Murakami's writing has also been featured in *The New Yorker* magazine consistently since 1999. His reception in Australia has been perhaps less avid, although he has been critically appraised. His works have at various points appeared in popular rating lists, for example, in 2014, *1Q84* was numbered at #56 and *Kafka on the shore* at #95 (Dymocks 2014) (a drop from #63 in 2012; Dymocks 2012) in the Dymocks Booklovers Annual Top 101 booklist. In its debut year, *Colorless Tsukuru Tazaki and his years of pilgrimage* came in at #75 (Dymocks 2016).

It is worth noting that Murakami is also somewhat unique in the production of literature in Japan: the usual practice for a Gunzo Prize winner like Murakami is that the publishing house requests a particular kind of material and the author produces it. However, with his massive rise in fame, Murakami has been allowed the freedom to write what he wants to write and when he wants to write it (Shimizu 2006, 10). This contributes to the idea of Murakami as his own man – rather than the literary establishment or market stooge – a perspective that is strongly propagated within reviews, critical discussions, and even by Murakami himself within interviews. Another common trend is connecting Murakami's writing with biographical details and his intentions as stated in interviews.

Murakami's position within the Japanese literary world and the question of 'canon' have been the target of a great deal of debate. Early criticisms, particularly propelled by Miyoshi Masao and Ōe Kenzaburō (Chozick 2008, 62), claimed that his work was un-Japanese and light-weight. There has also been a discussion about whether Murakami lacks the social commitment and social conscience necessary in a writer, as demonstrated by the ahistoricity of his works (Karatani 2011) and his lack of engagement with Japanese social issues. This idea of the 'un-Japanese Murakami' raises the question of to which national literature, if any, Murakami's actual writing might belong.

This question of Murakami's 'Japaneseness' also often sits at the centre of scholarship regarding the cultural reception of his works. However, there are two different focuses in audience reception: the relationship between Murakami and the United States of America, and his reception in various Asian countries. Regarding Murakami's place in America versus Japan, Chozick (2008) argues that Murakami's writing has a kind of universal exoticism: intriguingly familiar and unfamiliar to both American and Japanese readers. Suter's (2008) landmark book also made an argument similar to Chozick, reading Murakami as a cultural mediator between Japan and America, and as such, as an enactor of Japanese-American cultural cross-representation. With regard to Murakami's Asian reception, Baik (2010) positions his popularity in China as evidence of his 'stateless' writing, attractive to a global middle class hungry for 'cool' without ideology or national ties. Likewise, Kawamura (2006, 15) argues that the reception of Murakami in countries such as South Korea has been strong, as the lack of nation in his writing separates him from the wounds of historical colonialism. Thus, Murakami is often positioned outside of national paradigms, as a universal insider/outsider.

In this chapter, however, I will focus on how Murakami and his works are constructed within Australian book reviews. This follows Damrosch's (2003, 24) invitation to explore how works are reframed as they move across the spheres of world literature. The two novels targeted within the book reviews are *1Q84* (2010) and *Colorless Tsukuru Tazaki and his years of pilgrimage* (2013). These novels are somewhat unusual for Murakami, as *1Q84* is a split narrative between male and female leads, and *Colorless* is in third person rather than his usual first person. *1Q84* is a massive work – three volumes in the original Japanese – whereas *Colorless* is a short one. Also, strikingly, both of these novels include explicit descriptions of Japanese landmarks and social issues. Therefore, these two works are departures from Murakami's common trends, although they still fit conceptually into the 'Murakami canon', as will be discussed later in this chapter.

The corpus and methodology

Five book reviews for each novel were chosen for this analysis. The reviews are a combination of print reviews that were subsequently published online and online-only content. All of the websites are aimed at an English-speaking audience.[1] The reviewers themselves are either regular reviewers, Japanese studies specialists, or authors in their own right. This combination suggests that reviews as a genre straddle an interesting space. Some are aimed at largely informing the audience of the novels and how to approach them, others are advocating for the books, and others are more focused on explaining the Murakami phenomenon beyond any individual novel. As such, the reviews must address a number of different audiences and manage a range of aims and intentions. Even with the rise of internet reviewers and crowd-review platforms, professional reviews continue to command a large audience and authority within the reading world. As such, although there are many within the reading public who may disregard or disagree with the conclusions of reviewers, they continue to act as gatekeepers and authorities, as well as representatives of the literary sphere.

Analysis of these reviews was undertaken through an iterative thematic analysis. Key terms and concepts were identified and then clustered to create a set of themes, which was subsequently reviewed and re-clustered to best reflect broad trends across the reviews as well as those specific to each novel or reviewer.

Murakami as Japan

Consistently across the reviews, we see a portrait emerging of Murakami that essentialises and emphasises his Japanese-ness, the exception being Hearn's (2011) *1Q84* review. There are many aspects to this construction; however, I focus here on two: connecting Murakami to Japanese literary and cultural traditions, and Murakami as writing works that explore Japanese society and issues. These different aspects combine to create a picture of Murakami as an exoticised Other, available for consumption but removed from the lived experience of the reader. I will argue that this demonstrates how strongly national paradigms determine the reception and construction of non-Australian authors.

A Japanese cultural heir

A key manner in which Murakami is positioned as writing 'Japanese literature' is by viewing him as the heir of a specific cultural and literary tradition. This is generally communicated by the reviewers through references to Japanese cultural products. Such references are often used to explain the effect or nature of Murakami's writing. However, what is being implied is that there is something about his writing that is innately Japanese, which therefore makes comparison to practices such as Noh plays and woodblock prints (Broinowski 2012), or Kabuki (Clark 2011), or Japan's literary canon such as Kawabata or Tanizaki (Jose 2014), not only appropriate but explanatory. These references are also notably historical Japanese cultural products. This creates an implicit continuity: a single, connected Japanese cultural tradition that stretches back into history and on into the future, with Murakami as the current iteration. On the other hand, this can also be read as creating an ahistorical Japan, in which creative works from all periods of modern Japan are collapsed into a timeless, essentialised 'Japanese culture'. The choices in references are also interesting given that these reviews are aimed at a general audience, who are not guaranteed to be familiar with these specific authors or practices. Therefore, perhaps these references are as much about creating the sense of an exotic 'Japan' and establishing the 'insider knowledge' of the reviewer as explaining Murakami to the reader. For example, Wright's (2014) reference to the *wabi-sabi* spirit in the review's title requires definition and explanation in the first paragraph. There is also a more contemporary Japanese artistic example used by Broinowski (2014): she makes a comparison to a pair of video scenes of Japan that had been exhibited at Sydney's Museum of Contemporary Art, as these videos and Murakami's writing display 'a similar aesthetic'.

Another aspect of this is the decision to identify Murakami's ethnicity. Half of these reviewers thought it was necessary and relevant to identify Murakami as being Japanese. What is more, in four of these instances, 'Japanese' was positioned as the first descriptor, 'Japanese writer', as opposed to, for example, 'writer who is Japanese'. Of course, perhaps it is equally striking that half of the reviewers took Murakami's Japaneseness either for granted or not worth mentioning. It is also worth noting that in the case of Broinowski's (2012) and Rabalais's (2014) reviews, Murakami and Japan are either explicitly or implicitly positioned as separate or outside of the West. There is a dichotomy being created here between the 'us' of the Australian reading public (which is aligned with London and the English-speaking world) and the West, against the 'them' of 'Japan'. Broinowski's (2012) use of the phrase 'bizarre fantasies' to describe woodblock prints also appears to be an engagement with a 'weird Japan' discourse. Indeed, as Rabalais

(2014) states, Murakami has two audiences: the West and his 'native Japan'. Here the West is once again positioned as a 'universal point of reference' against which Japan is identified and self-identifies as particular (Sakai 1989, 97, 105). This positioning of Murakami as 'exotic' and aligning Australia with the West may also highlight the somewhat precarious position Australian literature finds itself in within the world literature paradigms; if it is not part of 'the West', then it is in a highly marginal position.

It is important to note that although Murakami is presented as a somewhat exoticised figure, it is within fairly globally dominant constructions of 'Japaneseness' which are likely to be familiar to the reader to some extent. This combination is very similar to how Chozick (2008) presented Murakami's reception in America; however, it also fits with one of Damrosch's (2003, 12) main points about the reception of foreign works: they are reinterpreted on a continuum that ranges from difference and 'sheer novelty' to 'gratifying similarity'. This sense of similarity is reinforced through the significant emphasis on the influence of Western artistry on Murakami's writing style. International comparisons made include: Shakespeare, Bach, Dostoevsky, Chekhov, Tolstoy, Jung, Kafka, Sibelius, Wittgenstein, Orwell, Dickens, Agatha Christie (Broinowski 2012), Orwell, Chekhov, Stieg Larsson (Clark 2011), and Auster (Wright 2014).

The effect of this is that, of course, Murakami is presented as being very different, but also very familiar by being likened to authors within the literary canon. Therefore, the more broadly read audience of the reviews can understand Murakami's style through references to familiar names, whilst also embracing the idea of engaging with a different cultural tradition. Thus, Murakami is both of the West and very much not so.

A window on Japanese society

As mentioned previously, the construction of 'Murakami as Japan' has another major trend within the reviews, and that is the idea that Murakami's works provide a window into Japanese society. Even as these reviews paint Murakami as a universally popular author, he is also positioned as creating exceptional, 'foreign' works. Thus, the issues and ideas that Murakami is exploring are read as specific to the Japanese cultural context and separate from the lived experiences of both the reviewers and their Australian readers. Broinowski (2012) and Jose (2014) particularly emphasise this. For example, Broinowski (2012) describes *1Q84* as being a 'thoroughly Japanese narrative' and 'a guide to contemporary Japanese culture'. Indeed, she claims that through Murakami's writing 'you enter the Japanese mind, with its concerns about privacy, restraint, secrecy, motivation, the seeming, the instinctive, and the unspoken'. Jose (2014) focuses more on the idea that Murakami is challenging Japanese cultural issues and its wartime past, as 'the author probes Japan's wartime past in North Asia and its consequences in the present most deeply'. In some ways Jose lends legitimacy to this interpretation of Japan-centric significance through his comment that *Colorless* was 'read in Japan as an indirect response to the earthquake, tsunami and nuclear disaster at Fukushima in 2011'. Rabalais (2014) similarly positions Murakami's novels as concerning 'identity and friendship in contemporary Japan'.

This construction is within itself quite multifaceted. At times, it serves as a thematic descriptor, as in the sense that Murakami is dealing with Japanese society through his works: 'mind-melting meditation on love, sex, abuse, Japanese society, loneliness and literature', (Flynn 2011). At others, it is an explanation for how to understand the works themselves: for example, Wright (2014) sets a paragraph aside to explain how the novel makes more sense within the Japanese context of life transitions from university to the corporate world, and therefore, this work is 'most pertinent in a Japanese context'. This suggests that there is something to his works that is vitally connected to his 'native' context, and that as outsiders, 'we, the reader' might not understand. This also serves as an argument for why 'we' should be reading his works, but also translated texts more broadly: they allow you to immerse in a cultural context and mindset not of your own.

There are many assumptions present here: that there is a mind that is 'Japanese', that Murakami has this mind, that Murakami is targeting Japanese society in his works, that this is being communicated in his novels, and that reading him helps outsiders understand 'Japan'. Of course, none of these can really be taken for granted.

In some cases, the reviewers also make comment on Japanese linguistic elements, such as puns, key Japanese terms, and the meaning of the character names in *Colorless Tsukuru Tazaki and his years of pilgrimage*. Jose (2014) explores the debates regarding the perceived 'un-Japaneseness' of Murakami's writing style, but maintains that as influenced by American literature and culture as Murakami may be, he is 'equally an author formed from and immersed in the culture of his own language'. Overall, the role of the translators is little mentioned in the reviews, except for passing mentions such as Davies (2014) suggesting that some of the linguistic stumbles are 'possibly the product of the translation from Japanese to English' and Josephine (2011) on the mammoth effort to translate *1Q84* quickly despite its sheer length. But otherwise there is little to no discussion of the translators themselves. Indeed, based on some reviews, the reader could be left with the impression that Murakami writes in English. Yet, by speaking of the specifically Japanese society that Murakami is addressing, these reviewers are highlighting 'Japan' as different or exceptional, for example, Broinowski's (2014) description: 'weird, dark underside of Japan's well-lit, orderly, quotidian society'. Here, Broinowski seems to be speaking to generally accepted ideas about Japan, especially the idea that the Japanese may appear orderly and ordinary, but something dark lurks beneath the surface.

The effect of this is that Murakami is positioned as something Other, but also as somewhat exceptional, an opportunity for the English-reading public to reach beyond their own lives. However, it also works to essentialise and marginalise Murakami's works, as well as making a number of assumptions regarding his own intentions as an author.

Murakami as uniquely Japan?

More broadly, the positioning of Murakami as specifically Japanese has a number of different effects in his reception. In some ways, it serves the important aim of legitimising Murakami as an author worthy of attention, and, indeed, as mentioned previously, as an argument for reading translated works from other cultures: reading his works gives mainstream English-speaking Australians the opportunity to experience worlds not of their own. However, the construction of Murakami as 'Japanese' is fascinating given the context that one of the main consistent criticisms has been Murakami's *un*-Japanese-ness. This accusation is based on a range of observations, though particularly his heavy use of Katakana and 'Americanised' writing style/content (Ichikawa 2010, 37, 56), and his so-called 'translation-Japanese' (Doi 2014, 99), sometimes referred to as a 'translation novel' (Matsuoka 1993, 435). Also contributing to this is the actual content of his works, such as heavy use of American popular cultural references (Kawamura 2006, 118) and the perceived lack of commitment on his part to dealing with Japanese society (Miyoshi 1991). It is therefore particularly striking that Broinowski (2012) and Jose (2014) actually overrule this narrative. Indeed, although an acquaintance of Broinowski (2012) claims that 'Murakami owes his celebrity abroad to thinking and writing just like a foreigner', Broinowski maintains within her review that 'people outside Japan can read *1Q84* . . . as the thoroughly Japanese narrative it is'. This can be read as a kind of privileging of the outsider, who is, by their removal, better equipped to recognise and identify a culture, over and above the 'insider'. This also reflects Damrosch's (2003, 6) claim that when a work is received into other contexts it is not inevitable that it will suffer 'a loss of authenticity or essence', but that it may actually gain it in many ways. In this way, perhaps Murakami is never more Japanese than when his works leave Japan.

As already mentioned, Murakami is often seen as an 'Americanised author'. In particular, he is read as being similar to the Lost Generation authors of the 1920s (such as F. Scott Fitzgerald and Ernest Hemingway) (Matsumoto 2010, 16–18), and this is an impression promoted by Murakami's claim that in his teen years he never read Japanese literature (Kuroko 1993, 157). However, there has been a recent push to reconsider the simplicity of defining Murakami as either a Japanese or American author. The argument made by theorists such as Miura (2013, 15) and Hirabayashi (2011, 47) is that the popular cultural references Murakami includes (such as the Beach Boys) are not representative of American popular culture, but rather the global popular culture that happens to be influenced by American and British cultural products.

What the above discussion demonstrates is that Murakami's position with regard to national and cultural boundaries is never fully comfortable, so given this, why do these reviews position him so strongly as 'Japanese'? Although to some extent this is obviously prompted by the reviewers' personal intentions and Murakami himself, the larger influence here, I believe, is actually the tension with national literature paradigms as mentioned at the beginning of this chapter. Although there are many perceived limitations to the concept of national literatures, within

Australia there is still a fundamental tendency to understand works within their specific literary and cultural context. In the same way that works by Australian authors must be first and foremost 'Australian fiction', so too must Murakami be a Japanese author, and therefore the Japanese cultural context becomes vital in order to understand his works and his success. Just as academics seek to 'underline the unique social, historical and political foundations and boundaries of Australian literature' (da Silva 2014, 2), book reviewers are doing the same to Japanese literature, with Murakami being subject to redefinition and reinterpretation, or in the words of Damrosch (2003, 24), 'manipulation and even deformation', into a figure who is utterly Japanese. If Murakami does not carry something innately Japanese, then the idea of 'Australian literature' loses even further ground in an increasingly globalised world. I would not say that the reviewers are necessarily doing this intentionally, but rather, the language of national literary paradigms continues to be unconsciously fundamental to Australia's own literary identity.

The Murakami brand

Of course, having established this 'Japanese portrait', there are many other 'Murakamis' that are also constructed within these reviews. The second major theme is that of the multifaceted 'Murakami Brand'. He is constructed as a popular big-seller, a Nobel Prize for Literature heir apparent, and the subject of an obsessive fandom. Overall, these different portraits serve to give an account of Murakami's place in the *international* literary consumption sphere, thus demonstrating that the Australian reception of foreign works is strongly shaped by this international context.

Murakami: the big seller

There is a strong emphasis in a number of the reviews on the sheer extent of Murakami's popularity both at home and at a global scale. He is variously referred to as a best seller (Broinowski 2012; Clark 2011) and a brand (Rabalais 2014), and there are various references to his fanatical fanbase (Davies 2014; Flynn 2011; Hearn 2011). This emphasis across the reviews on his global popularity constructs Murakami as more than a quaint point of interest for Japanophiles, but rather as an international event. As such, even for those readers who are not familiar with this particular author, he is established as someone that we *should* know, as he is a 'big deal' worldwide. Almost uniformly, the reviews for *1Q84* also mention Murakami's sales figures: referring to 'mammoth sales figures' (Flynn 2011), 'already an international best seller' (Broinowski 2012), or specifically 'four million copies' (Josephine 2011).

This idea of 'big seller', however, comes with some somewhat negative perceptions, which is particularly present in Broinowski (2014) and Jose's (2014) *Colorless* reviews. This can clearly be seen in the shift in Broinowski's (2012, 2014) attitude. In her *1Q84* review, she discusses the design of the book, focusing on both its cover and the internal content (e.g., page numbers and the listing style for Murakami's works) as an interesting series of design choices which reinforce the themes of the novel. However, years later, similarly striking design choices for *Colorless* are framed as marketing tricks. Here, the 'striking cover design' is part of a marketing strategy intended to attract new readers. As she puts it, '[T]here is nothing enigmatic about such clever marketing, nor about releasing the novel at midnight like a new iPhone' (2014). This likening to the iPhone also speaks to the position of Murakami's fiction as a middle-class, consumer object, valued as a designer product to be owned. Jose (2014) focused on the use of colours within the narrative and how these were integrated into the marketing campaign with 'colour-themed stickers' for people to decorate their copy, thus turning the book into a 'decorator object'. Again, the emphasis here is on the perceived monetary aims: an 'engaging device for launching a novel'; '[T]he colour thing is a gimmick, as exciting to Murakami's marketers as it is challenging to his translators'. What both of these reviewers appear to be highly conscious of here is that Murakami is big business; here the image of Murakami as literary and cultural outsider is undercut by the massive marketing machine that carries his works into their Western reception.

Another reviewer, Flynn (2011), seems to shift between excitement and cynicism in this regard. Flynn quips that with the excitement around the release of *1Q84*, the reader might think J.K. Rowling had just released a new work, *Harry Potter: Vampire hunter*. This comparison aligns Murakami with popular fantasy, a young fanbase, and the 'pulpy' demand for vampire-themed content. The cynicism of this joke aside, Flynn also celebrates that in the ongoing crisis over traditional print, a major 'publishing event' with such excitement over a book like this can even take place. This suggests perhaps some friction within Flynn's attitude; there is a desire for novels to achieve success, but perhaps also only certain 'types' of books.

What appears to sit at the centre of this criticism is the quality of the work itself: if *Colorless* had been received as a better book, then perhaps the extensive marketing would be more forgivable? This speaks to the sense that develops in the reviews, for *Colorless* especially, that Murakami is now largely selling on his name alone: all hype and no delivery. Indeed, Davies (2014) suggests, 'everyone's favourite Japanese writer might need a bit of a breather', and Rabalais (2014) calls it an 'insubstantial version of what we have come to expect when we open a Murakami book' – I will return to the 'Murakami book' comment later in this chapter. Within the context of a book that under-delivers, the massive hype around the concept of 'Murakami' within the consumer market becomes worthy of suspicion.

However, what is not mentioned by the reviewers is that it is a very specific set of countries in which Murakami is popular: those with a large and, especially in the case of China, growing middle class. Kawamura (2006, 37–38) makes the point that Murakami's works serve as a guidebook for how to live in a Westernised, internationalised, post-industrialised country. Therefore, it is worth noting that Murakami's 'universal popularity' is not necessarily as broad as the figures might appear to initially suggest.

Within the Australian context of these reviews, however, this idea of Murakami as a big seller has some unique meanings. The first is that as residents of a fellow comfortably middle-class-driven country, Australians are positioned alongside the lining-up Londoners as the likely audience for an internationally recognised writer. Moreover, it could be interpreted as being quite important that Australian readers understand the importance of Murakami in the global system if we are to keep pace with the other Western consumer powers. Again, in other words, Australians should read Murakami because everyone else is, even if he is now a product of clever marketing.

Murakami as respected author

The counter-point to the idea of Murakami's extensive popularity is the positioning of him as also being an author highly respected by the literary establishment. This is similarly connected to the idea of the Murakami brand, but shifts the focus away from the sheer numbers, to his position as someone *worthy* of our attention and respect.

The first aspect of this is the discussion of Murakami's literary prizes, and especially talk of the Nobel Prize for Literature. This solidifies within the reviews the idea that Murakami is more than just a big seller: he is someone who writes literary works of value, and that this is something that has been acknowledged more broadly. For example, Broinowski (2012) notes that '[M]any expect him soon to add the Nobel to his literary prizes', and again in her *Colorless* review, '[T]he hints from reviewers and publishers about a future Nobel Prize for Murakami's impressive oeuvre are becoming broader'. Flynn (2011) mentions both the Novel prize and Murakami's other literary prizes. What these references tell the reader is that not only has Murakami already won a number of prizes, but that those who know about these things expect even greater fame and prestige.

However, the much more broadly used technique is the construction of the idea of the 'Murakami novel' and discussions of the 'Murakami canon'. This idea emphasises that Murakami is doing something unique with his writing, and that this 'specialness' is part of his success and worth. Murakami has developed a reputation for the use of similar symbols or characters across his works (Shimizu 2006; Yamasaki 2013; Suzumura 2015), to the point that even casual readers of his works are likely to notice. As such, many of the reviewers mention this particular trait of his, as well as sometimes making direct connections to previous works: 'familiar obsessions with beautiful ears and mysterious cats appear' (Hearn 2011), '[A]depts of his work will find most of the familiar tropes' (Flynn 2011), '[T]hemes that Murakami has explored in the past inform much of the surreal world' (Josephine 2011), 'this novel is trademark Murakami' (Clark 2011), 'familiar ingredients' (Broinowski 2014), 'long list of feckless Murakami protagonists' (Wright 2014). Although not always explicitly stated, there develops from this narrative the concept of the 'Murakami novel': carrying with it a particular set of traits and style. Indeed, this sensation is so strong that reviewers such as Davies (2014) can write the broad generalisation that '[T]o open the cover of a

Murakami novel is to become completely immersed' un-ironically. This develops the sense that there is also something unique about Murakami's writing, though the books themselves are at times very similar. The strongest example of this is in Broinwoski's *Colorless* review, in which she provides the following description of a Murakami plot:

> Often there is a disingenuous, solitary young man whose parents are remote or absent, a large old house, an elegant older woman, a wise male friend, a worldly girlfriend. As well there is jazz, a particular piece of classical music, casual clothes carefully chosen, a demanding exercise regime, food and wine sparingly consumed at home or in small restaurants, and details of journeys by car or train, often to a dark forest. But all is not as it seems. Inexplicable events and strange physical sensations soon begin to worry the young man who, typically, is too diffident to unburden himself to others.
>
> (Broinowski 2014)

Although Broinowski is being humorous in the above paragraph, she is not wrong: she could legitimately be describing any number of Murakami's novels.

Of the reviewers making these comparisons, Wright (2014) is the only one to explicitly mention the idea that Murakami actually writes two distinct types of novels: 'ingenious, pyrotechnical tour de forces' and 'simpler more intimate novels', '[W]hile the former novels deal with the blurring of dream and reality, the latter tend to be fuelled by the blurring of the romantic and the platonic, often in the context of emotional rescue'. Davies (2014) makes a similar point, though with a less explicit distinction, between his major works and *Colorless* as a smaller and quieter work: '[T]his is more a folk song than symphony, and like any good folk song it feels instantly familiar'. It is striking that these two works that I am discussing here are also from these two different categories: *1Q84* is certainly a sprawling, reality-bending trip, whilst *Colorless* is far shorter and focused on relationships.

As already mentioned, this construct of the 'Murakami novel' or 'novels' serves as argument for uniqueness. Of course, this construction plays a major role within the reviews in making Murakami a knowable entity (and perhaps is also an inside joke with his fans). There is also at times perhaps some cynicism here: the implication that Murakami is simply recreating that which has already successfully sold. However, interestingly, the argument for Murakami's uniqueness ties strongly into the issue of the Nobel Prize for Literature. By definition, this prize is awarded 'to the person who shall have produced in the field of literature the most outstanding work in an ideal direction' (Facts on the Nobel Prize in Literature 2016, n.p.). Therefore, it is not enough to write good literature; the works must be original and pushing literature in a direction that the prize committee defines as 'ideal'. Arguably this description aligns very closely with the descriptions the reviewers are providing. This is not to say that the reviewers are making an undercover effort to win Murakami the Nobel Prize for Literature, but rather that the evaluative concepts that are used to identify important and valuable literature are the same for Australian book reviewers as the global literary establishment. Murakami is being described as having a unique writing style, and moreover as having created a new type of novel called a 'Murakami novel', identifiable and specific to him, but which speaks to a massive global audience. In this sense, the construction of this uniqueness is serving a similar purpose to the discussion of his sales figures: he is special and worthy of attention, but also universally beloved.

The Murakami fandom

The final aspect of the Murakami brand that warrants discussion here is the sheer scale and commitment of his fans. The broadly accepted term for them has become 'Harukists' (Kuroko 2015), carrying connotations of obsessive commitment to Murakami and his works, and the term is now used in English coverage of Murakami's global presence (Kato and Wong 2017; Kelts 2012). A number of the reviewers mention Murakami fans, either as a potential audience member by speaking directly to them as 'you', or indirectly as an entity of which the reader may not be aware.

The Harukists are employed here to explain a number of different aspects of the Murakami brand. One major aspect is the sheer purchasing power that he therefore commands, as it is brought to our attention that if Murakami mentions a novel or piece of music, it will immediately become a best seller in Japan (Broinowski 2014). However, another is the sense that he has a devoted public who experiences and perceives his works differently: his fans will overlook issues or flaws in his works that a new reader will not (Hearn 2011). Therefore, in order to straddle the gap between the fandom and the disappointing works Murakami appears to be producing, a number of reviewers recommend that their readers go and read Murakami's great works first, and then return to these newer releases (Flynn 2011) in order to understand what the 'fuss' is about (Davies 2014). To some extent this appears to be an attempt to explain Murakami to those less familiar, but perhaps also to validate the reviewer's own mixed feelings about his newer offerings.

As mentioned above, this speaks to the problem that emerges when an author or creator becomes so popular and widely respected: they cannot be evaluated purely on their own merit, but instead as a known brand. This is similar to a point that one of Murakami's translators made to Flynn (2011): earlier works had chapters removed when translated, and that would *never* be done now due to 'Murakami's fame'. Doi (2014, 3–5) makes a counter-point to this: Murakami's works are not themselves evaluated; he receives a positive or negative response based entirely on the reviewer's personal opinion of *him* and his works overall – the author has overridden the work.

These narratives of uniqueness, as well as all but universal popularity, do not necessarily contradict one another. However, they are not the same 'Murakami' being constructed, but rather a multifaceted 'Murakami brand'. Arguably, one of the main effects of the discussion on Murakami's global, but also cult-like, popularity is one of keeping pace: we (the English-speaking, Australian reading public) should care about Murakami because everyone else does.

Conclusion

This chapter has focused on two key 'Murakamis' being constructed in these reviews: 'Murakami as Japan' and the 'Murakami brand'. The different techniques employed do not necessarily contradict each other, but they do demonstrate the tension present within the various aims or goals of the reviewers. As mentioned previously, within critical discussions more generally, we have seen an increasing emphasis on world literature over national literature paradigms. Indeed, Arimitsu (2014) argues that in Australia the concept of 'national literature' has all but disappeared due to Australia's multicultural context. This stands in direct contrast, however, to some of the major Australian literature specialists who argue that national paradigms are still an unacknowledged, fundamental assumption. Moreover, what is demonstrated in the construction of 'Murakami as Japan' within these reviews is that national literature thinking is indeed incredibly influential in how foreign works are understood and received within Australia. Yet, this idea of the 'Murakami brand' is strongly outward looking, focused on the global consumer market and his popularity. Therefore, Murakami cannot be just one thing: he must be an example of a specific cultural context, but also part of a massive world literary system, and perhaps a kind of global literary canon.

This also speaks to broader issues in the reception of translated texts. As already mentioned, a major part of the world literature system as Damrosch positions it is that a text will be significantly transformed when it is received within another culture. Yet for Australia this is not a direct relationship: we receive Murakami via his American translators and often later than other countries. Therefore, when Australians read Murakami, they are reading him as an already established global might, valued by the insular American fiction market and fashionable amongst our global 'equals'. Moreover, in world literature paradigms that focus on the idea of centre-periphery (such as Casanova), Australia is in some ways equally, if not more, periphery than Japan ever was. Yet, due to Australia's alignment with America and Europe, Japan can be Othered into a quaint object of fascination, separate from the 'Us' and the West.

It is worth stating here that this analysis is not actually intended as a criticism. There are aspects of these reviews that are worth examining and challenging. However, the approach of these reviews is reflective of the nature of the genre and the challenge these authors face in producing their texts. These reviewers must make Murakami Haruki a knowable entity and give the reading audience a sense that they 'get' the author. In some cases, the aim seems to be to create a relatively gentle review, creating knowledge rather than a criticism, in others there is a bid to go much deeper into critical discussions. Yet all of these reviews are managing a range of audiences, spanning from the committed fan who may take offence to the newly introduced who has never even heard of Murakami before.

There is a tension present here, with Murakami made over many times, as utterly Japanese, as a writer of popular fiction, as a Nobel Laureate-to-be, or even as the object of marketing overhype. Yet, in order to sustain the narrative of Australian literature as unique, Murakami's works as Japanese literature become unconsciously vital. Meanwhile, Murakami's importance and reception must also be placed on a global scale. As such, the Australian reception of Murakami is as much about the Australia's national literary paradigms and its relationship with the rest of the world as the actual works themselves.

Acknowledgment

The research for this chapter was partially undertaken whilst in residence at Waseda University, Tokyo, as a Japan Foundation Fellow, as well as through the generosity of the Tokyo Foundation and The University of Queensland's QPJE funding.

Note

1 The two *The Monthly* reviews are currently behind a paywall; however, this was not previously the case.

References

Arimitsu, Y. 2014. 'Nation, Identity, and Subjectivity in Globalizing Literature', *Coolabah*, 13: 1–12.

Baik, J. 2010. 'Murakami Haruki and the Historical Memory of East Asia', *Inter-Asia Cultural Studies*, 11 (1): 64–72.

Broinowski, A. 2012. 'Quests for Love in Japan's Proust', *Australian Book Review*, accessed 5 July 2016, www.australianbookreview.com.au/abr-online/archive/2012/67-march-2012/807-haruki-murakami-1q84.

———. 2014. 'Haruki Murakami's New Novel', *Australian Book Review*, accessed 5 July 2016, www.australianbookreview.com.au/abr-online/123-october-2014-no-365/2159-haruki-murakami-s-new-novel.

Chozick, M. R. 2008. 'De-Exoticising Haruki Murakami's Reception', *Comparative Literature Studies*, 45 (1): 62–73.

Clark, B. 2011. 'Little People Take Over Big Brother', *News*, accessed 5 July 2016, www.news.com.au/entertainment/books-magazines/little-people-take-over-big-brother/story-fna50uae-1226179538233.

da Silva, A. S. 2014. 'The Nation or the Globe? Australian Literature and/in the World', *Journal of the Association for the Study of Australian Literature*, 14 (5): 1–6.

Damrosch, D. 2003. *What Is World Literature*. Princeton and Oxford: Princeton University Press.

Davies, N. 2014. 'Book Review: "Colorless Tsukuru" by Haruki Murakami', *Adelaide Now*, accessed 5 July 2016, www.adelaidenow.com.au/lifestyle/sa-lifestyle/book-review-colorless-tsukuru-by-haruki-murakami/news-story/cd253e05db4c6407dbb7658f2b5e47be.

Dixon, R. 2007. 'Australian Literature: International Contexts', *Southerly*, 67 (1–2): 15–27.

———. 2012. 'Scenes of Reading: Is Australian Literature World Literature?' in P. Kirkpatrick and R. Dixon (eds.), *Republics of Letters: Literary Communities in Australia*. Sydney: Sydney University Press, 71–84.

Dixon, R. and Rooney, Brigid. 2013. 'Introduction: Australian Literature, Globalisation, and the Literary Province', in R. Dixon and B. Rooney (eds.), *Scenes of Reading: Is*

Australian Literature a World Literature. Melbourne: Australian Scholarly Publishing, ix–xxxvi.
Doi, Y. 2014. *Ima, Murakami Haruki o yomu koto [Reading Murakami Haruki Now]*. Nishinomiya: Kwansei Gakuin University Press.
Dymocks, 2012. 'Top 101 2012', accessed 30 July 2016, www.dymocks.com.au/top-101/2012.
———. 2014. 'Top 101 2014', accessed 30 July 2016, www.dymocks.com.au/top-101/2014.
———. 2016. 'Top 101 2016', accessed 12 January 2019, www.dymocks.com.au/top-101/2016.
'Facts on the Nobel Prize in Literature', 2016. accessed 28 November 2016, www.nobelprize.org/nobel_prizes/facts/literature/index.html.
Flynn, C. 2011. 'Labyrinth of Love and Loss', *Sydney Morning Herald*, accessed 5 July 2016, www.smh.com.au/entertainment/books/labyrinth-of-love-and-loss-20111028-1mnt2.html.
Halford, J. 2018. 'Reading the South Through Northern Eyes: Jorge Luis Borges's Australian Reception, 1962–2016', *Australian Literary Studies*, 32 (2).
Hearn, L. 2011. '1Q84 Books 1, 2 and 3 by Haruki Murakami', *The Monthly*, accessed 5 July 2016, www.themonthly.com.au/issue/2011/november/1320388074/lian-hearn/1q84-books-1-2-and-3-haruki-murakami.
Hirabayashi, M. 2011. 'Murakami Burando wa naze ureru no ka' [Why Does the Murakami Brand Sell?], in K. Imai (ed.), *Murakami Haruki sutadiizu: 2008–2010 [Murakami Haruki Studies: 2008–2010]*. Tokyo: Wakakusashobō.
Ichikawa, M. 2010. *Akutagawa sho wa naze Murakami Haruki ni ataerarenakatta ka? Gitai suru Nippon no shōsetsu [Why Was Murakami Haruki Not Given the Akutagawa Prize? Mimicking Japanese Novels]*. Tokyo: Gentosha.
Jose, N. 2014. 'Through Colourful Doors of Perception', *Sydney Morning Herald*, accessed 5 July 2016, www.smh.com.au/entertainment/books/through-colourful-doors-of-perception-20140807-101hkp.
Josephine, I. 2011. '1Q84 Book Review', *Readings*, accessed 5 July 2016, www.readings.com.au/review/1q84-by-haruki-murakami.
Karatani, K. 2011. 'The Landscape of Murakami Haruki: Pinball in the Year 1973', in S. Lippit (ed.), *Weatherhead Books on Asia: History and Repetition*. New York: Columbia University Press, 117–150.
Kato, Y. and Wong, Tessa. 2017. 'Nobel Prize: Chronicle of Wound-Up "Harukists" as Murakami Fails to Win', *BBC News*, accessed 26 January 2019, www.bbc.com/news/world-asia-41521260.
Kawamura, M. 2006. *Murakami Haruki o dō yomu ka [How to Read Murakami Haruki?]*. Tokyo: Sakuhinsha.
Kelts, R. 2012. 'The Harukists, Disappointed', *The New Yorker*, accessed 26 January 2019, www.newyorker.com/books/page-turner/the-harukists-disappointed.
Kuroko, K. 1993. *Murakami Haruki: za rosuto warudo [Murakami Haruki: The Lost World]*. Tokyo: Daisanshokan.
———. 2015. *Murakami Haruki hihan [Murakami Haruki Criticism]*. Tokyo: Ātsuandokurafutsu.
Matsumoto, K. 2010. *Murakami Haruki: Toshi shōsetsu kara sekai bungaku e [Murakami Haruki: From Town Novel to World Literature]*. Tokyo: Dansan bunmeisha.
Matsuoka, N. 1993. 'Murakami Haruki and Raymond Carver: The American Scene', *Comparative Literature Studies*, 30 (4): 423–438.

Miura, R. 2013. *Murakami Haruki to posuto modan Jappan: Gurōbaruka no bunka to bungaku [Murakami Haruki and Postmoden Japan: The Culture and Literature of Globalisation]*. Tokyo: Sairyusha.

Miyoshi, M. 1991. *Off Center: Power and Cultural Relations Between Japan and the United States*. Cambridge: Harvard University Press.

Mostafa, J. 2011. 'Our Hunger for Translated Literature', *Overland*, accessed 18 January 2019, https://overland.org.au/2011/04/our-hunger-for-translated-literature.

Murakami, H. 2010. *1Q84*. Tokyo: Shinchosha.

———. 2013. *Shikisai o motanai Tazaki Tsukuru to, kare no junrei no toshi [Colorless Tsukuru Tazaki and His Years of Pilgrimage]*. Tokyo: Bungeishunjū.

Rabalais, K. 2014. 'Colorless Tsukuru Tazaki and His Years of Pilgrimage', *The Monthly*, accessed 5 July 2016, www.themonthly.com.au/issue/2014/september/1409493600/kevin-rabalais/'colorless-tsukuru-tazaki-and-his-years-pilgrimage'.

Sakai, N. 1989. 'Modernity and Its Critique: The Problem of Universalism and Particularism', in M. Miyoshi and H. D. Harootunian (eds.), *Postmodernism and Japan*. Durham and London: Duke University Press, 93–122.

Shimizu, Y. 2006. *Murakami Haruki wa kuse ni naru [Murakami Haruki Becomes a Habit]*. Tokyo: Asahi Shinso.

Suter, R. 2008. *The Japanization of Modernity: Murakami Haruki Between Japan and the United States*. Cambridge: Harvard University Asia Center.

Suzumura, K. 2015. *Murakami Haruki wa denkineko no yume o miru ka? Murakami neko ansorojii [Does Murakami Haruki Dream of Electric Cats? The Murkami Cat Anthology]*. Tokyo: Sairyusha.

Whitmore, A. 2018. 'Australia's Taste for Translated Literature Is Getting Broader, and That's a Good Thing', *The Conversation*, accessed 18 January 2019, http://theconversation.com/australias-taste-for-translated-literature-is-getting-broader-and-thats-a-good-thing-94402.

Wright, E. 2014. 'Haruki Murakami's Pilgrimage Infused with the Spirit of Wabi-Sabi', *The Australian*, accessed 5 July 2016, www.theaustralian.com.au/arts/review/haruki-murakamis-pilgrimage-infused-with-the-spirit-of-wabisabi/news-story/9eb4e2327c10cb769b3dc88a2306dd2d.

Yamasaki, M. 2013. *Murakami Haruki to kanojo, Hokkaidō . . . [Murakami Haruki and Girlfriends, Hokkaido]*. Tokyo: Sairyusha.

11 Why introductory Japanese? An Australian case study

Chihiro Kinoshita Thomson

Right assumptions?

As lecturers of Japanese, we would naturally assume that the students in tertiary Japanese language classrooms are there to learn the Japanese language. We might assume that they are serious about learning Japanese to the advanced levels. We might also assume that in Australian universities, students enrol in introductory Japanese courses to perhaps learn Japanese and use it in travel, in future careers, or to gain course credit. However, after some research, I have reason to debate these assumptions. Doubt has arisen for various reasons that I encountered in my years of teaching introductory Japanese at UNSW.[1] Firstly, the majority of introductory Japanese students at UNSW are non-Arts students who cannot major in Japanese. Secondly, the majority of students are already in the later stage of their university career when they start the introductory course, not allowing sufficient time to thoroughly learn the language before graduation. Some of these students do not appear to be too concerned about gaining high marks or even passing the Japanese course in which they are enrolled. There must, therefore, be other additional reasons for them to be enrolled in the introductory Japanese course than becoming proficient in the language.

In this chapter, I argue that Japanese language learning at UNSW has shifted largely from instrumentally motivated endeavours aiming to attain future jobs, high course marks and other pragmatic gains, to individual consumption of the learning experiences of Japanese language, which signals to us a change in the way in which the Japanese language is viewed and experienced in Australia. I also argue that the influence of Japanese popular culture is prominent among the introductory Japanese students and this could relate to an engagement with 'cool Japan' impacting the self-identity of those who study Japanese. I first introduce a brief history of Japanese language education in Australia, including the variety of rationales used to support the study of Japanese in Australia. I will then discuss student motivation in language learning by examining some data arising from UNSW introductory Japanese classrooms. Although the findings in this chapter are limited to the UNSW context, based on a UNSW case study, I will speculate that the findings may be more broadly representative of Japanese language learners in other Australian tertiary institutions. I will contend that, based on these findings, it may be necessary for a new rationale to be developed for Japanese language education in the Australian university context. This discussion of Japanese language education makes an important contribution to our understanding of the shared Japan-Australia cultural space, which may reach out to other parts of the world through experiences of overseas students studying in Australia.

Japanese language education in Australia

The learning of Japanese in Australia started in about 1906 on a small scale at a time when Japan was swept up by Meiji Imperialism and the White Australia Policy was rolling out in Australia. This was the time when Japan claimed victory over Qing China in 1895 and another victory over Russia in 1905. Although in World War I (1914–18), Japan was Australia's ally, Japan was still considered a threat to Australia and the Australian military started teaching Japanese for strategic purposes in the 1910s. With the outbreak of hostilities in World War II (1934–45), Japanese was in fact used both for intelligence gathering and interrogation of prisoners as well as inspection of documents and letters. In this era, learning of Japanese was strategic and pragmatic (Shimazu 2004).

This war period was followed by the era in which Japan became Australia's number one trading partner. Soon after the surrender of Japan and the end of WWII in 1945, diplomatic relations between Australia and Japan were re-established in 1952. Australia had the foresight to sign the 1957 Australia-Japan Agreement on Commerce, which contributed to Japan becoming Australia's number one trading partner in 1967. Japan held this position for over 40 years until China took over the position in 2010 (Anderson 2016). Against this background, both economic and people-to-people interactions between the two countries intensified with an increasing direct investment from Japan to Australia and expansion of tourists from Japan in the 1970s–80s. About the same time, Australian policies became more multicultural, and the government recognised Japanese as one of the most important business languages in the National Policy on Languages (Lo Bianco 1987, 18)[2] and as one of the priority languages in The Australian Language and Literacy Policy (Dawkins 1991). The number of learners of Japanese rose, and Japanese became the most widely studied foreign language in Australia (Spence-Brown and de Kretser 2010). In this era, the Japanese language was considered important for the nation's economic gain (Shimazu 2010).

The early 21st century has seen the downturn of the Japanese economy, as well as the diminishing importance of Japanese as the language of business. However, despite the sluggish economy of 1990s onwards, the number of learners of Japanese has remained stable. The learner population steadily increased in the late 1980s and 90s, was placed third at its peak and is currently fourth in the world, according to the 2015 Japan Foundation survey results (The Japan Foundation 2016). The Australian learner population is large in comparison to its total population, as seen in Table 11.1, the largest among the top five countries, which together hold 77% of the total learner population in the world. It may be noteworthy that Australia was the only country in the top five that experienced an increase of

Table 11.1 Numbers of learners of Japanese in top five countries in 2015

Country	Population	Learners	Per Capita Ratio
China	1,427 million	953,283	1/1,446
Indonesia	267 million	745,125	1/348
South Korea	51 million	556,237	1/91
Australia	25 million	357,348	1/67
Taiwan	24 million	220,045	1/109

Note: Population is sourced from Wikipedia (2019) and Worldmeters (2019). Learners are sourced from the Japan Foundation (2016)

learner population between 2012 and 2015 (The Japan Foundation 2012, 2016). We can thus conjecture that the reducing presence of Japan as an economic powerhouse has not impacted the learning of Japanese in Australia.

Another important characteristic of Australian Japanese language education is that the learners are clustered in primary education and in introductory proficiency level. Ninety-seven percent of all learners in Australia are in primary (58.5%) and secondary schools (38.7%), according to the 2015 survey by the Japan Foundation (2016).

Changing rationales for studying Japanese

More recently, the National Statement for Languages Education in Australian Schools advocated language education which integrated language and culture for all Australian students and states:

> This involves the integration of language, culture and learning. Inter-cultural language learning helps learners to know and understand the world around them, and to understand commonality and difference, global connections and patterns.
>
> (MCEETYA 2005, 3)

Japanese is linguistically distant from English in a number of aspects, the distance is evidenced by its categorisation as one of the most time-consuming languages for English speakers to learn by the US Foreign Service Institute (U.S. Department of State 2019) and Japanese comes with cultural and historical traditions that are dissimilar to those of Australia. Yet the presence of Japan and Japanese in everyday life in Australia in the form of cars, motorbikes, sushi, ramen and Pokémon makes it possible to get school children interested in comparison between the two languages and two cultures. It helped that Japanese language education in Australia developed a well-established infrastructure with teachers' associations, school curriculum guides and teaching resources. Unlike some other language groups, the Japanese teacher cohort changed from predominantly Australian Anglo teachers who had been to Japan on exchange in the 1970s, to a combination of Anglo and Japanese nationals, to now a multicultural cohort with a range of Anglo, Japanese, Korean and Chinese teaching Japanese (Armour Personal communication September 5, 2017). This successful integration of teachers has been very productive in moving Japanese language education forward. Japanese language education further offers an easy access point to wider Asia with the rise of the Asian Century. Japan has become the first 'Asia' that many Australian children come into contact with. As one in ten school children are said to be learning Japanese (Spence-Brown and de Kretser 2010), the role that Japanese has been playing in this respect is significant. In this era, the learning of Japanese has been instrumental in raising world citizens for Australia's national benefit (Matsuda 2009).

Throughout these changes, Japanese has been considered useful to Australia; consequently, policies have advocated for schools and universities to introduce Japanese. Japanese has been considered a strategic tool for Australia's security, a pragmatic tool for Australia's economy and an intellectual tool for Australia's education. It is clear that the policy-makers view the learning of Japanese language, or for that matter, all languages, to be an investment for the nation's future, as stated below:

> Our learners are the future of our nation. Developing in them language skills and inter-cultural understanding is an investment in our national capability and a valuable resource.
>
> (MCEETYA 2005, 2)

These investments into pragmatic, commercial, intellectual and cultural capital, in terms of Japanese language, have perhaps paid off, given that Australia and Japan currently enjoy a strong relationship and a 'special friendship' as described by the former Australian Minister for Foreign Affairs, Julie Bishop, in February 2016 (Bishop 2016), as well as having systematic and successful frameworks for economic collaboration and extensive, well-developed human networks. The recent popularity of Japan as a tourist destination is evident from the rise of Australian visitors from 226,751 in 2010 to 376,200 in 2015 (ANA 2016), and the fact that Australians have become the top spender per capita among visitors to Japan in 2018 (Japan Tourism Agency 2019), all add support to Bishop's claim. The impact of these policy changes on individual children and students cannot be ignored, as evidenced in the sudden surge of learners of Japanese in primary schools, that is, an increase of 20% from the 2012 to 2015 after the implementation of the Australian National Curriculum (The Japan Foundation 2016).

Australia's university students of Japanese

I now turn our focus to university learners. University Japanese classrooms in Australia are different from school classrooms in that the students choose to study Japanese, while in schools, students often do not have a choice and are made to take Japanese under the language requirement of the education authorities, or are perhaps told by their parents to take Japanese. In this sense, policy-makers' intentions do not have a strong hold on university learners' motivations and choices.

I teach Japanese at UNSW, which hosts one of the largest tertiary Japanese programs in Australia. Assuming that the UNSW Japanese program is somewhat typical of major Australian universities in metropolitan areas, what I present here may have relevance in a wider context.

Firstly, a definition of Australian university learners of Japanese, in the case of UNSW in particular, is required. Many Australian universities in large cities, including UNSW, host a large number of international students and local students of Asian backgrounds. At UNSW, roughly one-third of the student population is international students and many of them are from neighbouring Asian countries, such as China, Indonesia, Singapore, Malaysia and Vietnam (UNSW Sydney 2018). International students are prominent in the Japanese language courses as well. Combined with local students of Asian backgrounds, the great majority of the students in Japanese courses at UNSW are of Asian background, and this creates classrooms full of diverse languages and cultural expectations, creating a multilingual and multicultural space.

Another notable trend in our Japanese courses is the generally equal number of enrolments by male and female students.[3] Noting that science and engineering attract more male students in general, and that USNW has strong enrolments in science, technology, engineering, medicine (STEM) disciplines (see below), a higher ratio of male students in UNSW Japanese classes could have been expected, despite the fact that participation of male students in general in non-compulsory language study is said to be less than female students; for example, Bradshaw (2007) shows in Victoria, the Year 11 male participation rate in language study was 32.6%, with 31.3% in Year 12, in 2005. However, this has not been the case at UNSW.

The disciplinary orientations of the learners are also of interest here. The data from the Introductory Japanese A course in 2017, which finished with 424 students, shows that while a major in Japanese studies is offered by the Faculty of Arts and Social Sciences (which includes education and media), the majority of the students come from the non-arts faculties (Table 11.2). Most notably, less than 20% of the students are from arts/education/law/media, and STEM students constitute more than 40%, followed by the business-oriented majors (25%). Furthermore, our enrolment records show that the trend of having more students from non-arts faculties and more students from upper stages has been consistent over at least the past several years.

One could speculate that these non-arts students are taking Japanese in order to enhance their employability in their professions. However, their later year course choices make this less likely. Although this is a "Gateway course" which is meant for Stage 1 students (the first year of the university program), ongoing students are the minority. While Stage 1 arts students are likely to continue with Japanese to higher stages, provided they have at least three full years ahead, and they are in the arts program which allows them to major in Japanese studies, other groups, such as Stage 3 (later stage near graduation) business students and Stage 3 STEM

Table 11.2 Introductory Japanese A course students by faculty by stage (2017)

Discipline	Stage 1	Stage 2	Stage 3 and beyond	Total
Arts/education/law/media	58	9	4	71 (17%)
Business/commerce/economics	30	45	26	101 (25%)
Science/tech/engineering/medicine	60	52	56	168 (41%)
Architecture/design	11	26	9	46 (11%)
Combinations	22	3	1	26 (6%)
Total	181	135	96	412 (100%)

Note: The total number of enrolment (424) includes stage unknown (12). The data is sourced from the enrolment list of the students.

students, for example, are less likely to continue studying Japanese after the initial one or two courses. Since they are already at Stage 3 in their program, they do not have enough room to major in Japanese studies, even if they wish to do so. These students are most likely using the introductory Japanese course to satisfy the general education requirement or as an elective. They would thus not reach the level of Japanese that could be advantageous in seeking professional positions.

As stated above, Japanese is considered one of the most time-consuming languages to learn for speakers of English (U.S. Department of State 2019). The Japanese course takes up 5 face-to-face hours per week and many more hours of self-study in comparison to other general education options of 3 hours per week or online courses without any face-to-face hours. If these learners are aiming for easy credits, they would likely not choose Japanese. At the same time, students probably realise that an introductory Japanese course would not give them sufficient Japanese skills to use in their future careers. We do sometimes witness general education students changing their program of study in order to accommodate more Japanese courses, even if that means elongating their time in the university and postponing graduation. But such cases are rare. So, what are the underlying motivations for taking Japanese for these students?

Japanese popular culture

One reason may be found in the wide interest in Japanese popular culture, including manga, anime, J-drama, J-pop, J-fashion, J-video games and so on. Many of the current learners of Japanese are enthusiastic fans of Japanese popular culture, and their interest in it is intertwined with their interest in Japanese language and culture (Northwood 2014; Tsutsui 2010).

In 2012, the Japan Foundation's worldwide survey results show that the top five reasons and purposes cited for Japanese language study were: 'interest in Japanese language study' (62.2%); 'communication in Japanese' (55.5%); 'interest in manga, anime, J-pop, etc.' (54.0%); 'interest in history, literature' (49.7%) and 'future employment' (42.3%) (The Japan Foundation 2012). The survey report concludes that general interest in Japan was more predominant than utilitarian motivations. The report also concludes that Japanese popular culture has made its clear mark throughout the world. Considering the data collection method of this large-scale institutional survey, individual reasons and purposes of learning Japanese were never asked directly of the learners themselves. Most likely, a Japanese language teacher answered the survey questions on behalf of the learners of their institution. Thus, the extent to which Japanese popular culture has penetrated throughout the world could be much wider and deeper than the survey results suggest.

A past Australian study surveying students of Japanese in four Sydney area universities has also found that Japanese popular culture plays a significant role in Australian tertiary learners' reasons to continue studying Japanese (Northwood and Thomson 2012, 342). Figure 11.1 shows that four out of the top five reasons directly relate to Japanese popular culture. 'Interest in culture' most likely includes an interest in popular culture, and further, what students 'Like Reading' would inevitably include manga and what they 'Like Listening' to would predominately include J-pop songs. 'Travel to Japan' may also relate to popular culture, considering many visit Akihabara, Studio Ghibli and other popular culture-related spots during their stay in Japan, while one of the major reasons for their visit is winter skiing (Inbound Insight 2018).

Student interviews in the same study revealed that students in introductory classes, who may not be committed to learning Japanese, are already engaged in popular culture activities such as listening and singing J-pop songs, watching anime and J-drama, playing computer/video games and reading manga. Some

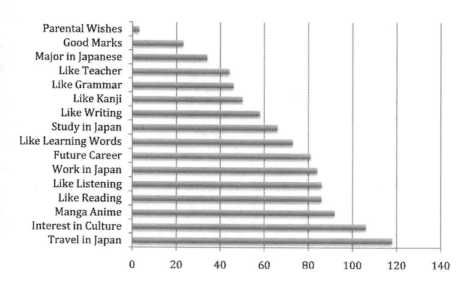

Figure 11.1 Reasons to continue studying Japanese of university learners

Source: (N = 136, multiple answers) (Northwood and Thomson 2012, 342)

stated that they watch Japanese dramas in 'every spare moment' they have (Northwood and Thomson 2012, 348). Armour and Iida's Australian study verified that for those who had or were engaged in learning Japanese, their motivation for their learning came directly from their consumption of popular culture, namely anime and manga (Armour and Iida 2016).

UNSW students' interest in popular culture is vividly apparent in their responses to class surveys run since 2007 as a part of the UNSW introductory Japanese curriculum. Every year in our second week lecture, students pick one or more names of Japanese people they know and write them in either Romanization or *Hiragana*, a set of Japanese syllabaries they are learning at the time. Table 11.3 shows the top ten names the students wrote in 2007. Ayumi Hamasaki, a pop diva, came in first in the survey by a large margin. The overwhelming majority of the names are icons of Japanese popular culture: J-pop music and J-drama stars and anime and manga characters, followed by creators of Japanese popular culture. The introductory Japanese students were, at the beginning of the semester, already familiar with a wide variety of key names of popular culture, and some are familiar with game creator Shigeru Miyamoto and manga character Kaname Chidori.

Table 11.4 shows the summary of the same class survey results in the ten-year span between 2007 and 2016.[4] In 2013, Ayumi Hamasaki, who was top of this chart for six consecutive years since the start of this exercise in 2007, had her position taken by Naruto Uzumaki, a character of an extremely popular manga series *Naruto*, which started its series in 1999. *Naruto*'s main series ran up to Vol.

Table 11.3 Japanese names that Introductory Japanese students knew in 2007

Category	No (votes)	Top three names in the category (votes)	Top ten names (votes)
Singers and actors	48(150)	Ayumi Hamasaki (50), Hikaru Utada (17), Mika Nakashima, Ken Watanabe (6)	
Anime and manga characters	31(39)	Naruto Uzumaki (5), Hajime Kindaichi (2), Kaname Chidori (2)	1. Ayumi Hamasaki (50) 2. Hikaru Utada (17) 3. Hidetoshi Nakata (8) 3. Hayao Miyazaki (8)
Anime, manga, and game creators	11(16)	Hayao Miyazaki (8), Osamu Tezuka (1), Shigeru Miyamoto (1)	5. Mika Nakashima (6) 5. Ken Watanabe (6) 7. Takuya Kimura (5)
Sports stars	8(20)	Hidetoshi Nakata (8), Shunsuke Nakamura (3), Ichiro (3)	7. Naruto Uzumaki (5) 7. Ken Hirai (5) 7. Nagiko Fukuda* (5)
Other celebrities	22(29)	Akira Kurosawa (4), Shinzo Abe (4), Musashi Miyamoto (2)	*Japanese teacher's pseudonym
Others	61(74)	Incl. Japanese teachers	
Total	193(348)		

Note: Respondents (*n* = 272), number of different entries (193), total votes (348) (Modified from Thomson 2010, 165).

Table 11.4 The top five names that introductory Japanese students knew by year between 2007 and 2016

	2007 [193] (348)	2010[1]	2011	2012 (436)	2013 (225)	2014 (397)	2015 (337)	2016 [242] (344)
1	Ayumi Hamasaki 50	Ayumi Hamasaki	Ayumi Hamasaki	Ayumi Hamasaki 30	Naruto Uzumaki 12	Naruto Uzumaki 17	Naruto Uzumaki 13	Naruto Uzumaki 8
2	Hikaru Utada 17	Hikaru Utada	Tomohisa Yamashita	Naruto Uzumaki, Takuya Kimura 15	Tomohisa Yamashita 10	Yoko Ono 9[2]	Hayao Miyazaki 9	Shinzo Abe, Eiichiro Oda, Hikaru Utada 6
3	Hidetoshi Nakata, Hayao Miyazaki 8	Shun Oguri	Hayao Miyazaki		Ayumi Hamasaki, Yuko Oshima, Hikaru Utada 8	Ayumi Hamasaki 6	Shinzo Abe 8	
4		Takuya Kimura	Hikaru Utada	Hikaru Utada 13		Takuya Kimura, Hayao Miyazaki 5	Ichigo Kurosaki 6	
5	Mika Nakashima, Ken Watanabe 6	Thelma Aoyama	Keisuke Honda	Tomohisa Yamashita 10			Toma Ikuta, Shun Oguri 5	Yui Aragaki, Tomohisa Yamashita 5

Note: The numbers below the years show [varieties of entries] (No. of respondents).

[1] I only have the ranking for 2010/2011 surveys.
[2] At the time of the classroom survey in 2014, the Museum of Modern Art in Sydney had the Yoko Ono Exhibition, which could have prompted a number of votes.

188 *Chihiro Kinoshita Thomson*

72 and finished in 2015, while side stories are continuing to be published according to *Naruto*'s official site (Naruto.com, n.p.). The series has been translated in more than 35 countries and has sold more than 75 million copies worldwide (Wikipedia, *Naruto*). *Naruto* has been made into TV, manga and anime and aired internationally. From 2013 until 2017, Naruto has been the top name that students state as a Japanese person they know, despite Naruto being a fictitious character.

The number of enrolments in the Introductory Japanese course fluctuate over the years, and therefore so do the numbers of respondents. It so happens that the numbers of respondents in 2007 and in 2016 are very similar. However, the spread of the entries is much larger in 2016. In 2016, the top name, Naruto Uzumaki, gathered only 8 votes, while in 2007, Ayumi Hamasaki received 50 votes. The 344 votes are spread among 242 names in 2016. This demonstrates increasingly diverse contact points with Japan. Speculations may be made on the reasons for this development. Perhaps the increasingly easy access to Japanese popular culture via the Internet and social media assisted its penetration into Australian youngsters' everyday lives deeply and widely, so that they each develop their own distinct world of Japanese popular culture, rather than merely following popular trends, showing Australia's divergent engagements with Japanese popular culture.

In this brief examination of Japanese popular culture and Japanese language learners, we have found that (1) Japanese popular culture provides important reasons and purposes for learners of Japanese to pick up and continue learning Japanese; (2) Japanese learners, at the introductory level, or even before entering into Japanese courses, are engaged in Japanese popular culture activities; (3) they are increasingly familiar with a wider variety of Japanese popular culture icons, and the diversity of their experience appears to be intensifying and (4) their Japanese experiences come largely from the virtual world of manga and anime.

Introductory tertiary learners' experiences in Japanese classes

In searching for answers to the reasons students come to our Japanese classes, I now turn to examine our introductory learners' experiences in Japanese classes. I draw upon their voices from an online questionnaire targeting students in the Introductory Japanese A course at the end of the first semester in 2016, and the end of the term course evaluation by the students conducted every year.

Table 11.5 summarises the survey respondents. Mirroring the 2017 student population discussed above, the majority of the respondents are overseas students, males, in STEM disciplines, not in the first year, and taking Japanese either as an elective or general education option. Although the majority of the respondents answered that they will continue their study of Japanese in the second semester, they are the 30% of the enrolled students who made the effort to voluntarily respond to the survey, who I would assume to be keener than the average students.

The answers to the survey question, 'What first interested you in Japanese?' showed that the majority of the respondents became interested through popular culture, such as anime, manga and drama (52/99), suggesting the above assumptions are valid.

Table 11.5 Respondents of the survey (99 respondents; about 30% response rate)

Nationality	Australian: 47		Overseas: 52
Gender	Female: 47		Male: 52
Discipline	STEM: 41	Business: 26	Arts: 20
Stage	Stage 1: 30 Stage 2: 42	Stage 3: 18	Stage 4: 7
Program	Majoring in Japanese: 15	Elective: 28	General education: 55
Second semester	Continuing: 55	Discontinuing: 44 (want to continue, but can't: 32)	

We may assume that popular culture fans are potential learners of Japanese. However, not all consumers of popular culture become learners of Japanese. Armour and Iida (2016) found that 55% of Australian fans of anime and manga they surveyed have studied Japanese. Of those, 48% have self-studied.

The survey then asked, 'Why did you take up Japanese?' The respondents chose many options as their reasons for taking up Japanese. Out of 540 responses, 136 were directly related to pop culture, such as 'wanting to be able to enjoy anime' (46), and 'wanting to be able to read manga' (33). Other reasons include 'wanting to travel in Japan in the future' (60), 'wanting to prepare for the future career' (30) and 'wanting to live in Japan in the future' (19). These reasons related to Japanese popular culture, future travel to Japan and making Japanese friends show the learners' inclination to invest in their future. They want to learn Japanese so that they will gain something later. As Norton Pierce (1995, 17) states, 'learners will expect or hope to have a good return on that investment – a return that will give them access to hitherto unattainable resources'. In other words, learning Japanese can be considered an investment to make these learners more efficient consumers of popular culture, better travellers and more favourable friendship candidates.

It is notable that a good number of respondents chose 'wanting to make friends in class' (29). This reason is a little different from others, as it does not project the future use of Japanese. The learners who chose this reason were concerned about the classroom experience itself. They were interested in gaining membership in a classroom community while studying Japanese.

Table 11.6 lists the answer choices to the next question, 'Why do you want to continue?' which was asked to those who answered that they would continue studying Japanese in the second semester.

The choice, 'Because learning Japanese is fun' (40) attracted the most responses, more than 'Because I want to learn more Japanese' (36). Although the difference between the two choices is small, the 'fun' factor is embedded in other responses related to classroom experiences marked in boldface in the table. This survey conducted at the end of the semester has most likely reflected the characteristics of the classrooms in which the respondents had studied. This particular introductory course emphasises a variety of interactions among the members of the classroom communities, which include not only classmates and the class teacher, but also more advanced learners from upper level courses who act as mentors, Japanese

Table 11.6 'Why do you want to continue?' $N = 55$ (Multiple responses)

Because learning Japanese is fun.	**40**
Because I want to learn more Japanese (grammar, Kanji, speaking. . .)	36
Because I can feel my Japanese is improving.	32
Because I like going to Japanese classes.	**28**
Because I would like to be able to speak with Japanese people in the future.	27
Because I like learning languages.	25
Because I like the teachers.	24
Because I am travelling to Japan at the end of this year/in the future.	22
Because I like the teaching methods.	**20**
Because I would like to be able to use Japanese in my future career.	20
Because I can see my friends in class.	**14**
Because I want to make new friends.	**14**
Because I like using Japanese with my classmates.	**14**
Because I have Japanese friend(s).	10
Because I am trying to change my program to include Japanese.	10
Because I did very well in Intro. Japanese A.	10
Because it is my major/requirement in my program.	9
Because I would like to study in a graduate program at a Japanese university in the future.	9
Because my friend(s) is continuing to Intro. Japanese B.	**8**
Because I have some free room in my program/timetable.	5
Because I have Japanese family member(s)/partner.	4

exchange students and others (Thomson and Mori 2014). In transition from 'Why did you take up Japanese?' to 'Why do you want to continue?' the impact of the classroom learning experiences of the interactive classroom community is visible. To many of the respondents, their Japanese classes are a fun place, where they see their friends and chat with them, perhaps using Japanese, and that motivates them to continue with learning the language.

The prominence of the 'fun' factor stands out also in the word cloud created using the end-of-semester course evaluation comments in response to 'What was the best feature of the course?' by students of Introductory Japanese A courses in 2014, 2015 and 2016 (see Figure 11.2).

In the course evaluation comments, the students expressed their enjoyment:

- Lectures and seminars are interesting and enjoyable.
- A lot of fun during the whole semester.
- Learning a language was made fun and interactive.

Their fun derived from their engagement in interactions (including tests) with classmates and teachers:

- Very interactive and promoted individuals to learn through interactions with their peers.
- The active participation and the interaction between student and the teachers.
- The best feature of this course was the interaction test with partner.

Why introductory Japanese? 191

Figure 11.2 Word cloud of student evaluation comments (2014–2016)
Source: Author's own

The results draw a picture of a Japanese classroom where the students are engaged in having fun with classmates and teachers. As early as 1973, Kidd described three types of learning orientations of adult learners, which are goal orientation, activity orientation and learning orientation (Kidd 1973). These students may be considered activity oriented, drawing meaning from consumption of activities, rather than pursuing goals or enjoying learning itself. This relates to Kubota's study (2011) on Japanese learners of English, which proposed a view of language learning as *consumption*, as opposed to the notion of future *investment* (Norton Pierce 1995). Northwood and Thomson also speculate that many of the learners of Japanese in their study were *consuming* Japanese language as well as *consuming* the language 'learning' itself (Northwood and Thomson 2012). The interactive and fun nature of the course accentuates the students' inclination to focus on the *leisure* and *consumption* aspects of the experiences (Kubota 2011).

Motivation and investment in language learning

Language learning motivation research has a long history and for many years was led by the view of instrumental motivation vs integrative motivation posed by Gardner and Lambert (1959) and later developed into the socio-educational model of motivation (Gardner 2010). In a nutshell, the discussion was around whether students were motivated to learn a language in order to have instrumental (pragmatic) gains, such as getting a good job and good academic results, or motivated to integrate into the target culture and society by making friends. Recent developments in motivation research are in Dornyei's L2 Motivational Self System (Dornyei 2009). While Gardner's model argues for learners finding motivation externally, whether it was instrumental or integrative, Dornyei's system finds motivation within the learners. It discusses one's 'Ideal L2 Self', an ideal second language speaker whom one aspires to become, one's 'Ought to L2 Self', a second language speaker whom one has to become and the L2 Learning Experiences. A learner might picture himself speaking fluently in Japanese with a Japanese business partner at an imagined future meeting in Tokyo (Ideal Self). Another learner might be pressured by her parents to get a good mark in a Japanese class and picture herself being at the top of the class (Ought to Self). If these persons are whom they would like to become, the gap between the Ideal/Ought to Self and the present-self needs to be filled. This desire to fill the gap, self-discrepancy, motivates the learners (Higgins 1987), and their L2 learning experiences either assist or hinder their motivation.

While Gardner's model enticed motivation for the learners to be integrated into the real target community, Dornyei's system invites the learners to create and invest in their own imagined future communities, which are not immediately tangible and accessible, but can be connected through the power of the imagination (Kanno and Norton 2003). The strength of Dornyei's system arises from the language learning experiences of individual learners, which are dynamic and influence development of their views of their own L2 Selves. Thus, when learners have a good learning experience, for example, having fun in classrooms, their imagination may expand and their Ideal Self may further develop. Dornyei's system perhaps affords the learners to aim to become their Ideal L2 'Classroom-Selves' in their classroom as their target community, in which they aspire to be ideal classroom learners.

So, why do students come to introductory Japanese classes?

We have looked at a variety of aspects of Japanese language education and learners of Japanese in the search for an answer to this question, 'If they are not coming to learn Japanese seriously to the advanced level, why do they enrol in introductory Japanese classes?' Policy-makers may argue that the learning of Japanese is good for nation building, although rationales behind why it is good have shifted over time. Policy-makers and the government invest in Japanese language education and expect learners of Japanese also to invest in learning of Japanese, hopefully for a win-win scenario; that is, learners have financial, social, intellectual or cultural gain, while the nation also gains from having a strong economy or secure borders or by creating world citizens.

This scheme appears to have worked so far with the current strong and healthy relationships between Australia and Japan; however, the picture drawn by the

UNSW introductory Japanese classes seem to be different. As Heller (2003) puts it, tensions often emerge between governments and corporate-based identities and language practices, and between local, national and supra-national identities and language practices. The majority of the students surveyed in this study are not seriously learning Japanese; they are 'casual' learners who discontinue after one or two semesters, whether it is by their own choice or by the structural constraints placed by the system. At this stage of their university career, they do not seem to be investing their time to fully master Japanese so that they can pursue what the policy-makers intended over time, such as translating military documents (in the 1940s), having a successful career in a trading company dealing with Japanese clients (in the 1980s) or becoming a world citizen equipped with intercultural sophistication (hopefully the contemporary goal). Many of them are just wanting to enjoy Japanese popular culture, while perhaps consuming Japanese language and Japanese learning experiences, which further equip them with the skills of consumption of popular culture, and have fun while doing so. Their motivation does not seem to be instrumental in a sense that they do not aim for economic or academic gain. However, it is instrumental in another sense that they want to gain access to interact with popular culture. Their Ideal Self does not likely reside in the international business community or in military intelligence, but in the imagined 'virtual' community of Japanese pop culture, where they exist alongside Naruto, members of AKB48 and Pikachu,[5] or in their immediate classroom community in which they aspire to be the ideal classroom learners.

They learn Japanese to close the gap between the present-self and Ideal (virtual) Self, although in reality, they can easily watch anime and read manga in translation, whether it is in English or Chinese. They can certainly conduct business with Japanese people in English. Even if they still want to learn Japanese, they can do so on the Internet, and, as Armour and Iida (2016) point out, many popular culture fans self-study Japanese without coming to classes.

I propose one interpretation of why students come to our Japanese classes. They come to consume the classroom experiences. They might pick up Japanese because of their popular culture interests, but as they participate in classroom practices, they find it fun. The overseas students in the STEM discipline in the survey, for example, enjoy coming to the class, which becomes a place to belong. Unlike the outside world, whether it is on campus or off campus, in the Japanese classes, they are not considered a minority. Lack of social support for overseas students in Australian tertiary institutions has been reported (e.g., Khawaja 2008; Hellesten 2002). The Japanese classes have become the target community where the overseas students along with Australian students engage with others, occasionally use Japanese and gain social support.

The introductory students are investing in their own identity by being a part of the community. As Norton Pierce (1995) notes, 'an investment in the target language is also an investment in a learner's own social identity, and identity which is constantly changing across time and space' (Norton Pierce 1995, 18). These students are investing in their identity of being 'students of Japanese', which could be perceived as *cool*. They are also proactively investing in an identity of being

Japanese popular culture-loving '*Otaku*', which again can be perceived to be *cool*. The negative connotation of the Japanese term オタク has not necessarily transferred to the English term '*Otaku*', which actually carries a positive connotation. These students are consuming Japanese language and Japanese learning experiences while investing in building their *cool* identity.

As Iida and Armour (forthcoming in 2019) argue, these students who pick up Japanese because of popular culture may change and develop further interests. They cite a case of a student who took up Japanese out of interest in Japanese popular culture, continued learning Japanese and then became a Japanese teacher. She attributes her continuation to the influence of her Japanese teacher, not to popular culture alone. In other words, her classroom experiences contributed to her decision. It seems to be true for non-*Otaku* students as well that they enjoy being in Japanese classrooms, which become their community, a place where they nurture friendship through the medium of learning of Japanese. If not mastering Japanese, they are learning to interact with each other in a multicultural classroom community.

A new rationale?

If these learners do not necessarily attend Japanese classes to learn Japanese to the advanced levels, it is worth rethinking the rational for the teaching of Japanese in such classes. The language classroom has a unique socio-educational environment where the learners have to speak and interact with their classmates substantially more than they would be required to in classrooms in other subjects (Nikitina and Furuoka 2007). Introductory Japanese classes are a super-diverse multicultural, multilingual space where students from all disciplines meet. Provided that not all students have a serious desire to reach high levels of Japanese proficiency, a new rationale may lie in the educational benefit of intercultural learning that arises from being part of the multicultural, multilingual and multidisciplinary community with abundant opportunities to interact with each other, as well as learning the Japanese language itself. Even if the main goal is the learning experience and sense of community, students may still acquire 'cool' identity as learners of Japanese, while attaining intercultural competence. Ways in which the Australian students experience Japan, Japanese and Japanese popular culture have become extremely diverse, allowing each student to develop their own world view of Japan. Engagement with the learning of Japanese has diversified to include a large cohort of learners who consume Japanese language classroom learning experiences and a large group of Japanese popular culture fans who self-study Japanese, rather than joining formal learning opportunities, while another group of Japanese popular culture fans do not study Japanese.

Further, we might note that the overseas students in introductory Japanese courses come to Australian universities to study in their own discipline (e.g., STEM, business) while polishing their English. They return to their own country equipped with their disciplinary expertise, improved English and some Japanese skills as well as their intercultural experiences in the Japanese classrooms. In the

UNSW classrooms, these overseas students, Australian students and teachers of Japanese experience a shared Australia-Japan cultural space, where Japanese is taught and learned from Australian perspectives. In this sense, Australian classrooms offer the 'third space' (Bhabha 1994), that is neither their home country nor Japan, for overseas students to learn Japanese, which impacts their self-identity and will be taken back to their home countries.

Conclusion

Australian governments advocate Japanese language learning as an investment and therefore direct considerable resources into the field. The UNSW survey, however, demonstrates that a substantial number of students learn Japanese as an act of consumption rather than for utilitarian purposes. The learners surveyed in this study provide insight into how they consume the Japanese language and their learning experiences while they build their own identity and their own social capital both within and outside of their diverse classroom community. The consumed classroom experiences of learning Japanese in UNSW and perhaps other parts of Australia by international students may lead to unintended re-shaping of their world view. The views of policy-makers and these learners are intertwined and paint a new picture of Japan-Australia relations. While it is difficult to pin down one single new rationale for teaching Japanese, as the diversification of learner engagement with Japan and Japanese intensifies, teaching rationales will inevitably become complex, reflecting a changing relationship between perceptions of the two countries.[6]

Notes

1 UNSW, Sydney, formerly known as the University of New South Wales.
2 The policy notes that Indonesian/Malay, Japanese and Mandarin/Chinese in particular are important for the conduct of business.
3 The 2019 enrollment list in the Introductory Japanese A-1 course shows 47% males and 53% females.
4 Detailed records for 2008 and 2009 are unavailable.
5 *Pokemon Go* has already made this virtual community a pseudo reality!
6 Acknowledgement: I would like to thank Dr William Armour, the members of my postgraduate study group and the editorial team for their constructive comments given to the earlier version of this paper.

References

ANA. 2016. 'Gaikokujin kankōkyakusū toshibetsu kunibetu rankingu', *ANA Travel and Life*, accessed 19 February 2019, https://www.ana.co.jp/travelandlife/infographics/vol08/.

Anderson, K. 2016. 'Does Making Japan Still Matter: Teachers, Study-Abroad and Relevance', in C. K. Thomson (ed.), *2014 Local Connections: Global Visions: National Symposium on Japanese Language Education Proceedings*. Sydney: Japan Foundation, 14–25.

Armour, W. and Iida, S. 2016. 'Are Australian Fans of Anime and Manga Motivated to Learn Japanese Language?' *Asia Pacific Journal of Education*, 36 (1): 31–47.

Bhabha, H. K. 1994. *The Location of Culture*. London and New York: Routledge.

Bishop, J. 2016. 'Remarks at the 40th Anniversary of the Basic Treaty of Friendship and Cooperation Between Australia and Japan', 21 November, accessed 19 February 2019, http://foreignminister.gov.au/speeches/Pages/2016/jb_sp_160216.aspx?w=tb1CaGpkPX%2FlS0K%2Bg9ZKEg%3D%3D.

Bradshaw, J. 2007. 'Are Second Language Classroom Gendered?' in H. Marriott, T. Moor and R. Spence-Brown (eds.), *Learning Discourses and the Discourses of Learning*, Chapter 18. Monash University ePress, accessed 19 February 2019, http://books.publishing.monash.edu/apps/bookworm/view/Learning+Discourses+and+the+Discourses+of+Learning/134/xhtml/chapter18.html.

Dawkins, J. 1991. *Australia's Language: The Australian Language and Literacy Policy*. Department of Employment, Education and Training. Canberra: Australian Government Publishing Service.

Dornyei, Z. 2009. 'The L2 Motivational Self System', in Z. Dornyei and E. Ushioda (eds.), *Motivation, Language Identity and the L2 Self*. Clevedon: Channel View Publications, 9–42.

Gardner, R. C. 2010. *Motivation and Second Language Acquisition: The Socio-Educational Model*. New York: Peter Lang Publishing.

Gardner, R. C. and Lambert, W. E. 1959. 'Motivational Variables in Second Language Acquisition', *Canadian Journal of Psychology*, 13 (4): 266–272.

Heller, M. 2003. 'Globalization, New Economy, and the Commodification of Language and Identity', *Journal of Sociolinguistics*, 7 (4): 473–492.

Hellsten, M. 2002. 'Students in Transition: Needs and Experiences of International Students in Australia', Paper presented at the 16th Australian International Education Conference, Hobart, Tasmania, accessed 20 February 2019. http://aiec.idp.com/uploads/pdf/Hellsten_p.pdf.

Higgins, T. 1987. 'Self-Discrepancy: A Theory Relating Self and Affect', *Psychology Review*, 94 (3): 319–340.

Iida, S. and Armour, W. S. Forthcoming, 2019. 'The Voices of Adult Anime/"Manga" Fans in Australia: Motivations, Consumption Patterns and Intentions to Learn the Japanese Language', East Asian Journal of Popular Culture.

Inbound Insight. 2018. 'Nihon nara dewa o jūshi. Dēta kara wakaru Ōsutoraria-jin no tokuchō', 27 September, accessed 19 February 2019, https://inbound.nightley.jp/nationality/australia/2821/.

The Japan Foundation. 2012. '2012 Nendo Nihongo Kyōiku Kikan Chōsa Gaiyō Bassui', accessed 5 February 2016, www.jpf.go.jp/j/project/japanese/survey/result/dl/survey_2012/2012_s_excerpt_j.pdf.

———. 2016. 'Japanese-Language Education Survey (News Flash)', accessed 19 February 2019, www.jpf.go.jp/j/about/press/2016/dl/2016-057-2.pdf.

Japan Tourism Agency. 2019. 'Results of the Consumption Trends of International Visitors to Japan Survey for the October–December Quarter of 2018 (Preliminary Report)', accessed 19 February 2019, www.mlit.go.jp/kankocho/index.html.

Kanno, Y. and Norton, B. 2003. 'Imagined Communities and Educational Possibilities: Introduction', *Journal of Language, Identity, and Education*, 2 (4): 241–249.

Khawaja, N. G. 2008. 'A Comparison of International and Domestic Tertiary Students in Australia', *Journal of Psychologists and Counsellors in Schools*, 18 (1): 30–46.

Kidd, J. R. 1973. *How Adults Learn*. New York: Associated Press.

Kubota, R. 2011. 'Learning a Foreign Language as Leisure and Consumption: Enjoyment, Desire, and the Business of *eikaiwa*', *International Journal of Bilingual Education and Bilingualism*, 14 (4): 473–488.
Lo Bianco, J. 1987. *National Policy on Languages*. Canberra: Australian Government Publishing Service.
Matsuda, Y. 2009. *Tabunka Shakai Ōsutoraria no Gengo kyōiku Seisaku*. Tokyo: Hitsuji Shobou.
MCEETYA. 2005. 'National Statement for Languages Education in Australian Schools: National Plan for Languages Education in Australian Schools 2005–2008', accessed 19 February 2019, www.curriculum.edu.au/verve/_resources/languageeducation_file.pdf.
Nikitina, L. and Furuoka, F. 2007. 'Language Classroom: A "Girls' Domain"? Female and Male Students Perspectives on Language Learning', *MICOLLAC 2007*, 1–12, ERIC Document, accessed 19 February 2019, https://files.eric.ed.gov/fulltext/ED508640.pdf.
Northwood, B. 2014. 'Passion, Persistence & Learning Japanese', in D. Y. Lee (ed.), *Proceedings of the 18th Conference of the Japanese Studies Association of Australia*, Peer-reviewed Full Papers, The Australian National University.
Northwood, B. and Thomson, C. K. 2012. 'What Keeps Them Going? Investigating Ongoing Learners of Japanese in Australian Universities', *Japanese Studies*, 32 (3): 335–355.
Norton Pierce, B. 1995. 'Social Identity, Investment, and Language Learning', *TESOL Quarterly*, 29 (1): 9–31.
Shimazu, T. 2004. *Ōsutoraria no Nihongo kyōiku to Nihon no Tai Ōsutoraria Nihongo Hukyū*. Tokyo: Hitsuji Shobou.
———. 2010. *Gengo Seisaku to shite "Nihongo no Hukyū" wa Dō Atta ka*. Tokyo: Hitsuji Shobou.
Spence-Brown, R. L. and Kretser, A. D. 2010. *The Current State of Japanese Language Education in Australian Schools*. Carlton South, VIC: Education Services Australia Ltd.
Thomson, C. K. 2010. 'Understanding Australian Learners of Japanese', *The Otemon Journal of Australian Studies*, 36: 157–170.
Thomson, C. K. and Mori, T. 2014. 'Japanese Communities of Practice: Creating Opportunities for Out-of-Class Learning', in D. Nunan and J. Richards (eds.), *Language Learning Beyond the Classroom*. New York: Routledge, 272–281.
Tsutsui, W. M. 2010. *Japanese Popular Culture and Globalization*. Ann Arbor, MI: Association for Asian Studies.
UNSW Sydney. 2018. '2018 at a Glance', accessed 20 February 2019, www.unsw.edu.au/sites/default/files/documents/2018-At-a-Glance.pdf.
U.S. Department of State. 2019. 'The Foreign Service Institute Language Difficulty Ranking', accessed 19 February 2019, www.state.gov/m/fsi/sls/c78549.htm.
Wikipedia contributors. 2019. 'List of Countries by Population (United Nations)', *Wikipedia, The Free Encyclopedia*, accessed 19 September 2019, https://en.wikipedia.org/wiki/List_of_countries_by_population_(United_Nations).
Worldmeters. 2019. 'Countries in the World by Population', accessed 28 March 2019, www.worldometers.info/world-population/population-by-country/.

12 Mobility and Children Crossing Borders

Ikuo Kawakami

Introduction: Sofia's story

"日本の方ですか" (Are you Japanese?) When I first met Sofia, a sixteen-year-old female student with Slavic features, at Milpera State High School in Brisbane, she asked me this question in very natural Japanese. The high school provided intensive English programs for newly arrived migrant students like Sofia, whose English proficiency was insufficient.

Sofia explained her story with a PowerPoint presentation in class as follows:

> I am Russian. I had to leave my country when I was seven years old because of family reasons. Then my mother and I moved to Japan. Because of this, I lived in Japan ten years. I got all my education in Japan, so my first language is Japanese. But I also speak Russian. English is my third language. I hope that in the future I'll be a good English speaker, so now I'm studying for that goal. After high school, I want to return to Japan and go to university to realise my dream, (which is) to be a graphic designer, because in Japan I can get (a) more thorough education in that area.

After I asked her to send me a copy of the PowerPoint presentation that she made to show at a conference in Sydney, she sent it to me by e-mail in Japanese;

> パワーポイントですが、内容が役に立って幸いです。もちろん（学会に）出していただいて構いません。またご質問がありましたら、ご一報ください。喜んでお答えします。
>
> I am glad that the content of my PowerPoint presentation would be helpful. Of course, you may show it at conferences. Please let me know if you have any questions. I would be very happy to answer them.

This episode has many implications. As we are in an era where 'mobile lives' are increasingly prominent (Elliott and Urry 2010, 1–23), it is not rare to meet students like Sofia anywhere in the world. However, is it sufficient to describe Sofia as a Russian-born Australian student, or a Russian student who speaks Japanese as her first language? Neither of these descriptions fully and accurately represent this female student who moved to Australia from Japan, because those terms do not characterise Sofia's world of everyday life (Berger and Luckmann 1966, 19) which includes her subjective thoughts, feelings and internal discord.

Anthropologist James Clifford notes that 'mobility' has a definitively vital place in our incomplete modern world, and insists that we should study people and society from a viewpoint of 'mobility' (Clifford 1997). Therefore, he also suggests, anthropological ethnography should be studied and reported based not on the settled place, but on 'mobility'. Sociologist John Urry emphasises the 'mobility paradigm' in social science, which means that social studies should also be studied from a viewpoint of mobility (Urry 2007). Applied linguist David Block discusses the identity of language learners in the postmodern age from the viewpoint of post-structuralism, insisting on the need for a shift from a fixed essentialised version of identity based on nationality, race, ethnicity, gender and age, to a social constructivism version of identity that is more fluid and unstable (Block 2007).

These studies suggest that we need to adopt such an approach and viewpoint in studying people on the move; however, these researchers only discuss the mobile lives of adults such as migrants, sojourners and refugees, not the lives of a child like Sofia. This chapter focuses on children who were born and raised in plurilingual and pluricultural environments since their childhood. Children constitute a large proportion of today's mobile population of migrants and refugees, and they mostly have no choice in making the journey across multiple cultural and linguistic borders into new environments in their daily lives.

Therefore, this chapter challenges the way we explore the world of everyday life that such children subjectively experience beyond the discourse commonly used in discussing migrant children in both Australia and Japan. In the next section, I introduce an analytical concept I have used to explore the world of everyday life of these children.

Children Crossing Borders as an analytical concept

'Children Crossing Borders' (CCB) is a concept I have used to analyse and explore the mobile lives of children who have been raised in plurilingual and pluricultural environments (Kawakami 2011, 6). CCB focuses not on the children themselves, but on their experiences and memories in relation to spatial mobility, linguistic mobility and language-education category mobility. Language-education category mobility means that children move between places where different languages are used for different educational purposes. For instance, some children read books and write diaries in their parent's language at home, while at school they learn in a different language likely used predominantly in the host society. In Australia, children of Japanese parents attend Australian local schools where they learn subjects in English on weekdays, while they attend Japanese Saturday school on the weekend where they learn subjects in Japanese. In some cases, they may go to Japan and attend a local school where they would study in Japanese. In other countries, children may move among three different places where more than two different languages are used at educational institutions. Such institutions may include religious facilities where a different language is spoken. In these situations, children have to learn and think in more than two different languages.

Children who have been raised in such plurilingual and pluricultural environments have experiences of crossing national borders or different cultural spaces both inside and outside their home. These experiences of spatial mobility allow children to recognise other lives and to encounter people who are different from them. These children also have experience of using different languages or mixed languages depending on whether they are at home or at school and other places. At the same time, they may have experiences of miscommunication with others in different languages. Such experiences might be unpleasant for children and cause them to realise their own language (in)competence. The miscommunication with 'others' by these children may lead to children perceiving other children as different and unlike them.

As for children of Japanese parents in Australia, when they go to Japan, they try to understand the people and society of Japan based on the experiences that they have had or on what they have imagined before going to Japan. Unfortunately, what they have imagined of Japanese society is not always consistent with the reality in Japan. Therefore, they need to adjust their perceptions of Japan, and such experiences may influence their consciousness, leading to a reconstruction of their identity.

Spatial mobility, linguistic mobility and language-education category mobility are all closely linked, and experiences within each of these mobility domains all combine to make the children think about their life and identity on the move (see Figure 12.1). The meaning of experiences and memories in each mobility domain would be stored in each silo as represented in the figure below and at the same time updated by mobility in daily life as presented on the horizontal line in the figure and the biographical move between the present and the past along a biography continuum that includes one's family history. Therefore, experiences and memories arising from three domains of mobility are the central concept of CCB. In other words, the CCB concept does not represent a child who really exists, but the experiences and memories of the child on the move (Kawakami 2013).

In the next section, I present a case study analysing the life of one 'child on the move' from the perspective of these three mobility domains.

Case study of Wen Yuju

Wen Yuju (温又柔) is a female novelist and essayist working in Japan. She was born in Taiwan of Taiwanese parents in 1980, and her family moved to Tokyo when she was three years old. She was brought up and lived in Japan for over thirty-five years. During her childhood, her parents used a mix of Chinese and Taiwanese at home.

Her first book of essays, *Taiwan umare, Nihongo sodachi* (『台湾生まれ日本語育ち』 [Born in Taiwan and raised in Japanese], 2015, Tokyo: Hakusuisha),

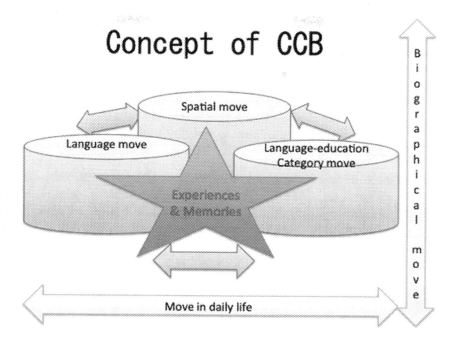

Figure 12.1 Concept of CCB
Source: Author's own

received the 2016 'Japan Essayist Club Award'. The cover of the book has a slogan, which reads *Watashi wa Nihongo ni Sunde imasu* [*I Live in the Japanese Language*]. In this book, she describes the details of her life, feelings, emotions, anger and sorrow within the plurilingual and pluricultural environments she has lived in since childhood. From my point of view, this is not simply a book of essays, but academic literature involving CCB in the sense that she has depicted her inner world constructed by the three mobility domains mentioned above. Below, I present an analysis of her life story as described in her book and examine her inner world through the lens of these mobility domains.

Mobility and language during childhood

Wen remembered that she used words in a mixture of (Mandarin) Chinese and Taiwanese when she was in Taiwan in her early childhood. In Taiwan, adults around her told her to speak this way and so she imitated these words because she could not differentiate Chinese from Taiwanese.

She explained that she was a talkative child in Taiwan, but after moving to Tokyo with her family at the age of three and attending kindergarten at the age of five, she suddenly found that the languages she used at home were different from the language used outside her home and she became a quiet child.

Her parents made her watch Japanese animation TV programs in Japanese. After six months, she was able to speak Japanese just like the characters on the TV programs and so managed to make friends at kindergarten. As she began to talk with friends in Japanese, she gradually understood more and more of the Japanese conversations in the programs she was watching. She writes that she was rapidly absorbing Japanese.

She describes one episode at her kindergarten as follows:

> ゴメンネは自分よりも小さい子、ゴメンは自分と同じ歳の子、ゴメンナサイは先生にむかって言うもの。[1]
>
> I use 'gomen ne' to apologise to a child younger than me, 'gomen' to a child the same age and 'gomen nasai' to the teachers.
>
> (Wen 2015, 12–13)

She also explains that 對不起 (duìbuqǐ) in Chinese is the only word to express apology, but in Japanese 'Gomen ne', 'Gomen' or 'Gomen nasai' should be used depending on the person on the receiving end. She described how she started acquiring Japanese grammar and learned about Japanese social hierarchy in kindergarten.

When she entered elementary school, she first began to learn how to write in Japanese. In Year One, her teacher made comments on her Japanese diary and kindly tried to encourage her to write more. Wen felt happy to read her teacher's comments and she increasingly became absorbed in writing Japanese. She loved writing in Japanese. However, when she wrote about her family in her diary, Wen notes:

> （わたしは）、まるで「翻訳家」のように、母の放つ中国語や台湾語を日本語に「整えて」から、「書く」のだ。おかげで、わたしの文にあらわれる母は、本物の母よりずっと日本語が流暢だった。
>
> [I] 'wrote' my mother's words in my diary after 'translating' her Chinese and Taiwanese into 'correct' Japanese. So, in my diary, my mother would appear to be more fluent in Japanese than my real mother.
>
> (Wen 2015, 227)

Wen's Japanese proficiency progressively improved. Finally, Wen found herself speaking only in Japanese even when she was at home with her parents. Although she could understand every word that her parents said to her, her ability to reply in Mandarin or Taiwanese at home rapidly decreased.

Perception of languages: Mandarin, Taiwanese and Japanese

Wen recognises how her mother's words were, for her, a special language. She calls it 'Mummy Language', which is one language consisting of a mix of Mandarin, Taiwanese and Japanese and so grammatically incorrect. In her book Wen expresses her mother's words in Mandarin or Taiwanese as sounds written in katakana and kanji, while her Japanese words are written in hiragana as follows:

ティアー・リン・レ・講話、キリクァラキリクァラ、ママ、食べれないお菓子。
Cause I was listening to you chattering, I missed a chance to eat sweets
(Wen 2015, 32).

When she was a child, Wen was deeply critical of her mother's use of the Japanese language because her own Japanese language proficiency was so much more advanced than her mother's. Wen said that after learning how to write in Japanese at the age of seven, she found a 'translator' in herself. The 'translator' became an 'inspector' who examined the languages she heard (Mandarin and Taiwanese) and determined whether they should be translated or not. If the 'inspector' judged them to be meaningless noise, those particular words of her mother were excluded from her diary.

Wen became rapidly immersed into a monolingual world where only Japanese was used, and she has continued her routine of writing in her diary in Japanese almost every day since she was 13 years old. Wen began to learn Mandarin at her high school, although she did not fully understand the language differences between Mandarin spoken in mainland China and Taiwanese spoken in Taiwan. She initially thought they were the same; however, when she entered university, she came to understand the differences between the two kinds of Chinese language. Wen continued to take Mandarin classes at university, and the teacher of her Chinese class pointed out that her language was not appropriate and corrected it, even though she had listened to both Mandarin and Taiwanese at home throughout her childhood. Upon hearing such comments on her Mandarin, she felt sad. She heard the same comments on her Mandarin from a Chinese teacher in a short program of Chinese language at a university in China. Afterwards, her motivation to learn Mandarin declined, but she steeled herself to speak it more. She lost confidence in her pronunciation since she thought her Mandarin had a southern provincial accent. Furthermore, she became tense during Chinese classes as she could not understand what was 'correct' Mandarin. At the age of nineteen, Wen felt completely frustrated with her language ability and remembered the bitterness she once experienced when she was five years old in kindergarten when she could not make herself understood in Japanese. She recalled the times when she had used 'ガッコウ' [school] for '幼稚園' [kindergarten] and 'ミライ' [future] for '今度' [next time] when she played with the other children in a sandpit at kindergarten.

Wen returned to Taiwan with her parents when she was in her third year of elementary school. She had so thoroughly engrossed herself in Japanese that when she played with her cousins in Taiwan, although she could understand their conversations in Taiwanese, she could not respond spontaneously to them in the same language. Instead she would keep silent. One of her younger cousins asked, 'She can't understand us, can she?' Wen was suddenly very agitated and felt a sense of humiliation. All she could do was just watch them in silence. At the same time, she felt a sense of a heart-rending sadness due to the degenerated state of her Taiwanese.

In addition, Wen's thoughts about the Japanese language that she used had also changed. At the age of twenty-three, Wen found that she could no longer write her diary in Japanese despite having continued to write her diary in Japanese almost every day for over ten years. She was struck by the question of why she was writing in Japanese, as if it were her own language since birth, although at the same time she was a 'foreigner' in Japan. She found she could no longer write in Japanese and go on pretending to be a Japanese person. Japanese language was merely a medium that she had at her disposal to express herself. She began to wonder if Japanese was just a language she could use or if in fact she could only express herself in Japanese.

Languages and identity

Wen was clearly thinking about her identity in various situations, using Mandarin, Taiwanese and Japanese. For example, she has the right to vote at national elections in Taiwan because of her Taiwanese nationality, but she wonders if it is 'appropriate' for her to vote as she does not even live in Taiwan. Another relevant episode was when Wen used to teach Japanese to children with Chinese backgrounds as a language teacher at elementary and junior secondary schools in Tokyo. The children told her that her Mandarin was funny, so she responded, 'I will do my best to learn Mandarin and so, do your best to learn Japanese'. The children laughed at her Chinese, claiming that it was more childish than theirs. However, among those children, there was one child who was a grandchild of returnees in Japan from China. Wen thought about how the child was closer to Japanese than she herself in terms of ancestry, but the child could speak Chinese and Wen, who is Taiwanese, could speak Japanese.

Wen began to wonder who the Japanese really are and whom the Japanese language belongs to. She writes that she continues to think about her own *nihongo* (or Japanese language) in situations when everyone seems to be deluded into believing that the Japanese language belongs only to Japanese people. She concludes that she regards herself as a new Taiwanese who writes in Japanese. Yet even with that decision, she could not release herself from the idea that Japanese language should be synonymous with 'National Language' and Japanese people. Finally, she realised that it was not until she decided to weave Mandarin and Taiwanese into her writing in Japanese that her own Nihongo could be free from the idea that Japanese language should only be a 'National Language'.

Wen is also sure that the *nihongo* she continues to use will also be woven into her mother language, Taiwanese (Pennycook and Otsuji 2015). She notes:

ワ・エ・ツゥ・シ・リップンウェ。（わたしは日本語に住んでいます）記憶に向かって、わたしは耳を傾ける。もう二度と、聴こえないふりをしない。わたしの住処には、ずっと昔、日本がやってくるよりももっと前から台湾で奏でられてきた言語も鳴っている。

Wa e tu shi rippunwe [I am residing in Japanese]. I listen to my memories. I will never pretend not to hear anymore. My home is alive with language are that was spoken in Taiwan from way back before I came to Japan.

(Wen 2015, 220)

Wen's great-grandparents' generation used the Taiwanese that was found in the Fujian province in the southern part of mainland China, but her grandparents' generation born in the 1910s in Taiwan had received Japanese language education under Japanese colonisation. After Japanese colonisation, when the Chinese Nationalist Party under Chiang Chung-cheng established a temporary government in Taipei in the late 1940s, Mandarin became the national language of Taiwan and thus Wen's parents' generation was educated in Mandarin at school. Wen tells a story of her mother who used Taiwanese at home and went to school and learned Mandarin. Apparently, the teachers would hit her when she did not use Mandarin. The national language of Mandarin was hammered into the heads of these children. Drawing upon this experience, Wen wrote about how she hesitated to regard Mandarin as a language of her country of Taiwan. She resisted referring to Mandarin as the language of a country where children were forced to learn by the government.

Meaning of CCB through analysis of Wen's case

In this section, I explain the meaning of 'Children Crossing Borders' as an analytical concept for Wen's case by focusing on her experiences and memories influenced by spatial mobility, linguistic mobility and language-education category mobility.

(1) Spatial mobility

Wen was born in Taiwan and moved to Tokyo at the age of three. This spatial mobility forced her into plurilingual and pluricultural environments while growing up. During her time in Japan, she sometimes returned to Taiwan with her parents and played with her cousins. Additionally, in Wen's case, spatial mobility includes her time in China, where she learned Mandarin. Studying abroad in China is thus another stage of spatial mobility.

(2) Linguistic mobility

The spatial mobility resulted in her linguistic mobility. When growing up, she heard Mandarin and Taiwanese at home and Japanese at school. She also heard Mandarin and Taiwanese in Taiwan and Chinese in mainland China. It is noteworthy that she repeatedly moved between languages in her daily life.

(3) Language-education category mobility

Wen was educated in Japanese from kindergarten to university. She also learned Mandarin at high school and university in both Japan and China. When she immersed herself in Japanese at school, she had negative feelings toward her mother's mixed language at home whilst progressively losing confidence in her own Mandarin.

As Figure 12.1 shows, Wen's mobility domains are closely connected and so experiences and memories within these domains work together to profoundly influence her life. Not only do the mobility domains influence daily life along the horizontal continuum, but also the influence on biographical and family history on the vertical continuum (see Figure 12.1) makes her experiences more meaningful, as the accumulation of those experiences and memories constructs her identity. By analysing the life of those who have been brought up in plurilingual and pluricultural environments through the concept of CCB, it becomes possible for us to fully understand feelings, conflict and the reality of life on those on the move.

Studies on students called 'Japanese' in Australia

Recently in Australia, many researchers have focused on young people growing up in Japanese-English bilingual environments in Australia where one or both parents are Japanese (Oriyama 2010; Koshiba and Kurata 2012; Yoshimitsu 2013; Moloney and Oguro 2015). In these studies, young people are referred to as 'Japanese-background students', 'Japanese Australians' or 'Japanese heritage learners' and their lives have been studied in the Australian context as Australian residents. In other words, the everyday lives of these young people have not been studied from the viewpoint of (1) spatial mobility, (2) linguistic mobility and (3) language-education category mobility used in the CCB conceptual frame. In this chapter, I will review these studies and expose the limits of their approach. In so doing, I propose a new approach in the study of Japanese-English bilingual youth in Australia.

For instance, Oriyama (2010) examined the role of schooling and ethnic community contact in identity formation and Japanese language maintenance of Japanese Heritage Language (JHL) youths through interviews and questionnaires. The schooling in this study refers to Japanese language community schools or a full-time private Japanese school [*nihonjin gakko*] focusing on the Japanese community in Sydney. Data was collected through structured individual interviews containing seventy questions and questionnaires consisting of twenty-four questions with nineteen JHL youths aged between fifteen and twenty-two. The questions focused on individual and socio-psychological factors such as family and educational background, language use and environment, identity, beliefs and language proficiency. Based on her findings, Oriyama (2010, 245) distinguishes four types of identity of JHL youths: Japanese, Japanese and Australian, Japanese and father's ethnicity (other than Australian) and Australian. In conclusion, she emphasises the importance of the role of heritage language schooling and ethnic community in identity construction and heritage language maintenance for these young people.

During the interviews, Oriyama investigated the perceptions of these young people by asking questions such as, 'What do you think of Japan and Japanese culture? What do you like and dislike about it?', 'Do you think your way of thinking and behaviours are closer to Japanese or Australians?', and, 'Do you want your future children to learn Japanese? Why?' (Oriyama 2010, 269–270). These questions, however, force students to think about Japan, Japanese culture and Japanese language from a monocultural and monolingual point of view. The questions mirror a fixed and essentialist viewpoint and presuppose culture and identity as static. Such questions are problematic and do not capture the fluid and multiple dimensions of identity of young people who have been raised in plurilingual and pluricultural environments.

Koshiba and Kurata (2012) published a case study on ten university students at an Australian university whom the researchers classified as 'Japanese home-background speakers'. The students were educated in Australia and children of parents who were either both Japanese or with one Japanese parent and a parent from another cultural background. The researchers examined the language identity (Block 2006) of the students based on the concepts of language expertise, language affiliation and language inheritance developed by Rampton (1990). Two instruments were employed as part of the methodology: a questionnaire survey, as well as group interviews. The data collected was analysed against several factors related to their background, such as information about their parents, length of residence in Australia, their age when living in Japan, country where they received elementary and secondary schooling and their formal study of Japanese. Based on this data, the researchers explored how such factors played a role in these university students' language identities.

Throughout the study, the researchers discuss a sense of language expertise in Japanese, a sense of affiliation to Japanese language and a sense of language inheritance of these 'Japanese home-background speakers'. The researchers concluded that the Japanese home-background speakers in the study were 'highly complex individuals who had various motivations for investing in Japanese, and may have complex and sometimes contradictory perceptions about their language identities' (Koshiba and Kurata 2012, 373).

It is noteworthy that these students' conscious use of Japanese language is influenced by their self-perception, the expectations placed on them by others and their plurilingual abilities. However, as with Oriyama's study above, the theoretical framework in this study using language expertise in Japanese, affiliation to Japanese language and Japanese inheritance presumes Japanese language and Japanese culture to be static and essentialised. The researchers have not sufficiently addressed the consequences of mobility on the lives of these students within a fluid, contradictory and complex context of plurilingual and pluricultural environments. The CCB as an analytical concept would contribute to problemising this context further to yield deeper and more reliable results.

Yoshimitsu (2013) conducted a study on 'Japanese-background students' taking Japanese classes at an Australian university. The researcher collected data from four students through interviews. Narratives of these four students encompassed their parents, birthplace, residence in Australia, language used at home and attendance at a Japanese school in Australia. For instance, one student, Yuka, was born in Japan of Japanese parents and migrated to Australia with her parents at the age of four, without attending pre-school in Japan. She communicated with her parents in Japanese but did not attend the Saturday Japanese School, as it was located some distance away and, as a result, was educated from elementary through to secondary school in English in Australia. She also took Japanese classes at secondary school and completed a Japanese subject for university entry requirements.

Yoshimitsu (2013, 137–138) notes 'it is interesting to find out how these Japanese-background students engage in the Japanese language classroom at university and what norms are operating in their learning behaviour'. To achieve this, in the study, Yoshimitsu adopted Neustupný's academic contact research theory and language management theory (Neustupný 2004) as a basis for analysing the interview data. Results suggest that the Japanese language acquisition process of 'Japanese-background students' differed from each other. As a result, each learner had different imagined norms of Japaneseness which he or she inherited from their parents or the Japanese community. Such expressed norms and peer-pressure norms imposed by non-Japanese peers in Japanese classes influence the behaviours of these students. In conclusion (Yoshimitsu 2013, 150–151), the researcher pointed out that the students' observation of their norm deviation is a dynamic process.

Language management theory used in this study leads us to focus on heritage language learners' language management, and the narratives of the 'Japanese background students' seem to be examined only for that goal. Again, mobility and its impact on the lives of these students were not fully analysed and understood. As a result, this study is an example of a limited approach focusing only on language management within the domestic context of Australia.

Moloney and Oguro (2015) tried to explore the multilingual identity development of adolescent 'Japanese Australians' who used and learned Japanese as a heritage language. They discussed this theme, showing two cases drawn from the data of in-depth interviews. They focused on the stories of two female university students, Maki and Akiko, in Sydney. All of Maki's family were born in Japan, and moved to Hong Kong when Maki was one year old. Maki learned English at school in Hong Kong. Her parents communicated with her in Japanese, but she replied to them in English. At the age of seven, Maki and her family moved to Australia where she entered an Australian school, continuing her education in English. She started learning Japanese as a subject at secondary school and also took private lessons in Japanese for three years. However, she gave up taking the Japanese Background Speakers Course designed for native speakers of Japanese because of her poor Japanese skills. It was not until she entered university that she resumed her Japanese language learning. The researchers concluded Maki displayed ambivalence about herself and her identity. Maki states:

> Japanese by blood, by nationality I like to consider myself Japanese at the heart as well. I am very traditional . . . there are parts of me that I picked up from Australia; I think I have different qualities in different things. . . . It's kind of difficult to say where I am. But I think I've decided to be Japanese and

to stand up for being Japanese as well. I describe myself as being Japanese, with a bit of international qualities.

(Moloney and Oguro 2015, 128)

In the case of Akiko, her parents were born and grew up in Japan. Akiko was born in Australia and has always lived in Australia. She spoke Japanese at home and learned English at school. She attended Saturday morning school (Japanese language community school on weekends) to study Japanese from Years One to Nine. She took Japanese as a subject at secondary school, but she was not permitted to take the Japanese Background Speakers Course at senior secondary school levels because her Japanese proficiency level was deemed insufficient for the course by the school. In Akiko's case, the researchers explained her multiple identities between Japan and Australia, quoting:

I am a mixture of qualities from both sides: I love both places. I'd like to work sometime in Japan, but don't think I could live there, because of the environments. I love it here, more space.

(Moloney and Oguro 2015, 130)

The researchers describe Maki's and Akiko's parents as 'first generation Japanese migrants to Australia' and use 'Japanese as a heritage language' when describing the use of Japanese by children growing up in Australia in families (Moloney and Oguro 2015, 129). They conducted interviews with the aforementioned two students and then analysed the interview data. However, before analysis, the researchers determined a number of crucial characteristics to be examined, such as the importance of Japanese language for personal relationships and the development of reading and writing skills for participation in aspects of Japanese culture. These characteristics indicate that the researchers of this study, Moloney and Oguro, believe Japanese language, in particular reading and writing skills, are indispensable for the children's identity formation as Japanese. Therefore, the conclusion reached was that the two young women's Japanese language development was strongly associated with their sense of identity as Japanese. It was the researchers who described the students as 'Japanese' or 'Japanese Australian' and asked them about their identities and to conclude their identities as multiple with attachment to Australia and Japan. The presuppositions of this conclusion seem to be based on the image of Japanese in Japan as well as Australians in Australia and the image of 'Japanese heritage learners' between Japan and Australia. This kind of perspective also emerges from a fixed and essentialist viewpoint. In other words, the researchers have concluded that the identity of Akiko and Maki is binary consisting exclusively of Japanese and Australian identities from a perspective of fixed settlement rather than continuing mobility within their lifetimes.

It is evident that these previous studies (Koshiba and Kurata 2012; Moloney and Oguro 2015; Oriyama 2010; Yoshimitsu 2013) have a common approach and presuppositions about these young people. For instance, the researchers regarded language, culture and identity as static and immobile, and their way of understanding the lives of these young people were based on a binary and essentialist definition of Japanese and Australian. As a result, the reality of these young people's mobile lives and their cognitive discord are neglected and not sufficiently explored. Therefore, a new, different point of view is needed to grasp the world of everyday life of those living mobile lives.

One example of a new approach is Thomson's (2013) research based on in-depth interviews with six university students who have been raised in Australia with connections to Japan at an Australian university. Thomson argued that it is difficult to place the students into a singular category because of their plurilingual and pluricultural backgrounds and that we should positively evaluate their linguistic competence through the lens of plurilingualism (Coste et al. 2009). She also indicated that there are many children who have given up attending Saturday Japanese Schools (Japanese language community schools on weekends) and Japanese learning itself because it is difficult for them to keep learning Japanese at home. She also noted that even university students attending a distinguished university in Australia have demonstrated psychological conflict regarding their identities and how to live with their diverse backgrounds and trajectories. Thomson suggests that there are many areas to explore in the world of everyday life of these mobile young people.

In 2003, Shiobara published research into the lives of children of Japanese descent attending a Japanese Saturday school in Canberra. His research is unique, as it focuses on the memories of these children. Shiobara worked as one of the teachers at the school and discussed the memories of children based on his teaching experiences there. He noted that children learnt Japanese culture in class and through the cultural events pre-selected by the Japanese teachers and children's parents, who believed such activities to be essential aspects of Japanese culture. Through these school activities, children accumulated memories of Japanese culture. He also reported that the memories he calls 'Essential Memories' of Japanese culture would become 'Hybrid Memories' mixed with various experiences in the future of children's lives in Australia. In this discussion, he criticises this fixed notion of multiculturalism in Australia and argues for a deeper understanding that truly reflects the pluricultural lives of these children in Australia (Shiobara 2003, 126–127).

Shiobara (2003) asserts that the memories of these children are important. Yet, this approach is limited in that it does not include the viewpoint of the children themselves, nor does it reflect on the mobile lives they lead. We need an alternative approach to understanding mobility, not from the domestic viewpoint of those settled within Australia, but from the viewpoint of people who themselves are leading mobile lives. In the next section, I will examine the life of a young man who has grown up in both Japan and in Australia with an emphasis on this mobility.

Case study of a Vietnamese refugee

I conducted in-depth interviews among the second generation of Vietnamese refugees entering Japan in the 1980s. The purpose of the research was to find out more about life in plurilingual and pluricultural environments in Japan.

Nguyen Nhat Hai (25 years old at the time of the interview) was born in 1988 as a second son of a Vietnamese family in Japan. His father came to Japan as a refugee in the early 1980s. His mother and elder sister joined his father after the father's arrival in Japan.

The home language was Vietnamese and as his brother, sister and he grew up attending a local Japanese school, they used Japanese between themselves. At the time, he wondered why his parents were not good at using Japanese language. On the other hand, his parents tried to teach their children Vietnamese language at home, but he was not eager to learn Vietnamese because his pronunciation was always corrected. His parents also urged him to study hard at school. So, during his teens, he studied hard while enjoying baseball at school, and he worked part time at a supermarket after school. Half of the money he earned he gave to his mother and the rest of it was saved for his future.

After graduating from high school, he decided to go to Australia to study and applied at the Australian Embassy for a visa. However, it was at this point that he suddenly realised he did not have a passport. After a long negotiation with the Australian Embassy during which he produced a re-entry visa[2] issued by the Japanese government, he finally received a permit to enter Australia.

In Australia, he entered a language school to learn English. In his class, he introduced himself as being Japanese, but his classmates who came from Vietnam told him that he was a Vietnamese because of his Vietnamese name and that it was wrong to hide it. This incident led him to choose a way to live as a Vietnamese in Australia and made him think about his life and identity. He decided that he could live as a Vietnamese anywhere. While staying at a relative's home in Australia, he met many young Vietnamese who were born in Australia and talked with them in English as well as Vietnamese. Doing so helped his Vietnamese improve. He entered university in Australia and studied business and international relations.

After graduating from university, he returned to Japan. In the interviews I asked him why he returned to Japan. He said that he did so because he was born in Japan and his Japanese was better than his Vietnamese or English. He also said that he would retain his Vietnamese name in Japan and believed his language skills in English and Vietnamese would be an advantage in gaining employment in Japan. At the time of my interview he stated that he planned to naturalise as a Japanese citizen like his older brother. He also said he would keep his Vietnamese name even after naturalisation in the same way that his brother had done.

In the domain of spatial mobility, Nguyen Nhat Hai experienced moving between Japan and Australia. Through the biographical domain, he became aware of his parents' migration from Vietnam to Japan and understood the experiences of people who came from Vietnam and resettled in Australia. Through his spatial mobility, he expanded his life world. In the domain of linguistic mobility, he grew up in contact with Vietnamese, Japanese and English languages. In using and learning these languages, he appreciated his parents' linguistic struggle with Japanese, and despite his struggles in learning Vietnamese at home, he came to realise the value in communicating in Vietnamese with people from Vietnam in Australia. In the domain of language-education mobility, he experienced learning Japanese at school in Japan, learning and thinking in Vietnamese at home and learning in English at schools in Australia. Through the domain of language-education mobility, he reconsidered his ethnic roots and identity by learning Vietnamese in Japan and Australia, and through acquiring Japanese at school in Japan, he was able to live and work in Japan. Although he could improve his English competence and expand his knowledge at schools in Australia, he chose to live in Japan. The experiences he had in Australia prompted him to live in Japan rather than in Australia.

The case of Nguyen Nhat Hai provides us with much to consider under the umbrella of mobility. Firstly, the languages of Vietnamese and Japanese influenced the world of his everyday life from his childhood. Secondly, his mobility experiences gained through his departure from Japan, his study at Australian schools using English and his encounters with people of Vietnamese background in Australia influenced his life course. Thirdly, this mobility led him to reflect on life as a person with Vietnamese background and how to represent himself strategically using the different language resources he had acquired.

Concluding remarks

Within the field of Japanese language acquisition, the subjective world of the everyday life of people on the move has not been examined in detail. In the present era of increasing mobility, more people than ever with different backgrounds and experiences live and travel between Japan and Australia. Within the broader study of Japan and Australia, and globally, this mobility and its ramifications on personal lives and society in general are impossible to ignore (Kawakami 2012).

In this chapter I have presented some examples such as the writer Wen Yuju, who states that she wants to be a 'new' Taiwanese writing Japanese and that she wishes to be Japanese as well as Taiwanese. Nguyen Nhat Hai emphasises that he would continue to use his Vietnamese name even after being naturalised as a Japanese citizen. Sofia, whose mother was Russian, says her first language is Japanese and would like to study in Japan after graduating from an Australian school. It would be insufficient to call Wen Yuju a Taiwanese heritage learner, Nguyen Nhat Hai a Vietnamese heritage learner, Sofia a Russian heritage learner (García and Li Wei 2014). It would be meaningless to categorise these individuals by their nationality, ethnicity or language of their parents alone, as is often seen in research to date.

In order to overcome the limitations of these studies, we need a new viewpoint removed from the notion of a static domestic resident of a particular country to a category that includes mobility and recognises these individuals as 'people on the move'. Urry (2007, 17) emphasises a 'mobilities paradigm' from which to study a twenty-first-century society characterised by many kinds of mobility involved in the daily lives of people. This approach is needed to broaden and deepen our analysis of the experiences of people who have been raised in plurilingual and pluricultural environments. To do that, 'Children Crossing Borders' is an effective and indispensable analytical concept that focuses on the core of one's experiences and memories that are shaped by spatial, linguistic and language-education mobility.

For this reason, it is not sufficient to examine the lives of people on the move only within the social context of the country where they reside. Their lives and languages are developed in multiple places and through interactions with various people and through various networks. Their experiences and interactions in these occasions and places are embedded in their lives and languages. At the same time, their experiences and memories accumulate as their identities developed, constantly being reconstituted through multiple contexts.

In summary, it is necessary for us to recognise and engage with multiple trajectories in space, time and place, to reflect on how mobile individuals interact with people throughout their lives and to try to understand their subjective world of the everyday rather than look at their lives as static domestic residents in one country and only by line of descent or within the context of their heritage language education. As in the case of Wen Yuju, Nguyen Nhat Hai and Sofia, many participants in past research studies must have had a much richer, pluralistic world of experience not captured by that research. A deeper analysis would have uncovered a world of feelings, conflict and affection. Such a world will emerge through analysis using a CCB approach. It is important that we apply this approach to the reality of people moving and living between Japan and Australia. More of this type of research will contribute to a rethink of the rich experiences outside of fixed and limited notions of the world within national borders to include the mobile lives of those living between different linguistic and cultural worlds.

Notes

1 *Gomen ne* is used to express apology to a younger child than me, *gomen* is to a child the same age and *Gomen nasai* is used towards teachers.
2 Vietnamese refugees in Japan are issued travel documents with re-entry visas because in most cases they do not have a Japanese or Vietnamese passport.

References

Berger, P. and Luckmann, T. 1966. *The Social Construction of Reality*. London: Penguin Books, http://perflensburg.se/Berger%20social-construction-of-reality.pdf.
Block, D. 2006. *Multilingual Identities in a Global City: London Stories*. New York: Palgrave Macmillan.
———. 2007. *Second Language Identities*. London and New York: Continuum.
Clifford, J. 1997. *Routes: Travel and Translation in the Late Twentieth Century*. Cambridge, MA: Harvard University Press.
Coste, D., Moore, D. and Zarate, G. 2009. *Plurilingual and Pluricultural Competence*. Language Policy Division. Strasbourg: Council of Europe.
Elliott, A. and Urry, J. 2010. *Mobile Lives*. Oxen: Routledge.
García, O. and Li Wei. 2014. *Translanguaging: Language, Bilingualism and Education*. Basingstoke: Palgrave Macmillan.
Kawakami, I. 2011. *Idō suru kodomotachi no kotoba no kyoikugaku [Language Pedagogy for Children Crossing Borders]*. Tokyo: Kuroshio Shuppan.
———. 2012. 'Children Crossing Borders and Their Citizenship in Japan', in N. Gottlieb (ed.), *Language and Citizenship in Japan*. New York: Routledge, 79–97.

———. (ed.). (2013) *'Idō suru kodomo' to iu kioku to chikara, kotoba to aidentiti [Memories and Powers of Having Been 'Children Crossing Borders', Their Languages and Identities]*. Tokyo: Kuroshio Shuppan.

Koshiba, K. and Kurata, N. 2012. 'Language Identities of Japanese Home- Background Speakers and Their Language Learning Needs', *Japanese Studies*, 32 (3): 357–375.

Moloney, R. and Oguro, S. 2015. 'To Know What It's Like to Be Japanese': A Case Study of the Experiences of Heritage Learners of Japanese in Australia', in I. Nakane, E. Otsuji and W. S. Armour (eds.), *Languages and Identities in a Transitional Japan: From Internationalization to Globalization*. New York: Routledge, 121–140.

Neustupný, J. V. 2004. 'A Theory of Contact Situations and the Study of Academic Interaction', *Journal of Asian Pacific Communication*, 14 (1): 3–31.

Oriyama, K. 2010. 'Heritage Language Maintenance and Japanese Identity Formation: What Role Can Schooling and Ethnic Community Contact Play?' *Heritage Language Journal*, 7 (2): 237–272.

Pennycook, A. and Otsuji, E. 2015. *Metrolingualism: Language in the City*. Oxon: Routledge.

Rampton, B. 1990. 'Displacing the "Native Speaker": Expertise, Affiliation and Inheritance', *ELT Journal*, 44 (2): 97–101.

Shiobara, S. 2003. 'Essensial-na 'kioku'/Hibrido-na 'kioku': Kyanbera no nihonjin esunikku-sukuuru wo jirei ni' [The "Essential" Memory/The "Hybrid" Memory: A Case Study of a Japanese Ethnic School in Canberra], *Journal of Australian Studies (Ōsutoraria Kenkyu)*, 15: 118–131.

Thomson, C. K. 2013. 'Idō suru kodomo' ga tokubetsu dewa nai basho' [The Place Where 'Children Crossing Borders' Are Not Special'], in I. Kawakami (ed.), *'Idō suru kodomo' to iu kioku to chikara, kotoba to aidentiti [Memories and Power of Having Been 'Children Crossing Borders', Their Language and Identity]*. Tokyo: Kuroshio Shuppan, 144–165.

Urry, J. 2007. *Mobilities*. Cambridge: Polity Press.

Wen, Y. 2015. *Taiwan Umare, Nihongo Sodachi [Born in Taiwan and Raised in Japanese]*. Tokyo: Hakusuisha.

Yoshimitsu, K. 2013. 'Japanese-Background Students in the Post-Secondary Japanese Classroom in Australia: What Norms Are Operating on Their Management Behaviour?' *Electronic Journal of Foreign Language Teaching*, 10 (2): 137–153.

Coda

IT'S TIME: a personal journey through Australia-Japan relations

Roger Pulvers

I was born in 1944, raised and educated in the United States. From the year I entered primary school, 1950, to the year I graduated from high school, 1961, both Australia and Japan played a minuscule part in my life and the lives of other young Americans.

Our view of Japan came primarily from movies about the war or its aftermath. Movies taking up the war depicted Japan as a nation of fanatic screaming demons recklessly rushing toward brave American soldiers and the well-deserved deaths of the former. Movies set in postwar Japan, however, were not entirely unsympathetic to Japanese people. Yet Hollywood's angle was curiously oblique: the Japanese were, down to the last man and woman, definitely the most inscrutable, most unfathomable and, if left to themselves, most untrustworthy of all people, white or nonwhite. The Japanese cultural and technological presence that was to become so evident around the world a few decades later was nonexistent. The only thing "Made in Japan" that the average American cherished was cheap and clever toys. The only Japanese film that enjoyed popularity was "Godzilla." But since it was dubbed, I thought it was an American film when I saw it in 1956 at my local Los Angeles cinema. After all, it carried the title "Godzilla, King of the Monsters!" and featured Raymond Burr, whose part had been edited into the original so that Americans could "identify." (Americans to this day have a hard time "getting into" films that don't feature their compatriots in central roles.)

No one living in L.A. and in their right mind would buy any other car than an American-made one. (It wasn't until the 1960s that the hippie end of my generation longed for the VW Beetle.) And while the Pulvers family often ate the American equivalent of Chinese food at Wan-Q on the corner of Pico Blvd. and Wooster St. (we lived in sight of Pico Blvd., in the burning heart of Jewish Los Angeles), I didn't sample a single Japanese dish until I arrived in Tokyo in September 1967. Wan-Q, with its tropical décor that included chairs made out of driftwood and a real stream and waterfall, was a landmark in Jewish-Chinese L.A.; and either the Oriental waiters dressed in gaudy Hawaiian shirts or the colourful proprietor,

Mr. Benny Eng, would be sure to enquire if a customer was Jewish to know if they should "hold the pork." (We were strictly nonkosher, so we generally pigged out on their overly sweet sweet-and-sour pork.) Being much too young to drink, I wasn't given the chance to indulge in the Wan-Q's "tropicocktail" intriguingly called "Vicious Virgin" at this iconic Los Angeles restaurant that boasted: "We feature Chicago style and authentic Cantonese foods." I never did come to know how Chicago-style Chinese food differed from that in "other parts of China" or what having a vicious virgin would do for you.

It may seem strange to begin a discussion about Australia and Japan in the United States. But America isn't the elephant in the room in which Australia and Japan come together. It is the room itself.

Japan played no part in our everyday world until the country's superior vehicles and electronic goods took America by storm in the 1980s and the country came to consider Japan a serious commercial rival. (This is a pattern in American life: Americans are wont to ignore far-off places until they present a perceived threat and can be duly demonized and dealt with accordingly.)

Speaking of ignoring far-off places, you could hardly find a country more ignored and neglected – neglect can be a by-product of taking a person or country for granted – than Australia. Most Americans couldn't identify Australia on a map or didn't know what language was spoken here. Those who knew a few things about Australia – that there are kangaroos here and that Australians wished to keep their country racially "pure white" – fondly thought of this vast cattle country as "the Texas far away from home."

And so I can tell you in all honesty that, though as I was equally ignorant of things Japanese as things Australian during my formative years, which includes those at university, I was more aware, in the full sense of the word, of Japan than of Australia.

From the 1970s onward I have often been asked to comment on the level of ignorance of Australian life on the part of the Japanese. I always found this level exaggerated toward the low end, particularly in comparison with the gross ignorance that characterised the American awareness of everything Australian.

By the time the 1960s were coming to a close, people around the world were generally aware that Australia was a self-styled white enclave in Asia and that an Australian prime minister had presumably coined the ugly phrase "All the way with LBJ," a sinister little rhyme that equated strategic obsequiousness with sexual incontinence.

I was hit by a stroke of luck, however, in the northern spring of 1972, and this jolted me out of my apathetic ignorance of Australia.

I had received a letter from the head of the department of Japanese at the Australian National University in Canberra, an institution of which I had never heard. Prof. Sydney Crawcour was coming to Kyoto, where I had been living since late 1967, and asked to meet me. The long and short of it is that after a meal at a restaurant on Hanamikoji in Gion famous for its eel, he offered me a lectureship. Here I had only started learning Japanese myself some four-and-a-half years earlier by what in Japanese is called *dokugaku*, or self-education, and I was supposed to go "down under" and teach students the language and literature, some of whom had begun learning the language and reading its literature before I had. My M.A. in Soviet studies and my postgraduate work in Warsaw wouldn't do me a bit of good.

I had been writing plays for two years with no prospect of getting them on a stage in Japan. They were in English for one thing, and for another, there was no professional theatre troupe in Kansai at the time. I figured that, since English was spoken in Australia – I had somehow acquired that sliver of awareness – then I might have the chance to see a production of one of my plays there someday.

The very next day I phoned Prof. Crawcour and accepted his offer. And so, on the evening of 13 August 1972, I flew to Tokyo and that night boarded a flight to Sydney. I transferred to a domestic flight to Canberra the next morning and checked into University House on the edge of the ANU campus.

That evening I was to go without dinner due to what might be called the "dialect barrier," a wall of misunderstanding often higher than its cousin once removed, the language barrier. An elderly gentleman living at Uni House had informed me that it was time for "tea," if I wanted it. Having visited but never lived in the United Kingdom, I didn't know that "tea" was the mot habituél for dinner . . . and so I politely declined. The other shock to my system was going outside that night and looking up to the heavens. As astronomy had been my passionate hobby since my early teen years, I knew my way well around the stars. Never having been in the southern hemisphere and knowing, of course, that the lay of the sky was different, it nonetheless came as a shock of disorientation. I felt as if I was losing my balance standing on the dewy Uni House lawn as I gazed up to the stunningly beautiful Canberra night sky.

But the biggest shock of arrival came thanks to a book I had purchased earlier that year at a used bookshop across from Kyoto University. It was titled *Australia for the Tourist* and was published "under the authority of The Minister of State for External Affairs, Commonwealth of Australia," and bore the name of the minister, Patrick McMahon Glynn, as well as the place and date and of publication, Melbourne, Australia, July 1914. In fact, I have my treasured copy of *Australia for the Tourist* before me as I write, and I wish to quote a passage or two from it for you.

Under the chapter subtitle "Advance Australia – A Striking Story," we find . . .

> Here is a vast Territory, rich in soils and minerals, which has been added to the British Empire without war or violence, a Commonwealth not won by the sword or sprung from lust of territory; in whose bloodless records there is no stain of external or internal strife. The conquerors have been the hardy explorers and pioneers, whose sole battles have been waged in subduing nature. There is no ancient civilisation to hurl back reproaches for its extinction, no people worthy to live who have been forced out of existence. The process by which Australia has risen has resembled a natural growth rather than a deliberate creation. It has been won not by clash of arms but by the triumphs of brain and muscle, and the highest human virtues.

Reading the trusty government-issued guide in my rented two-room home in the northern district of Kyoto, I felt a surge of both relief and excitement. I was going to a country that had come into the world "naturally," one boasting the "highest human virtues" and one, unlike the United States that I had left, that had not prosecuted wars of ethnic cleansing on people "worthy to live."

As I read on I felt a sense of unbridled elation at my choice of destination, learning that Australians had . . .

> . . . transformed what was a mere haunt of aborigines into a populous, prosperous and peaceful country, peopled by a race which fully appreciates Nature's gifts and resources and which applies intelligence and ingenuity to making the best use of them.

Isn't this what I, just turned 28 years old and hoping to make a small mark somewhere in the cultural world, was craving – intelligence and ingenuity in a populace? I was certainly a genius in choosing this ideal country to be my new home: an accidental genius!

Further study proved my guide to be spot on when it came to the way in which Australians fully appreciated Nature's gifts and resources. For I learned that Australia had sufficient resources to ensure prosperity for a minimum of five hundred years. Why did they need me to teach their young people an exotic and allegedly fiendishly difficult language like Japanese? After all, virtually all Japanese people were convinced that no foreigner could really learn to understand their language anyway. As for the Australians – if my precious guide, with its state-sponsored imprimatur, was to be believed – wouldn't it be much better to teach young Australians how to swing a shovel and sing the lyrics of "Don't Cry For Me Argentina" in order to keep Australia "populous, prosperous and peaceful" forever and ever? What else did they need to know?

Revelation in the Pine Break

Now, you may rightfully be wondering what an official guide to Australia published in 1914, no doubt bought by an early Japanese visitor to this country and abandoned at a used Kyoto bookshop as scarcely worth the glossy paper it is printed on, has to do with relations between Australia and Japan today. Let me assure you that it has everything to do with them.

When I settled into my new home in the Northbourne Flats on the edge of the Pine Break in Braddon – a home which, by the way, is still standing but boarded up and earmarked for demolition – I listened every night to ABC broadcasts on the little transistor radio I had bought at Haneda Airport the night of my departure from Japan. I was shocked to hear the prime minister, William MacMahon, speaking on the radio of the need to curb the immigration of "non-European" people; for, as he went on to say, "We know that those people are more prolific than we are." The clear implication was that liberalising immigration policy was akin to introducing racial "pollution" into the population. (It is interesting to note that, as of 2019, the agendas of certain political classes in Australia have not moved far off from this base, nor have they deviated from the goal of, to quote my guide book, "fully (appreciating) Nature's gifts and resources and (applying) intelligence and ingenuity to making the best use of them.")

It wasn't until the leadup to the general elections in December 1972 that I began to realise that there could be another Australia, one with a more progressive and advanced social system than the one I had become used to in my native America.

Through the window of my flat I could see gatherings of people enjoying picnics in the Pine Break. These were not ordinary Sunday revellers, by any means. You could tell by the men with long sideburns and shirts billowing out of their pants, and the women in loose batik mumus hanging down to bare feet, that these were largely academics on one of their many days off, those who might be called "The Lumpen Professoriat of the Limestone Plains," with a sprinkling of even more geeky public servants. They had clearly gathered under the tall pine trees on a mission. Drinking cask red wine so astringent that it produced a grimace – the "claret" otherwise known as "Public Service Plonk" – and chewing on slabs of what resembled a variety of non-radioactive yellowcake with the highly dubious name "Coon Cheese," they were locked in heated discussions. I had never seen people standing so close to each other and pointing their index fingers into each other's collarbones since the time of my Bar Mitzvah reception in 1957.

Only in the country for some three months and curious about this verbal commotion, I wandered out and stood on the edge of the crowd until someone was kind enough to notice me and offer me what they called a "Chico Roll." Could this, I wondered, be a roll like a bagel named after one of the Marx Brothers? If so, I had truly come to my home away from home. (As it turned out, the only thing the Chico Roll had in common with a bagel was that it would roll a few feet if you used it to play lawn bowls.)

It was a placard sitting face up on a picnic table that made everything clear to me. The placard had only two words on it, followed by an exclamation mark. Those two words put everything into perspective for me, including the ominous import of my official guidebook to Australia and the relevance of the remarks of the nation's soon-to-be ousted prime minister that I had heard on the radio. The placard read . . . IT'S TIME!

It wasn't long after the election of Gough Whitlam as prime minister in early December that I came to know what it was time for. With a speed surpassing that of the issuance of executive orders by another elected leader, who shall remain anonymous, Prime Minister Whitlam freed from jail those young men who had refused to fight an unjust war in Vietnam. During his first year in office, more than two hundred bills were passed into law, totally reforming the nation's social security system, education, health care and indigenous and women's rights, to name a few fields of reform. And when Deputy Prime Minister Jim Cairns called Richard Nixon a "maniac" for his decision to carpetbomb Hanoi that Christmas, I sat in my little kitchen with my ear to the transistor radio with tears flowing down my face. I had been in the country for less than half a year and thought for the first time that I wanted to be an Australian.

Prime Minister Whitlam's fate created a link to my own. On 11 November 1975, I again found myself listening to my little radio when ABC news broadcast the fact that the prime minister had been dismissed by the governor-general. Incensed by this affront to democracy, I pounded the table and said out loud to myself, "That's it. It's time!"

The next day, a Wednesday, I took myself to the Department of Immigration and applied for Australian citizenship. I had left the United States for Europe before antiwar protests had raged across the country and had never taken part in a protest. Now that I considered myself an Australian – though I was not naturalised until July 1976 – I was going to make up for it. Days later I joined protesters on the steps of Parliament House holding up a placard I had made at home that read: KHEMLANI VOTES LIBERAL! Khemlani was, needless to say to Australians of an older generation, Tirath Hassaram Khemlani, the dodgy financial broker at the centre of the trumped-up Loan's Affair, the ruse perpetrated on the Australian voter by anti-Whitlam forces to discredit the Labor government. I even started to write a musical titled "O Khemlani!" but abandoned it when the Labor Party lost the election in a landslide on 13 December.

Forgive me for taking the liberty of running the topic of Japan-Australia relations through my own experiences. I am trying to get to the point of my logic's destination by employing the means described in an old Japanese proverb: *isogaba maware*, or "if you are in a hurry, go the long way around."

If Gough Whitlam and his "comrades," as he often called them, pronouncing the "a" as in "Asia," had been able to take his agenda to their aspired conclusions, then Australia would surely have become a northern-European-style social democracy and a republic. These two things alone would have distanced the nation spiritually and socially from its two historical mentors, the United States and the United Kingdom. Such a move would have clarified the position of Australia in the minds of people not only in Japan but also in the rest of Asia, and would have altered the loci of relations between our country and Asia once and for all. This is where the "old" Australia depicted in my guidebook comes back to haunt us with its enforced relevance.

Sand shoes deeply dyed

Japanese people during the 1970s often asked Australians how they felt about the *hongoku*, or home country. When I was confronted with this question, I assumed that they were talking, in my case, about the United States. But what they meant was Britain. It was assumed by many Japanese that Australians naturally thought of Britain as their natural homeland. We have only ourselves to blame, of course, for this hideous misappropriation of identity and loyalty, for such a viewpoint was, for a long time, inculcated in us in our schools and other institutions. Until 1981 British subjects living in Australia for six months could vote in our elections and referendums, as well as serve in the public service. Seven million Australians, one-tenth of the population of the nation at the time, came out to see the British Royal Couple on their visit to this country in 1963; and Prime Minister Robert

Menzies wrote of it, "It is a basic truth that for our Queen we have within us, sometimes unrealised until the moment of expression, the most profound and passionate feelings of loyalty and of devotion . . . the common devotion to the throne is part of the very cement of the whole national structure." How can we blame Japanese for believing that we cherished our tie with the mother country as any dutiful offspring would?

I had another rude awakening awaiting me, one closely related to the contents of my official 1914 guide to Australia.

In August 1973 my translation of a play by the most famous of Polish playwrights, Stanislaw Ignacy Witkiewicz, was produced by the Totem Theatre of Alice Springs. Witkiewicz had written the play, "The Metaphysics of the Two-Headed Calf," as a result of the trip he had made here in 1914. As far as I know, "The Metaphysics of the Two-Headed Calf" remains the only play written by a major European playwright set in and about Australia. Thanks to a grant from the then Australia Council, I travelled to the Red Centre of Australia to see the production, exactly one year after arriving here.

I found in The Alice a town that, in more ways than one, was largely unchanged from the country at the time of the Polish playwright's visit and the publication of my precious official guidebook.

Alice Springs, August 1973. Heavy rains that winter had brought flowers and frogs out of the ground that seemed to have been waiting years to greet the light of day. The light in the outback there was more intense than anywhere I had been, the clearest air a lens that allowed you to see all the way to the desert's red horizon.

The atmosphere in this little town was equally transparent. I took a Pioneer Bus tour of the local sights. Pioneer was part of the then Ansett transportation empire. As we drove around the town, the bus driver, in company uniform – short pants, tall white socks, black leather shoes, a singlet and Pioneer cap – shared his personal insights with us passengers through his pin mike, pointing out as we passed a group of Aboriginal men standing beside a car that "they probably stole it" and that the new hospital "admitted Aboriginal children first . . . your sons and daughters couldn't get in there even though it's you and me bloody paying for it in the end."

Indigenous Australians were suffering from one of the highest incidences of infant mortality in the world; many of them in Alice Springs lived in and around the dry Todd River bed; the local lockup was full of Aboriginals young and old, some of them painting pictures given by jailers to white agents who sold them in the well-patronised little art galleries of the town for their own profit. I bought one thing in a gallery, not a contemporary painting. It was a beautiful dot painting of an emu on the back of a tortoise shell. I learned later that it was hundreds of years old and originated in the far north of Australia. It cost $10. I gave it to the Australia Museum in Canberra when it opened, to be displayed with the sign "Donated by a Friend of Japan."

There were centenary celebrations at Uluru over the "discovery," in August 1873, of Ayers Rock. In those days the present name, Uluru, was unknown to white Australians, many of whom seemed to believe that Europeans were the first real people to happen upon this magnificent monolith, one of the most awesome objects I have seen in my life, described by its 19th-century white "discoverers" with the trite throwaway epithet, "a giant pebble growing out of the ground."

The trip to Alice Springs affected me deeply. My sand shoes had been dyed deep red by the soil surrounding Uluru. I put them in the washing machine, but the colour would not come out. I held them in my hands and stared at that colour. That ochre became a symbol to me: that I was indelibly becoming an Australian myself.

I am taking the long way around to my destination point. But the fact of the matter is, if we do not redress our racist attitudes toward our indigenous peoples and recognise fully the crimes we committed against them, the people of the world – and particularly the nations in Asia – will never look upon us an exemplar nation, let alone consider us the beacon of democracy that we make ourselves out to be. We can be a nation with a social system envied by people in Asia. But only if we rid ourselves of our biases toward all non-European ethnic groups, beginning with our own first Australians, will they see us as a model to emulate.

From my first years here, I threw myself into Australian culture with the vengeance of the convert. I went down to Melbourne in December 1972 and saw plays at LaMama and the Pram Factory. Those visits led to my own plays being performed at the former, the cradle of new Australian drama, and in 1979 I directed one of the last plays at the Pram Factory before that iconic venue closed its doors for good. I established ties with directors at the Nimrod Theatre, when it was still located on Nimrod St. in Kings Cross. I was fortunate enough to write regularly for *The Canberra Times*, *The Australian* and *The National Times*; cover the Adelaide Festival for ABC radio and *Newsweek*; and frequently talk about Japanese literature, Polish theatre, Russian poetry and American politics on our radical radio show of the time, "Lateline," which in 1977 morphed into "Broadband," in the company of brilliant broadcasters such as Richard Neville, Bob Debus and Mark Aarons. I wrote and directed two hour-long radio specials, one on Mishima Yukio titled "The Decline and Fall of the Japanese Male," and the other "General MacArthur in Australia."

I bring this up at the risk of it sounding like a boast. But I simply want to explain that I became fiercely dedicated to my new country and desperately desired to be a part of what was being called its "new cultural nationalism." The 1970s were politically, socially and culturally our own Australian era of glasnost, a decade before it appeared in the Soviet Union. The word "glasnost" comes from the Russian word for "voice," and Australians of all ethnicities, orientations and persuasions were finally being given a voice that they had been obliged to repress under the old Anglocentric cultural regime.

I read everything Australian that I could get my hands on. We had Judith Wright, David Campbell, A.D. Hope and Rosemary Dobson living in Canberra. To me it was like Moscow on the Molonglo, and I befriended them all and admired them immensely as poets and individuals. I plunged into the study of native flora and fauna. Once, a friend browsing over my library at home shouted into the kitchen, "Hey, who wrote this play? What a bizarre title for a play!" When I came into the room I saw him leafing through a monograph I had read titled *The Cloacal Temperature of the West Australian Bobtail Skink*.

It certainly looked for a time as if Australians were rewriting their national narrative, transforming what was once a "haunt of displaced white people to a distant and unknown region" into a country that genuinely valued the beauty of its unique environment and the ethnic riches that it possessed, both indigenous and nonindigenous.

The tale of two narratives

I was blessed to have been able to witness the same kinds of transformations in Japan from the 1960s to the 1980s that I saw in Australia in the 1970s. Every aspect of Japanese cultural expression – from stage performance to screen, from industrial design to fashion and food – was enriched, enhanced and opened to the world during that time, in a similar opening up that had occurred in the Meiji Era. But that era's movement had been, with the exception of graphic art and design, one way. This one saw Japan's cultural messages being taken around the world and assimilated.

Both Australia and Japan were demonstrating that the liberalisation of public consciousness and a true cosmopolitanism based on the values of universal social democracy were achievable aims. People and countries could change their societies for the better, become more tolerant through the reinvention and recreation of the narratives of their nation. One thing can be said of Australia in the seventies and Japan from the mid-sixties to the eighties: How people looked at themselves and expressed themselves did matter!

This was the most wonderful thing that I discovered about the two countries that I had come to love, neither of which was the one I was born and raised in.

So, if the keyword here is "narrative," what should this be for these two countries, longitudinally linked, in the 21st century? Sadly, though the individual national narratives of Australia and Japan are in gentle flux and spluttering ahead (despite the two governments' best efforts to brake the progress), the two nations are dangerously becoming locked into a mutual narrative that has its roots deeply planted and entangled in the century that has just passed away.

Above all, relations between Australia and Japan depend less upon the depth of knowledge we possess concerning the other country than on the profundity of our understanding of ourselves. That is why it is so vital for Australians and Japanese to delve into their own pasts first and create a narrative that faithfully and honestly reflects the realities, not the myths, within them. Only when we know ourselves can we reach out with sincerity and goodwill to others.

This behooves Australians and Japanese to put themselves, including the charity or lack thereof of our very motives, under the electron microscope of scrutiny and public debate.

Electron beams, in the form of art and national discourse, both penetrate and are focused onto the surface that is the past and present. The beams create images. These images form the basis of our new narrative.

Up to now, the images of these narratives have been severely bent in the public eye to give the appearance of Australia as a loyal sacrificial lamb forever indebted to two benevolent shepherds. In our century, when the pivot of history is clearly and irrevocably turning to Asia, with our two shepherds' crooks shrinking to the point where they will be unable to reach us poor little lambs, we Australians will be obliged to create a narrative for ourselves that will allow us to stand culturally and politically on our own feet, to accommodate the cultural, social and political values of Asian powers (Indonesia, Korea, Vietnam) and superpowers (Japan, China, India) without the quasi-religious rhetoric that is part of our colonial and, by association, imperial past. We will occupy a moral high ground only if and when we create a society of our own that is tolerant, open and socially democratic. All the talk about "Western values" and "freedom" rings very hollow in Asian ears – and so it should – if we continue to cling to the narratives that bind us to the narratives of the United States and the United Kingdom. We will only be admired in Asia when we cease to be America's Lassie, going wherever and whenever we are called by our master, or Britain's subject, the wild colonial boys guarding a cultural outpost of an empire long ago driven into the dust. Just as vast numbers of people in Holland, Scandinavia and Germany speak English, because such a skill is essential to their prosperity, we Australians should aim, in a generation, to produce countless speakers of Chinese, Japanese, Korean, Indonesian and Vietnamese. Those young bilingual Australians will rewrite our narrative and create a truly unique culture for us, one that is a part of Asia not in name only.

We need to present ourselves as an independent Asia-oriented republic in Asia; as an English-speaking independent entity welcoming of the new century's order; as players of a diplomatic role between the United States on the one hand and the established and rising powers of Asia – China, Japan, Korea, India, Vietnam and, perhaps, most of all, Indonesia – on the other. Asian languages: compulsory! Asian history: compulsory! Asian dramas on our televisions. Asian films in our cinemas. With this, our traditional distrust of Asia, inherited from Europe and America and as a result so ingrained in us, will diminish.

This by no means indicates that we are faced with a Sophie's choice between our traditional allies and our new friends. Loyalties need not be drastically divided in order to be multifaceted. Those who say that if we reorient toward Asia we will forever damage our ties with the United States are only striving to protect their own social status and profit. Our present narrative hangs over our heads: that Orientals represent a threat to "our" way of life.

Our way of life is in flux. It is constantly being reimagined, reinvented, redefined and reidentified, whether the powers-that-be like it or not. It has happened that way in the forty-seven years since I arrived in Australia and it continues to happen, more rapidly than before, because our young people are interconnected with people elsewhere by social media that do not depend upon the established tightly controlled Anglophonic-centric press.

We are a different country in so many ways from the one I first encountered in 1972. All we have to do is recognise this new Asian identity as our mainstream, not as an "ethnic" tributary to the mainstream that merely makes us more colourful and entertaining, but as the most important part of our essential identity. Australia is no longer the country described in my quaint but pernicious guidebook. We are a different people, a wiser nation. We only have to be able to instil those differences into our new narrative. This role belongs to our artists and educators. But we need our leaders to open the doors for us.

Hiroshima and Nagasaki

And what of the Japanese narrative as we are about to enter the second decade of our century?

Like Australia, Japan had once been an isolated Asian backwater in a mighty European-dominated ocean of scientific, industrial and technological power. In Japan's case it was a deliberate isolation that kept them in that backwater. But beginning with the Meiji Restoration in 1868, the country, in the space of less than two generations, became a cultural and industrial powerhouse and a respected world leader. Everyone loved Japan in Europe, in America, and in the as yet not modernized non-Christian world. The Chinese looked up to the Japanese, sending tens of thousands of their best and brightest to the country to learn the fanciest trick of all: how to modernize and yet retain your traditions and customs. The working Japanese principle was *wakon yosai*, or "the Japanese spirit together with Western scientific and technological ingenuity." This was, and in many ways still is, the key to Japan's successes right through to our own time, though the *yosai* has become *wayosai*, or Japanese-Western scientific and technological ingenuity.

But the Japanese narrative of progress and pride formulated in the Meiji Era and expanded freely in the Taisho Era was manhandled by ultra-nationalists and shattered by a new type of "divine wind," a tailwind for Japanese forces that blew destruction into countries in Asia and the Pacific. The brilliant experiment of Taisho Democracy that roughly covered the decade and a half following the death of Emperor Meiji in 1912 was trampled underfoot by military boots; and the sparkling narrative that shone so brightly around the world as a model for a nonwhite, non-Christian, non-European nation to take its place on the heights of progress and modernity was snuffed out and buried.

In 1945, with their narrative, socially, politically and ethically left in ruins, the Japanese began to reinvent themselves. Japan would never impose its nationalistic aspirations on other countries, thanks to the guarantees of Article 9 of the new Constitution. Freedom of religion now guaranteed that State Shinto, an artificial construct in its very foundations, was defunct. Universal suffrage, combined with a new model of democratic education, would see to it that autocracy and imperialism based on notions of racial superiority in Asia would never return. The postwar narrative for Japan was non-belligerency, free elections based on universal suffrage, a free press and friendship with all countries.

And yet, this narrative, while pursued with sincerity and passion by many sectors of the society, was never accepted by the diehards who cherished the notion that Japan had the "right" to be the head honcho in Asia. They hankered for the Meiji model and the prestige that it once engendered around the world. The militants among them – Prime Minister Abe Shinzo being in their ranks – ever aspire to a Japan whose military might stands on par with that of the first two decades of the Showa Era.

By all rights, the catastrophic tragedies of Hiroshima and Nagasaki should have been at the core of the postwar narrative. If Japan did have a moral right, it was the right to say that only Japanese knew the heinous truth of nuclear power.

The nuclear catastrophes of Hiroshima and Nagasaki were, however, compartmentalised, localised and encapsulated, to prevent what happened in those two cities from becoming an integral part of the national narrative. Japan could have led the world in the cause of nuclear disarmament, but instead chose to be "enfolded into the embrace of the strong," with arms provided by the very country that inflicted the two holocausts on them, the United States of America. Cultural leaders of the calibre of Oe Kenzaburo and Inoue Hisashi, to name only two, wished for their country to "claim" the holocausts. Had their compatriots done so, Japanese could have produced the world's most persuasive voice for nuclear disarmament and peace.

It's time for Japanese people to open the doors to that compartment, to claim the two local catastrophes as national ones and break the walls around the capsule created by the diehards of forget. No matter how much time has elapsed, it is never too late.

In my early years in Japan, the thing that excited me most was the spirit of positive rebellion in the arts and the society in general, the swiftness and depth of the transference of ideas from the creators of the culture and the intellectuals to the populace. In the United States I had been used to two strictly bifurcated cultures: one characterised by the rigorous intellectual debates in the halls of the universities and on the pages of the quality press, and the other by appalling ignorance of the most basic tenets of progressive knowledge among the vast majority. This bifurcation exists, with even greater invidious contrast than when I was young, in present-day America . . . and it has come to take its ugly place in our own Australian national dialogue as well. Our national dialogue, as heard in our media, is increasingly sounding like two loud monologues simultaneously incanted. The very centre of the lines of argument has shifted markedly to the right, just as it has in the United States. With the exception of The Greens, even progressive Australian politicians stand to the right of their counterparts when I first came to this country in 1972.

The alternative

In Australia we are, at some time, going to become a republic. We are, at some time, going to recognise the vital role that our indigenous peoples can play in the recreation and reidentification of our national character. We are, at some time, going to form strong bonds of mutual respect – not just strategic ties based on perceived threats of terror from rogue individuals, groups or states – with the nations of Asia.

In Japan, people are, at some time, going to come to terms with their sordid deeds leading up to and during World War II. They are going to play a major role in the social and cultural modernisation of other Asian countries, just as they once so admirably did.

I believe this deep in my bones . . . and yet, have no idea how and when this may be achieved in either country. Authors and playwrights and film directors don't give answers, and even when they do, those answers are often as misconceived and self-serving as those of others. But they do often pose the right and essential questions and set the scene, as it were, for the upcoming dramas.

To me, the set for both countries' dramas is this. First for Japan. Japan is

> the largest secular democracy in the world. Japanese are not blinded by religious dogma as it encroaches on social policy in the United States, Russia, Iran and Australia, or by an ideological dogma such as the one dominant in China.
>
> [T]he country in the world that implicitly understands and appreciates the history and culture of both China and the United States, thanks to long and intense contact with both countries and profound assimilation of their cultures into its own.

In Australia's case, we are

> a nation that is largely secular in outlook, despite our Christian heritage.
> [A] nation that knows and understands China and the United States very well and has the potential to interpret events in those countries dispassionately.

Both Australia and Japan have the ability in the future to provide their good offices in diplomacy. Both countries are logical mediators in a clash of hegemonies between China and the United States and a confrontation of sovereignties dressed as religious conflict between Muslim nations and the West.

Both Australia and Japan are able to engage with countries in our region and around the world with a flexibility that will protect real national interests while guiding developments toward reconciliation and peaceful settlements of disputes. If the tyranny of distance and isolation have any advantage, even in our interconnected world, it is the ability to stand aside and mediate between face-to-face rivals.

If you think this is pie-in-the-sky, well perhaps it is. I have the stubborn habit of looking up to the sky and hoping to see light. But please do contemplate the alternative, a development of events based on old national narratives and seriously outdated models of what the present Australian and Japanese governments call "security" but is really motivated by the lust for military and short-term economic power. There is only one conclusion to that old drama . . . and that is the destruction of all culture, all peaceful social intercourse and, at worst, our species in the bargain.

I personally have great hope for the Australia-Japan relationship, so long as we free ourselves from the hand-me-down biases and noxious myths of the past.

Australians and Japanese can guide each other in this. Australians can help Japanese become more open and tolerant to those who are different from themselves. Japanese can help Australians take themselves and their culture more seriously and have pride in it.

If it's time for anything, it is for this.

Honorary Professor Roger Pulvers
University of Queensland

On the streets of our town

Japan in Australia

©*Vera Mackie*

The nineteenth-century Strand Arcade in Sydney's central business district hosts the storefront of Japanese-Australian fashion designer Akira Isogawa. Akira[1] first came to Australia in 1986 on a working holiday visa, came back again to study English, and then went on to study fashion design at the Sydney Institute of Technology. While establishing his fashion business, he supported himself in various jobs such as guide for tourists from Japan or kitchen hand in Japanese restaurants.[2] Now, he regularly displays his clothes at Paris fashion shows and sells them around the world. They are worn by people like actor and director Cate Blanchett and model Naomi Campbell. Akira's life exemplifies some of the themes of this book on Japan in Australia. Although he has been based in Australia for the last three decades, he is in constant movement between Australia, Japan, Europe and North America, and his work is embedded in global circuits of production, distribution, commodity consumption and cultural consumption.

There are several reference points in Akira's work. First is his Japanese heritage. He talks of his mother's and other relatives' *kimono*, which provided inspiration and, indeed, the material basis for his early designs (Safe 2018, 56). Media profiles of Akira often refer to aesthetic concepts like *wabi-sabi* or belief systems such as Zen Buddhism (Entor 2003; Safe 2018, 198–199), while Akira called his 1997/1998 Spring/Summer collection '*Satori*' – the word for Buddhist enlightenment. He uses particular Japanese techniques such as '*shibori*' (tie-dyeing) and '*kasuri*' (*ikat*, or resist-dye weaving). One series of clothes was known as '*origami*', an adaptation of paper-folding techniques to fabric ('About' n.d.; Safe 2018, 100–199).

Another reference point is Paris. He regularly shows at Paris fashion shows, and his collections are known by the names of the seasons in French '*Printemps/Été*' (Spring/Summer) and '*Automne/Hiver*' (Autumn/Winter), as is the practice in the Paris fashion shows. The French words for the seasons have also been adopted for some of his exhibitions, as is the practice in the Paris fashion shows.[3] This French connection also places him in the company of élite designers such as Rei Kawakubo (and her brand Commes des Garçons), Issey Miyake and Yohji

Figure BM2.1 Akira's store in the Strand Arcade, Sydney
Source: Photograph by Vera Mackie

Yamamoto, who operate between Japan and Paris (Mackie 1999). The association is reinforced when Akira reports that he likes wearing clothes by Commes des Garçons (Entor 2003).[4]

There are further reference points in other parts of Asia, which provide artisanal labour for his collections – *batik*, embroidery and beading from Bali; silk and embroidery from China and beading, embroidery and fabrics from India (Safe 2018, 100–199). Akira's clients can afford to pay for clothes painstakingly designed by Akira in his Marrickville studio and then drawing on materials and labour from the third world. He comments that the 'number of hours someone has spent on manual work like this makes it priceless' ('About' n.d.). 'Craftsmanship' is a word which recurs in his accounts of his work: 'Richly embellished fabrics echo Eastern influences, and I have great respect for their traditions. Inspiration can be found from the past – re-using vintage textiles and sometimes creating replicas of them, incorporated with specific craftsmanship' ('About' n.d.).

A further reference point is Australia. His Australian collections are often known under the label 'Resort', and he mentions the Australian lifestyle and climate – particularly Sydney (Birrell 2016). He has used fabric designs by Australian Florence Broadhurst (1899–1977); he has collaborated with Australian underwear manufacturer Bonds on a special set of 'Chesty Bond' cotton singlets and with the Australian Wool Corporation on a lightweight wool gauze fabric (Safe 2018, 74–75, 114–115, 202–227). He has created costumes for the Sydney Dance Company and the Australian Ballet and has collaborated with the Australian Chamber Orchestra (Safe 2018, 202–227). In 2005 Australia Post issued a postage stamp with Akira as one of its 'Australian Legends'. He has also been awarded several prizes by the Australian fashion industry (Safe 2018, 234–235). In 2018 and 2019 the Museum of Applied Arts and Sciences in Sydney held a retrospective of Akira's work (Safe 2018).[5]

Just down the Pitt Street Mall from the Strand Arcade is the two-story Uniqlo store. Uniqlo is known as a leading 'fast fashion' brand, originating in Japan, but now a global retail empire. In juxtaposing Akira and Uniqlo, it is worth revisiting some questions I raised about fashion in the context of the Tokyo Vogue exhibition at Brisbane City Art Gallery in 1999.

> Once we start thinking about the making of clothing, we start to wonder about who did the making? Who designed the garment? Who wove the cloth? Who cut it? Who marketed it? Who sewed it? Who transported it? Who will buy it? Who will wear it?
>
> (Mackie 1999, 24)

These questions can throw into relief the ways in which both the élite garments from Akira's Strand Arcade store and the mass-produced clothes from Uniqlo's Pitt Street store are embedded in global processes, in the 'highly segmented institutions of fashion production at the global level' (Skov 2003, 216). Indeed, similar questions could be posed of the production, dissemination and consumption of the other cultural products I discuss below.

Uniqlo's owner, Yanai Tadashi, is one of the richest people in Japan and, indeed, the world. While Akira's clothes are created with an artisanal, handcrafted ethic, which could perhaps be characterised as 'slow fashion', Uniqlo's 'fast fashion' is mass produced, with the company often being accused of exploitative working conditions.[6] A few years ago it was reported that 70 percent of Uniqlo's clothes were manufactured in China, and Indonesian workers also produced clothes for Uniqlo for a time (Durisin 2013; Clean Clothes Campaign 2019).[7]

Uniqlo pursues two parallel marketing strategies. It made its name on generic, basic fashion items like t-shirts, knitwear, separates and underwear, in some ways similar to US chains like The Gap and Urban Outfitters. The low-cost items were particularly popular in Japan during the recession years. As Uniqlo became a global brand, these generic fashion items could be said to be, in Koichi Iwabuchi's terms, 'odourless' or '*mukokuseki*' (without a clear national identity) (Iwabuchi 2002, 24–28).

Uniqlo also, however, capitalises on Japanese cultural references. In 2019, the company sold a series of t-shirts displaying details from Katsushika Hokusai's (1760–1849) woodblock prints, including the iconic 'Great Wave off Kanagawa'

Figure BM2.2 The Uniqlo Store in Sydney
Source: Photograph by Vera Mackie

from the series 'Thirty-Six Views of Mount Fuji', using indigo-like hues. Uniqlo also enters into collaborations with such organisations as the Museum of Modern Art in New York, adding artistic cachet to 'fast fashion' and 'Japan cool', but printed on basic cotton t-shirts.[8] For a time in 2015, the New York flagship store

Figure BM2.3 The Uniqlo Store in New York
Source: Photograph by Vera Mackie

was decorated with a gigantic face in Kabuki actor makeup, marking a collaboration with the Shochiku entertainment corporation. In its original incarnation in Japan, the company name 'Uniqlo' was written in white roman script on a red background. Its international branches use both roman script and the Japanese katakana script. So far, I have not noticed many local references in Uniqlo's Australian capital city stores, except perhaps the use of Merino wool. Rather, one can see similar products on display in New York, Singapore, Sydney or Denver.

Further down the street from the Pitt Street Mall in Sydney is the Galeries Victoria Building. This houses the Kinokuniya bookshop which stocks books, magazines and manga in Japanese and English as well as Japanese stationery. Kinokuniya is a major site for disseminating Japanese popular culture (and, indeed, high culture). It also connects with local audiences with its excellent collection of Australian fiction and scholarship and by hosting exhibitions in its small gallery. The same building also houses the Japanese chain restaurant Yayoi, the sushi train (*kaiten sushi*) restaurant Hotaru and the noodle restaurant Ichibanboshi. On the ground floor of Galeries Victoria is a branch of the 'Super Dry' fashion brand. Super Dry is actually a British brand, but it styles itself with a Japanese inflection with the name '*Sūpā Dorai*' in Japanese katakana script, and the barely comprehensible Japanese translation '*Kyokudo Kansō Shinasai*'.[9]

In the same building is the Muji store. The name 'Muji' is the English abbreviation of 'Mu-jirushi Ryōhin' (No Label, Quality Goods), a subsidiary of the

Japanese Seiyū supermarket company. Many of Muji's items are simple, generic 'basics' like t-shirts, but at a higher price point than Uniqlo. Muji makes a point of using natural fibres for its clothes. Its interior design items, too, are characterised by the use of natural products and minimalist design. Despite its more upmarket image, though, Muji has also been accused of exploiting third-world workers by subcontracting to factories in places like Myanmar (Chamberlain 2017).

Still in Sydney's central business district, walk further down Pitt Street and then head west towards Chinatown. On the way you will pass by more sushi train restaurants, take-away sushi bars and *rāmen* shops.[10] You will then come across Tetsuya's restaurant. Tetsuya Wakuda fuses French and Japanese techniques and now has a Michelin-starred branch restaurant in Singapore. Like Akira, Tetsuya came to Australia in the 1980s, and is identified with Australia just as much as Japan. He is ubiquitously known by his given name 'Tetsuya'. He is also known for sourcing Australian ingredients of premium quality (Harden 2018), and sells his own range of sauces and dressings. The Michelin stars add the connotations of élite French cuisine.

> Tetsuya is part of an elite group of international chefs that has influenced other chefs through their personal styles and unique approaches to food. His culinary philosophy centres on pure, clean flavours that are decisive, yet completely refined. His amazing technique, Asian heritage, sincere humility, worldwide travels and insatiable curiosity combine to create incredible, soulful dishes that exude passion in every bite.
>
> (Trotter n.d.)

Tetsuya was awarded the Order of Australia in 2005. His restaurant displays works by Japanese-Australian sculptor Akio Makigawa (1948–1999), who spent much of his working life in Melbourne, where several of Makigawa's other works can be found.[11]

Once you get to Chinatown, you can find shops selling Japanese cosmetics, fashion, food and popular culture – anime, manga, J-Pop, computer games and 'character' goods such as figurines depicting popular anime characters.[12] Such popular cultural products are now embedded in the everyday lives of youth in contemporary Australia.[13] Youth are also enthusiastic participants in local comic conventions and costume play (cosplay, *kosupure*) events.[14] The appreciation of such East Asian popular cultural forms is a major impetus for Japanese study in Australian universities (Kinoshita-Thomson in this volume, McLelland 2017).

Also in Chinatown is one of several branches of Daiso Japan.[15] Daiso Japan is a version of the ubiquitous '100 yen shops', which flourished in Japan in the recession years from the late twentieth century. In their Australian incarnation, the goods are generally priced at AUD$2.80. Like Uniqlo, they have a range of relatively 'odourless' everyday mass-produced items, but also stock specifically Japanese items like rice bowls, tea cups, teapots and popular culture items like cute *emoji* stickers. They also display *maneki-neko* (welcoming cat figures) and

Figure BM2.4 Sculpture by Akio Makigawa, Melbourne
Source: Photograph by Vera Mackie

daruma – which unaccountably have both eyes painted in![16] In its Australian incarnation, Daiso includes the word 'Japan' in its name, possibly to distinguish itself from the China-based chain Meisō/Miniso.[17] A quick perusal of the labels of the goods on sale in a local store revealed, though, that most Daiso Japan products are actually manufactured in China.

If we were to walk around other state capital cities, such as Melbourne, we would also see branches of Uniqlo, Muji and Daiso Japan. Until recently, one of Melbourne's arcades housed the boutique of Yasuyo and Mamoru Kondō's distinctive fashion brands Moshi Moshi and Kondo Tricot. Like Akira, the Kondōs negotiated between Japanese, English and French. One of their brands had the name 'Moshi Moshi' (hello), one of the Japanese words which is recognisable in English. Their other brand name combined their surname 'Kondō', with the French word for knitware, 'tricot', because they specialised in jersey separates, which draped stylishly and were easy to take care of. For some years a Gothic Lolita fashion shop called 'Shibuya' was found at the top of Melbourne's Elizabeth Street, taking its name from one of Tokyo's major shopping and entertainment districts (Mackie 2009). Several public buildings in Melbourne also have sculptures by Akio Makigawa, who, as noted above, spent much of his professional life practising in Melbourne. Makigawa's sculpture in Melbourne's Swanston Street is thoroughly integrated into the city. It is at the front of a coffee shop, located beside some steps where citygoers stop to eat lunch, check their phones, or watch the passersby.

Move south from Melbourne's central business district and you can walk by the National Gallery of Victoria's Ian Potter Centre, which hosted the *Akira Isogawa: Printemps Été* exhibition in 2004 and the National Gallery of Victoria International, which has an impressive collection of Asian art, including a print of Hokusai's 'Great Wave off Kanagawa'.[18] Move on to the inner suburbs and you can visit the Made in Japan store, which sells Japanese ceramics and second-hand *kimono*, and Kazari, which deals in Japanese antiques, prints, furniture, textiles and vintage *kimono*.

Thus, one aspect of 'Japan in Australia' is the way in which it is imprinted on the very streets of our cities, from high fashion to mass-produced Japanese 'goods', from haute cuisine to supermarket sushi.[19] The editors of this collection comment on the contributors who have 'interrogated definitive notions of Australia and "Australianness", and Japan and "Japaneseness"'. They refer to 'a blurring of lines and smearing of borders that emphasise an interconnectedness that is transnational, translingual and transcultural' (Hayes and Chapman in this volume). When we talk about Japan and Australia, we are no longer simply talking about a bilateral relationship between two hermetically sealed entities called 'Australia' and 'Japan' but rather a series of connections which bring together Australians, Japanese and Japanese-Australians in global chains of connectedness, through the production, distribution, dissemination and consumption of fashion, artistic works, cultural products and cuisine in our everyday lives.

Notes

1 While it is usual to refer to Japanese names in the order of family name followed by given name (Isogawa Akira), I will use the order of given name followed by family name (Akira Isogawa), as that is how he is known in Australia and in international fashion circles. Indeed, he is most widely known just by his given name 'Akira', his eponymous brand name. The name 'Akira' may have seemed familiar to Australian consumers of popular culture who would have known of Ōtomo Katsuhiro's post-nuclear cyberpunk apocalypse animated movie *Akira*, which was widely screened in Australia (Ōtomo 1988; Freiberg 1996). I will also use English word order for other creative

practitioners who are widely known by given name followed by family name in English language sources.
2 On working holiday visas; see Kumiko Kawashima, 'Japanese Working Holiday Makes in Australia and Their Relationship to the Japanese Labour Market', *Asian Studies Review*, 34 (3): 267–286.
3 *Akira Isogawa: Printemps Été*, National Gallery of Victoria 2004/ 2005; *Akira Automne/Hiver '10* Japan Foundation Gallery, Sydney 2010. The catalogue of Akira's 2019 retrospective includes Akira's calligraphy of the words '*Haru/Natsu*' (Spring/ Summer) in Japanese hiragana script, which seems to bring together all of his different cultural reference points (Safe 2018, 186).
4 Roger Leong (in Safe 2018, 15) also notes that Akira's clothes evoke early twentieth-century designers such as Paul Poiret, Callot Soeurs and Madame Paquin who referenced Orientalism in their clothes, suggesting the complex interplay of European and non-European art and culture over long periods of time (Geczy 2013).
5 Other exhibitions of Akira's work include participation in the *Tokyo Vogue* Exhibition at Brisbane City Gallery in 1999 (see English 1999), a Sydney Festival exhibition at Object Gallery in 2003 and participation in the *Future Beauty: 30 Years of Japanese Fashion* exhibition (alongside Yohji Yamamoto and Comme des Garçons) at The Barbican in London in 2010 and the Queensland Gallery of Modern Art in 2014.
6 Akira proclaims a commitment to environmental sustainability and comments that his business has become smaller in order to focus on 'quality not quantity' (Safe 2018, 233).
7 It should also be noted, though, that Uniqlo also tries to be associated with social justice issues (Uniqlo Sustainability 2018).
8 On the marketing of 'Cool Japan', see Miller (2011), McLelland (2017).
9 This possibly references the Japanese beer, Asahi Superdry.
10 On Japanese cuisine in Australia, see Hamada and Stevens (2011).
11 For a sense of the scale and scope of Japanese-Australian diasporic art practice, see Japan Foundation (n.d.), Steains (in this volume), Pulvers (in this volume), Fukui (2014), Kanamori (2017), Fukui and Kanamori (2017). In this discussion I hope to operate outside binaries of 'Australian' and 'Japanese' art practitioners and wish to include Japanese nationals active in Australia, Australians of Japanese descent (including those recently naturalised) and Australians who engage with Japanese artistic forms. Members of each of these groups may be active across national boundaries in Australia, Japan and other locations.
12 'Chinatowns' in Australian cities often display the products of a range of East Asian cultures, with the rise of K-Pop and other Korean cultural forms being particularly noticeable.
13 In earlier generations, Australian children watched dubbed Japanese cartoons like *Astro Boy* and *Kimba the White Lion*, television shows about samurai and ninja and the dubbed version of the series *Monkey* (based on the Chinese Buddhist epic *Journey to the West* (*Xiyouji* in Chinese, *Saiyūki* in Japanese) (Chapman 2015; Hausler in this volume).
14 On *kosupure*, see King (2013a, n.p., 2013b, n.p., 2015, n.p.).
15 In Japanese it would be rendered as 'Daisō', with a long vowel.
16 Daruma is the Japanese name of the Bodhisattva Bodhidharma, who is said to have prayed in a cave until he eventually lost the use of his legs. In Japan, daruma dolls are ovoid figures with a weight in the base so that the doll will always right itself. This is a metaphor for perseverance. They are usually sold with blank white eyes. The purchaser paints in one pupil in black as a sign of commitment to a goal. Once the goal has been achieved, the other pupil will be painted in.
17 The origins of 'Meisō' or 'Miniso' are more complex, arising from a collaboration between Japanese designer Miyake Jun'ya and Chinese entrepreneur Ye Guofu. The logos for Miniso and Meisō mimic the red background and white script of Uniqlo. The Chinese name 名創優品/Míngchuàng Yōupǐn/Meisō Yūhin has echoes of 無印良品/

Mujirushi Ryōhin/Muji. Meisō/Miniso has huge coverage in China and other parts of Asia and is also starting to be seen in Australian cities.

18 While beyond the scope of this essay, several Australian public galleries, including those of South Australia, Victoria, New South Wales and Queensland, include significant collections of Asian art. Of particular mention is the Asia-Pacific Triennial of Contemporary Arts, held at the Queensland Art Gallery and now the Queensland Gallery of Modern Art since 1993.

19 At the time of writing, Woolworths in Australia sells a brand of take-away sushi called 'Sushi Izu', described as 'Hybrid Sushi: Traditional Style with a Modern Twist'.

References

'About'. n.d. *Akira*, accessed 26 May 2019, akira.com.au.

Birrell, A. 2016. 'The Quiet Power of Akira Isogawa', *Vogue Australia*, 18 May, accessed 26 May 2016, www.vogue.com.au/fashion/news/the-quiet-power-of-akira-isogawa/news-story/0cc3f99d203820614d5ae8957d61dabf.

Chamberlain, G. 2017. 'How High Street Clothes Were Made in Myanmar for 13p an Hour', *The Guardian*, 5 February, accessed 5 June 2019, www.theguardian.com/world/2017/feb/05/child-labour-myanmar-high-street-brands.

Chapman, D. 2015. 'Suburban Samurai and Neighbourhood Ninja: Shintarō and Postwar Australia', *Japanese Studies*, 35 (3): 355–371.

Clean Clothes Campaign. 2019. 'Former Uniqlo Garment Workers Attend Flagship Store Opening in Denmark to Highlight Uniqlo's Wage-Theft', *Clean Clothes Campaign*, accessed 5 June 2019, https://cleanclothes.org/news/2019/04/02/former-uniqlo-garment-workers-attend-flagship-store-opening-to-highlight-uniqlo2019s-wage-theft.

Durisin, M. 2013. 'The Story of Uniqlo: The Japanese Clothing Chain That's Taking Over the World', *Business Insider*, 27 April, accessed 5 June 2019, www.businessinsider.com.au/the-story-of-uniqlo-2013-4?r=US&IR=T#the-first-uniqlo-opened-its-doors-in-hiroshima-japan-in-1984-1.

English, B. L. (ed.). 1999. *Tokyo Vogue; Japanese/Australian Fashion*. Brisbane: Griffith University, Queensland College of Art.

Entor, C. 2003. 'Primal Colours', *Lucire*, n.p., accessed 4 June 2019, http://lucire.com/2003/spring2004/0704fe0.htm.

Freiberg, F. 1996. 'Akira and the Post-Nuclear Sublime', in M. Broderick (ed.), *Hibakusha Cinema*. London: Kegan Paul International.

Fukui, M. 2014. 'When Blossoms Fall', *Griffith Review*, 46.

Fukui, M. and Kanamori, M. 2017. 'The Creation of Nikkei Australia: Rediscovering the Japanese Diaspora in Australia', *Journal of Australian Studies*, 41 (3): 388–396.

Geczy, A. 2013. *Fashion and Orientalism: Dress, Textiles and Culture from the 17th to the 21st Century*. London: Bloomsbury.

Hamada, I. and Stevens, C. 2011. 'Fitting Japanese Cuisine into Australia: Imperfect Translations', in J. Breaden, S. Steele and C. Stevens (eds.), *Internationalising Japan: Discourse and Practice*. Oxford: Routledge.

Harden, M. 2018. 'Tetsuya Wakuda Is Coming to Melbourne for One Night Only', *Gourmet Traveller*, 25 August, accessed 5 June 2019, www.gourmettraveller.com.au/news/restaurant-news/tetsuya-wakuda-cooks-in-melbourne-16387.

Iwabuchi, K. 2002. *Recentering Globalization: Popular Culture and Japanese Transnationalism*. Durham: Duke University Press.

Japan Foundation. n.d. 'Directory of Japanese Arts & Culture in Australia', accessed 4 June 2019, https://artdirectory.jpf.org.au/.

Kanamori, M. 2017. 'You've Mistaken Me for a Butterfly: With an Afterword by Vera Mackie', *Japanese Studies*, 37 (3): 387–394.

King, E. 2013a. 'Explainer: What Is Cosplay?' *The Conversation*, 31 December, accessed 9 June 2019, https://theconversation.com/explainer-what-is-cosplay-20759.

———. 2013b. 'Girls Who Are Boys Who Like Girls to Be Boys', BL and the Australian Cosplay Community', *Intersections: Gender and Sexuality in Asia and the Pacific*, 32 (July), http://intersections.anu.edu.au/issue32/king.htm.

———. 2015. 'Cosplay, Crossplay and the Importance of Wearing the Right Underwear', *The Conversation*, 7 August, accessed 9 June 2019, https://theconversation.com/cosplay-crossplay-and-the-importance-of-wearing-the-right-underwear-45045.

Mackie, V. 1999. 'The Worlds of Japanese Fashion', in B. L. English (ed.), *Tokyo Vogue; Japanese/Australian Fashion*. Brisbane: Griffith University, Queensland College of Art, 19–26.

———. 2009. 'Transnational Bricolage: Gothic Lolita and the Political Economy of Fashion', *Intersections: Gender and Sexuality in Asia and the Pacific*, 20, accessed 5 June 2019, http://intersections.anu.edu.au/issue20/mackie.htm.

McLelland, M. (ed.). 2017. *The End of Cool Japan: Ethical, Legal and Cultural Challenges to Japanese Popular Culture*. Oxford: Routledge.

Miller, L. 2011. 'Cute Masquerade and the Pimping of Japan', *International Journal of Japanese Sociology*, 20.

Ōtomo, K. 1988. *Akira*. Tokyo: TMS Entertainment.

Safe, G. 2018. *Akira Isogawa: Unfolding a Life in Fashion*. Sydney: Museum of Applied Arts and Sciences and Melbourne: Thames and Hudson.

Skov, L. 2003. 'Fashion – Nation: A Japanese Globalization Experience and a Hong Kong Dilemma', in S. Neissen, A. M. Leshkowich and C. Jones (eds.), *Re-Orienting Fashion: The Globalization of Asian Dress*. Oxford: Berg, 215–242.

Trotter, C. n.d. 'About Tetsuya', *Tetsuya*, accessed 5 June 2019, www.tetsuyas.com/page/about_tetsuya.html.

Uniqlo Sustainability. 2018. 'Uniqlo', accessed 5 June 2019, www.uniqlo.com/en/sustainability/.

Index

Note: Figures are noted by *italic* page numbers, tables by **bold** page numbers.

Aboriginal: can migrant belong 132; Lucy Dann 135; Preston's art shifts 44, 59; Stolen Generations 135
academic realism 47
adult learners' orientations 191
after-school television 123–124
ageing/desire for youth 99, 108–109
Allied Occupation: of Japan 17; Japanese, swimming 82
Ame no Uzume Den: god, Japanese mythology 26; Shunsuke Tsurumi 26
Ame no Uzume Den (Tsurumi 1991) 15
American domination 151
Anglophonic-centric press 224
anime 118, 164, 184, *185*
An Intellectual History of Wartime Japan ([1986] 2010) 25
Armanno, Venero (2006): *Candle Life* 96, 100–105, 109
Article 9 225
Article Nine Association 26
artisanal labour 230
Asian: media cultures 150, 151; movie 120
Asian Australian Studies Research Network 134
Astro Boy 113
Atsuo, Nakamura 118
1957 Australia-Japan Agreement on Commerce 180
Australian-Asian hybridisation 102
Australian baseball: American servicemen 64; coin toss 74; equipment irregularities 74; inadequate lighting 74; non-conventional rules 73; only minor sport 78
Australian Baseball Council 71

Australian book reviews: Broinwoski's *Colorless* review 173; *Colorless*, tsunami, Fukushima 2011 167–168; corpus and methodology 165; foreign works: 'sheer novelty' to 'gratifying similarity' 167; identify Murakami as Japanese 165–166; Murakami, exoticised figure 166, 167; 'Murakami novel' 172, 174; reviewers mention 'Harukists' 174; West audience, native Japan 167
Australian Federal election 1949 84
Australian multiculturalism 131
Australian 'national literature' 163
Australian nationhood: Britain natural homeland 220; whiteness, Britishness, Australianness 17
Australian press 86
Australian ships: *Cypress* 6–7; *Eamont* 7; *Lady Rowena* 6
Australian Society of Artists 54
Australian veterans 84
Australian women 86
Australian Women's Weekly 124, 125
Australia's Asia: Walker, Sobocinska 17
Australia trans-Asian 19, 149, 153–159

Bachmann, Ingeborg: 'The Thirtieth Year' 108
Ball, W. Macmahon 83
Basic Treaty of Friendship and Cooperation 18
Basile, Giambattista: *The Pentamerone* 98; 'Sun, Moon, and Talia' 98
BBC to ABC 123
Beadsley, Aubrey 49

Index 241

Beaurepaire, Sir Frank 83
Bell, Clive: *Art* (1914) 57
Black, John Reddie (1826–1880): Ishii Black 8; *Kairakutei Burakku* 8; *rakugoka* 8
Blair, Mrs Teruko 16
"Blood-bath" if Japs in Olympics 85
Brah, Avtar: *Cartographies of Diaspora* (1996) 140
Breen, George 86, 90, 91
Bridging Australia and Japan: Sisson, David 6
Brisbane 70
Brisbane Exhibition Ground 70
British Commonwealth Occupation Force: Australian-led, in Japan 84
British Commonwealth Occupation Force (BCOF) 16
Broadhurst, Florence (1899–1977) 230
Brooke, John Henry (1826–1902) 8
Broome: Japanese pearl diving 12; Lucy Dann home 135
Brundage, Avery 82
Buddhism 116, 121, 126
Bunny, Rupert (1864–1947) 48
bushidō, code of conduct 93

Calwell, Arthur: Minister for Immigration 82; women, Remembrance Day 86
Canberra: embassy of Japan 17; Japan Society of Sydney 18; tour ends 75; two matches played 70, 71, 73
Canberra Manuka Oval 71
Canberra-maru 31, 38, 39
Candle Life: intertextuality, other artists 101, 104; Japanese literature not featured 104
cane fields 12, 21n7
Carradine, David 120
Carter, Angela: *The Infernal Desire Machines of Doctor Hoffman* (1972) 100
Carter, Norman (1875–1963) 49
Cassatt, Mary 49
Castor, Mike: American sports promoter 65; Giants tour profits donated 70
Ceremonial Performance 137
Cézanne, Paul 47
Chan, Jackie 120
Chardin, Jean Baptiste Siméon (1699–1779) 46
Cheng'en, Wu: *Journey to the West* 18, 116
chiaroscuro 46

Chicago White Sox 64
Chidori, Kaname 186, **186**
'Children Crossing Borders' (CCB): experiences, memories 201–205; language identity 203–205, 209; language inside, outside home 200; mobility domains 200–201, *201*, 205–207; monolingual 203, 207; plurilingual, pluricultural 199, 207, 212; Wen Yuju analysis 200–206
Chinese Nationalist Party 205
Citizen's League for Peace in Vietnam 26
Civilian Internment Interpretive Board: Cowra Japanese War Cemetery (CJWC) 133, 137; history of civilian internees 133
Clifford, James 199
Coetzee, J. M. 99
Commonwealth Immigration Restriction Act (Willard 1923, 108–118; see also Clark and Ely 1888) 12
Composition (1899) 47
contract labour 12
cosplay 234
Courtesan of the Motoya Looking at the Face of a Komusō Reflected in Water (c1769–1770): Suzuki Harunobu (1725–1770) 51, *53*
Cowra Breakout 133
Cowra Japanese War Cemetery (CJWC): Ceremonial Performance 137; Civilian Internment Interpretive Board 133; Indonesian political prisoners buried 139; *In Repose* 137
'Creation of Nikkei Australia: Rediscovering the Japanese Diaspora in Australia': Masako Fukui 133; Mayu Kanamori 133
cross-border: interaction 131; mobility 149
cultural fusion 17, 139
cultural issues: Australian 54; racially "pure white" 216
culturally odour-foul 113
culturally odourless 113, 231
cultural mixing 151
'cultural odor' 152
Cypress 6–7

Daiso Japan: manufactured in China 234–235; 'odourless' mass produced items 234
Da Tang Sanzang qujing shihua ('The Poetic Tale of the Procurement of

Scriptures by Tripitaka of the Great Tang') 117
Davidson, Bessie (1879–1965) 47
Day, Ikyo 135
death, spirits 138
declining birth rate 152
Degas, Edgar 49
de Goncourt, Edmond: *Manette Salomon* (1867) 45; renowned *Japoniste* 48
de Goncourt, Jules: *Manette Salomon* (1867) 45
Derain, André 47
deterritorialisation 131
de-Westernized 150, 151, 153
Dicinoski, Ewar: buried Toowong Cemetery, Brisbane 8, *9*; naturalised Japanese in Australia 8; Royal Tycoon Troupe 8
diplomacy roles 227
disarmament 226
dokugaku (self-education) 216
Dow, Arthur Wesley: *Composition* (1899) 47, 57

Eamont 7
École Nationale des Beaux-Arts 1890 49
economic sanctions 15
Eguchi: requests drug 102; visits inn, special service 96
Ehonsaiyūki 117
élite garments 231
emigration 6
emoji 234
equestrian events 86
erotic novels 100, 101
'Essential Memories' 210
ethnic identity 134
European fairy tale 97
exploitation 8, 106, 231, 234
Exposition Universelle 1867, 1878 49

Federal Congress of the Returned Soldiers' League 82
Fenollosa, Ernest: *Epochs of Chinese and Japanese Art* (1912) 57
Flynn, Greg 125
friendship through bat and ball: gifts 72–73; profits donated, RSL 70; tour slogan 68
'From Eggs to Electrolux' (1927): Margaret Preston 46
Fry, Roger: *Vision and Design* (1920) 54

Fukui, Masako: 'Creation of Nikkei Australia: Rediscovering the Japanese Diaspora in Australia' 133; 'Japanese living in Australia' 132

gag-dubbing 121
'Gateway course' 183
German Secessionists 47
'Ghandhara/Monkey Magic' 123
globalization: deal with transnationally 154; impact 116; migrant populations 161; social media, interconnected 224; speed 115
Glynn, Patrick McMahon: *Australia for the Tourist* 217
Godiego: 'Ghandhara/Monkey Magic' 123; Japanese band 123
'Godzilla' 215
goodwill mission - through bat and ball 63, 68
Goto, Count [i.e., Gotō Shinpei] 29, 31
graves: Cowra Japanese War Cemetery (CJWC) 133; Japanese in Australia 15; Japanese War Cemetery 16
'Great Wave off Kanagawa' 231, 236
Grimm Brothers: 'Briar Rose' (1812) 98
gymnastics 87, 89–90, 92

Hajime, Furusawa 15–16
Hall, Bernard (1859–1935) 46
Hamasaki, Ayumi 186, **186**, **187**
Harada, Tsuneo (Cappy): California native 69; gifts presented 72–73; Yomiuri team manager 68
Harries, Elizabeth Wanning 99
Haruki, Murakami: 'Americanised author' 169; *Colorless Tsukuru Tazaki and his years of pilgrimage* 164, 165; 'Harukists'/fans 174; highest Google spike line 161–162, *162*; *IQ84* 164, 165; Japan in Australia's literature 19; *Kafka on the Shore* 164; *Kaze no uta o kike [Hear the wind sing]* 1979 163; lacks social commitment 164; Murakami as Japanese 161, 169; 'Murakami Brand' 170; popular rating lists 164; possible Nobel Prize for Literature 172; reception in US vs Asia 164
Harunobu, Suzuki (1725–1770) 49; *Courtesan of the Motoya Looking at the Face of a Komusō Reflected in Water* (c1769–1770) 51, *53*

Hayes, Helen M.: *The Buddhist Pilgrim's Progress* 119
The Heart of the Journey: Kanamori's creative role 137; Lucy Dann, Japanese Aboriginal 135
The Heathen Japee *11*
Helsinki Olympics 85
Heysen, Hans (1877–1968) 57
hiragana 203
Hironoshin, Furuhashi 86–87
Hiroshige, Andō (1797–1858) 49, 55
Hiroshima 225, 226
Hōchi Shinbun 71
Hokusai, Katsushika (1760–1849): block print t-shirts 231; t-shirts, woodblock prints 231; woodblock artist 49, 55, 117
Holland, Sir George 67
hone o uzumeru kakugo -preparedness to bury one's bones: *In Repose*, meditation 138
hongoku (home country) 220
horse racing 14
House of the Sleeping Beauties (1967) 96–99
Hughes, W.S. Kent: Australian POW 84, 87; Chairman, Australian Olympic 87
hybridisation 131

Ichirō, Sawada 82
immigration: "non-European" 218; war brides 16
Immigration Museum in Melbourne 156
Immigration Museum Tokyo 156
Immigration Restriction Act 6, 12
Indigenous Australians 221, 222
Indonesian political prisoners 139
In Repose: Cowra Japanese War Cemetery 137; Japanese ghosts, Australia 140; living to dead 141; silent histories 138
Inter-Asia: Asia, interconnected 150; Social Science Research Council 150; studies 157
Intercolonial Exhibition in Melbourne 9
International Exhibition in London 1862 8
1862 International Exhibition London 49
International Olympic Committee (IOC): August, 1950 voted Japan, Germany 85; 1951 Copenhagen, Helsinki Olympics 85; President, Avery Brundage 82
internment: Civilian Internment Interpretive Board 133; Japanese 1941 15; Japanese repatriated 134; marginalisation, exclusion 133; no apology 138; no compensation 15; US Japanese 133
internment camps: residence determined 15; returned to Japan 15
intertextuality 18
Introductory Japanese classes: course evaluation word cloud *191*; learner demographics 188, **189**; Why continue? **190**, 191
Isogawa, Akira: *Akira Isogawa: Printemps Été 2004* 236; exhibit, Museum of Applied Arts and Sciences 231; fashion designer 229–233; *kimono* 229; 'Resort' collection 230; Strand Arcade store *230*
Iwabuchi, Koichi: 'resilient borders' 131; *Resilient Borders and Cultural Diversity: Internationalism, Brand Nationalism, and Multiculturalism in Japan* 130–131

'Japanese as a heritage language' 209
Japanese colonisation 205
Japanese Consul General 64
Japanese-English bilingual 206
Japanese Heritage Language (JHL) 206
'Japanese home-background speakers' 207
Japanese immigrant 12
Japanese immigration 66
Japanese imperialism 20
Japanese language education: changing rationales 180, 181, 188, 194–195; consumer learners 20, 191, 195; introductory class, super-diverse 194; militarily strategic 180; Pop names students know 186, **186**, **187**; Senkichi Inagaki 19; student motivation UNSW 179; time-consuming to learn 181, 184; university learners, disciplinary areas 182–184, **184**
'Japanese living in Australia' 132
Japanese Olympic athletes 89–91
Japanese pop culture 184–185, *185*, 234
Japanese women 144
Japanese woodblock prints: asymmetrical composition 48; *ukiyo-e* 44–45
'Japan in Australia' 130, 133–135, 158
Japan Professional Baseball League 1936 64
Japonisme 8, 14; Australian 45; fascination with Japan goods 44–45; *Sleeping Beauty* film 109; Sleeping Beauty film, orientalism 105–106
Jo, Takasuka 13

244   Index

Jong, Erica: *Fear of Flying* (1973) 100
Journey to the West (Xiyouji): Chinese tale, *Monkey* 113; English, *A Mission to Heaven* 119; Japanese television 18, 117–118; monk Xuanzang pilgrimage 116; *Saiyūki* reinterpreted, British 120
Jun'ichirō, Tanizaki: 'The Gourmet Club' (Tanizaki 2001) 105

Kanamori, Mayu: *The Heart of the Journey* 137; interpretive internment board 133; migrant, Aboriginal 132; Nikkei artist 19, 132; *In Repose* 132, 137; You've Mistaken Me For a Butterfly 143
Kandinsky, Wassily 47
kanji 203
karate 120
karayukisan 6
karayuki-san prostitutes 12, 143
Kashima Maru 70
kasuri (*ikat*, or resist-dye weaving) 229
katakana 203
Kato, Megumi: *Narrating the Other: Australian Literary Perceptions of Japan* (2008) 100
Katsushika, Hokusai 231
Ken, Shindō 30
Kenkichi, Ōshima 85
Kimba the White Lion 113
Kinichi, Asano 91; Japanese Track and Field 82; Olympic prep 83
Kitano-maru 38
KlockWorx 110
Kneen, Krissy: *The Adventures of Holly White and the Incredible Sex Machine* (2015) 100, 109; erotic fiction 101
Kojiki: English translation 15; Uzume nonviolent 26
Kojiro, Nonami 13
Kondō, Mamoru: Moshi Moshi, Kondo Tricot 235–236
Kondō, Yasuyo: Moshi Moshi, Kondo Tricot 235–236
Kung Fu 120
kuyo: appease the souls 138; to Japanese spirits 139; non-traditional Japanese 137

Lady Rowena 6–7
Lang, Andrew: *The Blue Fairy Book* in 1889 98
language-education category mobility: monolingual 203, 207; multiple languages 205–206
language incompetence 200, 203–204
Language learning motivation 191–192
Language management theory 208
Lee, Bruce: *Enter the Dragon* 120
Leigh, Julia 18; explicit sexual 98; 2011 film *Sleeping Beauty* 10, 96, 100, 104–105
'Lenton and Smith's Great Novelty for the Colonies-The Great Dragon Troupe of Japanese–12 Wonders from Yeddo' 8
like-but-unlike 161
Lindsay, Lionel (1874–1961): *Japonisme* experiment 14; *Woodcuts Exhibition 1923* 55
linguistic mobility 205
Lister, William Lister (1859–1943) 46
London Camberwell School of Art and Crafts 1916 57

MacArthur, General Douglas: Japanese participation 82; support Japanese Olympics, 1950 84
'Made in Japan' 215
Mahākapi Jātaka 116
Makigawa, Akio (1948–1999) 234, *235*
Manchurian Incident (1931) 33
maneki-neko (welcoming cat figure) 234
Manette Salomon (1867) 45
manga 164, 184, 185, 186
marginalised subjects 131
marketing tricks 171
Marks, Alexander 7–8
Marquet, Albert 47
Marquez, Gábriel García (1927–2014): *Memoria de mis putas tristes* (Memories of My Melancholy Whores 2004) 99, 103, 105
martial arts, Japanese 120
Masaji, Tabata 84
Masāki, Sakai: critique of 124; 'Monkey Dance' craze 118
Masako, Natsume 118
Masamichi, Count Soejima 83
Masao, Maruyuma 25
mass-produced fashion 231
Masuda (Matsuda) 77
matches in Australia 70, 71, 73
Matisse, Henri 47; *The Black Table* (1919) 57–58; *French Window at Collioure* (1914) 57–58
Matuzō, Nagai 83
Maugham, Somerset 58
Mayu Kanamori: 'Creation of Nikkei Australia: Rediscovering the Japanese Diaspora in Australia' 133
McCubbin, Frederick (1855–1917) 46

media coverage: ABC radio 83; *The Age* 125; *The Argus* 67, 71, 75, 76, 77, 83, 89, 90; *The Australian Story* 81; *Australian Women's Weekly* 124, 125; Giants tour, Radio Australia 18; *Hōchi Shinbun* 71; *Monkey* 124; *Queensland Times* 84; *Rolling Stone Australia* 125; *The Truth* 85; *Yomiuri Shinbun* 69, 71, 78
Meiji Era 223, 225
Meiji Imperialism 180
Meiji Restoration in 1868 225
Melbourne 12, 19; Akio Makigawa sculpture *235*; Japanese businessmen 12
Melbourne Olympic Invitation Committee 82
1956 Melbourne Olympics: Japan at 81; Japanese Olympic athletes 89–91; Japanese participation key 85; Japan invited to participate 78; positive Australia, Japan relations 17; seven nations withdraw 87–88
'Memorandum on Chinese Immigration' 12
Menzies, Prime Minister Robert 84
mestiza 136
Meteor Garden 152
Mieko, Takamine 118
migrant: belong in Aboriginal country 132; conditions to accept 152; exclusion, mis-interpellation 131; Japanese to Australia 8; loss of place, belonging 140; negotiate, Indigenous 138
'Migrant Diplomacy' 156
Mikado (1885) 45
mimetic style 45, 48, 59
mixed race: *The Heart of the Journey* 135, 137; identity, Australia 19th–20th century 135; Indigenous 137
Miyamoto, Shigeru 186
'mobile lives': identity of language learners 198; mobility, not settled place 199
'mobilities paradigm' 212
mobility, language education: home, school, Saturday school 199, 201
mobility and children: language, culture, identity, static 207, 209, 212; mobility domains 200–201, *201*, 205–207
'mode of circulation' 162
Monet, Claude: *Waterlilies and the Japanese Bridge* (1897–1899) 49
Monkey: BBC to ABC 123; high esteem, 2000's 125; history 126; Japanese production, Chinese folktale 113; Japanese television, impact 18; oriental aesthetic reinvented 113; racism viewers/critiques 124, 125; sexual overtones 122; sound track 122–123;

transcultural 116; VHS copies 125; Waley translation, *The Journey to the West* 119
monkey lore 116
'Monkey Magic' 123
monoculture 207
Moses, Ken 77
movement: Aesthetic 45; Art Nouveau 49; Arts and Crafts 45, 57
Mr Masuda (Matsuda): Japanese horse buyer 14
'mugukjeok' 152
Muji 233–234
'mukokuseki' (no clear national identity) 152, 231
Munich Style 46
Murakami, Yasukichi 141; Kathleen and Y on buggy *142*; Tatura Internment Camp 1944 139; *Through a Distant Lens* 139
Murdoch, James (1856–1921) 14
Musée Guimet 48
Musume Dōjōji 30

Nabokov, Vladimir: *Lolita* 99
Nagasaki 225, 226
Nakashima, Leslie 88
Nanjin Massacre 37
natal land 141
Natal test 12
National Gallery of Victoria Art School 46
National Policy on Languages 180
National Studies of Southeast Asia 150
nationhood 131, 222
nation-state 150
Nemureru bijo 97–103
'new cultural nationalism': Asian powers 224; Australia 1970's 222; create a culture with Asia 224; Japan 1960's–1980's 223; liberalisation public consciousness 223
New South Wales Baseball Association 64
New York Giants 64
nihonga (Japanese Language) 204
Niji [Rainbow] 30
Nikkei Australia: Civilian Internee Project 133; Cowra Japanese War Cemetery (CJWC) 133; project, reconnect history 134
Nikkei identity: intercultural relations 19; Japanese, diasporic people 133; Japanese Australian 130; 'Japanese living in Australia' 132; 'Nikkei Australian' 132, 133–135, 140
Nippon Television: celebrity cast 118; *Saiyūki* series 117

Nishi, Haruhiko: best diplomat 65; Japanese Ambassador 73
Nobutsuna, Sasaki (1872–1963) 30
Northcliffe, Viscount 29
notan (systems of light and dark) 57
Number of Learners of Japanese **181**

Occupied Japan 82
O'Doul, Frank: coach Auckland Oaks 65; Japan Baseball Hall of Fame 78n1
Olson, Lawrence 31
Olympic gymnastics: Japan dominates 1960's 92; Kondō Takashi, coach 89; Ono Takashi, gold 85, 89–91
Olympic media coverage 88; *Asahi, Mainichi, Yomiuri Shinbun* 88; Kokusai Denshin Denwa (KDD) 88; Leslie Nakashima, UPI, Japan Times 88
Olympic wrestling: Ikeda Mitsuo, gold 89; Ishii Shōhachi, gold 85; Kasahara Shigeru, silver 89; Sasahara Shōzō, gold 89, 91
oriental cool: Australians after WWII 126; Japanese martial arts 120; Japanese pop-culture 114–115, 118
'origami' 229
'Otaku' (cool) 194
Otomo, Takumi 64, 73

Parkes, Sir Harry 9
Peace Treaty 63, 65
pearling industry: Japanese dominate 6, 12; Nonami Kojiro 13; Tomitaro Fujii, last diver 15
Perrault, Charles: *La belle au bois dormant* 97, 98
Picasso, Pablo 55
pluricultural environment 199
plurilingual: identity 203, 204–205, 207, 212; migrant, refugee children 199
plurilingualism 210
political policy 83
pop music 123
POWs 84, 86, 89
Preston, Margaret (née McPherson 1875–1963) 14; Aboriginal patterns 44; *Circular Quay* (1925) 56; Coloured Woodprints 56; *métier* (body of work) 46; *Nasturtiums* 51, *52*, 57; printmaker 44, 54, 55; *Red Bow* (1925) 56; *Still Life: Lobsters* (1901) 46; *Still Life with Teapot and Daisies* 1915 50, *50*, 51; *Sydney Bridge* (c1934) 56, *56*; *Western Australian Gum Blossom* (1928) 57, *58*; *Wheel Flower* (c1929) 56, 57; Wood-Blocking as a Craft 56; *Woodcuts Exhibition* 1923 55

racial-nationalism: sense of belonging, racialised groups 132; White Australia ideology 16
racism: acts of exclusion 131; "pure white" 216; racial diversity increasing 126; racial "pollution" 218; towards Indigenous 222; viewers/critiques *Monkey* 124, 125
Radio Australia 18
Redmond, Sir Barry (1813–1880) 9–10
Redon, Odilon 47
Remembrance Day 82
resilient borders 131
Returned and Services League (RSL) 66–67, 68
Reynell, Gladys (1881–1956) 48
Rolling Stone Australia 125
Rolph, Ian 124
Rose, Murray 81; Australian freestyle 86, 90; friends with Yamanaka 90–91
Royal College of Art in London 46
ryōsai kenbo 29

Sacher-Masoch, Leopold von: *Venus in Furs* (1870) 100, 101
Saeki, Roy 71
Saiyūki (Monkey): BBC alterations 119; Chinese tale 113, 116; English version, *Monkey* 120; gender swap 118; Japanese tv version 117; special effects 118; transcultural medium 126
Sakoku Edict 8
sakoku period: 1633–1866 6, 20n1; opening markets 45
1904 Salon d'Automne 47
Samurai 113, 114; introduced Japanese culture 126; Japanese drama 120
Sāñchī 116
San Francisco Peace Treaty 1952 16
School of Design, Painting and Technical Arts 46
Schooner *Julie* 7
seclusion policy 7
Second Sino-Japanese War 37
Seidensticker, Edward 97
senbazuru 87
'shibori' (tie-dyeing) 229
Shigeru, Kasahara 89
Shikibu, Murasaki 99
Shingorō, Takaishi 83
Shiro, Kishibe 118
Shisō no kagaku 25
Shōhachi, Ishii 85
Showa Era 226
Shōzō, Sasahara 89, 91

silent histories 138
Sissons, David (1925–2006) 5, 6, 7
Slade school London 49
Sleeping Beauty: Walt Disney 98
Sleeping Beauty film: disquieting eroticism 107; exploitation of women 106; *Japonisme* 106
sleeping beauty service: exploitation of young women 106; Les Belles Endormies 102
Smith, Sydney Ure (1887–1949): *Art in Australia* 54, 55; entrepreneur, publisher 54; *The Home: An Australian Quarterly* 54
Social Change and the Individual: Japan Before and After Defeat in World War II ([1970] 2015) 25
social interactions: chopsticks training 75; cocktail party 73; secure 1964 Olympics for Tokyo 82; wreath laying 70, 72, 76
social media 224
Sōseki, Natsume (1867–1916) 14
South Korean media 152
spatial mobility 205
sports: baseball most popular 63–64; 1954 Baseball Tour of Australia 17; 1956 Melbourne Olympics 17; re-establish relations 17; teach morals 85; Yomiuri Giants' Baseball tour 17
Spowers, Ethyl 55
Stead, David G.: *The Rabbit in Australia* 29
Stolen Generations 135
Streeton, Arthur 57
1940 Summer Olympics 82
Sun Wukong 116
Super Mario Brothers 152
swimming records 86
Sydney Sports Ground 70

Tadashi, Yanai 231
Taisho Democracy 225
Taisho Era 225
Takao, Inoue 118
Takashi, Kondō 89
Taki, Seiichi: *Three Essays on Oriental Painting* (1910) 57
Tamura, Keiko 17
tanka 30, 33, 35
Tanner, Edgar S. 83
Tavan, Gwenda (2005, 3) 17
Tchukarin, Victor (USSR) 90
Teague, Violet (1872–1951) 14
'Thirty-Six Views of Mount Fuji' 231

ticket prices 76
Tokugawa period (1603–1868) 6, 117
Tokutarō, Hanayagi (1878–1963) 29
Tokyo Metropolitan Museum of Arts 156
1964 Tokyo Olympics 91–92
Tomotoshi, Katagi 106
Torres Strait 12
Toulouse-Lautrec, Henri de: *Divan Japonais* (1892–93) 49
trade: delegation 66; dispute 14; growing with Japan 83, 180; between Japan and Australia 10
TRaNS: Trans-Regional 150
trans-Asia 149–159
transculturality: defined 115; theories, Berry and Epstein 114
Transnational Asia: An Online Interdisciplinary Journal 150
transnationalism 131
translation process 120–121
Tsurumi, Kazuko (1918–2006): *Canberra-maru* 31, *32*; Musume Dōjōji 30; *Niji* [Rainbow] 30; Picturesque Dancer 27, *28*; *Social Change and the Individual: Japan Before and After Defeat in World War II* ([1970] 2015) 25
Tsurumi, Shunsuke: *The Intellectual History of Wartime Japan, 1931–1945* 33
Tsurumi, Shunsuke (1922–2015): absence in records 30; *Ame no Uzume Den* 26; *An Intellectual History of Wartime Japan* ([1986] 2010) 25; *Canberra-maru* 31, *32*; *A Cultural History of Postwar Japan 1945–1980* (1987) 25; perceptions of Australia 36; perceptions of Yūsuke 35
Tsurumi, Yūsuke (1885–1973): *Canberra-maru* 31, *32*; impressions of Australia 33–36; Japanese Diet 15; Japanese representative, education 27, *28*
Tsūzokusaiyūki ('Popular Journey to the West') 117

ukiyo-e: *Ehonsaiyūki* illustration 117; Japanese art revolution 49; Japanese woodblock prints 44–45; techniques 50
Uniqlo: exploits third-world workers 234; Kabuki face 232, *233*; mass-produced clothes 231, *232*; uses natural fibres for clothes 234
USSR 85
Utamaro, Kitagawa (1753–1806) 49, 55
Uzumaki, Naruto 186, **186**, **187**, 188

vanitas, still life 46
Victoria and Albert Museum 49

wabi-sabi 229
wakon yosai (Japanese spirit together with Western scientific and technological ingenuity) 225
Wakuda, Tetsuya: fuses French and Japanese, chef 234; Order of Australia 2005 234
Waley, Arthur: British flavor, *Monkey* 120; translation of *The Journey to the West* 119–120
Walt Disney 98
war brides: assimilate Japanese 16; entertained Giants 73; migration from Japan 153; Sydney attendants 71
Weir, David: rewrite Monkey, English 120–121; television writer 120, 123
'Western values' 224
White Australia Policy *(hakugōshugi)*: Japanese language learning, strategic 20, 180; non-European exclusion 6; open Japanese immigration 16; 1960's in effect 115
Whitlam, Gough 219
William, Harold (Williams 1958, 179) 14
Witkiewicz, Stanislaw Ignacy: "The Metaphysics of the Two-Headed Calf" 221
Wölfflin, Heinrich: *The Principles of Art History* (1915) 57
woodblock: artist, Hokusai Katsushika 117; artist, Margaret Preston 44–57; prints 44; technique 56, 57
Woodcuts Exhibition 1923 55
wool: buyers 73; exports 10; industry 66
world literature theory: centre-periphery 162; circulation models 162
World War II: moving past 126; rebuilding relations 16, 63
worship of virgins 99

Xindiao Da Tang Sanzang Fashi Qujingji ('The Newly Printed Record of the Procurement of Scriptures by the Master of the Law, Tripitaka, of the Great Tang') 117

Yamanaka-san, Tsuyoshi 81
Yang, William: *Fruit: A New Anthology of Contemporary Australian Gay Writing* 100; Japan 100
Yasuda, Shoji 68
Yasunari, Kawabata (1899–1972): 'Fairy Tale for Old Men' 96–97; *House of the Sleeping Beauties* (1967) 96–100; Nobel Prize for Literature 97; Order of Culture 1961 97
Yeo, William: New South Wales, RSL 66–67; politically motivated 78; protest tour 66–67, 76; tour ill-timed 76
Yomiuri Giants: Australian experience 71–72; baseball tour, Australia 1954 63, 65–70; donation, RSL 70; end of tour 75, 76; fair attitude 71; goodwill mission 63, 69, 70; Japanese professional baseball 63; Kaname Yonamine 64; member selection 69; pitcher Takumi Otomo 64; rebuilding relationships 63, 65, 68; tough opposition 67; *Yomiuri Shinbun*, owner 64, 68
Yomiuri Shinbun: goodwill mission 69; interview of Giants 78; no attendance reported 71
Yonamine, Kaname 64
You Only Live Twice 120
You've Mistaken Me For a Butterfly 143; Okin, raped 143; reference, Madame Butterfly 143
Yuju, Wen: CCB analysis 200–206; experiences, memories 201–205; *Taiwan umare, Nihongo sodachi* 200
Yukiko 100, 103–104
Yukio, Mishima (1925–1970) 97, 104
Yusunari, Kawabata 99

Zhu Bajie 116